Why countries choose different exchange rate arrangements and how these arrangements affect domestic monetary policy control and macroeconomic stability are questions of substantial interest to policymakers and researchers alike. The countries of the Pacific Basin region offer a wide variety of examples for the comparative study of the implications of different exchange rate arrangements. The essays in this volume examine the degree of financial interdependence and the conduct of exchange rate and monetary policy among Pacific Basin countries. The essays address four broad issues: the degree of regional financial market integration in the Pacific Basin, the implications of choosing different exchange rate regimes for domestic macroeconomic stability, the effect of exchange rate intervention policy on the conduct of domestic monetary policy, and the prospects for a yen currency bloc. Some of the essays focus on the national experience of specific countries in the Pacific Basin; others adopt a cross-country comparison approach.

Exchange rate policy and interdependence

Exchange rate policy and interdependence

Perspectives from the Pacific Basin

Edited by

REUVEN GLICK
Federal Reserve Bank of San Francisco

MICHAEL M. HUTCHISON
University of California, Santa Cruz

Published by the Press Syndicate of the University of Cambridge
The Pitt Building, Trumpington Street, Cambridge CB2 1RP
40 West 20th Street, New York, NY 10011-4211, USA
10 Stamford Road, Oakleigh, Melbourne 3166, Australia

© Cambridge University Press 1994

First published 1994

Printed in the United States of America

Library of Congress Cataloging-in-Publication Data
Glick, Reuven.
Exchange rate policy and interdependence : perspectives from the
Pacific Basin / Reuven Glick, Michael M. Hutchison.
p.   cm.
Includes index.
ISBN 0-521-46110-3
1. Foreign exchange – Government policy – Pacific Area.   2. Monetary
policy – Pacific Area.   I. Hutchison, Michael M.   II. Title.
HG3997.55.G58   1994
332.4'56'099 – dc20   93-47205
                                                              CIP

A catalog record for this book is available from the British Library.

ISBN 0-521-46110-3 hardback

Contents

v

Contributors

Menzie D. Chinn
University of California,
Santa Cruz

Michael P. Dooley
University of California,
Santa Cruz

Charles Engel
University of Washington,
Seattle, and National
Bureau of Economic
Research, Cambridge,
Massachusetts

Jeffrey A. Frankel
University of California,
Berkeley, and National
Bureau of Economic
Research, Cambridge,
Massachusetts

Reuven Glick
Federal Reserve Bank of
San Francisco

Arthur Grimes
Reserve Bank of New Zealand,
Wellington

Michael M. Hutchison
University of California,
Santa Cruz

Takatoshi Ito
Harvard University,
Cambridge, Massachusetts,
and Hitotsubashi University,
Tokyo

Sung Y. Kwack
Howard University,
Washington, D.C.

Julia Lowell
RAND Corporation, Santa
Monica, California

Donald J. Mathieson
International Monetary Fund,
Washington, D.C.

Michael Melvin
Arizona State University,
Tempe

Ramon Moreno
Federal Reserve Bank of
San Francisco

Michael Ormiston
Arizona State University,
Tempe

Bettina Peiers
Arizona State University,
Tempe

vii

John Pitchford
Australian National University,
  Canberra

Helen Popper
Santa Clara University, Santa
  Clara, California

John H. Rogers
Pennsylvania State University,
  University Park

Stephen J. Turnovsky
University of Washington,
  Seattle

Tsutomu Watanabe
Bank of Japan, Tokyo

Jason Wong
Reserve Bank of New Zealand,
  Wellington

Preface

The implications of different exchange rate policy arrangements have long been a central issue in international economic analysis. Because of the diversity of historical backgrounds, stages of economic development, and financial market environments among countries in the Pacific Basin, this region provides an ideal laboratory for a comparative study of exchange rate arrangements and their implications for monetary policy. Moreover, the Pacific Basin has become widely recognized as the most dynamic region in the world economy. Much attention has focused on issues related to international trade with Pacific Basin countries. Only recently have exchange rate and financial policy issues come to the forefront, as countries in the region have become more integrated with one another and with the rest of the world through international capital as well as trade movement.

This volume is a collection of essays originally prepared for a conference titled "Exchange Rate Policy in Pacific Basin Countries" sponsored by the Center for Pacific Basin Monetary and Economic Studies at the Federal Reserve Bank of San Francisco on September 16–18, 1992. The conference brought together academics, central bankers, and other policymakers and researchers to review and compare the experiences of Pacific Basin countries. The essays in this volume provide a comprehensive analysis of the theoretical issues associated with exchange rate policies as well as the individual experiences of Pacific Basin countries.

The September 1992 conference was the third in a series sponsored by the Federal Reserve Bank of San Francisco on Pacific Basin monetary issues as part of its Pacific Basin program. Since 1974 the program has promoted cooperation among central banks in the Pacific Basin and sponsored research on major monetary and economic policy issues in the region. The research agenda has been supported by the contributions

ix

of the Bank's own research staff as well as through international conferences. This work has been published in the Bank's *Economic Review,* academic journals, and conference volumes. Previously published conference volumes include *Financial Policy and Reform in Pacific Basin Countries,* edited by Hang-Sheng Cheng (Lexington Books, 1986), and *Monetary Policy in Pacific Basin Countries,* edited by Hang-Sheng Cheng (Kluwer Press, 1988). The Center for Pacific Basin Monetary and Economic Studies was established by the Bank in 1990 to open the program to greater participation by visiting scholars. The program was also augmented by the creation of a formal network of researchers in other central banks, universities, research institutes, and international organizations who share the Bank's recognition of the importance of Pacific Basin nations in the world economy.

This book is the joint product of many people. Besides the authors of the chapters, special thanks are due to Ramon Moreno, who provided detailed comments on earlier drafts of several papers, and Mary Racine, for her work as production and copy editor. Our deepest gratitude goes to Hang-Sheng Cheng for his role in ensuring the success of the conference and providing the guiding hand for the Bank's Pacific Basin program since its inception.

Finally, any opinions expressed in this volume are those of the respective authors and do not necessarily reflect the views of the organizations with which they are associated. Nor do they reflect the views of the Federal Reserve Bank of San Francisco or of the Board of Governors of the Federal Reserve System.

Exchange rate policy and interdependence

CHAPTER 1

Overview

Reuven Glick and Michael M. Hutchison

Since the collapse of the Bretton Woods system of fixed exchange rate parities in the early 1970s, countries have been largely on their own in making choices about their exchange rate arrangements. Most countries have moved away from pegging to a single currency toward either pegging to a basket of currencies or adopting a more flexible arrangement under which the domestic currency is frequently adjusted. In large part this movement was prompted by a desire to liberalize financial markets, maintain some national autonomy over macroeconomic policy, and at the same time avoid the need for a system of widespread international capital controls.

This is especially true among Pacific Basin countries, which in the past fifteen years have undertaken substantial financial reform, removing barriers to domestic and international capital flows. Under these circumstances, national economies have become increasingly influenced by foreign developments. Greater international interdependence has complicated the conduct of domestic monetary policy and led to greater exchange rate flexibility as individual countries have sought to insulate themselves from foreign disturbances.

Because of the diversity of historical backgrounds, stages of economic development, and financial environments, the Pacific Basin region offers a wide variety of approaches to exchange rate policy. Some countries still peg their currency to a single foreign currency, while some peg to a basket of currencies. Other countries allow varying degrees of flexibility in their exchange rates. The Pacific Basin region thus provides a useful set of country experiences for a comparative study of exchange rate arrangements and their implications for the conduct of monetary policy. Why countries have adopted different exchange rate policies and how these different policy approaches have affected their national econ-

1

omies are questions of substantial interest to policymakers and researchers alike.

The essays in this volume examine the conduct of exchange rate and monetary policy among Pacific Basin countries. They address four broad issues, with some essays focusing on the national experience of specific countries in the Pacific Basin and others adopting a cross-country comparison approach.

First, how closely linked are financial markets in the Pacific Basin? The extent to which individual countries are linked to foreign economies and are able to insulate themselves from foreign disturbances is dependent upon the degree of international capital mobility. Three essays in the volume quantify the degree of capital mobility and asset market linkages among Pacific Basin countries. Chinn and Frankel focus on the interest rate linkages of financial assets and the relative importance of the U.S. and Japanese markets in the region. Engel and Rogers examine the linkages in equity markets and the persistence of stock return differentials in the region. Dooley and Mathieson develop an alternative measure of capital mobility that does not depend on observed domestic interest rates.

Second, what are the implications of choosing different exchange rate regimes? The optimal choice of exchange rate arrangements depends on a variety of factors. These include the degree of capital mobility, structure of the economy, relative magnitudes of external disturbances, and policymakers' objectives. What is the experience of Pacific Basin countries? How have exchange rate policies influenced the dependence of these economies on developments abroad?

Five essays in the volume look at these issues. Turnovsky provides an analytical overview of exchange rate theory and its policy implications from several theoretical perspectives. Moreno examines the link between exchange rate regimes and domestic insulation from external shocks for Korea and Taiwan. Pitchford considers the importance of the exchange rate regime for the transmission of trade price shocks in the case of Australia. Grimes and Wong consider the New Zealand experience and discuss how the exchange rate is used to guide monetary policymakers in achieving their ultimate objective of price stability. Popper and Lowell look at the experience of Australia, New Zealand, Canada, and the United States and infer the extent of concern by monetary authorities about the exchange rate by measuring the influence of foreign developments on domestic prices.

Third, to what extent have countries been able to sterilize the effects of their exchange rate intervention policy on their monetary policy? Virtually all central banks in the Pacific Basin region have active intervention policies, in some cases designed to peg currency values and in others simply to moderate currency movements. How actively have central banks intervened in foreign exchange markets? What have been their objectives? What are the ultimate effects on the conduct of monetary policy?

Three essays examine these issues. Glick and Hutchison consider Japan's experience over the post–Bretton Woods period and estimate the nature of the Bank of Japan's intervention policy over time and its impact on the control of money aggregates. Watanabe analyzes how intervention operations by the Bank of Japan have acted as a signal about the future stance of monetary policy. Kwack examines the extent to which Korea was able to sterilize the effects on its money supply of large current account surpluses in the late 1980s.

Fourth, what are the prospects for a yen bloc? Two essays evaluate the prospects for a yen currency bloc among Pacific Basin countries. Ito discusses different interpretations of a yen bloc and examines the present overall international use of the yen, as well as the financial and trade relations of Japan with neighboring countries in the Pacific Basin. Melvin, Ormiston, and Peiers evaluate the portfolio demand for international currencies and assess the desirability of forming a yen currency area from the point of view of investors.

Using this organizational framework, we turn to a discussion of the individual essays.

1.1   International financial market integration

In recent years almost all countries in the Pacific Basin have attempted to promote greater economic efficiency by undertaking steps to liberalize their domestic financial systems and remove restrictions on international capital flows. Hong Kong and Singapore were the first to begin liberalizing their financial systems by removing or relaxing interest rate regulations and abolishing exchange rate controls in the mid-1970s. Significant financial reforms have been undertaken in Japan and Malaysia since the late 1970s and in the Philippines, Australia, New Zealand, and Indonesia since the early 1980s. More recent movements toward liberalization have occurred in Thailand, Korea, and Taiwan. Although the timing and the extent of liberalization steps have varied across countries, virtually all countries in the region have allowed domestic and foreign market forces to play a greater role in their financial markets.

To what extent has this liberalization process increased the integration of financial markets and the international mobility of capital within the Pacific Basin? In Chapter 2, Chinn and Frankel address three relevant questions: (i) Have nominal interest rates in Pacific Basin countries become more strongly linked to foreign rates as a result of the removal of capital controls and other barriers to international capital mobility? (ii) To the extent that barriers remain, are interest differentials attributable to country factors (such as capital controls, differential tax treatment, default risk, and imperfect information) or to currency factors (such as expectations of exchange rate changes or exchange rate premia)? (iii) To what extent are interest rates linked to the United States versus Japan? They find that though interest rate linkages with the United States have become stronger over the period 1982–92, the region is still far from achieving complete financial integration, particularly in the lesser developed countries. For countries with well-developed forward markets, they attribute most of the remaining barriers to integration to currency factors. Although U.S. rates remain the dominant foreign influence for most countries, for the Association of Southeast Asian Nations (ASEAN) in particular, there is some evidence of a greater Japanese role.

As local equity markets have grown in the region, the opportunities for international investors seeking higher return or diversification have expanded. Engel and Rogers in Chapter 3 explore the extent to which equity markets in the Pacific Basin have equalized real returns on investment opportunities using data on stock market indexes over the period 1983–91. Consistent with the Chinn and Frankel work on interest rates, Engel and Rogers find substantial differences in real return prospects for equity investors across countries. They also ask whether real returns differ among countries because (ex ante) nominal rates of returns are different or because (ex ante) purchasing power parity fails to hold. They find that the real return differences are largely accounted for by nominal return differentials. Moreover, there does not appear to be any relation between the type of exchange rate arrangement and the relative magnitudes of nominal return differentials and purchasing power parity deviations. Engel and Rogers's evidence implies that there are still important restrictions to the flow of financial capital among Pacific Basin countries that prevent the equalization of returns. The authors suggest that the observation of real return differentials might be attributable to differences in the relative riskiness of equity investments.

In light of prevailing implicit or explicit regulatory controls, Dooley and Mathieson (Chapter 4) question the usefulness of observed domestic interest rates in measuring the degree of capital mobility and extent of international financial market linkages. They construct an alternative measure of capital mobility, not based on observed domestic interest rates, but derived instead from the response of money demand to private capital flows. This measure gives results that are sometimes counter to the conventional wisdom about which countries are more integrated with world capital markets.

Dooley and Mathieson also discuss the implications of increased capital mobility for the choice of exchange rate arrangements and the conduct of monetary policy. They maintain that the choice of exchange rate arrangements is best viewed as a response by policymakers to their loss of control over growing private sector international arbitrage activity. To the extent that a country desires to maintain control over domestic monetary conditions, it must choose between permitting greater exchange rate flexibility and imposing increasingly restrictive controls on international capital flows. Moreover, changes in the degree of capital mobility have affected various monetary policy instruments. Dooley and Mathieson point out that the effectiveness of credit ceilings and allocation rules is weakened by the private sector's access to alternative sources of credit, through either nonbank financial intermediaries or foreign sources.

1.2 Choice of exchange rate regimes

Increasing economic interdependence implies that countries are subject to a broader range of shocks. Which exchange rate regime best insulates an economy from foreign shocks? What form of exchange rate arrangement helps provide discipline to policymakers and perhaps lends credibility to announced policies? Some of the basic economic theory on these issues is addressed in Chapter 5 by Turnovsky. Surveying the theoretical literature on exchange rate management and implications for monetary policy, he classifies these models into four categories: (i) dynamic portfolio models, (ii) new classical stochastic models, (iii) rational intertemporal models, and (iv) target zone models.

In Turnovsky's view, the principal policy insight from dynamic portfolio models is the implication for the long-run interdependence between monetary and exchange rate policies. Choosing to target the money growth rate implies a particular long-run domestic rate of inflation and, given the rate of inflation abroad, a corresponding long-run rate of exchange rate depreciation. If instead the monetary authorities choose to target a particular level or path for the exchange rate, this implies a corresponding money growth rate, and hence a loss of control over monetary policy.

What are the advantages of choosing to peg the exchange rate as opposed to allowing the exchange rate to float? One of the strongest arguments for pegged exchange rates is that they enforce discipline on domestic macroeconomic policies, which in turn may help to stabilize inflation expectations. Linking to a stable foreign currency limits the rate of domestic inflation, which in turn constrains monetary and fiscal policy. By "credibly" committing themselves to a fixed exchange rate arrangement, policymakers may hope to import some of the credibility for stable monetary control presumably associated with foreign policies. This presupposes that a country desiring to peg its exchange rate has a history of high and volatile inflation attributable to political/economic policy instability. The disciplining effects of a currency peg may be small or absent in an already well-managed economy.

In other cases, political pressures may make tighter monetary and fiscal policies infeasible and limit the ability of the government to commit credibly to a pegged exchange rate. With open capital markets, a more flexible exchange rate is often the only practical policy option, since attempts at fixing the exchange rate would inevitably invite speculative attacks on the rate. Thus, fixed exchange rates are consistent with a high degree of capital mobility only if domestic monetary policy objectives are sacrificed, a difficult political choice for many policymakers.

The implications of new classical models are particularly rich for exchange rate policy. With these models, Turnovsky discusses how the choice of exchange rate regime can depend on a host of economic and political factors, such as the nature of disturbances, the structure of the economy, the information available to agents, and policymakers' preferences. Whether economic disturbances are predominantly domestic or foreign, nominal or real, temporary or permanent, all influence the choice of exchange rate regime. A flexible exchange rate regime, for example, generally works better to insulate the domestic economy from foreign inflation than do fixed exchange rates by permitting the value of domestic currency to appreciate so as to limit the effect on domestic prices. Structural characteristics of the economy, such as the degree of international capital mobility and wage rate flexibility, also affect the insulating properties of the exchange rate regime. The less the degree of wage flexibility, for example, the greater the effect of a change in the nominal exchange rate on the real wage and thus on output, and hence the greater the desirability of exchange rate flexibility. Also important are policymakers' preferences regarding domestic price stability, output fluctuations, and the stability of the terms of trade, all of which can reflect political factors.

An important result of the theoretical literature is that because of the diverse nature of shocks facing an economy, neither purely flexible nor perfectly fixed exchange rates are generally "optimal." Rather, some intermediate degree of flexibility is generally best able to stabilize the economy in response to economic disturbances. The optimal degree to which exchange rates should be "managed" or "flexibly fixed" varies with changes in the nature of disturbances, economic structure, or political objectives.

However, the practical problems involved in discerning the source of shocks and identifying the relevant structural characteristics make it difficult for policymakers to apply theoretical criteria for adjusting the exchange rate. Thus, the choice of exchange rate regimes by policymakers is ultimately an empirical one involving "learning by doing." Pacific Basin countries provide a wide range of experience and learning paths in such a choice. Some countries have followed gradual regime transitions, moving from fixed exchange rates to more flexible exchange rates slowly over time. Others have undertaken major institutional and policy reforms affecting their exchange rate arrangements virtually overnight.

In Chapter 6, Moreno considers how exchange rate regime shifts in Taiwan and Korea affected macroeconomic discipline and domestic vulnerability to external shocks. Both countries maintained adjustable pegs to the U.S. dollar for most of the 1970s. In the case of Taiwan, large current account surpluses, together with liberalization of international trade and financial transactions, made continued pegging to the dollar undesirable. Consequently, it moved to a managed float policy against the dollar in 1979 and a free float in 1989. Korea also allowed its exchange rate to adjust more flexibly in the 1980s because of balance-of-payments disequilibria. It adopted a basket currency peg with undisclosed currency weights in the 1980s followed by a more explicit managed float against the dollar in 1990.

Moreno uses a vector autoregression model to identify the underlying sources of disturbances, which are generally unobservable, and focuses on how the change in exchange rate regime affected domestic price stability in each economy. He finds that Korea and Taiwan appear to be more insulated from foreign shocks with greater exchange rate flexibility. Taiwan is less insulated than Korea, however, because of its greater international trade openness and higher capital mobility.

Reflecting in large part the desire to improve macroeconomic performance in the face of large trade shocks and structural rigidities in the economy, Australia adopted a flexible exchange rate regime at the end of 1983. In Chapter 7, Pitchford analyzes several episodes of major foreign price shocks experienced by Australia and compares the effect of these shocks on the domestic economy during the periods of fixed and floating exchange rates. He concludes that the lack of exchange rate flexibility in response to external price shocks in the 1970s exacerbated

Australia's macroeconomic adjustment problems during that period. The policy of flexible exchange rates maintained for most of the 1980s better insulated the economy from the nominal trade price shocks Australia has traditionally experienced. The insulation benefits manifested themselves in the form of lower domestic inflation and a more stable real economy despite substantial wage and price rigidity.

New Zealand switched dramatically from a fixed exchange rate to a freely floating exchange rate policy in March 1985. This change was necessitated by the lesson that a fixed exchange rate and an independent monetary policy could not be maintained following the removal of international capital controls in the early 1980s. The strong private capital inflows under the fixed rate regime frustrated the central bank's ability to control the monetary base. The floating of the exchange rate in turn allowed the central bank to maintain control over bank reserves. This has played an important operational role since 1988, when the Reserve Bank of New Zealand established a low rate of price inflation as the overriding goal of monetary policy.

Nonetheless, the exchange rate still plays an important role in New Zealand's monetary policy. In Chapter 8, Grimes and Wong describe how the exchange rate is used to guide monetary policy in achieving New Zealand's long-run inflation goal. While not an end in itself, this policy has resulted in a high degree of exchange rate stability. The price level stability objective for monetary policy stated in the Reserve Bank of New Zealand Act of 1989, combined with an operating procedure consistent with this objective, seems to have established the credibility of the policy with the private sector. Desired exchange rates, for example, are met without any significant official exchange market intervention, and private capital flows appear to have had a stabilizing influence.

Grimes and Wong argue that the present operating procedure comes close to being an "optimal" regime for New Zealand. They empirically test the relative merits of using a monetary aggregate, exchange rate, or some combined rule as an intermediate target for the monetary authorities. Using a vector error correction model approach, they find that the dominant influence on inflation in New Zealand has come from the exchange rate and international price variables, though money aggregates also have some influence. This implies that the exchange rate path, rather than the path of money aggregates (or a combination of the two, with greater weight to the former), provides the better intermediate target for policymakers.

Popper and Lowell focus their analysis in Chapter 9 on the exchange rate regimes of the United States, Japan, Canada, and Australia. All four countries are wealthy and developed and have relatively open capital markets. They also officially maintained floating exchange rate regimes through most of the 1980s. However, they differ greatly in terms of the openness of their goods markets, the extent of their economic dependence on trading partners, and the sources of the economic disturbances they experience.

Popper and Lowell explore the extent to which these countries, in fact, have implicitly targeted their exchange rates. They do so with a model that treats the exchange rate as an objective of monetary policy, along with output and price variability. Their model implies that domestic prices depend negatively on depreciations of the domestic currency (and positively on foreign inflation) to the extent that monetary policy authorities care about exchange rate stability and attempt to offset depreciations. A central bank caring strongly about exchange rate stability will offset a depreciation (or foreign inflation) with tighter monetary policy, hence lowering domestic prices or inflation. This implies that the behavior of prices in response to exchange rate changes ultimately depends on the extent to which the central bank targets the exchange rate. Popper and Lowell find some evidence of exchange rate targeting in the case of Canada, but not in that of Australia and Japan. There is weak evidence of targeting for the United States, but only vis-à-vis the yen.

1.3   Intervention and sterilization policies

An exchange rate policy implies a systematic effort by the monetary authorities to influence the level or rate of change of the exchange rate. A variety of policy instruments are potentially available to influence the exchange rate, including foreign exchange intervention, domestic monetary policy, various forms of controls on international trade and capital flows, and official announcements of future policies.

Foreign exchange market intervention and domestic monetary policy are generally perceived as the primary instruments available to central banks in their pursuit of an exchange rate policy. To some extent, the same exchange rate objectives can be accomplished with either foreign exchange intervention policy or domestic monetary policy. Foreign exchange intervention that is unsterilized is equivalent to domestic monetary policy to the extent that both affect the domestic monetary base: the former typically involves the exchange of domestic money for foreign currency assets, while the latter typically involves the exchange of domestic money for domestic government securities.

In some countries with relatively undeveloped domestic financial markets, the foreign exchange market may be the primary means through which the central bank affects the money supply. Few disagree that unsterilized intervention has a significant influence on the market exchange rate. By changing the monetary base, monetary intervention influences broader monetary aggregates, interest rates, prices, the exchange rate, and usually real variables as well in the short term.

With sterilized intervention, however, the exchange of domestic money for foreign currency assets is offset by an accompanying exchange of domestic securities for domestic money, leaving the monetary base unaffected. Because it amounts to an exchange of domestic securities for foreign securities held in private portfolios, "pure" sterilized intervention (not associated with changes in other current or anticipated future fundamentals) can have a lasting effect on the exchange rate only to the extent that investors view the securities as less than perfect substitutes (and the investors are risk averse) or institutional impediments limit the degree of capital mobility. If international capital is not fully mobile and/or domestic and foreign assets are imperfect substitutes, relative yields and the exchange rate will adjust in response to the change in the relative supplies of assets in portfolios.

The extent to which central banks are able to pursue an exchange rate policy independent of monetary policy depends on its ability to sterilize or offset the effects of international reserve changes on the monetary base. The scope for successful sterilized intervention and an independent domestic monetary policy is greater in countries with limited international capital mobility and/or without fully liberalized domestic financial markets. Limited capital mobility enhances the ability of the central bank to retain overall control over domestic monetary aggregates. Even if the markets for certain short-term financial assets are closely integrated with those abroad, domestic monetary policy can still be effective through its impact on the prices of other domestic assets that do not have a close foreign substitute.

In Chapter 10, Glick and Hutchison examine how the Bank of Japan (BOJ) intervention and sterilization policies affected its control of money aggregates. They show that the BOJ has actively intervened in the foreign exchange market over most of the floating rate period. Using both simple regressions and a vector error correction approach, they also measure the extent to which the BOJ has been able to sterilize the effects of this intervention on the monetary base. They find that the degree of sterilization is high in the short run, but is much less in the long run. This suggests a high degree of international capital mobility in the case of Japan after a period of portfolio adjustment.

Glick and Hutchison also find evidence of an asymmetric response pattern in the BOJ's policies: efforts to restrain yen depreciations generally have been greater than efforts to limit yen appreciations, and offsetting domestic credit operations have tended to be larger with intervention against yen appreciations than against depreciations. They argue that this behavior is consistent with monetary control in pursuit of general price stability in the face of a long-term appreciation of the yen. With sterilization less than complete, they suggest that the intervention against the rise of the yen in the early 1970s and in the late 1980s contributed to the rapid growth of money aggregates during those periods. In the early 1970s this resulted in a surge in inflation. Only an apparent upward shift in money demand seems to have prevented this money growth from resulting in a sharp increase in goods market inflation in the late 1980s.

Recent models suggest that sterilized as well as unsterilized intervention may influence exchange rates by altering expectations in the exchange market. One way it might do so is by "signaling" market participants about the direction of future monetary policy. Such intervention, however, is still not strictly independent of monetary and/or fiscal policies. Its success depends largely on how it informs the market about future policy changes and hastens the market's response. Such intervention must also be reinforced by the expected change in monetary policy, or else it will lose credibility. Moreover, such intervention affects the exchange rate only when the market does not anticipate policy changes; otherwise the information embedded in the signal is already discounted by the market.

Watanabe in Chapter 11 tests two implications of the signaling hypothesis of foreign exchange intervention: (i) intervention policy should be correlated with future economic policies that could affect exchange rate fundamentals, such as money aggregates, and (ii) intervention should not be fully anticipated. In this context, he also considers the possibility that the central bank has followed an unannounced but nonetheless predictable policy of targeting the exchange rate, perhaps within a tolerance band that changes over time.

Looking at BOJ behavior over the period 1973–92, Watanabe finds that the purchase (sale) of foreign currencies tends to precede a reduction (increase) in the BOJ discount rate, and the purchase (sale) of foreign currencies tended to precede an increase (decrease) in the growth rate of broad money. Intervention policy depended both on past movements of the exchange rate and on movements in the BOJ's target exchange rate that are unobservable to market participants. This suggests that intervention is at least in part unanticipated and able to influence the exchange rate by surprising market participants. Both findings are consistent with the signaling hypothesis.

Kwack argues in Chapter 12 that in the late 1980s domestic credit creation by the Bank of Korea was heavily influenced by the desire to sterilize the monetary effects of net foreign asset accumulation associated with current account surpluses. He concludes that the Bank of Korea was able to sterilize almost all of the effects of foreign reserve changes and to achieve its monetary policy goals. Because the market for government securities is not well developed in Korea, the Bank of Korea conducts open market operations with its own interest-bearing liabilities, called Monetary Stabilization Bonds. The success of Korea's sterilization policy during this period can be attributed in part to barriers to international capital mobility that apparently still remain despite some recent financial liberalization in the country. Limited substitutibility between Korean and foreign assets arising from other causes may play a role as well. In Korea the informal curb market is still an important source of finance, particularly for small businesses with little access to institutional credit.

Kwack also discusses how Korea took measures, such as raising domestic interest rates, opening domestic markets for foreign goods, and permitting the appreciation of the won, to reduce the rate of foreign asset accumulation by decreasing current account surpluses. He constructs a small-scale open-economy macro model of the Korean economy to quantify the effects of changes in various policy instruments.

1.4   Prospects for a yen bloc

As regional economic and financial integration proceeds in Europe and in North America, many wonder whether a similar economic bloc might form in the Pacific Basin. Most speculation has centered around the role of Japan as the dominant country in such a bloc because of its relative economic power within the region. There are several different definitions of a "yen bloc." Some interpret it as an area in which the yen is used extensively in international transactions. Others interpret it more broadly as a free trade zone or tariff union. It has also been interpreted as referring to a monetary arrangement whereby countries peg their currencies to the yen or adopt the yen as a common currency.

In Chapter 13, Ito discusses the various interpretations of a yen bloc and whether it is possible or probable that a yen bloc will emerge in Asia. He surveys the evidence related to the international use of the yen as an invoice, transaction, or reserve currency. He reports some evidence that countries in Asia are increasing their use of the yen as an invoice currency in international transactions. However, Japan still uses the yen as an invoice currency for exports and imports to a lesser extent than other developed countries use their national currencies for invoicing. This finding cannot be explained by Japan's close trade relationship with the United States or by its role as a major importer of raw materials and oil. While trade between Japan and other Asian countries increased substantially in the late 1980s, there is no apparent evidence of an intra-regional trade bias once account is taken of such factors as economic growth and proximity.

Many Asian countries peg their currencies to a basket of foreign currencies that includes the yen as well as the dollar. Typically the currency weights are unannounced by policymakers. Tying the exchange rate to a basket of currencies has the advantage of reducing the average fluctuation of the domestic currency vis-à-vis other currencies, thus reducing the risk of taking an open position in any individual currency. Leaving the weights unspecified gives policymakers somewhat more leeway to follow a "managed" or "flexibly fixed" exchange rate policy. Ito cites econometric evidence that the currencies of the smaller countries in Asia are in fact de facto pegged to the dollar and with few exceptions place relatively little weight on the yen. This is consistent with the observation that these countries typically export more to the United States than to Japan. He concludes that there is little current evidence that a yen-based exchange rate mechanism is forming in Asia.

What about the prospects for such a monetary arrangement in the future? How viable would it be? Ito discusses the extent to which combinations of countries in the Pacific Basin region fit the criteria of an optimum currency area. He discusses evidence on the prevalence of common shocks suggesting that East Asia is no less suitable than Europe for a move to a currency union. However, he also notes the political considerations that limit this prospect. These include the lack of consensus in Japan about whether the internationalization of the yen is in the country's best interest, as well as a concern among its neighbors about conceding too much regional political power to Japan. On balance, there is little evidence of a yen bloc at present, and not much likelihood of its forming in the near future.

In Chapter 14 Melvin, Ormiston, and Peiers examine the prospects for a yen bloc from a narrower focus. They analyze international portfolio demands for use of the yen by a group of Pacific Basin countries. They do so by assessing the risk-return rankings for different Pacific Basin currencies using the generalized stochastic dominance approach. In particular, they examine the distributions of returns on holding yen,

Australian dollars, U.S. dollars, German marks, and British pounds from the point of view of agents in selected Pacific Basin countries. Their portfolio analysis indicates that agents with moderate or high levels of risk aversion generally prefer the distribution of returns associated with holding U.S. dollars or interest-bearing assets. Like Ito, they find little support for a dominant yen and little reason for a yen bloc.

PART I
INTERNATIONAL FINANCIAL MARKET INTEGRATION

CHAPTER 2

Financial links around the Pacific Rim: 1982–1992

Menzie D. Chinn and Jeffrey A. Frankel

2.1   Introduction

The rapid steps Europe has taken toward economic integration, and their many effects, have been extensively studied. There exists a belief that economic links among Pacific countries are also increasing rapidly, and a suspicion that Japan is at the root of it, but these issues have been less extensively studied. Some recent tests regarding bilateral trade suggest that there is not in fact an increasing bias toward intraregional trade within East Asia and that the Pacific-wide grouping which includes North America is the most natural "trade bloc."[1] But there are signs that Japanese *financial* influence is increasing in East Asia. Capital flows within the region, particularly foreign direct investment by Japan in Southeast Asia, are growing. The yen is playing a greater role in the region, as reflected in trade invoicing, loan denomination, reserve holdings, and exchange rate policies. The role of the dollar is still dominant, however.

This essay investigates the extent to which Pacific financial markets are becoming more tightly linked, by analyzing the co-movements of interest rates in a number of countries around the Pacific. International equalization of interest rates has a number of important policy impli-

The authors thank Thomas Cargill, Masahiro Kawai, and William Maloney for comments, Yunqi Li for research assistance, and Carlton Strong of Morgan Guaranty for graciously providing data. We are grateful for the support of the Group for International and Comparative Economic Studies and faculty research funds granted by the University of California, Santa Cruz, the Institute for Business and Economic Research of the University of California, Berkeley, the United States–Japan Friendship Commission of the U.S. government, and the Center for Pacific Basin Monetary and Economic Studies of the Federal Reserve Bank of San Francisco.

[1] See Frankel (1993) and other chapters in the same volume.

cations. It would imply, for example, that national monetary authorities had lost the ability to affect domestic demand through independent monetary policies and that countries would be able to finance investments easily despite shortfalls of saving. Earlier studies of these issues in the Pacific context include Cheng (1988), Glick (1987), and Glick and Hutchison (1990).

Here we focus on three basic questions. (i) As a result of financial liberalization and innovation, particularly the removal of capital controls and other barriers to international capital mobility, are interest rates in Pacific Rim countries becoming increasingly linked to world financial centers? (ii) To the extent that barriers remain and interest rates continue to be set independently, what is the nature of these barriers? Do they tend to be associated with country boundaries (such as capital controls, differential tax treatment, default risk, imperfect information, or risk of future capital controls) or with currencies (expectations of exchange rate changes and an exchange risk premium)? (iii) To the extent that interest rates in Pacific countries are now influenced by interest rates in world financial centers, is the power of Tokyo in the region gaining over that of New York?

We shall use the term "financial links" to refer to the ease with which capital moves from one country to another and the extent to which capital controls and the other country barriers have been broken down. We shall use the term "currency links" to refer to the perceived stability of the exchange rate between two countries. Arbitrage will not equate interest rates internationally unless *both* financial links and currency links are very strong. One or the other alone will not do it. Either country barriers such as capital controls or the perceived possibility of exchange rate changes will be sufficient to drive a wedge between two countries' interest rates.

Convergence of Pacific Rim interest rates is not as widespread a trend as one might think.[2] Neither the mean of onshore–offshore interest rates nor the standard deviation of those rate differentials shows any sign of a declining trend. As already noted, there is no reason to believe that interest rates should converge with integration unless one believes that *both* country barriers and the perceived likelihood of exchange rate changes were tending toward zero. To see this, notice that the differential for interest rates of common maturities can be decomposed as follows:

---

[2] The Pacific Rim countries examined in this study are Australia, Canada, Hong Kong, Indonesia, Japan, Korea, Malaysia, New Zealand, Singapore, Taiwan, Thailand, and the United States.

$$i - i^{US} \equiv (i - i^{US} - fd) + (fd - \Delta s^e) + \Delta s^e, \qquad (2.1)$$

where fd is the forward discount for a consistent maturity and Δs^e is the expected depreciation over a consistent horizon. This identity merely breaks the nominal interest differential into its constituent parts: country factors (including capital controls, differential tax treatment, default risk, localized information, risk of future capital controls), which give rise to the covered interest differential, $i - i^{us} - fd$, and currency factors (an exchange risk premium, $fd - \Delta s^e$, and expected depreciation, Δs^e),which give rise to the forward discount, fd.

While exchange risk and expected depreciation are difficult to assess, one can examine capital controls and country risk directly by looking at the country premium – otherwise known as the covered interest differential. (What we are here calling the country premium is sometimes called political risk.)[3]

We can examine covered interest differentials for only a subset of countries, those with relatively well-developed forward markets: Australia, Canada, Hong Kong, Japan, Malaysia, New Zealand, and Singapore. Figure 2.1 illustrates one finding of this essay: that capital mobility, defined as the absence of barriers to the movement of short-term capital across national boundaries, has indeed increased over the 1982–92 period for this subset of countries (measured by a three-month moving average series for the covered interest differential). The mean covered interest differential has moved from -1 percent to roughly zero on an annualized basis, while the standard deviation of interest differentials has shrunk to near zero.[4] Domestic financial liberalization in these countries is as much a part of the convergence process as international financial liberalization, as only market-determined interest rates are free to adjust to world levels in response to arbitrage.

This graph is merely suggestive, and summary statistics can be misleading. This essay examines more carefully each of these linkages in a variety of ways. In Section 2.2, we turn our attention first to the left-hand side of equation (2.1), discussing how the total interest differential has evolved over time for the Pacific Rim countries. Then we assess individual components on the right-hand side: the covered interest differential and the exchange risk premium.

---

[3] Aliber (1973), Dooley and Isard (1980), and Frankel and MacArthur (1988), among others, make this distinction between political and exchange risk. Sometimes political turmoil is associated with the country premium; this seems to be the case for Canada, where the covered interest differential widened in the immediate aftermath of the failure of the Meech Lake accords in June 1990.

[4] Malaysia drops out of the sample at 1990:04, which tends to reduce both the mean and standard deviation.

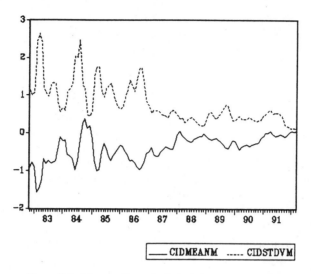

Figure 2.1. Mean and standard deviation of the three-month covered interest differential for a group of seven Pacific Basin countries.

In Section 2.3, we investigate whether local interest rates are becoming increasingly influenced by U.S. interest rates. We examine correlations between the U.S. Eurodollar rate and local onshore rates. The data on covered interest rates are relatively reliable, and we pursue further ways of assessing influence over time, including recursive and rolling regression analysis (Section 2.4). In Section 2.5, we investigate whether uncovered interest parity is becoming a better characterization of Pacific Rim linkages, which brings in the exchange risk premium. These tests use survey data from *Currency Forecasters' Digest* on exchange rate expectations for several Pacific countries. Finally, in Section 2.6, we evaluate the relative importance of the United States and Japan as financial influences on interest rates in the region.

Our key findings are as follows: Pacific Rim interest rates appear to be increasingly influenced by foreign interest rates (either U.S. or Japanese), as measured by co-movements. Some of these interest rates also appear to be increasingly influenced by covered interest rates, indicating increasing financial integration for some countries (Australia and New Zealand, most evidently). For certain other countries, the level of financial integration was high at both the beginning and end of the sample period, so that no trends were discernible (e.g., Hong Kong and Singapore). The statistical evidence for currency integration is much less strong, although for three out of the four countries studied (Australia, Canada, and Japan) the exchange risk premium is decreasing. There is also some evidence that covariation of Pacific Rim interest rates with Japan is increasing – though not for the English-speaking countries, Australia, Canada, and New Zealand. Most of the conclusions are limited in scope, since the results pertain to subsets of the overall group of Pacific Rim countries. Many East Asian countries are not far enough along on the path of financial liberalization to show clear signs of arbitrage activity vis-à-vis overseas financial markets.

2.2 Interest rate differentials and risk premia

2.2.1 *Interest differentials*

The first item we examine is the left-hand side of equation (2.1). We regress the *absolute value* of the interest differential on a constant and a linear time trend. Absolute values are used because this prevents positive and negative differentials from canceling out and making such countries appear open. While a regression of the absolute differential on a time trend is somewhat restrictive in form, it has the virtue of easy interpretation: the coefficient on the time trend is the average rate at which the differential shrinks in percentage points.[5] Table 2.1 shows the results for the period 1982:09–1992:03 (with the trend coefficient expressed in annualized terms). There are few clear cases of shrinking absolute interest differentials. When appropriately adjusted standard errors are used to account for what is obviously a high degree of serial correlation, only one country appears with a statistically significant downward trend (Japan).[6] The conclusion, based on this measure, is that important barriers remain, keeping countries' interest rates largely independent. The question is whether the barriers to integration are

---

[5] The interest rates examined are mostly end-of-month money market rates (e.g., interbank), of a three-month maturity. Three exceptions are the Korean series KO3, which is a monthly average of daily observations, the Indonesian one-month interbank rate, and the Thai overnight call money rate. Greater detail on sources and definitions can be found in the Data Appendix.

[6] One is tempted in this age of robust estimators to use the GMM Newey–West standard errors to conduct tests of statistical significance. This procedure is not appropriate in this case because the observed serial correlation appears to be of an autoregressive nature (usually AR(1)) rather than of a moving average type. The $N/3$ adjustment to the standard errors is consistent with a first-order autocorrelation coefficient of approximately .82, which is close to the average of the estimated autoregressive coefficients. Running the regressions in first differences results in little change in the point estimates but such large standard errors that nothing comes out significant.

Table 2.1. *Regressions of absolute interest differential with the United States on time trend, 1982:09–1992:03*

Currency	Constant	Trend	$\bar{R}^2$	DW	N	Sample
Australia	4.088** (0.467) [1.401]	0.212 (0.085) [0.147]	.04	0.149	115	82:09–92:03
Canada	0.306 (0.143) [0.428]	0.326** (0.026) [0.045]	.58	0.324	115	82:09–92:03
Hong Kong	1.532** (0.189) [0.566]	−0.094 (0.034) [0.059]	.05	0.873	115	82:09–92:03
Indonesia	6.082** (0.494) [1.482]	0.667** (0.090) [0.156]	.32	0.497	114	82:092–92:03
Japan	3.405** (0.241) [0.722]	−0.175** (0.044) [0.076]	.12	0.118	115	82:09–92:03
Korea (KO2)	−1.315 (0.951) [2.853]	1.206** (0.134) [0.233]	.56	0.257	63	87:01–92:03
Korea (KO3)	2.834** (0.304) [0.913]	0.649** (0.057) [0.099]	.54	0.134	111	82:09–91:11
Malaysia	1.556 (0.269) [0.807]	0.162 (0.049) [0.084]	.08	0.706	111	82:09–92:03
New Zealand	8.229** (0.743) [2.229]	−0.305 (0.135) [0.234]	.03	0.138	115	82:09–92:03
Singapore	2.561** (0.176) [0.529]	−0.049 (0.033) [0.057]	.01	0.330	112	82:09–91:12
Taiwan	2.367** (0.273) [0.819]	0.031 (0.049) [0.085]	−.01	0.602	110	83:01–92:02
Thailand	1.303 (0.433) [1.299]	0.405** (0.084) [0.145]	.18	0.176	103	82:09–91:11

Note: All parameter estimates in percent terms (annualized). Figures in parentheses are asymptotic standard errors; figures in square brackets are standard errors assuming $N/3$ independent observations. DW represents the Durbin–Watson statistic. ** indicates significance at 1% level using the adjusted standard errors.

associated with the countries themselves (capital controls, information costs, etc.) or with the respective currencies (anticipations of exchange rate changes).

2.2.2 *Covered interest differential*

The covered interest differential is our means of measuring the country premium. Frankel (1991) found that covered interest differentials, vis-à-vis the Eurodollar rate during the period September 1982 to January 1988, on average were as small for Hong Kong, Singapore, Japan, and Canada as for the financially most open European countries. The differentials were bigger and more variable for Malaysia, Australia, and New Zealand.

We now turn to the question of how the covered interest rate behavior has changed over the period 1982–92. Table 2.2 shows the results of regressing the absolute covered interest differential against a constant and a linear time trend, using the same ten-year sample period previously defined. As already noted, there are only seven currencies covered, since forward markets do not exist for other Pacific countries.

Australia and New Zealand show covered interest differentials that have diminished at a statistically significant rate, as one would expect from their programs of financial liberalization in the 1980s. Only one other country shows a downward trend, however, and it is not statistically significant. A significant *positive* trend appears for the case of Japan, an unexpected result in light of past findings by Otani (1983), Frankel (1984), and others that the large differentials of the 1970s fell to zero in the early 1980s.[7] The Australian results appear to be dominated by a spike in early 1983 (due to a large forward discount of the Australian dollar).

---

[7] In these data the covered interest differential is as high as 0.92 percentage points in September 1990. Similarly, the Gensaki–Euroyen differential peaks at 1.02 percentage points in February 1990, before declining back to zero at the end of 1991. The most likely explanation for these results is that the Gensaki was a more representative rate earlier in the 1980s, and it has since decreased in importance (Feldman, 1986: 42); CDs are thought now to be far more representative. While some have argued that there still exist frictions in Japanese financial markets that prevent perfect international arbitrage, such as Ministry of Finance administrative guidance of institutional investors buying dollar assets during 1987–9, the sign of the observed differential does not support this interpretation. We also tried the regression using the Japanese Euroyen interest rate in place of the Gensaki rate. The Euroyen rate seems to obey covered interest parity better, as one would expect. But there is a rise in the covered Euroyen differential to as high as 0.60% in mid-1989 (of the opposite sign from the onshore–offshore differential).

Table 2.2. *Regressions of absolute covered interest differential with the United States on time trend, 1982:09–1992:03*

Currency	Constant	Trend	$\overline{R}^2$	DW	N	Sample
Australia	1.572*	−0.190*	.12	1.306	115	82:09–92:03
	(0.243)	(0.046)				
	[0.759]	[0.080]				
Canada	0.121	0.020	.06	1.021	115	82:09–92:03
	(0.038)	(0.007)				
	[0.113]	[0.012]				
Hong Kong	0.100	0.028	.05	1.331	115	82:09–92:03
	(0.058)	(0.011)				
	[0.174]	[0.018]				
Japan	0.142	0.027*	.14	0.761	115	82:09–92:03
	(0.034)	(0.006)				
	[0.103]	[0.011]				
Malaysia	1.460*	−0.040	−.01	0.621	87	82:09–90:03
	(0.240)	(0.056)				
	[0.720]	[0.096]				
New Zealand	3.165**	−0.388**	.35	1.920	115	82:09–92:03
	(0.272)	(0.050				
	[0.816]	[0.086]				
Singapore	0.269	0.028	.05	1.082	112	82:09–91:12
	(0.055)	(0.010)				
	[0.164]	[0.018]				

Note: All parameter estimates in percent terms (annualized). Figures in parentheses are asymptotic standard errors; figures in square brackets are standard errors assuming $N/3$ independent observations. DW represents the Durbin–Watson statistic. * (**) indicates significance at 5% (1%) level using the adjusted standard errors.

In the cases where the absolute covered interest differential is increasing, the constant is quite small, indicating that integration has already occurred. Moreover, the rate of increase is also fairly small, thirty basis points per year at the most. We will examine the covered interest differentials more closely in Section 2.4.

2.2.3   The exchange risk premium

The exchange risk premium is defined as $f - s^e$. We cannot observe investors' expectations, s^e, directly. The most standard method for measuring expected returns and examining the exchange risk premium is to invoke rational expectations and to infer investors' ex ante expectations from the ex post behavior of the spot rate. This methodology usually leads to the finding that all or most of the observed variation in the forward discount is attributable to a time-varying exchange risk premium. But it has been argued that survey data offer a measure of expectations that, though far from perfect, may be more informative than ex post movements of the spot rate (Froot and Frankel, 1989). Survey data results for the five major currencies have showed a tendency for expected depreciation, as measured by the survey data, to move one for one with the forward discount, in contrast to the findings of the standard rational expectations approach.

Recently it has become possible to extend such tests to a variety of smaller currencies by means of data from *Currency Forecasters' Digest,* which reports forecasts of market participants (actually the harmonic mean of the responses) on a monthly basis. We will denote the survey data measure by $\hat{s}^e$. Analysis of such data for seventeen currencies has turned up more evidence of a time-varying risk premium than there was for the five major currencies.[8] Four of the currencies were for Pacific Basin countries. (Australia, Canada, Japan, and Singapore are the only countries for which we have both expectations and forward rate data.)[9] Only the Singapore dollar showed a tendency for expected depreciation to move one for one with the forward discount. For Australia and Canada there was evidence that some part of the variation in the forward discount is attributable to a time-varying risk premium. For Japan, the test at the three-month horizon supports the hypothesis of a varying risk premium while the test at the twelve-month horizon does the opposite.

Here we see how the exchange risk premium has changed in recent years among the Pacific countries for which the data are available. The results are reported in Table 2.3 for the 1988:02–1992:04 period.[10] It appears that, over this period, the exchange risk premium at the three- and twelve-month horizons fell for the Australian and Canadian dollars,

---

[8] Frankel and Chinn (1993). These data are proprietary with *Currency Forecasters' Digest* of White Plains, New York, obtained by subscription by the Institute for International Economics. Frankel and Phillips (1991; updated in Frankel, Phillips, and Chinn, 1992) apply the data to the question of European integration.

[9] Data for Hong Kong are also available on an alternate-month basis. The data indicate zero variation in the risk premium, since reported expectations of (nonzero) change in the exchange rate are constant over time.

[10] Unfortunately, we do not have expectations data spanning a period consistent with the interest and forward rate data. These data are timed somewhat differently than the other data used in this essay. The *Currency Forecasters' Digest* forecasts are usually compiled on the third Thursday of each month.

Table 2.3. *Regressions of absolute exchange risk premium with the United States on time trend, 1988:02–1992:04*

Currency	k	Constant	Trend	$\bar{R}^2$	DW; Q-stat	Het.	N
Australia	3	7.307**	−1.451*	.09	2.154	0.989	51
		(0.243)	(0.046)		10.86		
	12	1.777**	−0.278*	.08	2.171	5.662[a]	51
		(0.356)[b]	(0.122)[b]		12.92		
Canada	3	3.826**	−0.480	.11	na[c]	1.592	50
		(0.789)	(0.319)		16.23		
	12	2.005**	−0.239	.25	na[d]	2.723	49
		(0.737)	(0.276)		17.45		
Japan	3	7.578**	−0.173	.09	na[c]	1.930	50
		(2.082)	(0.839)		12.24		
	12	5.062*	−0.071	.41	na[c]	4.329*	50
		(2.290)	(0.886)		10.36		
Singapore[e]	3	1.130	1.283*	.23	na	3.764*	24
		(0.829)[b]	(0.575)[b]		8.62[f]		
	12	2.424**	0.668**	.25	na	2.622	24
		(0.522)	(0.227)		14.37[f]		

Note: All parameter estimates in (annualized) percent terms. k is the forecast horizon/maturity. Figures in parentheses are asymptotic standard errors. DW represents the Durbin–Watson statistic. Q-stat is the Ljung–Box Q-statistic for serial correlation of lag order 13. Het. is the F-statistic for heteroskedasticity. * (**) indicates significance at 5% (1%) level using the adjusted standard errors.
[a]Significant at 10%.
[b]White heteroskedasticity-robust standard errors.
[c]AR(1) correction.
[d]AR(1), AR(2) correction.
[e]Data reported on alternating months only.
[f]The Q-statistic is the Godfrey–Breusch Lagrange multiplier test for thirteen lags of residuals.

as well as the yen, although the trend term is statistically significant only in the first case. The risk premium for Singapore is increasing.

2.3 Integration: interest rate co-movements

One way to assess the strength of financial linkages is to measure the impact of foreign interest rates on local rates. To discern whether U.S.

financial influence is increasing or decreasing, we ran the following regression:

$$i_t = \alpha_0 + \alpha_1 i_t^{US} + \alpha_2(i_t^{US} \times \text{TIME}) + u_{2,t}, \tag{2.2}$$

where i is the local onshore rate, i^{US} is the U.S. Eurodollar deposit rate, and TIME is a linear trend term. Equation (2.2) is admittedly a rather blunt instrument by which to measure the effect of increasing integration, since it restricts the time variation in the slope coefficient to be a linear trend. (α_2 can be interpreted as the rate at which α_1 increases each period.) Moreover, the regression makes sense only under certain restrictive assumptions. To begin with, it must be assumed that the local country is small enough that it can take the U.S. interest rate as exogenous. The local rate[11] is related to the U.S. rate in a clear manner under the null hypothesis of complete integration; that is, capital controls are nonexistent and investors do not expect the exchange rate to change.[12] In that specific case (assuming debt instruments of similar attributes), $\alpha_0 = \alpha_2 = 0$ and $\alpha_1 = 1$. More loosely, one might plausibly interpret a parameter estimate for $\alpha_2 > 0$ as an indication of increasing impact over time.

The results of implementing regression equation (2.2) are presented in Table 2.4.[13] (We report results for two Korean series because of the difficulty of finding an adequate market-determined rate.) The key coef-

[11] Ideally, the local rate in these tests should be determined freely in financial markets. We tried to get close to market-determined interest rates if possible. It was not always possible, since many East Asian countries maintain repressed or highly regulated financial systems. South Korea is one country that has only begun to liberalize (which is why we do not use the highly regulated interbank rate). The Monetary Stabilization Bond rate (KO2) is the closest to an active market rate, the curb market no longer being as active as it was in the early 1980s. See Tseng and Corker (1991), Emery (1992), and Frankel (1992) for details. A government that sets domestic interest rates artificially will have to use capital controls to prevent international arbitrage; our tests will reject interest rate parity for such countries, just as they should.

[12] The assumption that the exchange rate follows a random walk, so that the rationally expected depreciation is zero, has been made in a study by Faruqee (1992) for the Pacific Basin countries of Korea, Malaysia, Singapore, and Thailand. The data are ambiguous on this point. Unit root behavior is rejected only for Hong Kong, which is to be expected given the pegged exchange rate regime. However, there is almost borderline rejection of a unit root in favor of trend stationarity for Australia, Indonesia, Malaysia, New Zealand, and Thailand (according to augmented Dickey–Fuller tests using four lags and a constant).

[13] Almost all the interest rate series appear to be nonstationary (i.e., $I(1)$), but fail to exhibit co-integrated behavior. This result is to be expected given the high frequency of the data and the short time span. Rather than imposing a first-differenced specification, we impose our prior that none of these countries would allow its interest rates to diverge without bound from the U.S. rate, and so we run the regressions in levels.

Table 2.4. *Regressions of local interest rate on U.S. interest rate and a trend-interaction term, 1982:09–1992:03*

Currency	Constant	Interest rate	Trend interaction	$\bar{R}^2$	DW	N
Australia	8.305**	0.466	0.027	.08	0.155	115
	(1.364)	(0.148)	(0.012)			
	[4.092]	[0.257]	[0.021]			
Canada	1.754	0.802**	0.046**	.74	0.342	115
	(0.439)	(0.048)	(0.004)			
	[1.317]	[0.083]	[0.007]			
Hong Kong	2.797	1.276**	0.012	.66	0.342	115
	(0.794)	(0.086)	(0.007)			
	[2.382]	[0.149]	[0.013]			
Indonesia	15.389**	0.037	0.041	.06	0.512	114
	(1.492)	(0.162)	(0.014)			
	[4.476]	[0.281]	[0.023]			
Japan	4.401*	0.157	−0.004	.04	0.037	115
	(0.663)	(0.072)	(0.006)			
	[1.989]	[0.125]	[0.010]			
Korea (KO2)	15.237**	−0.989**	0.126**	.63	0.599	63
	(0.690)	(0.110)	(0.014)			
	[2.070]	[0.191]	[0.023]			
Korea (KO3)	12.971**	−0.066	0.039**	.22	0.069	111
	(0.887)	(0.097)	(0.007)			
	[2.661]	[0.169]	[0.012]			
Malaysia	9.177**	−0.013	0.061**	.25	0.346	111
	(1.132)	(0.123)	(0.010)			
	[3.396]	[0.213]	[0.018]			
New Zealand	16.585**	0.059	0.071*	.10	0.165	115
	(2.112)	(0.229)	(0.019)			
	[6.336]	[0.397]	[0.033]			
Singapore	−0.615	0.809	−0.006	.65	0.303	112
	(0.555)	(0.605)	(0.005)			
	[1.665]	[1.048]	[0.008]			
Taiwan	0.496**	0.594*	0.032	.14	0.271	110
	(1.304)	(0.143)	(0.012)			
	[3.913]	[0.248]	[0.021]			
Thailand	1.312	0.997**	0.046	.18	0.128	103
	(1.915)	(0.205)	(0.016)			
	[5.745]	[0.355]	[0.028]			

Note: All parameter estimates in percent terms. Figures in parentheses are asymptotic standard errors; figures in square brackets are standard errors assuming $N/3$ independent observations. DW represents the Durbin–Watson statistic. Sample periods correspond to those indicated in Table 2.1. * (**) indicates significance at 5% (1%) level using the adjusted standard errors.

ficient on the interaction term is "annualized" so that it indicates how much the coefficient on the U.S. interest rate increases each year, on average.

The estimated trend in the effect is upward in three-quarters of the countries. Given the crude nature of the test, it is surprising how much of the total variation the interaction term picks up. For about two-thirds of the countries in the sample, this coefficient is positive and statistically significant using asymptotic standard errors. Using more appropriate standard errors that assume $N/3$ independent observations to account for the serial correlation (see note 6), one finds evidence of an increasing U.S. effect in only three cases – Canada, Malaysia, and Korea (for both of the two Korean market-determined interest rates). Negative coefficients on the interaction term appear in three instances – Japan, New Zealand, and Singapore.[14] The New Zealand result is suspect because of the extreme serial correlation. Estimating this equation in first differences eliminates the statistical significance of the interaction term.

For most of these countries the history of liberalization and structural change over the past ten years is more complicated than a simple linear time trend. Korea, for example, made a first start at liberalization in the early 1980s, backtracked in the mid-1980s, and has more recently started forward again. Two econometric approaches that are more sophisticated than the inclusion of a simple time trend are recursive and rolling regression techniques, which are nonrestrictive means of allowing for time variation in the slope coefficient.

We run the regression

$$i_t = \alpha_{0,t} + \alpha_{1,t} i_t^{US} + u_{3,t},\qquad(2.3)$$

where $\alpha_{i,t}$ is the coefficient at time t. The recursive regression procedure increases the sample size as it recursively updates the parameter estimates, and is more appropriate if one is seeking to replicate the updating of investors' knowledge of an existing structure. The rolling regression maintains the sample size (k = twenty-four periods is used here) as it updates and is more appropriate if one is seeking to discover how the structure has evolved over time. In either case, most of the recursive slope coefficients (α_1) trace out an inverted U-shape. Rather than blinding the reader with graphs of the coefficients for all the countries, we will merely observe that the results are in accord with the earlier ones: for Australia the coefficient is continuously rising beginning in 1986, while for Hong Kong and Singapore the coefficients are close to unity

---

[14] The regression for Japan is suspect, since the U.S. rate is less likely to be weakly exogenous with respect to the Japanese rate.

and relatively constant. The Hong Kong and Singapore findings are consistent with the regimes of pegged exchange rates and open financial markets that each maintained during this period.

2.4   Financial links to the United States: covered interest rate co-movements

Some countries, like Australia, are known to have undertaken sweeping financial liberalization in the 1980s and yet did not show (in Table 2.1) a downward trend in their interest differential that was statistically significant. A likely explanation is that even while capital controls were removed and financial links with offshore markets were growing, exchange rate variability continued to drive a large wedge between local and dollar interest rates. We now bring forward rate data into the regressions of the preceding section in order to remove currency factors from the calculation and zero in on other financial factors.

We consider the regression

$$i_t = \beta_0 + \beta_1(i^{US} - fd)_t + u_{4,t}, \qquad (2.4)$$

where fd is the forward discount, in U.S. dollars / foreign currency unit. Table 2.5 reports the results of simple ordinary least squares (OLS) regressions for six currencies. (Recall that there are only six currencies, besides the yen, for which data are available: Australian, Canadian, Hong Kong, New Zealand, and Singapore dollars and the Malaysian ringgit.) The β_1 coefficients are all of the correct positive sign and at a high degree of statistical significance. The three that have coefficients close to 1 are known to have had open financial markets throughout the sample period: Canada, Hong Kong, and Singapore.[15]

How have these relationships changed over the sample period? We ran these equations through recursive and rolling regression procedures to obtain time-varying parameter estimates. Recursive regressions increment the sample size recursively. Rolling regressions hold the sample size constant. The slope coefficients at the end of August 1984[16] and at

---

[15] Even the coefficients on these three are statistically significantly less than 1. (The standard errors are very small.) A small amount of fluctuation in the covered interest differential within a narrow range dictated by the bid-ask spread or other transactions costs could give this result. Notice that the proper test for efficiency in a technical, statistical sense is for $\beta_1 = 1$, not the joint null of $\beta_0 = 0$ and $\beta_1 = 1$, since the series appear integrated of order 1. See Brenner and Kroner (1992).

[16] The coefficient series start in 1982:11, but it takes a while for the series to settle down to reasonable estimates with some degrees of freedom. At 1984:08, there are only 22 degrees of freedom.

the end of the sample, March 1992, are reported in the rightmost columns of Table 2.5. The pattern of changes substantiates one's priors of increasing or high liberalization. In five of six cases the coefficient is higher at the end of the period than the beginning. In Australia and New Zealand, countries that undertook extensive programs of financial liberalization in the 1980s, the increase is substantial. In the cases of Canada, Hong Kong, and Singapore the coefficients were already high at the beginning of the sample period, so it is not surprising that the increase is small.

Several tests make use of recursive techniques to assess structural breaks. We used the one-step-ahead forecast F-test to find possible break points. The break in 1984 for New Zealand fits well with the devaluation of the New Zealand dollar, and the breaks in 1985, with the abolition of exchange controls in December 1984 and floating in March 1985 (Coats, 1988: 91). Hong Kong's end-of-1983 break matches the beginning of the pegged exchange rate for the Hong Kong dollar.[17]

2.5   Overall integration: does uncovered interest rate parity hold?

We examine one final measure of the strength of financial links: the degree to which domestic interest rates move with foreign interest rates adjusted for expectations of exchange rate changes, that is, the degree to which investors treat the domestic country's assets as perfect substitutes for U.S. assets. Perfect substitutability implies that uncovered interest rate parity holds: expected returns are equalized across currencies. It requires two conditions, both of which we have already tested individually: that covered interest parity hold and that there be no exchange risk premium.

To examine whether uncovered interest parity holds for the Pacific Rim countries we run the regression

$$i_t = \mu_0 + \mu_1(i^{US} - \Delta s^e)_t + u_{5,t}, \tag{2.5}$$

where Δs^e is the expected depreciation using the mean survey response. Equation (2.5) is exactly analogous to the regression equation in (2.4).

There is at least one econometric problem with implementing this test: the slope coefficient will be estimated with a downward bias due to measurement error in the right-hand-side variable. The ideal regres-

---

[17] Another measure of how much international interest rates (appropriately covered) influence domestic interest rates can be obtained by segmenting the sample into early (1982:09–1987:06) and late (1987:07–1992:03) subsamples and comparing the relationships implied by the results of vector autoregression techniques. These results can be found in Chinn and Frankel (1994).

Table 2.5. *Covered interest parity regressions,* $i = \beta_0 + \beta_1(i^{us} - fd) + u$, *1982:09–1992:03*

Currency	β_0	$\beta_1{}^a$	$\bar{R}^2$	DW	Q-stat; ARMA Spec	Break(s)	Proc	$\hat{\beta}_1$ st	$\hat{\beta}_1$ end
Australia	3.396* (0.499) [1.497]	0.707** (0.036) [0.062]	.77	0.825	119.56** AR(1)	1985	Recurs Roll	0.287 0.287	0.707 0.965
Canada	0.399 (0.137) [0.411]	0.943* (0.014) [0.024]	.98	0.851	223.70** AR(2)	1987, 1990	Recurs Roll	0.916 0.916	0.943 0.887
Hong Kong	0.376 (0.065) [0.195]	0.968* (0.008) [0.014]	.99	1.957	14.87	1983:08 –11	Recurs Roll	0.974 0.974	0.968 1.011
Malaysia[b]	0.860 (0.258) [0.774]	0.742** (0.029) [0.050]	.88	0.862	71**/14.8 AR(1)/—	1984:09 1985:04	Recurs Roll	0.707 0.707	0.742 0.550
New Zealand	2.997* (0.477) [1.431]	0.741** (0.029) [0.050]	.85	1.269	67.49** AR(3)	1983:07 1984:08	Recurs Roll	0.305 0.305	0.741 0.939

Singapore	0.023 (0.117) [0.351]	0.935* (0.019) [0.033]	.96	0.911	186.63** AR(3)	1987:02 1990:04	Recurs Roll	0.730 0.923	0.935 0.865

Note: All parameter estimates in percent terms. Figures in parentheses are asymptotic standard errors; figures in square brackets are standard errors assuming $N/3$ independent observations. DW represents the Durbin–Watson statistic. Q-stat indicates the Ljung–Box Q-statistic for lag order 13. ARMA Spec indicates the apparent ARMA specification for the residuals. Break(s) indicates likely breaks as indicated by a one-step-ahead recursive residuals test. Proc is procedure, either "recurs" (recursive) or "roll" (rolling regression). β_1, st is the $\beta_{1,s}$ coefficient at 1984:08. β_1 end is the $\beta_{1,t}$ coefficient at 1992:03. * (**) indicates significance at 5% (1%) level using the adjusted standard errors. Sample periods correspond to those in Table 2.2.

^{a}The significance levels for the slope coefficient are for H_0: $\beta_1 = 1$. Note that all the slope parameter estimates are statistically different from zero.

^{b}There are missing data for the period 1987:07–1987:10. The figures to the left (right) of the solidus are for the first (second) subperiod.

^{c}Sample ends at 1991:12.

sion would include the *true* market expectation of depreciation (Δs^e); this is observed only with error. We hope in future work to account for this errors-in-variables problem with an instrumental variables approach.

Table 2.6 reports the results of the OLS regressions over the 1988:02–1992:03 period for six countries. (We are able to add Korea and Taiwan to the list of countries tested in Table 2.3, because we are no longer using the forward rate.) The coefficient is significantly greater than zero in the cases of Korea and Singapore, and borderline in the case of Australia. These findings hold even when more conservative standard errors (indicated in square brackets) are used in conducting *t*-tests to take into account what is obviously high serial correlation. In every case, the null hypothesis of $\mu_1 = 1$ is always rejected, suggesting that uncovered interest parity does not hold. This is not very surprising, since each country has shown evidence of nonzero covered interest differentials, exchange risk premium, or both. Again, it is also likely that the coefficients are biased downward by measurement error.

It may be more interesting to see how the coefficients change over time. The rightmost columns of Table 2.6 report the slope coefficients at the end of January 1989 and at the end of March 1992. While for the cases of Australia, Japan, and Korea the estimated coefficient is higher at the end of the sample period than at the beginning, it would be foolhardy to attempt to lend much weight to the results because the estimates are so imprecise. Hence, no firm conclusions can yet be drawn.

2.6   Is Tokyo gaining influence at the expense of New York?

Our data and equation design can be used to shed light on a topical question – whether Japan is establishing a yen bloc.[18] Many signs point to increased Japanese financial and monetary influence in East Asia and the Pacific. The (quite imperfect) data available from Japan and the United States on their direct investment in Pacific Asia have been extensively discussed. The (equally imperfect) data on portfolio flows have been much less widely noted. Japanese statistics show flows of long-term capital to Asia, particularly the four Newly Industrialized Econ-

---

[18] Tests of monthly changes in the value of East Asian currencies in Frankel (1993) confirm the strong influence of monthly changes on the value of the dollar, most completely in Hong Kong, but also show that during some subperiods the yen has had a significant influence on the Singapore dollar, the Thai baht, and the Korean won. Other aspects of the yen bloc question, in particular quantification of the trade links and foreign direct investment within this region, are examined there as well and in other chapters in the same volume.

omies (NIEs), in 1988, the first year that the statistics were broken down into such geographical regions.[19] Subsequently, however, the figures on increases in liabilities to the region have dwarfed the figures on increases in assets, a reflection of loans from subsidiaries of Japanese banks in the NIEs back to Japan. (The figures for Australia show net flows of Japanese long-term capital throughout 1988–91.) Focusing just on securities, Japan on net purchased $725 million worth of foreign securities from the NIEs and $5,995 million from Australia, cumulatively during 1988–91. During this period, the United States on net *cashed in* foreign securities in both places, continuing its ten-year pattern of net capital inflows.[20] In theory, the influence of Japanese versus U.S. residents over financial conditions in Pacific Asia should depend on the respective magnitudes of their portfolio holdings. The U.S. authorities have not conducted a survey of portfolio investment abroad more recently than World War II (Stekler and Truman, 1992: 5), and apparently no statistics on accumulated stocks are available for Japanese investors. Nevertheless, it appears likely that Japanese investors have acquired more securities in Pacific Asia than have U.S. investors.

Several measures show an increase in the use of the yen in the region. The share of the yen in external debt of five major Asian debtors (Indonesia, Korea, Malaysia, the Philippines, and Thailand) almost doubled in the 1980s. The percentage of Southeast Asian imports denominated in yen increased from a mere 2.0 percent in 1983 to 19.4 percent in 1990 (though the percentage of exports denominated in yen showed little trend).[21] There was also some increase in the role of the yen in the exchange rate policies of a few East Asian countries, though it turns out to have been less than one might expect.[22]

Our regressions of local interest rates in East Asia and the Pacific against world interest rates can be extended to test the relative influence of the Tokyo and New York financial markets. We implement three tests, corresponding to the earlier tests of simple interest rate parity, covered interest parity, and uncovered interest parity: (i) regress the local interest rate on U.S. *and* Japanese interest rates and these interest rates interacted with a linear time trend; (ii) regress the local rate on

---

[19] Bank of Japan, *Balance of Payments Monthly*.
[20] *U.S. Treasury Bulletin*, Table CM-V-5, June issues.
[21] Japanese Ministry of Finance, *Annual Report*, as reported in Tavlas and Ozeki (1992:33).
[22] The yen share in official reserve holdings of Asian countries rose from 1980 to 1987, and then declined rather sharply in the last three years of the decade. The weight of the yen also rose in the implicit baskets of a few East Asian exchange rates, particularly from 1985, as discussed further later in this section (Frankel and Wei, 1994).

Table 2.6. *Uncovered interest parity regressions*, $i = \mu_0 + \mu_1(i^{US} - \Delta\hat{s}^e) + u$

Currency	$\hat{\mu}_0$	$\hat{\mu}_1''$	$\bar{R}^2$	DW	Q-stat; ARMA Spec	Sample	Proc	$\hat{\mu}_1$ st	$\hat{\mu}_1$ end
Australia	8.641* (1.238) [3.714]	0.271*** (0.080) [0.139]	.17	0.299	153.74** AR(1)	1988:02– 92:03	Recurs Roll	−0.031 −0.031	0.271 0.226
Canada	10.240** (0.968) [2.904]	−0.016** (0.106) [0.184]	−.02	0.038	204.31** AR(1)	1988:02– 92:03	Recurs Roll	0.235 0.235	−0.016 −0.082
Japan	5.975** (0.208) [0.624]	0.009** (0.024) [0.042]	−.02	0.040	253.48** AR(1)	1988:02– 92:03	Recurs Roll	−0.013 −0.013	0.009 0.081
Korea (KO2)	14.306** (0.194) [0.582]	0.132*** (0.028) [0.048]	.31	0.508	43.99** AR(1)	1988:03– 91:12	Recurs Roll	0.083 0.083	0.132 0.131
Korea (KO3)	14.327** (0.181) [0.543]	0.204*** (0.026) [0.045]	.57	0.502	48.06** AR(1)	1988:03– 91:11	Recurs Roll	−0.112 −0.112	0.204 0.105
Singapore	3.472** (0.399) [1.197]	0.213*** (0.043) [0.074]	.53	na	20.29[b]	1988:02– 91:09	Recurs Roll	0.262 na	0.213 na

Taiwan	7.247**	−0.006**	−.02	0.348	61.69**	1988:04–	Recurs	−0.027	−0.006
	(0.456)	(0.046)				91:12	Roll	−0.027	−0.183
	[1.368]	[0.080]							

Note: All parameter estimates in percent terms. Figures in parentheses are asymptotic standard errors; figures in square brackets are standard errors assuming $N/3$ independent observations. DW represents the Durbin–Watson statistic. Q-stat indicates the Ljung–Box Q-statistic for lag order 13. ARMA Spec indicates the apparent ARMA specification for the residuals. Proc is procedure, either "recurs" (recursive) or "roll" (rolling regression). $\hat{\mu}_{1,t}$ st is the $\hat{\mu}_{1,t}$ coefficient at 1989:01 and $\hat{\mu}_{1,t}$ end is the $\hat{\mu}_{1,t}$ coefficient at 1992:03 (unless otherwise constrained by the sample). * (**) indicates significance at 5% (1%) level using the adjusted standard errors.

^{a}The * (**) significance levels for the slope coefficient are for H_0: $\mu_1 = 1$; ($\cdot\cdot$) are for H_0: $\mu_1 = 0$.

^{b}The Q-stat reported is the Godfrey–Breusch Lagrange multiplier test for serial correlation of lag order 13, instead of the Box–Ljung Q-statistic, since there are missing data.

the covered counterparts of (i); and (iii) regress the local rate on the uncovered counterparts of (i). If the world's financial markets and monetary systems are perfectly integrated, we should not expect to be able to sort out any bilateral effects, such as from Japan to smaller countries in the region. Rather, countries would simply deposit savings into, or draw funds out of, an undifferentiated pool of world capital. But few countries in the Pacific follow a perfectly pegged exchange rate, and the majority still have serious barriers to capital mobility as well, as we have seen.[23] Even capital mobility between the United States and Japan faces minor friction and major exchange rate uncertainty. Thus, we may be able to pick up some differential effects of New York and Tokyo interest rates in the region.

The results of the first test are reported in Table 2.7. The coefficients on the interaction terms can be interpreted as the increase per year (on average) of the coefficient relating the local interest rate to the U.S. or Japanese interest rate. All the regressions exhibit a high degree of serial correlation, so the adjusted standard errors are the appropriate ones to use in conducting inference. One finding is that in almost every case the trend coefficients are of opposite sign, suggesting that one financial center is gaining at the expense of another. However, since the relevant parameter estimates are not always statistically significant, one cannot make too much of this result.

Perhaps the most interesting finding is that over the 1982–92 period New York seems to have gained influence at the expense of Tokyo in the English-speaking countries of the Pacific Rim (Australia, Canada, and New Zealand), while the reverse has occurred in a number of East Asian countries. The observed shift in influence from New York interest rates to Tokyo interest rates is highly significant in the case of Indonesia and somewhat less so in the case of Korea. It is positive but not significant for Malaysia, Singapore, and Hong Kong.

It would be interesting to try to distinguish whether the links to Tokyo and New York are attributable to country-specific factors, such as information advantages that might be afforded by common languages, cultures, or tax and legal systems, or to currency factors, such as the weights of the yen and dollar in a country's currency basket. To the extent that an Asian currency is linked to the yen or dollar, the two currency terms in equation (2.1) should disappear. Although Hong Kong remains pegged to the dollar, and the Philippines also remains (more loosely) tied to the dollar alone, there is evidence that some other East

---

[23] The major exception has already been noted: Hong Kong, which is pegged to the U.S. dollar *and* has open financial markets.

Asian currencies at times during the 1980s began to give some weight to the yen in the determination of their currencies.

Out of nine currencies, in 1979–80 there were signs of significant weight on the yen for only one, the Singapore dollar. Starting in 1981–2, the Malaysian ringgit also began to put significant weight on the yen. By 1985, more than half of the currencies studied did so. The role of the yen was particularly clear for the Indonesian rupiah during 1985–90. Toward the end of the sample period (January 1979 to May 1992), the influence of the yen in the implicit baskets of the nine East Asian countries appears to have diminished again. There is very little evidence that a campaign by the U.S. Treasury to push Taiwan and Korea away from a strict peg with the dollar, beginning in 1987, produced a de facto break that persisted to 1989–92. Overall, the dollar remains far more dominant than the yen, and the relative role of the yen even in the baskets where it is significant is still far less than the relative share of Japan in bilateral trade. Nevertheless, it is possible that, for a country like Indonesia, the highly significant increase in the influence of Japanese interest rates during the course of the ten-year sample period that appears in Table 2.7 can be attributed to the new role assigned to the yen in the determination of the value of the Indonesian rupiah in the second half of the 1980s.[24]

We now try to remove the currency factors from the interest rate regressions in order to see what remains. (Unfortunately, one of the countries for which the data are not available is Indonesia.) Table 2.8 reports the results of regressing the local interest rate on both the covered U.S. and Japanese interest rates, with the aim of discerning country-specific links. There is a strong a priori reason to expect high multicollinearity, since covered interest parity holds fairly well between dollar and yen interest rates.[25] Indeed, the correlation between the respective trend-interaction terms always exceeds .98. Thus, it should not be very surprising that none of the interaction parameter estimates is statistically significant. The two that are closest to significant, those for Malaysia and Singapore, continue to indicate that influence is shifting from New York to Tokyo.

Table 2.9 reports the uncovered interest rate results. There is some evidence of declining New York influence in Australia and Canada, and increasing influence in Korea. The sign on the Tokyo term suggests an

---

[24] The results on the implicit currency weights are reported in Frankel and Wei (1994). The case of Korea is discussed in Frankel (1992).

[25] Multicollinearity does not, of course, bias the coefficient estimates or their reported standard errors. It just makes it unlikely that there will be enough information in the data to answer the question at hand.

Table 2.7. Trends in the influence of New York vs. Tokyo interest rates, 1982:09–1992:03

Country	Constant	New York	New York interaction	Tokyo	Tokyo interaction	$\bar{R}^2$	DW	Q-stat
Australia	8.473* (1.143) [3.428]	-1.992** (0.277) [0.479]	0.429** (0.041) [0.071]	3.470** (0.411) [0.712]	-0.539** (0.054) [0.094]	.52	0.409	141.47**
Canada	0.535 (0.458) [1.375]	0.487* (0.111) [0.192]	0.086** (0.016) [0.028]	0.670* (0.165) [0.285]	-0.057 (0.022) [0.038]	.79	0.477	158.12*
Hong Kong	-4.115 (0.857) [2.570]	1.691** (0.208) [0.360]	-0.068 (0.031) [0.053]	-0.353 (0.308) [0.533]	0.104 (0.041) [0.071]	.71	1.047	41.35**
Indonesia	14.010** (1.483) [4.449]	1.852** (0.356) [0.616]	-0.267** (0.053) [0.091]	-2.337* (0.529) [0.916]	0.410** (0.070) [0.121]	.33	0.700	na
Korea (KO2)	16.294** (1.087) [3.262]	-0.754 (0.527) [0.913]	0.097 (0.077) [0.133]	-0.929 (0.704) [1.219]	0.086 (0.091) [0.158]	.64	0.671	57.01**
Korea (KO3)	10.079** (0.690) [2.070]	0.320 (0.143) [0.248]	-0.061 (0.026) [0.045]	-0.019 (0.231) [0.400]	0.124* (0.031) [0.053]	.69	0.204	194.35**
Malaysia	5.520 (1.262) [3.785]	-0.057 (0.286) [0.496]	-0.072 (0.049) [0.086]	0.700 (0.453) [0.784]	0.016 (0.059) [0.102]	.41	0.463	na

New Zealand	18.573**	−2.584**	0.379**	3.405**	−0.599**	.37	0.327	204.22**
	(2.063)	(0.500)	(0.074)	(0.742)	(0.098)			
	[6.291]	[0.866]	[0.129]	[1.285]	[0.169]			
Singapore	−2.768*	0.960**	−0.052*	0.174	0.056	.86	0.842	103.64**
	(0.413)	(0.093)	(0.014)	(0.142)	(0.019)			
	[1.239]	[0.161]	[0.025]	[0.246]	[0.032]			
Taiwan	−4.144	0.635	0.017	0.811	0.049	.45	0.422	109.01**
	(1.217)	(0.292)	(0.043)	(0.437)	(0.057)			
	[3.651]	[0.505]	[0.075]	[0.757]	[0.099]			
Thailand	−3.846	0.780	−0.069	1.363*	0.097	.78	0.461	na
	(1.114)	(0.232)	(0.039)	(0.363)	(0.049)			
	[3.341]	[0.402]	[0.068]	[0.628]	[0.085]			

Note: Figures in parentheses are asymptotic standard errors; figures in square brackets are standard errors assuming $N/3$ independent observations. DW represents the Durbin–Watson statistic. Q-stat indicates the Ljung–Box Q-statistic for lag order 13. * (**) indicates significance at 5% (1%) level using the adjusted standard errors. Sample periods correspond to those indicated in Table 2.1.

Table 2.8. *Trends in the influence of New York vs. Tokyo covered interest rates, 1982:09–1992:03*

Country	Constant	New York	New York interaction	Tokyo	Tokyo interaction	$\bar{R}^2$	DW	Q-stat
Australia	2.865 (0.645) [1.936]	-0.663 (1.807) [3.129]	-0.131 (0.324) [0.561]	1.320 (1.807) [3.129]	0.145 (0.319) [0.553]	.81	0.960	705.34**
Canada	0.395 (0.129) [0.386]	0.416 (0.365) [0.632]	0.010 (0.054) [0.094]	0.525 (0.356) [0.617]	-0.011 (0.054) [0.092]	.98	1.137	103.67**
Hong Kong[a]	0.361** (0.073) [0.218]	0.882* (0.403) [0.698]	0.032 (0.062) [0.108]	0.085 (0.394) [0.682]	0.031 (0.061) [0.106]	.99	1.965	16.71
Malaysia[b]	1.078 (0.297) [0.891]	1.296 (1.574) [2.726]	-0.343 (0.343) [0.594]	-0.473 (1.521) [2.651]	0.304 (0.332) [0.576]	.91	1.115	33.96** 7.24
New Zealand	2.166 (0.688) [2.064]	1.076 (2.419) [4.190]	-0.276 (0.412) [0.713]	-0.338 (2.406) [4.167]	0.288 (0.406) [0.703]	.86	1.464	32.35**
Singapore	0.102 (0.118) [0.354]	1.040 (0.529) [0.916]	-0.120 (0.083) [0.143]	-0.090 (0.510) [0.883]	0.110 (0.080) [0.139]	.97	1.169	66.91**

Note: Figures in parentheses are asymptotic standard errors; figures in square brackets are standard errors assuming $N/3$ independent observations. DW represents the Durbin–Watson statistic. Q-stat indicates the Ljung–Box Q-statistic for lag order 13. * (**) indicates significance at 5% (1%) level using the adjusted standard errors. Sample periods correspond to those indicated in Table 2.2.

[a] t-statistics calculated using asymptotic standard errors since there is no apparent serial correlation.
[b] The first figure for the Q-statistic is for the period 1982:09–1987:06; the second is for 1987:11–1992:03.

Table 2.9. *Trends in the influence of New York vs. Tokyo uncovered interest rates, 1988:02–1992:03*

Currency	Constant	New York	New York interaction	Tokyo	Tokyo interaction	$\bar{R}^2$	DW	Q-stat
Australia	11.143** (1.162) [3.486]	0.710 (0.317) [0.549]	-0.106* (0.043) [0.075]	-0.209 (0.280) [0.485]	0.048 (0.037) [0.064]	.44	0.362	86.98**
Canada	9.726** (0.807) [2.422]	0.631 (0.220) [0.381]	-0.094* (0.028) [0.048]	-0.319 (0.181) [0.313]	0.056* (0.024) [0.041]	.42	0.340	89.44**
Korea (KO2)	13.964** (0.227) [0.680]	-0.760 (0.248) [0.429]	0.118** (0.031) [0.054]	0.035 (0.116) [0.200]	0.009 (0.016) [0.027]	.58	0.806	46.80**
Korea (KO3)	13.695** (0.194) [0.582]	-0.760 (0.211) [0.365]	0.016** (0.026) [0.046]	-0.138 (0.101) [0.176]	0.021 (0.014) [0.024]	.78	0.657	51.85**
Singapore^a	3.433** (0.445) [1.334]	0.595 (0.246) [0.426]	-0.050 (0.030) [0.052]	-0.201 (0.156) [0.270]	0.027 (0.021) [0.036]	.53	0.243	21.68*
Taiwan	7.332** (0.601) [1.803]	0.177 (0.596) [1.032]	-0.018 (0.074) [0.128]	0.387 (0.401) [0.695]	-0.052 (0.054) [0.094]	-.06	0.343	62.73**

Note: Figures in parentheses are asymptotic standard errors; figures in square brackets are standard errors assuming $N/3$ independent observations. DW represents the Durbin–Watson statistic. Q-stat indicates the Ljung–Box Q-statistic for lag order 13. * (**) indicates significance at 5% (1%) level using the adjusted standard errors.
^{a}Data available only for alternating months.

43

increasing effect for five of six countries, but is not statistically significant. Here the imprecision is probably due more to measurement error in the survey data than to multicollinearity.

2.7   Conclusions

A series of criteria have been forwarded to evaluate the extent of financial and currency linkages among the Pacific Rim countries for which we have reasonable market-determined interest rates, and how the links have evolved over the period 1982–92. Our findings can be summarized as follows. The region is still far from achieving interest rate convergence. However, U.S. and local interest rates *do* appear to be increasingly correlated as time passes. Moreover, for countries with relatively well-developed forward markets, there is substantial evidence of declining covered interest differentials, indicating a greater degree of financial integration. The evolution of the exchange risk premium and the uncovered interest rate parity criterion indicate little evidence of (statistically significant) change in the degree of currency integration. With respect to the relative importance of the United States and Japan in the region, for a few countries like Indonesia there is some evidence of a shift during 1982–92 of influence from U.S. interest rates to Japanese interest rates, which may be attributable to a greater role for the yen in the region. Overall, however, the evidence for a "yen bloc" is much less than one would imagine from popular accounts.

Data appendix

Interest rates

Eurocurrency deposit rates. The U.S., U.K., and Japanese three-month Eurocurrency deposit rates are the arithmetic average of the bid and offer rates in London at close of market, as reported by Bank of America up to October 6, 1986, and Reuters' Information Services thereafter, and recorded by Data Resources International in the DRIFACS database.

Local market rates. Where both WFM and DRI are indicated under "Source," WFM is the source until 1989:10, at which time DRIFACS becomes the source. DRI indicates DRIFACS; WFM indicates *World Financial Markets;* and WFMr indicates Morgan Guaranty's database, as provided by Carlton Strong.

Country	Source	DRI code	Description
U.S.	DRI	FIP90Y	Financial paper, industrial firms, 90 days
U.S.	DRI	USD03	3-month Eurodollar rate
Australia	WFM, DRI	ADBBL90Q	90-day bank bill, quote
Canada	WFM, DRI	CACP90B,A	3-month prime finance company paper
Hong Kong	WFM, DRI	HKM03B,A	3-month interbank deposit rate
Indonesia	WFMr	—	1-month interbank deposit rate
Japan	WFM, DRI	JABGDS90Y	3-month Gensaki bond rate
Japan	DRI	JAD03	3-month Euroyen rate
Korea 2	WFMr	—	Monetary stabilization bond
Korea 3	Alternate	—	Avg. 1-, 3-, 5-year corp. bond, avg. of daily
Malaysia	WFMr	—	3-month interbank deposit rate
New Zealand	WFM, WFMr	—	3-month commercial bills to Dec. 1987; 3-month bank bills thereafter
Singapore	WFMr	—	3-month banker's acceptances to Aug. 1987; 3-month commercial bills thereafter
Taiwan	WFMr	—	90-day banker's acceptances
Thailand	WFMr	—	Call money rate
U.K.	DRI	UKM03B,A	3-month interbank deposit rate
U.K.	DRI	UKD03	3-month Europound rate

Exchange rates

All exchange rates (except those indicated below) are London 3 p.m., arithmetic average of bid and offer rates as reported by Barclay's until the end of March 1990, at which time the series is no longer recorded by DRIFACS. Thereafter, the London close rate is used, as reported by Reuters' Information Services. A consistent series is not used (i.e., the London close all the way) because the London close series begins only in 1986.

The exchange rates for Indonesia, Korea, and Thailand were obtained from the International Monetary Fund's *International Financial Statistics* database and are London midday rates.

Actual regression specifications

The interest rate regressions are actually run with the following specification:

$$\ln(1 + i) = \alpha_0 + \alpha_1 \ln(1 + i^{US}) + \alpha_2[\ln(1 + i^{US}) \times \text{TIME}].$$

The covered interest rate regressions are run analogously:

$$\ln(1 + i) = \beta_0 + \beta_1[\ln(1 + i^{US}) - (\ln F - \ln S)],$$

where F is the forward exchange rate (U.S. dollar / foreign currency unit) and S is the spot exchange rate (U.S. dollar / foreign currency unit).

References

Aliber, Robert Z. (1973). "The Interest Rate Parity Theorem: A Reinterpretation," *Journal of Political Economy* 81:1451–9.

Brenner, Robin, and Kenneth Kroner (1992). "Arbitrage and Cointegration." Unpublished manuscript, University of Arizona, Department of Economics, Tucson.

Cheng, Hang-Sheng, ed. (1988). *Monetary Policy in Pacific Basin Countries.* Norwell, MA: Kluwer for the Federal Reserve Bank of San Francisco.

Chinn, Menzie, and Jeffrey Frankel (1994). "Capital Barriers in the Pacific Basin: 1982–1992," *Journal of International Economic Integration* 9:62–80.

Coats, Warren, Jr. (1988). "Capital Mobility and Monetary Policy: Australia, Japan and New Zealand." In Hang-Sheng Cheng, ed., *Monetary Policy in Pacific Basin Countries,* pp. 81–94. Norwell, MA: Kluwer for the Federal Reserve Bank of San Francisco.

Dooley, Michael, and Peter Isard (1980). "Capital Controls, Political Risk, and Deviations from Interest-Rate Parity," *Journal of Political Economy* 88(2):370–84.

Emery, Robert (1992). "Central Banks' Use in East Asia of Money Market Instruments in the Conduct of Monetary Policy," International Finance Discussion Paper no. 426. Board of Governors of the Federal Reserve System, Washington, DC.

Faruqee, Hamid (1992). "Dynamic Capital Mobility in Pacific Basin Developing Countries: Estimation and Policy Implications" (International Monetary Fund) *Staff Papers* 39:706–17.

Feldman, Robert (1986). *Japanese Financial Markets: Deficits, Dilemmas, and Deregulation.* Cambridge, MA: MIT Press.

Frankel, Jeffrey (1984). *The Yen/Dollar Agreement: Liberalizing Japanese Capital Markets.* Policy Analyses in International Economics no. 9. Washington, DC: Institute for International Economics.

  (1991). "Quantifying International Capital Mobility." In D. Bernheim and J. Shoven, eds., *National Saving and Economic Performance,* pp. 227–60. Chicago: University of Chicago Press.

  (1992). "The Recent Liberalization of Korea's Foreign Exchange Markets, and Tests of U.S. versus Japanese Influence," *Seoul Journal of Economics* 5(Spring):1–29.

  (1993). "Is Japan Creating a Yen Bloc in East Asia and the Pacific?" In Jeffrey Frankel and Miles Kahler, eds., *Regionalism and Rivalry: Japan and the U.S. in Pacific Asia,* pp. 53–85. Chicago: University of Chicago Press.

Frankel, Jeffrey, and Menzie Chinn (1993). "Exchange Rate Expectations and the Risk Premium: Tests for a Cross-Section of 17 Currencies," *Review of International Economics* 1:136–44.

Frankel, Jeffrey, and Alan MacArthur (1988). "Political vs. Currency Premia in International Real Interest Differentials: A Study of Forward Rates for 24 Countries," *European Economic Review* 32:1083–1121.

Frankel, Jeffrey, and Steven Phillips (1991). "The European Monetary System: Credible at Last?" NBER Working Paper no. 3819. *Oxford Economic Papers* 44:791–816.

Frankel, Jeffrey, Steven Phillips, and Menzie Chinn (1992). "Financial and Currency Integration in the European Monetary System: The Statistical Record." In Francisco Torres and Francesco Giavazzi, eds., *The Transition to Economic and Monetary Union in Europe,* pp. 270–306. Lisbon: Banco de Portugal; London: Centre for Economic Policy Research.

Frankel, Jeffrey, and Shang-Jin Wei (1994). "Yen Bloc or Dollar Bloc: Exchange Rate Policies of the East Asian Economies." In Takatoshi Ito and Anne Krueger, eds., *Macroeconomic Linkage: Savings, Exchange Rates, and Capital Flows.* Chicago: University of Chicago Press and the National Bureau of Economic Research.

Froot, Kenneth, and Jeffrey Frankel (1989). "Forward Discount Bias: Is It an Exchange Risk Premium?" *Quarterly Journal of Economics* 104:139–61.

Glick, Reuven (1987). "Interest Rate Linkages in the Pacific Basin." (Federal Reserve Bank of San Francisco) *Economic Review* (Summer):31–42.

Glick, Reuven, and Michael Hutchison (1990). "Financial Liberalization in the Pacific Basin: Implications for Real Interest Rate Linkages," *Journal of the Japanese and International Economies* 4:36–48.

Otani, Ichiro (1983). "Exchange Rate Instability and Capital Controls: The Japanese Experience, 1978–81." In David Bigman and Teizo Taya, eds., *Exchange Rate and Trade Instability: Causes, Consequences and Remedies,* pp. 311–37. Cambridge, MA: Ballinger.

Stekler, Lois, and Edwin Truman (1992). "The Adequacy of the Data on U.S. International Finance Transactions: A Federal Reserve Perspective," International Finance Discussion Paper no. 430. Board of Governors of the Federal Reserve System, Washington, DC.

Tavlas, George, and Yuzuru Ozeki (1992). *The Internationalization of Currencies: An Appraisal of the Japanese Yen.* Occasional Paper no. 90. Washington, DC: International Monetary Fund.

Tseng, Wanda, and Robert Corker (1991). *Financial Liberalization, Money Demand, and Monetary Policy in Asian Countries.* Occasional Paper no. 84. Washington, DC: International Monetary Fund.

CHAPTER 3

Relative returns on equities in Pacific Basin countries

Charles Engel and John H. Rogers

3.1   Capital mobility

Equity markets have grown rapidly and restrictions on investments have declined equally rapidly in Pacific Basin countries in the 1980s. The return on equities now provides a good measure of the opportunity cost of capital in the eleven countries that are the focus of this study: Australia, Canada, Chile, Japan, Korea, Malaysia, Mexico, Singapore, Taiwan, Thailand, and the United States.

The purpose of equity markets is to allocate capital to its most efficient use. In the absence of uncertainty, efficient equity markets ensure that the marginal product of capital is equalized among its various uses. In the presence of uncertainty, equity markets price assets to reflect not only the expected return on the asset, but the riskiness of projects as well.

A great deal of attention has been focused in recent years on the international mobility of capital. If there are restrictions on capital flows between countries, then investors will not be able to allocate their resources toward their most desirable use. There appears to have been a global trend toward liberalization of capital markets and toward allowing foreigners access to local markets. However, there is no consensus as to whether these moves have achieved true integration of international capital markets.

Feldstein and Horioka (1980) questioned the degree of integration of international capital markets. They argued that if capital could flow freely between countries, savers would have no bias toward channeling their funds toward domestic projects. If capital markets allocated savings efficiently, the savings of residents of one country should be just as likely to be used to fund investments in foreign countries as to fund capital projects at home. So we should not expect to see a close relation between the level of saving in a country and the level of investment. There is no particular reason that high-saving countries should also be countries with excellent investment opportunities.

However, in examining a cross section of countries within the Organization for Economic Cooperation and Development (OECD) over the period 1960–74, Feldstein and Horioka found a strong correlation between national saving–GDP ratios and investment–GDP ratios. The simple correlation coefficient was greater than .90. The authors interpreted their findings as evidence of barriers to the international flow of funds: "If portfolio preferences and institutional rigidities impede the flow of long-term capital among countries, increases in domestic saving will be reflected primarily in additional domestic investment."

The findings of Feldstein and Horioka are surprising and have led many economists to search for ways to reconcile these conclusions with the observation that there are few restrictions on capital flows among OECD countries, and that transaction costs have fallen to very low levels. While many explanations for Feldstein and Horioka's results have emerged over the years, perhaps the most compelling has been offered by Frankel (1986, 1991). Frankel makes a distinction between portfolio capital and physical capital. Investment, as measured by Feldstein and Horioka, refers to the accumulation of physical capital. However, when economists speak of international capital mobility, they are not referring to the movement of physical capital. It is clear that moving actual machines and factories would be very costly. Nobody would describe such movements as "free." Mobility of capital, instead, refers to the movement of portfolio capital.

In essence, Feldstein and Horioka's theory is that international mobility of capital would equalize risk-adjusted ex ante real rates of return. With real rates of return the same across countries, there would be no reason for savers to channel their funds exclusively to home projects. Indeed, if a desirable investment opportunity arises abroad, the marginal product of capital, and therefore the real return on investment, is pushed up temporarily in that foreign country. Then capital will flow to that country until the real return there is drawn back into equality with ex ante real returns in other countries.

Thus, letting r^j_{t+1} equal the real rate of return between period t and period $t + 1$ in country j, and letting r^k_{t+1} be the analogous return for country k, the Feldstein–Horioka null hypothesis is that free international capital mobility implies

$$E_t r^j_{t+1} - E_t r^k_{t+1} = 0, \tag{3.1}$$

for all countries j and k. In this expression, E_t refers to the expectations that investors form at time t (so that, e.g., $E_t r^j_{t+1}$ is the expectation at time t of the real rate of return between time t and $t + 1$ in country j).

Frankel, however, notes that relationship (3.1) is really a condition that one would expect to hold if physical capital were free to move internationally. Then efficient markets would ensure that the real returns to owners of capital were the same, irrespective of the location of the capital.

However, as already noted, few economists interpret the notion of capital mobility as applying to actual machines and factories. If the ex ante return on capital is temporarily high in some country, economists do not envision entrepreneurs unbolting machines and disassembling factories to ship them to the country with the high rate of return. Instead, portfolio capital will flow to that country. Funds will be made available so that entrepreneurs can build new factories in the country where the marginal product of capital is high.

Frankel notes that free mobility of portfolio capital will result in the equalization of the nominal rate of return on investments, adjusted for expectations of currency depreciation. That is, when capital flows freely, investors should expect the same return on funds that are kept at home and funds that are sent abroad:

$$E_t i^j_{t+1} - E_t i^k_{t+1} - E_t d^{jk}_{t+1} = 0. \tag{3.2}$$

In this equation, i is the nominal rate of return. So $E_t i^j_{t+1}$ is the rate of return in country j, denominated in the currency of country j, that investors expect between time t and $t + 1$, while $E_t i^k_{t+1}$ is the analogous rate of return for country k. To make these two rates of return comparable, they must be converted into a common currency. We use the symbol d^{jk}_{t+1} to refer to the rate of depreciation of currency j relative to currency k between time t and $t + 1$. So $E_t d^{jk}_{t+1}$ is the expected rate of depreciation of currency j at time t. Equation (3.2) says that free mobility of portfolio capital implies that the expected nominal returns on investments in any two countries j and k, when expressed in a common currency, will be equalized.

What is the difference between expression (3.1), which states that ex ante real returns are the same, and equation (3.2), which indicates the equality of expected nominal returns? We can write the expected real return in country j as

$$E_t r^j_{t+1} = E_t i^j_{t+1} - E_t \pi^j_{t+1}. \tag{3.3}$$

Here $E_t \pi^j_{t+1}$ is the rate of inflation of country j's prices that is expected to occur between time t and $t + 1$. Using relation (3.3), we can write the difference in the ex ante real rates of return as

$$E_t r_{t+1}^j - E_t r_{t+1}^k = [E_t i_{t+1}^j - E_t i_{t+1}^k - E_t d_{t+1}^{jk}]$$
$$+ [E_t d_{t+1}^{jk} - E_t \pi_{t+1}^j + E_t \pi_{t+1}^k]. \qquad (3.4)$$

The first bracketed term on the right-hand side of equation (3.4) is the ex ante nominal return differential, as in equation (3.2). The ex ante nominal return differential does not equal the expected real return differential unless the second bracketed term on the right side of equation (3.4) is zero. That term is the expected change in the real value of currency j relative to currency k. Thus the real return condition expressed in equation (3.1) is equivalent to the nominal return condition in equation (3.2) if and only if ex ante purchasing power parity (PPP) holds.

So investment projects in one country may indeed have a higher expected real return than investment projects in another country, even if there is perfect international mobility of portfolio capital. That can occur as long as the expected change in the real exchange rate is not zero. Economists have long understood conditions under which ex ante PPP would not hold, and these conditions are not necessarily related to the presence or absence of capital controls. For example, Dornbusch (1976) examines the behavior of exchange rates and interest rates in a model with perfect capital mobility, but one in which PPP fails to hold because nominal goods prices are "sticky." That is, in Dornbusch's framework, equilibrium prices adjust toward PPP in the long run, but this adjustment occurs only gradually over time. Thus, deviations from PPP persist for long periods. In Dornbusch's extended Mundell–Fleming framework, national saving and investment rates can be highly correlated even in the presence of free portfolio capital mobility. Other authors (e.g., Razin, 1984) have emphasized that PPP need not be a condition of equilibrium in the market for goods when there are nontraded goods. Engel and Kletzer (1989) show that in general one should expect to find a high correlation between the level of saving and investment in countries when nontraded goods are present.

While Feldstein and Horioka and most of the subsequent related literature have focused on capital mobility in OECD countries, there has recently developed considerable interest in the nature of capital flows among Pacific Rim countries. In part that interest has arisen naturally from the increased capital flows among these countries, which were spurred by the widespread liberalization of capital markets and financial reforms that occurred in this region in the 1970s and 1980s.

(See Cheng, 1986, for a collection of papers that extensively study these issues.) Of particular interest for our purposes has been the concomitant expansion of local equity markets in the region. As these markets have developed, the opportunities for international investors seeking high return or diversification have expanded. In this essay, we explore the success of these equity markets in equalizing real returns on investment opportunities.

In particular, we focus on the issue raised by Frankel: Do real returns between countries differ because ex ante nominal rates of return are different or because ex ante PPP fails to hold? We develop a measure of the relative importance of these two components of real return differentials in explaining the average difference in expected real returns on equities across pairs of countries on the Pacific Rim.

Our findings show that generally it is the ex ante nominal return differentials that account for most of the difference in real return prospects for equity investors across countries. This result holds across most pairs of countries in the region, although it is not universal.

We focus on whether the exchange rate arrangements of the various countries influence the importance of nominal return differentials versus deviations from PPP in explaining ex ante real return differentials. Our findings are that there does not appear to be any consistent relation between the type of exchange rate arrangements and the relative strength of the two components.

In reaching the conclusion that most of the difference in real returns is attributable to the gap between expected nominal returns, we have not been able to adjust for risk. Hence, while our findings may imply that there are still important restrictions to the flow of financial capital among Pacific Rim countries that prevents the equalization of ex ante nominal returns, it is also possible that the differences in returns stem from the difference in the relative riskiness of the equity investments.

In Section 3.2, we present the methods we employ for measuring the relative strength of deviations from ex ante nominal returns equality versus ex ante PPP. Our methods are related to those of Frankel (1991, 1992), Chinn and Frankel (1992), Glick (1987), and Glick and Hutchison (1990), which focus on markets for lending rather than equity markets. In Section 3.3, we discuss the nature of restrictions on investments in equity markets in the Pacific Rim and the types of foreign exchange rate systems that prevail in these countries. We also discuss the data that we use in our empirical study. In Section 3.4, we present the results of our study and discuss the forces that lead to different degrees of influence of financial market versus goods market integration in the

Pacific Basin. In Section 3.5 we offer some conclusions and discuss the implications of our findings.

3.2   Decomposing the real return differential

In this section, we present a method for decomposing movements in the expected real return differential into a fraction attributable to changes in the ex ante nominal return differential and the rest to movements in ex ante deviations from PPP.

Initially, let us assume that we can measure expectations of investors completely accurately. Of course, in reality we cannot, so in a moment we will turn to how we derive a measure of expectations and what we do about the fact that the measure is not entirely accurate. First, however, assume that we observe $y_t = E_t r^j_{t+1} - E_t r^k_{t+1}$; $x_t = E_t i^j_{t+1} - E_t i^k_{t+1} - E_t d^{jk}_{t+1}$; and $z_t = E_t d^{jk}_{t+1} - E_t \pi^j_{t+1} + E_t \pi^k_{t+1}$. So y_t is the expected real interest differential, x_t the expected nominal interest differential, and z_t the expected deviation from PPP.

With these definitions $y_t \equiv x_t + z_t$. We would like to know what makes y_t differ from zero. That is, what makes the real interest differential at any time nonzero? Is it because x_t is different from zero, or because z_t is different from zero?

One way to think about measuring this is to calculate the average values of y, x, and z and then look at the ratio of the mean of x to the mean of y and the mean of z to the mean of y. One problem with this approach is that over time y might fluctuate between positive and negative. Its average might be low, but it may be substantially different from zero in every period. So looking at the mean of y might conceal the fact that the expected real interest differential is consistently nonzero.

We could avoid that problem by considering, for example, the average of the absolute values of y, x, and z or the average of the squared values of y, x, and z. But this approach does not solve another problem – suppose that x tends to be negative in periods when y is positive. Then it would be misleading to say that large values of the square of x are associated with large values of the square of y. When y is positive but x is negative, z is pulling y above zero and x is dragging it back down, so x is not responsible for making y nonzero.

An alternative decomposition is to calculate the sample noncentral second moments: $\hat{m}(y, y) \equiv \Sigma\, y_t^2/T$; $\hat{m}(x, y) \equiv \Sigma\, x_t y_t/T$; and so on (where T is the number of observations). Since $\hat{m}(y, y) = \hat{m}(x, y) + \hat{m}(z, y)$, it is natural to attribute to x the ratio $\hat{m}(x, y)/\hat{m}(y, y)$ of the average squared deviation of y from zero and to attribute to z the remainder, $\hat{m}(z, y)/\hat{m}(y, y)$. For example, suppose that every period $y = 5$, $x = 10$, and $z = -5$. Then, under this decomposition, we have that 2.0 (200 percent) of the average deviation of y^2 from 0 comes from x being different from zero, while -1.0 (-100 percent) comes from z. That makes sense here, because y is always positive but z is always negative. So z tends to draw y toward zero, but it is being pulled away from zero in the positive direction by the large positive values of x. But if, for example, every period $y = 5$, $x = 4$, and $z = 1$, the fraction of the deviation we attribute to x is $\frac{4}{5}$ and that to z, $\frac{1}{5}$.

In practice we cannot measure y, x, and z exactly. We will assume that we measure expectations with error and observe only y^0, x^0, and z^0, which are related to the actual expectations by the following equations:

$$y_t^0 = y_t + \epsilon_t^y,$$
$$x_t^0 = x_t + \epsilon_t^x,$$
$$z_t^0 = z_t + \epsilon_t^z.$$

The ϵ represent measurement error terms.

We would like to measure $\hat{m}(x, y)/\hat{m}(y, y)$, but we do not observe either x or y (or z). We propose using $\hat{m}(x^0, y^0)/\hat{m}(y^0, y^0)$ as an approximation to $\hat{m}(x, y)/\hat{m}(y, y)$. We can write

$$\frac{\hat{m}(x^0, y^0)}{\hat{m}(y^0, y^0)} = \frac{\hat{m}(x, y) + \hat{m}(y, \epsilon^x) + \hat{m}(x, \epsilon^y) + \hat{m}(\epsilon^x, \epsilon^y)}{\hat{m}(y, y) + 2\hat{m}(y, \epsilon^y) + \hat{m}(\epsilon^y, \epsilon^y)}.$$

Clearly, $\hat{m}(x^0, y^0)/\hat{m}(y^0, y^0)$ does not exactly equal $\hat{m}(x, y)/\hat{m}(y, y)$.

If the difference between our measured expectations and the true expectations is pure measurement error, it is probably plausible to assume that the measurement errors have means of zero and are uncorrelated with y, x, and z. Let $m(\ )$ represent the population moment that is consistently estimated by $\hat{m}(\ )$. Then our assumption is that the moments $m(j, \epsilon^k)$ for $j, k = x, y, z$, are zero. Imposing this (and replacing sample moments with population moments from the preceding equation), we have

$$\frac{m(x^0, y^0)}{m(y^0, y^0)} = \frac{m(x, y) + m(\epsilon^x, \epsilon^y)}{m(y, y) + m(\epsilon^y, \epsilon^y)}.$$

Thus, $m(x^0, y^0)/m(y^0, y^0)$ will equal $m(x, y)/m(y, y)$ as long as

$$\frac{m(\epsilon^x, \epsilon^y)}{m(\epsilon^y, \epsilon^y)} = \frac{m(x, y)}{m(y, y)}.$$

Intuitively, this condition is just that the measurement error of x contributes as much to the measurement error of y as x contributes to the deviation of y from zero.

Even if we do not accept the assumption under which $m(x^0, y^0)/m(y^0, y^0)$ equals $m(x, y)/m(y, y)$, so we do not believe that we can accurately measure the share of deviations of y from zero that are attributable to x, we can compare these shares across countries under much weaker assumptions. Much of our analysis of Section 3.4 consists of precisely this type of comparison. We ask, for example, whether countries with more flexible exchange rates tend to have larger ex ante real return differentials because of fluctuations in the ex ante nominal return differentials or in the ex ante deviations from PPP. We can make the fairly innocuous assumption that the noise-to-signal ratios are constant across countries,

$$\frac{m(\epsilon^x, \epsilon^y)}{m(x, y)} = \alpha$$

and

$$\frac{m(\epsilon^y, \epsilon^y)}{m(y, y)} = \beta,$$

but without imposing the requirement that $\alpha = \beta$. With these assumptions, we have

$$\frac{m(x^0, y^0)}{m(y^0, y^0)} = \frac{m(x, y)}{m(y, y)} \left(\frac{1 + \alpha}{1 + \beta} \right).$$

Under these assumptions, $m(x, y)/m(y, y)$ is not equal to $m(x^0, y^0)/m(y^0, y^0)$, but in all countries the measurement is off by a scale factor of $(1 + \alpha)/(1 + \beta)$. Thus, our measure correctly orders countries by the size of $m(x, y)/m(y, y)$, even if we cannot measure that ratio consistently.

We now turn to the construction of our measures of the ex ante real return differential, $y_t \equiv E_t r_{t+1}^j - E_t r_{t+1}^k$; the ex ante nominal return differential, $x_t = E_t i_{t+1}^j - E_t i_{t+1}^k - E_t d_{t+1}^{jk}$; and the ex ante deviation from PPP, $z_t = E_t d_{t+1}^{jk} - E_t \pi_{t+1}^j + E_t \pi_{t+1}^k$. Our measures of these variables are real time forecasts based on lagged values of $i_{t+1}^j - i_{t+1}^k - d_{t+1}^{jk}$, $d_{t+1}^{jk} - \pi_{t+1}^j + \pi_{t+1}^k$ and lags of the squares of $r_{t+1}^j - r_{t+1}^k$,

$i^j_{t+1} - i^k_{t+1} - d^{jk}_{t+1}$, and $d^{jk}_{t+1} - \pi^j_{t+1} + \pi^k_{t+1}$. For example, suppose that we wish to derive the expectation at time s of $r^j_{s+1} - r^k_{s+1}$. Then we perform the regression of $r^j_t - r^k_t$ on $i^j_{t-1} - i^k_{t-1} - d^{jk}_{t-1}$, $-d^{jk}_{t-1} - \pi^k_{t-1} + \pi^k_{t-1}$, and the squares of r^j_{t-1}, $-r^k_{t-1}$, $i^j_{t-1} - i^k_{t-1} - d^{jk}_{t-1}$, and $-d^{jk}_{t-1} - \pi^j_{t-1} + \pi^k_{t-1}$, with data on $r^j_t - r^k_t$ up to time s. We use time s data to forecast $r^j_{s+1} - r^k_{s+1}$. To forecast $r^j_{s+2} - r^k_{s+2}$, we reestimate the forecasting equation using data through time $s + 1$. Hence, we get "rolling" or "real time" forecasts of each of the variables.

We use only one lag of the various variables as forecasters, for several reasons. First, as we discuss in the next section, we examine a relatively short time series on equity returns. In part, this stems from the fact that the equity markets in many of the countries we examine have only fairly recently become very large and open to foreign investment. We also must use two years and one month of data to derive our first forecast. So the limited run of data constrains the number of lags that can be used in the forecasting equation. In addition, we do not want to overfit the equation. In preliminary work that is not reported here, we added some right-hand-side variables such as the deviation of last month's value of the return differential from its average over the prior six months. We found that such variables were usually not significant in the regressions and did not improve the forecasting performance.

The deviation of our measure of the agents' expectations from their true expectations will satisfy the properties stipulated earlier – that is, have a mean of zero and be uncorrelated with x, y, z and the other measurement errors – when two conditions are met. First, we assume that investors have rational expectations. Hence, they use all available information in an efficient way to construct their forecasts. We, as econometricians, do not know precisely which variables agents use in deriving their forecasts. The error we make in measuring the investors' expectations arises because we leave out variables from our forecasting equation that investors use in arriving at their expectations. So our second condition is that the marginal forecasting ability of the left-out variables be uncorrelated with the variables we include in the forecasting equation. (That is, the fitted values of the projection of the forecast equation errors onto the left-out variables should be uncorrelated with our included right-hand-side variables.)

An alternative way of measuring expectations would be to follow the lead of Frankel and Froot (1987), Froot and Frankel (1989), and Chinn and Frankel (1992) and use survey data. Although arguably there would still be some measurement error in expectations because the surveys might not cover comprehensively the relevant actors in the equity markets, it is a good bet that such surveys provide more accurate measures of expectations than the ones we construct. Unfortunately, we can find no surveys of investors' expectations of equity returns, inflation, and currency depreciation for most of the countries in our study.

3.3 Equity markets and foreign exchange markets in the Pacific Basin

We examine the behavior of equity returns from eleven countries that surround the Pacific Ocean – Japan, Canada, Australia, Chile, Korea, Malaysia, Mexico, Singapore, Taiwan, Thailand, and the United States. We use data on equity returns beginning in September 1983 (with the exception of Taiwan, whose data begin in January 1986). Our first forecast is for twenty-five months after the starting date of the data (October 1985 in most instances). The data end in 1991 for most countries, and in 1990 for the rest. Our stock return data are taken from the Datastream International tape for all countries except Chile and are middle of the month, end of trading day. Most of our information on the nature of restrictions on international investment in markets comes from either the 1990 edition of *Emerging Stock Markets Factbook* of the International Finance Corporation or the 1988 edition of the *Directory of World Stock Exchanges* compiled by the *Economist*.

Equity trading in Australia occurs on the Australian Stock Exchange in Sydney. Share trading began in Sydney in 1828, with shares of a single company being traded. Today there are essentially no restrictions on foreign investment in shares, and foreigners are allowed membership on the exchange. The only minor restriction is imposed by Australia's Foreign Take-over Act, which limits foreign ownership of a firm to 15 percent of the firm's value for a single investor. Our stock index data for Australia are from the All Ordinary Index.

Three-quarters of trades in shares in Canada occurs on the Toronto Stock Exchange. The only restrictions on foreign investment in Canada are limits on foreign control of certain companies such as banks. Foreigners are not allowed to be members of the Toronto Stock Exchange, but membership is open on the Bourse de Montréal. The Toronto Stock Exchange began trading in 1852, but informal trading began in Montreal in the 1820s. The stock return data for Canada come from the Toronto Stock Exchange Composite Index.

The Bolsa de Comercio de Santiago handles share trading in Chile. Trading began in Chile in 1893, and the markets have been relatively free since the liberalization that occurred in 1973. Chile underwent a severe financial crisis in the early 1980s, but the stock market apparently recovered by the mid-1980s. There are no restrictions on the remittance of income earned by foreigners on the Chilean stock market, but the initial capital invested must remain in Chile for at least three years. Foreigners are allowed membership in the stock exchange. Our Chilean stock return series is taken from *International Financial Statistics* published by the International Monetary Fund.

The Tokyo Stock Exchange has been trading since 1878. In accord with the general climate of financial liberalization following the December 1980 revision of the Foreign Exchange and Foreign Trade Control Law, there are essentially no restrictions on foreign investment. In February 1986, six foreign securities firms obtained regular membership at the Tokyo Stock Exchange, and foreign brokers won a recent battle to obtain seats on the exchange. In this essay, we use the Nikkei Dow Jones Average Index.

The Korean Stock Exchange was founded in Seoul in 1956. Until very recently there have been severe limitations on investments by foreigners. Investment and repatriation were subject to approval by the Ministry of Finance. However, foreigners could invest through international investment trusts, the Korea Fund, and the Korea–Europe Fund. In January 1992, a significant liberalization of the restrictions on foreign investment was initiated, although foreign ownership is still limited to less than 10 percent of the shares of any one company. Our Korean stock return data are constructed from the Korea South Composite Index.

In Malaysia, trading occurs on the Kuala Lumpur Stock Exchange. The market is essentially open to foreigners – they may obtain membership, and trading is subject only to the restriction that acquisitions exceeding M$5 million must be approved by the Foreign Investment Committee. Investment is also possible for foreigners through a mutual fund traded on international markets. We use the Financial Times Actuaries Index for our data on Malaysian returns.

Trading on the Malay Peninsula dates back to the late nineteenth century, and in 1930 the Singapore Stockbrokers Association became the first organized exchange. In 1960 the Malayan Stock Exchange was chartered with trading in Singapore and Kuala Lumpur. When Singapore seceded from the Federation of Malaysia in 1965, it remained in the exchange. The Stock Exchange of Singapore did not become an independent organization until 1973. There are virtually no restrictions on foreign investment (there are some requirements concerning the degree of foreign ownership of banks and newspapers), and foreign brokers are allowed membership on the Singapore exchange. Our stock returns are calculated from the Straits Times Index.

Mexico's share trading occurs at the Bolsa Mexicana de Valores in

Mexico City. Stock trading began there in 1894. Until the late 1980s there were a few significant restrictions on foreign investments. Foreigners were not allowed seats on the exchange, and foreign investors could not own shares in some industries: petroleum, petrochemical, development of radioactive materials, some mining, electricity, railroads, telegraph, radio and television, transport, national air transport and maritime companies, forest exploitation, and gas distribution. There has been considerable liberalization since Carlos Salinas became president, however. In addition, a Mexico Fund is traded on the New York Stock Exchange. For Mexico, we use data from the Financial Times Actuaries Index.

In Taiwan, the Taipei Stock Exchange Corporation began trading in 1961. Foreign nationals can trade under certain regulations, but otherwise investing for foreigners is limited to closed-end mutual funds traded on the U.S. and European markets. The Taiwan Weighted Index is the source of our stock returns for this country.

The Securities Exchange of Thailand (SET) trades securities in Bangkok. It began trading in 1975 and is now fairly open to foreigners, except for restrictions that prevent foreign interests from becoming majority shareholders. In addition, closed-end mutual funds are traded on international markets. We use the SET Index for our stock return data for Thailand.

There are several stock exchanges in the United States, the largest of which is the New York Stock Exchange (NYSE). The NYSE began using that name in 1863, but share trading began there in 1792. There are no rules for foreign investors that differ from those imposed on domestic residents. We use returns from the Standard and Poor's 500 Index.

Table 3.1, from the 1990 edition of the *Emerging Stock Markets Factbook*, indicates the rapid growth in the markets we focus on. In the 1980s generally there was a sharp increase in the number of firms whose shares were traded – particularly in the smaller markets – and the dollar value of shares traded expanded by a large factor in all eleven countries.

In the period covered by our study on expected stock market returns (post-October 1985), many of our countries maintained essentially freely floating exchange rates. The United States, Canada, Japan, and Australia can be characterized in this manner. The other seven countries can be said to have been under managed floating regimes during the period of our study. While some of these countries were officially pegging to a basket of currencies, many of the rest were in essence unofficially following such a policy (see the calculation of the basket weights in Frankel and Wei, 1992). All seven could be characterized as having

Table 3.1. *Growth of stock markets*

Country	Capitalization, 1980 ($U.S. millions)	Capitalization, 1989 ($U.S. millions)	No. firms listed, 1980	No. firms listed, 1989
Japan	370,000	4,392,597	1,402	2,019
United States	1,448,120	3,505,686	6,251	6,727
Canada	118,300	291,328	731	1,146
Australia	59,700	136,626	1,007	1,335
Singapore	24,418	35,925	103	136
Taiwan	48,634	237,012	102	181
Korea	3,829	140,946	352	626
Malaysia	12,395	39,842	182	251
Thailand	1,206	25,648	77	175
Chile	9,400	9,587	265	213
Mexico	12,994	22,550	271	203

a "managed float." Hence, we will pay special attention to the behavior of returns of the first four countries as compared with the other seven.

For most of the countries, the foreign exchange rate data are from the Datastream International tape. However, for Korea, Chile, Thailand, and Mexico, they are from *International Financial Statistics*. For Taiwan, they are from the EPS database of Academia Sinica in Taipei.

For all countries except Australia, we use the consumer price index as our measure of goods prices. For Australia, we use the wholesale price index. For all countries except Taiwan, the price data are from *International Financial Statistics*. For Taiwan, the source is the same as the exchange rate data.

3.4   Empirical results

We look at the bivariate returns for each pair of countries. This means that there are fifty-five relative rates of return we can study. There is an issue of whether we should examine each of the fifty-five relative rates separately, since they are not independent. For example, the forecast of the return on Australian equities relative to Japanese equities should equal the forecast of the Australian–U.S. return less the U.S.–Japanese return. A full simultaneous general equilibrium econometric model that forecasts each of the returns relative to the United States, for example, would not require any separate examination of the remaining forty-five relative rates of return. However, such a model would require that all information used to forecast any relative return be included in each relative return equation. Given our limited data set, such a full-blown simultaneous estimation is impractical. Hence, with estimation done equation by equation for each relative return, and with a small set of regressors included in the forecasting equation, separate information can be obtained from each of the fifty-five relative return forecasts. That is, we do not impose the constraint that our constructed forecasts of the Australian–Japanese relative return equal the Australian–U.S. return less the U.S.–Japanese return.

Table 3.2 contains some summary statistics for returns in the United States relative to the other countries. This table is useful for pointing out some of the regularities that run through many of the data. In the first block of the table, the variable USAJAPY is the ex post real return on equities in the United States relative to Japan. USAJAPX is the ex post nominal return on equities in the United States relative to Japan. USAJAPZ is the ex post real depreciation of the dollar. FORY is the forecast of USAJAPY, FORX is the forecast of USAJAPX, and FORZ is the forecast of USAJAPZ. MYY is the sample second moment of the forecast relative real return on equities. MXY is the sample cross-moment of the forecast relative real return on equities with the forecast nominal return on equities. MZY = MYY − MXY is the sample cross-moment of the forecast relative real return on equities with the forecast real depreciation of the currency.

The average forecast values of the variables of interest generally have the same sign as the average ex post values, although not in every case. The standard deviations of the forecasts, not surprisingly, are smaller than the standard errors of the ex post realizations.

The absolute size of the average real return differential is larger for Chile, Mexico, Thailand, and Taiwan relative to each other and the other seven countries than the real return differentials for those other seven countries relative to each other.

The absolute value of the nominal return differential (both ex post and ex ante) is very large relative to the average change in the real exchange rate. Furthermore, again both ex post and ex ante, the standard error of the change in the real exchange rate is small compared with the standard error of the nominal return differential.

It is very difficult to detect any pattern in the size of the second moments across countries. On the basis of the Dornbusch sticky-price model, one might have thought that those countries with highly flexible nominal exchange rates would have large real return differentials arising from large changes in the real exchange rate. However, MZY for the countries with floating exchange rates (the United States, Canada, Ja-

Table 3.2. *Summary statistics of return differentials*

Series	N	Mean	Std. error		
USAJAPY	100	− 0.0003376	0.055773	MYY =	0.0007949
USAJAPZ	100	0.0047692	0.037539		
USAJAPX	100	− 0.0051068	0.072914	MZY =	0.0000636
FORY	75	− 0.0035397	0.028159		
FORZ	75	0.0033539	0.019080	MXY =	0.0007313
FORX	75	− 0.0068936	0.031655		
USACANY	100	0.0064649	0.032131	MYY =	0.0002045
USACANZ	100	0.0008201	0.011928		
USACANX	100	0.0056448	0.032950	MZY =	− 0.0000082
FORY	75	0.0038543	0.013865		
FORZ	75	− 0.0002411	0.005052	MXY =	0.0002127
FORX	75	0.0040954	0.015298		
USAAUSY	99	− 0.0017089	0.064185	MYY =	0.0009744
USAAUSZ	99	− 0.0000962	0.031020		
USAAUSX	99	− 0.0016126	0.076461	MZY =	− 0.0000585
FORY	74	− 0.0076150	0.030479		
FORZ	74	0.0011029	0.009693	MXY =	0.001033
FORX	74	− 0.0087179	0.033464		
USACHLY	100	− 0.015285	0.075572	MYY =	0.0006420
USACHLZ	100	− 0.002504	0.019489		
USACHLX	100	− 0.012782	0.078293	MZY =	− 0.0000032
FORY	75	− 0.019970	0.015702		
FORZ	75	− 0.003948	0.010643	MXY =	0.0006452
FORX	75	− 0.016021	0.023228		
USAKORY	100	− 0.0054688	0.073486	MYY =	0.01187
USAKORZ	100	0.0015328	0.019311		
USAKORX	100	− 0.0070016	0.076148	MZY =	0.0003560
FORY	75	− 0.0045964	0.109580		
FORZ	75	0.0021502	0.011949	MXY =	0.01151
FORX	75	− 0.0067466	0.106950		
USAMALY	77	0.0017253	0.085450	MYY =	0.005234
USAMALZ	77	− 0.0034767	0.013595		
USAMALX	77	0.0052020	0.085686	MZY =	0.0002617
FORY	52	0.0253310	0.068427		
FORZ	52	− 0.0010558	0.010260	MXY =	0.004972
FORX	52	0.0263870	0.064615		
USAMEXY	87	− 0.020356	0.15218	MYY =	0.01252
USAMEXZ	87	0.0040949	0.066977		

Table 3.2 (*continued*)

Series	N	Mean	Std. error			
USAMEXX	87	−0.024451	0.17489	MZY	=	−0.007138
FORY	62	−0.017282	0.11147			
FORZ	62	0.018925	0.11897	MXY	=	0.01966
FORX	62	−0.036207	0.20105			
USASGNY	100	0.0033971	0.071192	MYY	−	0.001666
USASNGZ	100	0.0009013	0.013841			
USASNGX	100	0.0024958	0.069348	MZY	=	−0.0001333
FORY	75	−0.0062154	0.040616			
FORZ	75	−0.0007053	0.006031	MXY	=	0.001800
FORX	75	−0.0055101	0.044419			
USATWNY	59	−0.019109	0.15853	MYY	=	0.01107
USATWNZ	59	0.0050888	0.017570			
USATWNX	59	−0.024198	0.16116	MZY	=	−0.0002214
FORY	34	−0.063016	0.085524			
FORZ	34	0.0062237	0.012632	MXY	=	0.01129
FORX	34	−0.069240	0.084266			
USATHLY	46	−0.028213	0.10484	MYY	=	0.004645
USATHLZ	46	0.0006441	0.006523			
USATHLX	46	−0.028857	0.010267	MZY	=	0.0001394
FORY	21	−0.038668	0.057511			
FORZ	21	−0.0014036	0.003979	MXY	=	0.004506
FORX	21	−0.037265	0.056330			

Note: See text for variable definitions. Country abbreviations: USA, United States; JAP, Japan; CAN, Canada; AUS, Australia; CHL, Chile; KOR, Korea; MAL, Malaysia; MEX, Mexico; SNG, Singapore; THL, Thailand; TWN, Taiwan.

pan, and Australia) is not evidently any larger than that for countries with more controlled exchange rates. If anything, MZY is larger for the latter countries.

Table 3.3 contains our calculation of the share of deviations of the ex ante return from zero that we can attribute to deviations from ex ante PPP. Of course, the share attributable to deviations from zero of expected nominal return differentials is just 1 minus the share reported in Table 3.3. Most of the real return differentials can be attributed to nominal return differentials for the vast majority of the relative rates we examine. In fact, usually the expected change in the real exchange

Table 3.3. *Shares of real return differential "caused" by real exchange rate changes*

Country pair	Share	Country pair	Share	Country pair	Share
USAJAP	0.08	CANAUS	0.12	CHLSNG	0.03
USACAN	−0.04	CANCHL	−0.06	CHLTWN	0.0004
USAAUS	−0.06	CANKOR	−0.05	CHLTHL	−0.14
USACHL	−0.005	CANMAL	0.11	KORMAL	−0.27
USAKOR	0.03	CANMEX	1.31	KORMEX	0.12
USAMAL	0.05	CANSNG	−0.34	KORSNG	−0.60
USAMEX	−0.57	CANTWN	0.005	KORTWN	0.57
USASNG	−0.08	CANTHL	0.08	KORTHL	−0.20
USATWN	−0.02	AUSCHL	−0.15	MALMEX	−0.03
USATHL	0.03	AUSKOR	−0.25	MALSNG	−0.08
JAPCAN	−0.25	AUSMAL	−0.05	MALTWN	−0.01
JAPAUS	0.01	AUSMEX	−0.05	MALTHL	−0.07
JAPCHL	−0.10	AUSSNG	−0.07	MEXSNG	−0.23
JAPKOR	−0.16	AUSTWN	0.14	MEXTWN	0.20
JAPMAL	−0.32	AUSTHL	0.24	MEXTHL	−0.53
JAPMEX	−0.14	CHLKOR	−0.18	SNGTWN	0.06
JAPSNG	−0.16	CHLMAL	0.03	SNGTHL	0.14
JAPTWN	−0.02	CHLMEX	0.52	TWNTHL	−0.002
JAPTHL	0.01				

Note: For country abbreviations see Table 3.2.

rate has the effect of drawing the ex ante real return differential closer to zero than the ex ante nominal return differential.

There also does not appear, from Table 3.3, to be any relation between the role of the expected real exchange rate change in determining the real return differential and the type of exchange rate system operating in the various countries.

Table 3.4 reports tests of whether countries that tended to have high nominal exchange rate variability also tended to have higher shares of real return differentials caused by deviations from ex ante PPP. The dependent variable in these regressions is the shares of real return differentials caused by PPP differentials. The first equation regresses this share against the variance in the monthly log changes in the exchange rate for all fifty-five pairs of countries. Although the relation is positive, it is not statistically significant. When we add in the mean percent change as a way to control for exchange rates that had large secular changes during our sample period, the variance of changes still has a positive

Table 3.4. *Regression of m(z, y)/(m(y, y) on the variance of log changes of the exchange rate*

1. ZSHARE =	−0.05 + 14.7 VRALL
	(−0.98) (0.70)
2. ZSHARE =	−0.04 − 2.85 MEANALL + 5.10 VRALL
	(−0.78) (−1.14) (0.23)
3. ZSHARE =	0.05 − 128.5 VRUS
	(1.39) (−5.53)
4. ZSHARE =	0.03 + 2.85 MEANUS − 75.90 VRUS
	(0.90) (1.63) (−1.97)

Note: ZSHARE = $m(z, y)/m(y, y)$. VRALL represents the variance of log changes in the nominal exchange rate for each of 55 bilateral rates. MEANALL is the mean of log changes in the nominal exchange rate for each of 55 bilateral rates. VRUS is the variance of log changes in the nominal exchange rate for 10 bilateral rates relative to the United States. MEANUS represents the mean of log changes in the nominal exchange rate for 10 bilateral rates relative to the United States. Numbers in parentheses are t-statistics.

coefficient, but again is not significant. When we perform the same regressions using only returns on U.S. investments relative to the other countries, the relation is now negative – the more variable the exchange rate, the lower the share of real return differentials that we can attribute to real exchange rate changes. In the regression without the mean included, the negative relationship is strongly significant.

In short, we find that expected real rates of return are different across the Pacific Basin because expected nominal rates of return are different. There is not a strong relation between the behavior of nominal exchange rates and the share of ex ante real return differentials that we can attribute to expected changes in real exchange rates.

3.5 Conclusions

We have noted that expected changes in the real exchange rate do not seem to be the primary factor in determining the difference in real returns across Pacific Rim countries. This result seems to conflict with earlier findings of Frankel (1986, 1992), but several important caveats should be noted.

First, we do not control for risk. While we believe it is more appropriate to look at equities rather than interest-bearing assets if we are to determine the factors underlying patterns of investment in plant and equipment across countries, we must recognize that one important reason for the variation in equity returns from country to country is the difference in the riskiness of the investments. Hence, the fact that the expected nominal return differential accounts for most of the expected real return differential on stocks does not necessarily imply that restrictions to capital mobility are high. They may be low, and the market is simply properly rewarding risk-taking activity.

Second, our measures of expectations assume that investors have rational expectations. While that is a common assumption in empirical finance, the work of Frankel and Froot (1987) and Froot and Frankel (1989) calls it into question. Their analyses of survey data suggest that there are persistent biases in market participants' forecasts.

Third, even if expectations are rational, it is very difficult to measure the expectations without direct survey evidence. Hence, we are inevitably introducing large errors into our measures of expectations. While we have argued that there should be no inconsistency in large samples with our statistics, experience indicates that sample sizes for models in which expectations are constructed need to be very large before we can be confident of our measures. Here we are restricted by the data to use series that are no longer than seven years. In many cases, this may be insufficient to construct reliable statistics.

It appears that the expected real return differentials on equities across countries in the Pacific Rim are explained by expected nominal return differentials. Keeping in mind the qualifications just noted, we need to arrive at a finer understanding of why expected nominal differentials persist. Is it because of risk or because of barriers to international flows of capital? Risk could arise either because of differentials in the riskiness of projects or because of foreign exchange rate risk. Future research may uncover a relationship between exchange rate arrangements and the foreign exchange risk premium.

References

Cheng, H.-S., ed., (1986). *Financial Policy and Reform in Pacific Basin Countries*. Lexington, MA: Lexington Books for the Federal Reserve Bank of San Francisco.

Chinn, M., and J. Frankel (1992). "Financial and Currency Links in Asia and the Pacific." Unpublished manuscript, University of California, Santa Cruz.

Dornbusch, R. (1976). "Expectations and Exchange Rate Dynamics," *Journal of Political Economy* 84:1161–76.

Economist Publications (1988). *Directory of World Stock Exchanges*. Baltimore: Johns Hopkins University Press.

Engel, C., and K. Kletzer (1989). "Saving and Investment in an Open Economy with Non-Traded Goods," *International Economic Review* 30:735–52.

Feldstein, M., and C. Horioka (1980). "Domestic Saving and International Capital Flows," *Economic Journal* 90:314–29.

Frankel, J. (1986). "International Capital Mobility and Crowding-out in the U.S. Economy: Imperfect Integration of Financial Markets or Goods Markets? In R. Hafer, ed., *How Open Is the U.S. Economy?* pp. 33–67. Lexington, MA: Lexington Books.

(1991). "Quantifying International Capital Mobility in the 1980s." In B. D. Bernheim and J. Shoven, eds., *National Saving and Economic Performance,* pp. 227–50. Chicago: University of Chicago Press.

(1992). "Measuring International Capital Mobility: A Review," *American Economic Review* 82:197–202.

Frankel, J., and K. Froot (1987). "Using Survey Data to Test Standard Propositions Regarding Real Exchange Rate Expectations," *American Economic Review* 77:133–53.

Frankel, J., and S.-J. Wei (1992). "Yen Bloc or Dollar Bloc: Exchange Rate Policies of the East Asian Economies." Unpublished manuscript, University of California, Berkeley.

Froot, K., and J. Frankel (1989). "Forward Discount Bias: Is It an Exchange Risk Premium?" *Quarterly Journal of Economics* 104:139–61.

Glick, R. 1987. "Interest Rate Linkages in the Pacific Basin," (Federal Reserve Bank of San Francisco) *Economic Review* (no. 3):31–42.

Glick, R., and M. Hutchison (1990). "Financial Liberalization in the Pacific Basin: Implications for Real Interest Rate Linkages," *Journal of the Japanese and International Economies* 4:36–48.

International Finance Corporation (1990). *Emerging Stock Markets Factbook.* Washington, DC.

Razin, A. (1984). "Capital Movements, Intersectoral Resource Shifts and the Trade Balance," *European Economic Review* 26:135–52.

CHAPTER 4

Exchange rate policy, international capital mobility, and monetary policy instruments

Michael P. Dooley and Donald J. Mathieson

4.1 Introduction

This essay examines the degree of capital mobility confronting a sample of developing countries in the Pacific Basin. An accurate and timely assessment of changes in the degree of capital market integration is important because capital mobility has pervasive implications for economic performance under alternative exchange rate arrangements and monetary policy regimes. It seems likely that these differences are most pronounced during the early stages of integration. Unfortunately, well-known procedures for evaluating the degree of capital market integration among industrial countries are very difficult to implement during this crucial initial phase of economic transition. The approach taken in this essay requires a minimum of data for domestic interest rates and forward foreign exchange rates. While the approach is attractive because of minimal data requirements, the cost appears to be a difficult problem in identifying endogenous official behavior.

The pace of capital market integration is interesting because governments need a timely measure of integration in order to evaluate policy options. If changes in capital mobility are caused primarily by changes in administrative controls over international financial transactions, the degree of capital market integration can be measured by qualitative evaluation of the rules of the game and the pace of integration can be directly controlled by the government.

If the pace of capital market integration is determined largely by market forces, government policy might still be an important source of incentives for or against integration. In particular, if capital mobility

The views expressed in this essay are those of the authors and not necessarily those of the International Monetary Fund.

68

is determined by market reactions to incentives to arbitrage different rates of return, governments might still be able to *influence* the rate of integration indirectly but a much wider array of policy decisions will come into play. Perhaps the most important factor is the rate of taxation of domestic financial intermediation. Taxation in this context includes the wedge between international yields and administered yields on domestic instruments. In practice, an important determinant of the tax rate is the rate of domestic inflation both because narrow money typically pays no interest and because administered rates are adjusted slowly to an increase in the inflation rate. This implies that a country that wishes to integrate slowly with international markets has an additional incentive to follow conservative monetary and fiscal policies.

The main difficulty in identifying changes in capital mobility is that familiar measures of capital market integration among industrial countries involve comparisons of domestic and international interest rates (e.g., see Edwards and Khan, 1985; Chinn and Frankel, Chapter 2, this volume; Frankel, 1989; Glick and Hutchison, 1990). In general, data for forward exchange rates, offshore deposit rates, and market-determined domestic interest rates are available only *after* a high degree of capital mobility has been well established. For countries moving away from systems of strict controls on interest rates, it is difficult to determine marginal yields actually faced by savers and investors.

In some cases, curb interest rates have been used as a measure of domestic interest rates (e.g., see Edwards, 1988; Reisen and Yèches, 1991; Maloney, 1992). While these interest rates are available at times when there is a low level of integration and provide some information, it is not possible to determine the volume of transactions in these markets or the extent to which these rates are influenced by the risk associated with borrowers that are excluded from the controlled credit market. Glick and Hutchison (1990) found, for example, that in the case of Taiwan, the one country in their sample for which the only market interest available was a curb rate, the econometric analysis of open interest parity condition yielded implausible results.

Moreover, in making international comparisons, domestic currency interest rates must be adjusted for exchange rate expectations. In practice, this is a serious obstacle for countries in transition since forward exchange rates are typically not available to test covered interest parity conditions. Because the preliberalization exchange rate regime is usually an adjustable peg, the well-known "peso problem" limits the usefulness of ex post realizations as measures of expected exchange rate changes.

Another possible measure of capital mobility would be a qualitative evaluation of legal restrictions over capital movements (e.g., see Dooley and Isard, 1980). The difficulty with this approach is that changes in the intensity of legal restrictions are often associated with private initiatives designed to circumvent existing controls. Thus, a tightening of legal restrictions might be associated with an increase in capital market integration as the authorities respond to private initiatives with a lag and with decreasing effectiveness. Moreover, restrictions tend to stay on the books long after their effectiveness has been eroded by financial innovation.

For these reasons, the main objective of this essay is to develop an empirical measure of the degree of "capital mobility" for a selected set of Pacific Basin countries that does not depend on any measured domestic interest rate, either controlled or "curb," or qualitative evaluations of controls and to see how this measure has evolved over time. The measure of capital mobility chosen is the relative importance of an *estimated* domestic interest rate and the domestic currency equivalent of an international interest rate in explaining the economic behavior of residents of the countries selected.

An aspect of economic behavior that has received extensive empirical attention in these countries and elsewhere is the demand for money. For this reason, we follow Haque and Montiel (1990) in focusing on the demand for money as the economic behavior that might be influenced by domestic and foreign factors. In principle, any intertemporal behavior could be utilized to test the relative importance of international and domestic interest rates.

The empirical results reported in Section 4.6 provide some information about the degree of capital market integration for a sample of countries and about the evolution of capital mobility over time. In some cases, the measure of capital mobility developed here is consistent with our priors from examining legal restrictions on capital movements. For example, Myanmar is identified as a closed economy throughout the sample time period, while Indonesia is identified as an open capital market. For the other countries studied, the measured degree of capital mobility seems implausibly high, particularly early in the sample time period. Although the statistical techniques employed attempt to control for the simultaneous interactions between monetary policy and capital flows, the results reported may be distorted by the failure to identify a suitable reaction function for the monetary authority. More careful modeling of this interaction for individual countries is a topic for further research.

4.2   Capital mobility and exchange rate arrangements

Regardless of its origins, an increase in capital mobility has far-reaching implications for exchange rate policy. A government that wishes to maintain some control over the domestic interest rate must choose between an increasingly complex set of direct controls and greater flexibility in exchange rates. As Henry Wallich (1986: 5) pointed out, the adoption of floating exchange rates by the major industrial countries in the early 1970s "was a defensive maneuver on the part of national authorities by which they avoided what would very likely have become a system of widespread exchange controls. In a regulatory context, floating rates are not so much the opposite of fixed rates, but of a congeries of controls over international trade and payments." This interpretation of the move by industrial countries to floating exchange rates as a reaction to the increase in international capital mobility might provide lessons for countries facing similar circumstances today.

An alternative to fixed rates with increasingly restrictive capital controls would be to maintain the fixed exchange rate and allow international capital movements to determine domestic interest rates. This option was not seriously considered by the industrial countries but may be an option for very open developing countries. Indeed, the move toward monetary union in Europe can be interpreted as a reevaluation of this option for exchange rate arrangements among these countries given the de facto integration of their capital markets.

Our perspective on the implications of increased integration differs somewhat from that found in the traditional literature on the choice of an optimal exchange rate regime.[1] In that literature, the exchange rate regime and the degree of capital mobility (as implied by the structure of capital controls) reflect an optimal response by the authorities to the structure of shocks to the economy. As a result, the move to greater exchange rate flexibility in the 1970s and 1980s by the countries in the Pacific Basin region has been regarded as a response to the dominance of real as opposed to monetary shocks. Our hypothesis is that the timing of these regime changes is better explained by governments' loss of control over residents' transactions in international financial markets. In essence, we view the degree of capital mobility as a constraint on the authorities' decisions regarding their exchange rate arrangements and degree of openness to external transactions.

In the case of Pacific Basin countries that are now beginning a tran-

---

[1] See Mathieson (1988) for a review of the key results from that literature.

sition toward integration with international markets, our conjecture is that the *timing* of changes in exchange rate arrangements has been and will be determined largely by private initiatives to arbitrage international yield differentials. Governments can influence the speed of integration by controlling domestic inflation and by keeping administered interest rates roughly in line with international rates adjusted for inflation differentials. But, in the end, countries that have relied on regulation of internal and external markets will have to choose between fixed exchange rates and independent monetary policies as the major industrial economies have had to do.

4.3   Capital mobility and monetary instruments

Changes in the degree of capital mobility have also influenced the authorities' choice of monetary policy instruments. Mathieson (1988) documented the widespread use of credit ceilings as a principal monetary policy instrument in many developing and industrial countries in the Pacific Basin during the 1970s and early 1980s. Although the industrial countries subsequently switched to the use of market-based monetary policy instruments (e.g., open market operations), many developing countries in the region continued to rely on credit ceilings and credit allocation rules as key policy instruments.

In many of these developing countries, credit instruments have traditionally been seen as a means of controlling both macroeconomic activity, regardless of the exchange rate arrangements in place, and the distribution of resources through the financial system. Credit ceilings can be applied to lending by all financial institutions to the private sector or to lending to both the private and government sectors.

The key to the effectiveness of credit ceilings placed on the institutions in the regulated financial system lies in preventing domestic residents from accessing alternative sources of credit. Two alternative sources of credit typically have had the greatest potential for undermining the effectiveness of credit ceilings: the development of unregulated, domestic nonbank financial intermediaries and the availability of credit from foreign markets. In many developing countries, the informal financial sector has been a traditional source of short-term finance for small businesses, farmers, and households that have typically had limited access to the formal financial system.[2] It has often been difficult to apply

---

[2] This sector often encompasses moneylenders, rotating savings and credit associations (such as the tontine in Africa and the chit funds in India and Thailand), and finance institutions.

credit ceilings to these institutions, but during most periods the existence of these institutions did not significantly weaken the authorities' ability to influence macroeconomic activity. In part, this reflected the fact that large firms and state enterprises with access to the formal financial systems typically needed to raise funds on a scale that could not readily be provided by individual lenders on the informal market. During extended periods of highly restrictive credit policies, however, the borrowers from the formal financial sector would often either extend interfirm credits or encourage the development of informal markets for unsecured, short-term corporate liabilities as a means of obtaining short-term credits.[3] The authorities naturally tended to discourage the development of these markets either by making the contracts unenforceable or by direct intervention.

A second alternative source of credit has been external financial markets. Even for creditworthy countries, however, borrowing from external financial markets has been available only for large (often state-owned) enterprises and firms regularly engaged in international trade. Nonetheless, to prevent such firms from obtaining external credits during periods of restrictive credit policy, a variety of exchange and capital controls have often been employed by countries in the Pacific Basin (Table 4.1). The enforcement of such controls has been a linchpin in maintaining the effectiveness of credit ceilings.

4.4 Private incentives and capital market integration

During the 1970s and 1980s, monetary systems based on fixed or heavily managed exchange rates and credit ceilings came under increasing pressure for two reasons. First, the effects of financial repression on economic efficiency became increasingly evident, and this led to extensive financial liberalization in many countries. Since markets rather than the authorities determined the allocation of credit in such liberalized systems, this removed one of the pillars supporting the use of credit ceilings, namely to ensure consistency of the overall distribution of credit. Second, there have been growing linkages between domestic and external financial markets in both industrial and developing countries in the Pacific Basin region. In the industrial countries, these linkages were evident in the 1970s with the increasing use of offshore financial markets to conduct wholesale financial activities (e.g., syndicated lending and Eurobond issuance). In the 1980s, these linkages were tightened fol-

---

[3] In Korea, postdated corporate checks served as a form of short-term credit.

Table 4.1. *Capital controls for selected Pacific Basin countries*

Year	Required surrender of export proceeds	Advanced import deposits	Payments for invisibles	Foreign currency deposits by residents	Lending or borrowing financial institution	Tax or special reserve requirements on foreign borrowing
			Restrictions on			
1975	5	3	4	5	6	1
1976	5	3	4	5	6	1
1977	5	2	4	5	6	1
1978	5	2	4	5	6	1
1979	5	2	4	4	6	1
1980	5	2	4	4	6	1
1981	5	1	4	4	6	1
1982	4	1	4	4	6	1
1983	4	1	4	4	6	1
1984	4	1	4	4	6	1
1985	4	1	4	4	6	1
1986	4	1	4	4	6	1
1987	4	1	4	4	6	1
1988	4	1	4	4	6	1
1989	4	1	4	4	6	1
1990	4	1	4	4	6	1

Note: The table reports the number of countries with a particular control in place. The countries include Indonesia, Korea, Malaysia, Myanmar, the Philippines, and Thailand.

lowing the removal of capital controls and the liberalization of domestic financial markets.

In developing countries, a higher degree of "pseudo"–capital mobility was also evident. This did not necessarily mean that developing countries' residents could borrow in international markets; rather, it reflected the fact that the domestic residents of these countries had accumulated a large stock of external assets over time that they were able to repatriate during periods when domestic credit was severely restricted. To the extent that the authorities attempted to stabilize or fix the exchange rate, this repatriation of external assets led to an increase in the *net* stock of credit. While this may not be a good way to get flight capital back on a permanent basis, this phenomenon can undermine the effectiveness of credit ceilings. Moreover, Mathieson and Rojas-Suarez (1993) argued that for many developing countries in different regions of the world, the degree of pseudo–capital mobility was either at a high level or increased during the 1980s, and as a result the authorities have encountered growing difficulties in maintaining the effectiveness of capital controls.[4] Thus, even in the presence of capital controls, the willingness and ability of domestic residents to move funds in and out of the economy can imply increasing or high linkages between domestic and external financial conditions.

Given the central role played by capital mobility in theoretical analyses of the conduct of economic policy and given the extensive research carried out for industrial countries in evaluating international arbitrage conditions, it is surprising that relatively little empirical work has been done for developing and newly industrialized countries.

4.5   Empirical measurement of capital mobility

As discussed in Section 4.1, it seems important to supplement measures of capital mobility based on interest rate comparisons and qualitative evaluations of legal restrictions when dealing with economies in transition. An alternative measure of the effectiveness of capital controls or, alternatively, the degree of integration between domestic and external financial markets in countries in the Pacific Basin during the 1970s and 1980s can be analyzed using a modified version of a technique developed by Haque and Montiel (1990) (HM). The HM model assumes that the domestic market-clearing interest rate (i) can be expressed as a weighted average of the uncovered interest parity interest rate (i^*) and the domestic market-clearing interest rate that would be observed if the private capital account were completely closed (i'), or

$$i = \psi i^* + (1 - \psi)i'; \qquad 0 \le \psi \le 1. \tag{4.1}$$

Here ψ serves as an index of capital mobility. If $\psi = 1$, the domestic market-clearing interest rate equals its uncovered parity value and ex-

---

[4] Mathieson and Rojas-Suarez (1993) attribute this high or increasing degree of pseudo–capital mobility to the large differentials in the real rates of return that the residents of many developing countries saw on holding domestic and external assets during the 1980s, a "learning-by-doing" effect that may have reduced the cost of evading capital controls, the development of new financial products and services in the industrial countries and offshore markets, the lower risk of financial losses associated with holding deposits in the banking systems in the industrial countries relative to holding comparable assets in domestic banking systems, and the increasing sophistication of the techniques that have been used to finance the growing illicit trade in drugs and other goods.

ternal financial conditions are the primary determinants of domestic market interest rates. Conversely, if $\psi = 0$, external financial factors play no role in the determination of domestic interest rates and the capital account is effectively closed. As ψ moves from zero to unity, the effective degree of capital mobility naturally increases.

In order to identify the determinants of i', HM examine the rate of interest that would clear the domestic money market in the absence of private capital flows. The stock of money can be written as

$$M \equiv R + D \equiv R_{-1} + D + \Delta R$$
$$\equiv R_{-1} + D + CA + KA_G + KA_P, \tag{4.2}$$

where M is the domestic money stock, R is the domestic currency value of foreign exchange reserves, D is the stock of domestic credit, Δ is the first difference operator, and CA, KA_G, and KA_P are the domestic currency values of the current account, public sector capital account, and private sector capital account, respectively. The money stock that would have existed in the absence of private capital flows, which HM denote by M', equals

$$M' \equiv M - KA_P. \tag{4.3}$$

HM then determined i' from the money market equilibrium condition that

$$\ln(M'/P) = \ln(M^D/P), \tag{4.4}$$

where P is the domestic price level and ln is the natural logarithm operator. In their analysis, HM specified desired money holdings as a negative function of i and a positive function of income (y) and the lagged money supply $(M/P)_{-1}$.[5] The interest rate (i') that would then clear the money market was solved by using (4.4).

In our analysis, we use a broader definition of the real demand for money to allow for the effects of anticipated inflation and the yield on other close substitutes for narrow money. Thus,

$$\ln(M^D/P) = \alpha_0 - \alpha_1(i - \pi^e) + \alpha_2 \ln y$$
$$- \alpha_4 \pi^e - \alpha_5(r_D - \pi^e), \tag{4.5a}$$

where π^e is the expected rate of inflation, y the level of income, and r_D the rate of interest paid on time deposits. This formulation assumes

---

[5] This reduced-form equation could be derived from a stock adjustment model of the form

$$\ln(M/P) - \ln(M/P)_{-1} = \beta[\ln(M^D/P) - \ln(M/P)_{-1}],$$

with $\ln(M^D/P) = \alpha_0 + \alpha_1 i + \alpha_2 \ln y$, $\alpha_1 < 0$, $\alpha_2 > 0$, $0 < \beta < 1$.

that the real demand for narrow money (currency plus demand deposits) is influenced by the expected real returns on currency (whose real return is given by the [negative of] the expected rate of inflation $[\pi^e]$), on time deposits $(r_D - \pi^e)$, and other (implicit) money market instruments $(i - \pi^e)$. This implies that while the demand for money will be negatively related to the money market and time deposit interest rates, it could be negatively or positively related to expected inflation (depending on the size of α_4 relative to the sum of α_1 and α_5). If wealth holders adjust actual holdings of money to desired holdings gradually, then

$$\ln(M/P) - \ln(M/P)_{-1} = \alpha_3(\alpha_0 - \alpha_1(i - \pi^e) + \alpha_2 \ln y - \alpha_4 \pi^e \\ - \alpha_5 (r_D - \pi^e) - \ln(M/P)_{-1}). \qquad (4.5b)$$

This implies that if i' is the interest rate that equates $\ln(M'/P) = \ln(M^D/P)$, it is given by

$$i' = \frac{\alpha_0}{\alpha_1} + \frac{\alpha_2}{\alpha_1} \ln y - \frac{\alpha_5}{\alpha_1} r_D + \frac{\alpha_1 - \alpha_4 + \alpha_5}{\alpha_1} \pi^e$$

$$+ \frac{1 - \alpha_3}{\alpha_3 \alpha_1} \ln\left(\frac{M}{P}\right)_{-1} - \frac{\ln(M'/P)}{\alpha_3 \alpha_1}. \qquad (4.6)$$

Equation (4.6) can be substituted into (4.1) to obtain an expression for the unobservable i, and the resulting expression can then be substituted into (4.5) to obtain

$$\ln(M/P) = \alpha_0 \alpha_3 \psi + \alpha_2 \alpha_3 \psi \ln y + \psi(1 - \alpha_3)\ln(M/P)_{-1} \\ - \alpha_1 \alpha_3 \psi i^* + (1 - \psi)\ln(M'/P) \\ + \alpha_3(\alpha_1 - \alpha_4 + \alpha_5)\psi \pi^e - \alpha_5 \alpha_3 \psi r_D. \qquad (4.7)$$

4.6 Empirical results

To measure the degree of effective capital mobility for developing countries in the Pacific Basin region, we used annual data for seven developing countries from the mid-1960s to 1990 to estimate the parameters in equation (4.7). The size of the sample for each country was determined by the availability of consistent data from the International Monetary Fund *International Financial Statistics* and the desire to include countries that might exhibit differing degrees of capital mobility. The countries included are Indonesia, Korea, Malaysia, Myanmar, the Philippines, Sri Lanka, and Thailand.

The dependent variable in each regression is the natural log of the real money supply, as measured by M1 divided by the consumer price index (CPI). The independent variables are the lagged value of the log of real money stock, the log of real GDP (nominal GDP deflated by the CPI), the log of real M' (M1 minus the domestic currency value of private capital inflows),[6] the expected rate of inflation, and the uncovered foreign interest rate variable. Following Wickens's (1982) errors-in-variables approach to estimating rational expectations models, the expected rate of inflation is taken as the one-period-ahead rate of inflation.[7] The foreign interest parity rate is measured by the U.S. Treasury bill rate plus the one-period-ahead rate of change in the exchange rate.

The parameters estimated for equation (4.7) using nonlinear ordinary least squares (OLS) and instrumental variables estimation techniques are presented in Tables 4.2 and 4.3, respectively.[8] As in the original HM analysis, the results imply a relatively high degree of capital mobility for most countries. For four of the countries (Korea, Malaysia, the Philippines, and Thailand), the estimated ψs are not statistically different from 1. Indonesia and Sri Lanka have estimated ψs that are significantly different from both zero and 1. In contrast, the estimated value of ψ for Myanmar is not significantly different from zero. The low value of ψ for Myanmar suggests that its extensive current and capital account controls have effectively broken domestic and external financial market linkages.

For most countries in the group, the instrumental variables estimates of the speed of adjustment parameter (α_3) imply a relatively rapid adjustment of actual and desired real holding of money. In contrast, the income elasticities (α_2) show greater diversity, although many of the estimated values cluster around 1. The interest rate and expected inflation parameters (α_1, α_4, and α_5) suggest that the narrow money demands are relatively interest inelastic.

One key issue is whether these estimated relationships have been stable over the time period. Figures 4.1 to 4.6 plot the cusum and cusumsq test statistics developed by Brown, Durbin, and Evans (1974–5), which are designed to detect instability in the parameter estimates. The cusum test does not lead to the rejection of the hypothesis of

[6] Errors and omissions are included in the measure of private capital flows.
[7] Although we will examine OLS estimates of our model using this expectation formulation, this method provides consistent estimates only with a simultaneous equation estimation technique.
[8] These estimates were derived using the LSQ routine in the econometrics software package TSP.

Table 4.2. *Nonlinear ordinary least squares parameter estimates*

Country sample period	Indonesia, 1971–89	Korea, 1969–88	Malaysia, 1970–89	Myanmar, 1972–89	Philippines, 1964–89	Sri Lanka, 1965–89	Thailand, 1967–88
ψ	0.972 (5.03)	0.95 (28.82)	0.91 (23.03)	−0.000001 (−1.34)	1.11 (13.81)	0.76 (13.81)	0.91 (19.3)
α_0	−2.70 (−2.86)	2.42 (−2.06)	−4.10 (−3.50)	−4.24 (−0.88)	2.93 (1.67)	1.07 (1.23)	1.22 (1.09)
α_1	−0.002 (−1.66)	0.002 (1.32)	0.008 (1.25)	0.002 (0.32)	0.007 (1.81)	−0.005 (−1.35)	0.007 (1.59)
α_2	1.02 (20.17)	0.75 (12.46)	1.23 (10.76)	1.25 (2.65)	0.60 (4.32)	0.73 (9.29)	0.76 (8.56)
α_3	0.747 (14.07)	0.87 (4.85)	0.41 (2.64)	1.62 (2.64)	0.65 (3.71)	0.43 (3.43)	0.76 (3.33)
α_4	−0.004 (1.32)	0.01 (1.96)	−0.02 (−0.76)	−0.5 (−0.17)	0.0002 (0.55)	−0.02 (−2.03)	0.002 (0.35)
α_5	— —	0.02 (2.81)	−0.006 (−0.36)	−0.04 (−0.17)	—	—	—

Table 4.2 (*continued*)

Country sample period	Indonesia, 1971–89	Korea, 1969–88	Malaysia, 1970–89	Myanmar, 1972–89	Philippines, 1964–89	Sri Lanka, 1965–89	Thailand, 1967–88
Dummy variables	D1,[a] 0.152 (3.70)	D1,[c] −0.09 (1.66)	D1,[c] 0.09 (1.80)	—	D1,[f] 0.31 (5.65)	D1,[a] −0.12 (−2.81)	D1,[h] −0.13 (−2.82)
	D2,[b] 0.107 (2.68)	D2,[d] −0.08 (−1.66)			D2,[g] 0.18 (2.77)	—	—
					D3,[d] −0.08 (−1.61)		
R^2	.99	.99	.99	.99	.91	.98	.97

Note: *t*-statistics are given in parentheses.

[a] 1 in 1974–5 (period after first oil price increase).
[b] −1 in 1971, +1 in 1972 (effects of short-term liquidity crisis [1971] and subsequent recovery [1972]).
[c] 1 in 1981 (political crisis).
[d] 1 in 1973–4 (first oil price increase).
[e] 1 in 1984 (year before financial crisis).
[f] 1 in 1983 (inflows into banks due to nonbank crisis) and −1 in 1984 (outflows from banks due to problems of Banco Filipino [large savings bank]).
[g] −1 in 1985 (political boycott of state-owned banks).
[h] 1 in 1985–6 (financial crisis).

80

Table 4.3. *Nonlinear instrumental variables parameter estimates*

Country sample period	Indonesia, 1971–89	Korea, 1969–88	Malaysia, 1970–89	Myanmar, 1972–89	Philippines, 1964–89	Sri Lanka, 1965–89	Thailand, 1967–88
ψ	0.660	0.95	0.94	−0.000001	1.13	0.80	0.85
	(4.90)	(10.53)	(11.60)	(−0.53)	(8.85)	(9.35)	(5.45)
α_0	−1.84	0.51	−5.00	−3.89	3.51	−0.15	0.47
	(−0.90)	(0.22)	(−1.86)	(−0.69)	(1.71)	(−0.08)	(0.14)
α_1	−0.0002	−0.002	0.02	0.005	0.007	−0.008	0.01
	(−0.05)	(−0.38)	(0.80)	(0.47)	(1.44)	(−0.51)	(1.47)
α_2	0.979	0.85	1.32	1.22	0.55	0.85	0.82
	(9.25)	(7.10)	(4.93)	(2.15)	(3.43)	(5.03)	(3.14)
α_3	1.011	1.17	0.35	1.63	0.71	0.35	1.00
	(1.90)	(1.89)	(1.24)	(2.24)	(3.16)	(1.84)	(1.63)
α_4	−0.001	0.001	−0.01	−0.02	−0.001	0.004	0.008
	(1.16)	(0.04)	(−0.35)	(−0.77)	(−0.30)	(0.21)	(0.64)
α_5	—	0.01	−0.01	−0.02	—	—	—
	—	(0.58)	(−0.34)	(−0.84)			

Table 4.3 (*continued*)

Country sample period	Indonesia, 1971–89	Korea, 1969–88	Malaysia, 1970–89	Myanmar, 1972–89	Philippines, 1964–89	Sri Lanka, 1965–89	Thailand, 1967–88
Dummy variables	D1,[a] 0.152 (2.58)	D1,[c] −0.090 (0.08)	D1,[e] 0.090 (1.55)	—	D1,[f] 0.310 (3.55)	D1,[a] −0.12 (−1.28)	D1,[h] −0.13 (−2.85)
	D2,[b] 0.105 (1.64)	D2,[d] −0.080 (0.40)	—	—	D2,[g] 0.17 (1.50)	—	—
					D3,[d] −0.08 (−0.32)	—	—
Minimum distance function[i]	.00045	0.00033	0.0068	0.15 E-12	0.013	0.0052	0.00038

Note: *t*-statistics are given in parentheses.

[a] 1 in 1974–5 (period after first oil price increase).

[b] −1 in 1971, +1 in 1972 (effects of short-term liquidity crisis [1971] and subsequent recovery [1972]).

[c] 1 in 1981 (political crisis).

[d] 1 in 1973–4 (first oil price increase).

[e] 1 in 1984 (year before financial crisis).

[f] 1 in 1983 (inflows into banks due to nonbank crisis) and −1 in 1984 (outflows from banks due to problems of Banco Filipino [large savings bank]).

[g] −1 in 1985 (political boycott of state-owned banks).

[h] 1 in 1985–6 (financial crisis).

[i] Given by $F'[S^{-1} \otimes H(H'H)^{-1}H']F$, where F is the (stacked) vector of residuals from the nonlinear model, S the estimate of the residual covariance matrix, and H the matrix of instruments.

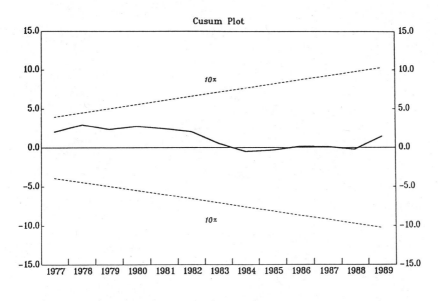

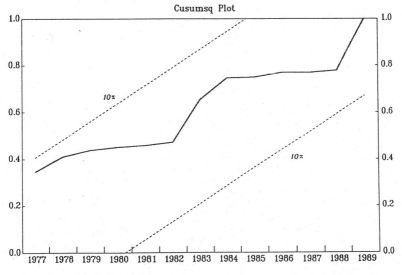

Figure 4.1. Indonesia.

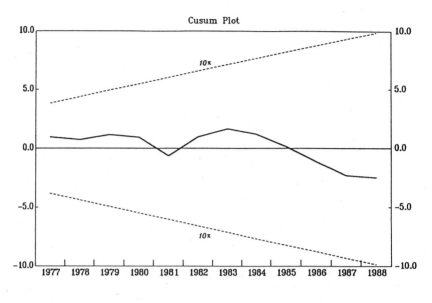

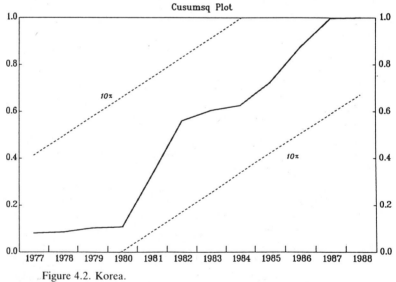

Figure 4.2. Korea.

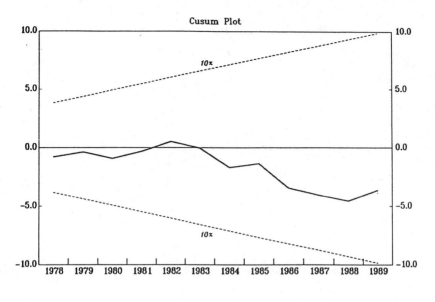

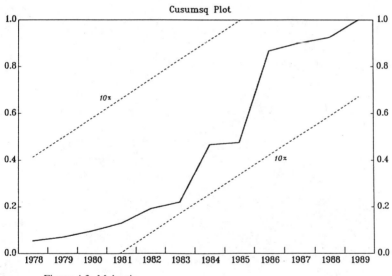

Figure 4.3. Malaysia.

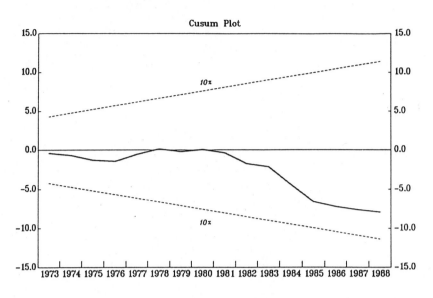

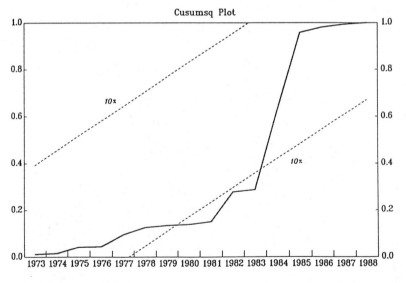

Figure 4.4. Philippines.

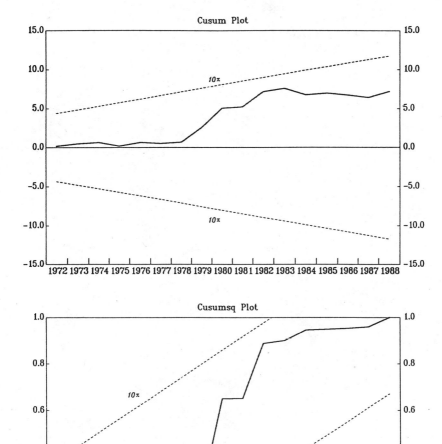

Figure 4.5. Sri Lanka.

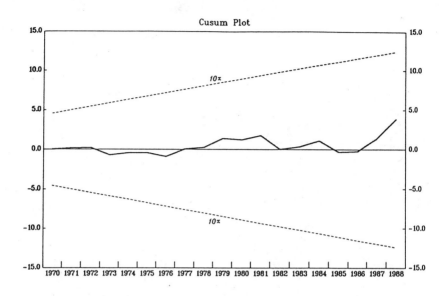

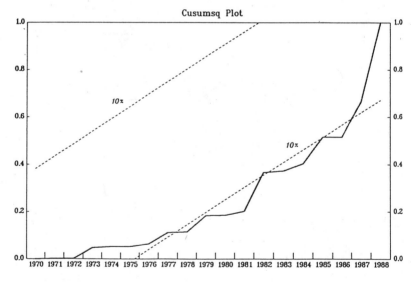

Figure 4.6. Thailand.

parameter stability (at the 10 percent confidence level) for any of the countries.[9]

In contrast, the cusumsq charts suggest some parameter instability (again at the 10 percent confidence level) for the Philippines, Sri Lanka, and Thailand.[10] For the Philippines the cusumsq statistic lies below the 10 percent significance line during the period 1980–3. For Sri Lanka, the lower bound is crossed in 1978, and for Thailand, the cusumsq statistic is below the lower 10 percent confidence limit throughout the period 1978–81. Moreover, the Malaysia cusumsq statistic has a value in 1978 that is very close to its lower bound. As Taylor (1990) has noted, such contrasting results between the cusum and cusumsq tests may be symptomatic of the low power of the cusum test.[11] Alternatively, they may also be suggestive of a shift in the residual variance rather than in the parameters in the structural model.

The parameter instability evident in the cases of the Philippines, Sri Lanka, and Thailand would be consistent with a rising degree of capital mobility (ψ). One way of allowing for this change is to incorporate a simple time trend into ψ in the form $\psi = \psi_0 + \psi_1 \times \text{TIME}$. For the Philippines and Thailand, such a formulation yielded values for ψ_1 that were insignificantly different from zero. Table 4.4 presents the results for Sri Lanka, which suggest that ψ rose from zero in 1965 to near unity by the end of the sample period (in 1988). As indicated in Figure 4.7,

---

[9] As discussed in Harvey (1991), the cusum test statistic is defined by

$$\text{cusum} (t) = \hat{\sigma}^{-1} \sum_{j=d+1}^{t} \bar{v}_j, \quad t = d+1, \ldots, T,$$

with $\hat{\sigma}^2 = (T - d - 1)^{-1} \sum_{t=d+1}^{t} (\bar{v}_t - \bar{v})^2$

and $v_i = \dfrac{Y_j - \chi'_j b_{j-1}}{(1 + \chi'_j X'_{j-1} X_{j-1})^{-1} \chi_j)^{1/2}}$,

where d is the number of parameters to be estimated, T is the total sample size, Y_j is the value of the dependent variable at time j, χ_j is a vector of values of independent variables at time j, X_{j-1} is a matrix composed of observations on the dependent variable from period 1 to $j - 1$, and b_{j-1} are estimated parameters based on data up to period $j - 1$.

[10] The cusumsq statistic is given by

$$\text{cusumsq} (t) = \sum_{j=d+1}^{t} \bar{v}_j^2 \Big/ \sum_{j=d+1}^{T} \bar{v}_j^2,$$

where the $\bar{v}_j$ are defined in the preceding note.

[11] Garbade's (1977) Monte Carlo studies lend support to this hypothesis.

Table 4.4. *Parameter estimates for Sri Lanka*

Sample period	OLS, 1965–88	Instrumental variables, 1965–88
ψ_0	−0.14 (−1.12)	−0.19 (−1.35)
ψ_1	0.05 (6.55)	0.05 (6.54)
α_0	−0.37 (−0.30)	−1.82 (−0.86)
α_1	−0.004 (−1.29)	−0.01 (−1.11)
α_2	0.84 (8.10)	0.95 (5.54)
α_3	0.43 (4.20)	0.36 (2.63)
α_4	−0.03 (−3.42)	−0.04 (−1.67)
α_5	—	—
Dummy variables, D1[a]	−0.05 (−1.61)	−0.04 (−0.97)
R^2	.99	—
Minimum distance function[b]	—	0.00002

Note: t-statistics in parentheses.
[a] 1 in 1974–5 (two years' flow, first oil price shock).
[b] Given by $F'[S^{-1} \otimes H(H'H)^{-1}H]F$, where F is the (stacked) vector of residuals from the nonlinear model, S the estimate of the residual covariance matrix, and H the matrix of instruments.

the cusum and cusumsq statistics for this new equation fall within the 10 percent boundaries.

The failure of a simple time trend to capture the evolution of ψ for the Philippines and Thailand could reflect the presence of a more complex pattern of evolution. One means of estimating a more complex pattern of change in ψ would be to employ a Kalman filter technique. However, there are two problems involved in estimating equation (4.7) using a Kalman filter. First, the right-hand side of equation (4.7) includes variables that are endogenously determined along with the left-hand-side variable in any general equilibrium setting. This creates the prospect

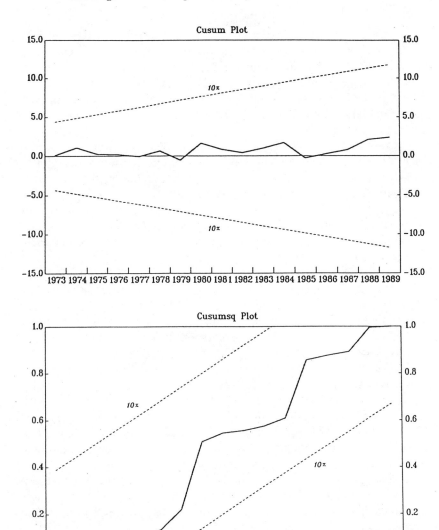

Figure 4.7. Sri Lanka; $\psi - \psi_0 + \psi_1 \times$ TIME.

of simultaneous equation bias in the Kalman filter parameter estimates unless this endogeneity is treated explicitly. A second problem is represented by the fact that while equation (4.7) is linear in the variables, it is nonlinear in the parameters. Nonetheless, an estimate of ψ could be obtained even without an explicit nonlinear estimate since the coefficient on $\ln(M'/P)$ will be equal to $1 - \psi$. However, identification of all parameters and their standard errors would require a nonlinear Kalman filter estimator.

To deal with the simultaneity problems, we employed the instrumental variables Kalman filter technique described in Harvey (1991: 412–16). This two-stage technique involves first regressing the left-hand-side variables on a set of instrumental variables.[12] The predicted values of these instrumental variables regressions were used in place of the original right-hand-side variables of equation (4.7). The application of a Kalman filter to these instrumented variables should be free of simultaneous equation bias.

To estimate all of the parameters in equation (4.7), we would need a nonlinear (or in Harvey's terms "extended") Kalman filter. Since we are interested primarily in the evolution of the ψ parameter, however, we can employ a standard Kalman filter (on the instrumented variables) with the knowledge that the parameter on $\ln(M'/P)$ in equation (4.7) equals $1 - \psi$.

Figures 4.8 and 4.9 report the estimated values of ψ for the Philippines and Thailand using both an OLS estimate (which takes the right-side variables of equation (4.7) as "exogenous") and the two-stage instrumented variables estimate. In each case, the OLS estimate implies a much higher level of capital mobility (especially at the beginning of the sample period). In addition, the instrumented variables technique shows a much larger increase in the value of ψ.

These figures also indicate that, at least in the 1980s, the sharpest increases in values of ψ have been accompanied by periods of high exchange rate variability measured either by the bilateral U.S. dollar exchange rate or the nominal effective exchange rate.[13]

[12] The set of instrumental variables consisted of the lagged values of each of the variables on the right-hand side of equation (4.7) (with the log of real money lagged two periods), the dummy variables included in each equation, a constant, a time trend, and the log of real U.S. GNP.

[13] The variance of the exchange rate was measured by first calculating for each month the variance of the exchange rate over the preceding twenty-four months. These monthly variances were then converted to an annual figure by taking the average value of the twelve monthly variances.

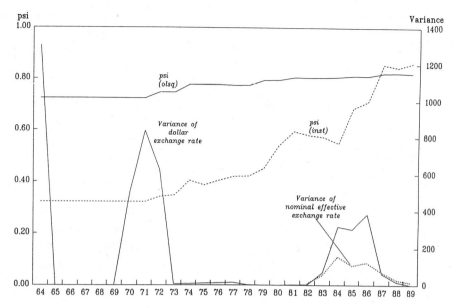

Figure 4.8. Philippines.

4.7   Conclusions

Our results indicate a surprisingly high level of capital mobility for all but one of the countries studied. The evidence that capital was almost perfectly mobile early in the time period seems inconsistent with the exchange control programs in place. It is, of course, possible that market forces have been more pervasive than generally believed and that perfect capital mobility is the correct characterization.

Another possibility is that we have not adequately modeled the simultaneous interaction between private capital flows and the net domestic assets of the central bank. Note that the hypothesis embodied in equation (4.3) is that all the components of M except private capital flows are set exogenously by the central bank. This allows the interpretation of i' as the domestic interest rate that would have prevailed if the capital account was completely closed. If, however, the authorities react to private capital inflows during the time period in order, for example, to maintain a yield differential in favor of domestic assets, then the estimated value for i' will be higher than the "true" closed economy value. Thus, to identify the exogenous or closed economy portion of

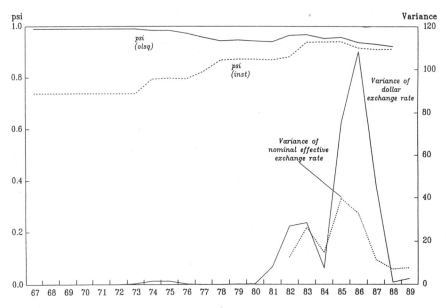

Figure 4.9. Thailand.

the monetary base it would be necessary to add a reaction or sterilization function to the model.

References

Brown, R. L., Durbin, J., and Evans, J. M. (1974–5). "Techniques for Testing the Constancy of Regression Relationships Over Time," *Journal of the Royal Statistical Society,* Series B37, pp. 149–63.

Dooley, Michael, and Isard, Peter (1980). "Capital Controls, Political Risk, and Deviations from Interest Parity," *Journal of Political Economy* 88:370–84.

Edwards, Sebastian (1988). "Financial Deregulation and Segmented Capital Markets: The Case of Korea," *World Development* 16:185–94.

Edwards, Sebastian, and Khan, Mohsin S. (1985). "Interest Rate Determination in Developing Countries: A Conceptual Framework," (International Monetary Fund) *Staff Papers* 32:377–403.

Frankel, Jeffery (1989). "Quantifying International Capital Mobility in the 1980s," NBER Working Paper no. 2856. Cambridge, MA.

Garbade, K. (1977). "Two Methods for Examining the Stability of Regression Coefficients," *Journal of the American Statistical Association* 72:54–63.

Glick, Reuven, and Hutchison, Michael (1990). "Financial Liberalization in the Pacific Basin: Implications for Real Interest Rate Linkages," *Journal of Japanese and International Economics* 4:30–48.

Haque, Nadeem, and Montiel, Peter (1990). "Capital Mobility in Developing

Countries: Some Empirical Tests." WP/90/117. International Monetary Fund, Washington, DC.

Harvey, Andrew C. (1991). *Forecasting Structural Time Series Models and the Kalman Filter.* Cambridge University Press.

Maloney, William (1992). "Testing Capital Account Liberalization without Forward Rates: Japan and Chile in the 1970's." Unpublished manuscript, University of Illinois at Urbana-Champaign.

Mathieson, Donald J. (1988). "Exchange Rate Arrangements and Monetary Policy." In Hang-Sheng Cheng, ed., *Monetary Policy in Pacific Basin Countries,* pp. 43–80 Norwell, MA: Kluwer.

Mathieson, Donald J., and Rojas-Suarez, Liliana (1993). *Liberalization of the Capital Account: Experiences and Issues.* Occasional Paper no. 103. Washington, DC: International Monetary Fund.

Reisen, Helmut, and Yèches, Hélène (1991). "Time-Varying Estimates on the Openness of the Capital Account in Korea and Taiwan." OECD Development Centre Technical Paper no. 42. Paris.

Taylor, Mark P. (1990). *The Balance of Payment: New Perspectives on Open Economy Macroeconomics.* Hants, England: Edward Elgar.

Wallich, Henry (1986). "A Broad View of Deregulation." In Hang-Sheng Cheng ed., *Financial Policy and Reform in Pacific Basin Countries,* pp. 3–12. Lexington, MA: Lexington Books.

Wickens, M. R. (1982). "The Efficient Estimation of Econometric Models with Rational Expectations," *Review of Economic Studies* 49:55–67.

PART II
CHOICE OF EXCHANGE RATE REGIMES

CHAPTER 5

Exchange rate management: a partial review

Stephen J. Turnovsky

5.1   Introduction

All countries, either explicitly or implicitly, have some form of exchange rate policy. This may involve doing nothing and letting the exchange rate fluctuate freely in response to market forces – a purely flexible exchange rate – or it may involve some kind of active intervention directed toward the attainment of certain specified objectives. Historically, a wide range of exchange rate policies have been adopted by individual nations in the world economy. In the recent past, the most dramatic change was the collapse of the Bretton Woods system in 1973, when the world moved generally from more fixed to more flexible exchange rate arrangements, although the regimes that individual economies chose to adopt were quite diverse.

This diversity of approaches to exchange rate policy is also characteristic of the Pacific Rim economies, which, while generally following the move toward more flexibility, have done so in a variety of ways and to various degrees. Thus, as Glick and Hutchison argue in Chapter 1 of this volume, the Pacific Rim region offers an excellent laboratory in which to compare various exchange rate arrangements and their consequences for monetary policy. Several of the developments are well documented by the relevant chapters in this volume. As discussed by Moreno in Chapter 6, during the 1970s both Taiwan and Korea maintained adjustable pegs to the U.S. dollar, and both economies adopted more flexible policies by the end of the decade. Taiwan moved to a managed float in 1979 and to a free float ten years later. Korea pegged to a currency basket during the 1980s and moved to a managed float

I am pleased to acknowledge the constructive comments I received on this essay from Reuven Glick and Michael Hutchison.

against the dollar in 1990. As noted by Pitchford in Chapter 7, Australia adopted a flexible rate regime at the end of 1983, switching from an adjustable peg. New Zealand moved from a fixed to a freely floating exchange rate policy in early 1985. Grimes and Wong describe in Chapter 8 how the exchange rate is now used as an intermediate target for achieving the monetary policy goal of a stable price level introduced by the New Zealand government in 1989. Finally, the evidence by Popper and Lowell presented in Chapter 9 examining exchange rate policies in the United States, Japan, Canada, and Australia reveals quite a diversity of policies among these economies insofar as exchange rate targeting is concerned.

Any rational monetary authority will choose its exchange rate policy (presumably in conjunction with other policy decisions) on the basis of some notion of what it perceives to be in the country's best interest. To determine what is a desirable or optimal policy requires an analytical framework embodying some criterion, or criteria, evaluating economic performance. Various approaches have been adopted by economists to address this issue, and the objective of this essay is to provide an overview and assessment of them. Our focus is on the theoretical aspects of these approaches and their implications for policymaking.

The theoretical analysis of exchange rate management has a long history and an extensive literature. Its origins trace back to the early debates of fixed versus floating exchange conducted by Friedman (1953), Meade (1955), Johnson (1969), and Kindleberger (1969) in the 1950s and 1960s. The first analytical treatment of the issue was carried out in the 1970s from a stabilization viewpoint (see, e.g., Turnovsky, 1976; Fischer, 1977; Flood, 1979). The approach undertaken by these authors was to develop a model of an economy subject to various sources of stochastic disturbances and to compare its stability, as measured by the variances of certain key variables such as the output level and/or price level, under the two regimes of perfectly fixed and perfectly flexible exchange rates. The choice between the two regimes from the standpoint of providing greater stability was shown to depend upon the sources of the underlying shocks affecting the economy.

However, both of these regimes represent polar forms of intervention policy. In the former case, the domestic monetary authority continually intervenes in the foreign exchange market so as to maintain the exchange rate at some fixed target level. In the latter case, the authority abstains from any active intervention, allowing the exchange rate to fluctuate freely in response to market forces. In between these two extremes is that of a "managed float," in which the monetary authority intervenes partly to offset movements in the exchange rate, so that the adjustment of the economy to changes in market pressure takes place through a combination of movements both in the exchange rate and in the adjustment of foreign reserves. The intensity with which the domestic monetary authority intervenes in the foreign exchange market thus becomes a policy decision.[1]

Targeting the exchange rate in an open economy parallels interest rate targeting in a closed economy. This, too, is a subject with a large literature. Analytical interest in this topic originated with Poole (1970) and his treatment of the "monetary instrument problem." He showed how the choice between targeting the interest rate, on the one hand, and targeting the money supply, on the other, from the viewpoint of stabilizing output depends on the origin of the shocks, very much as does the choice between fixed versus flexible rates. Indeed, since under conditions of high capital mobility, setting the interest rate is equivalent to targeting the rate of exchange depreciation, while control over the domestic money supply can be maintained only under a flexible rate, the two questions – interest rate versus money supply in the closed economy and fixed versus flexible rates in the open economy – are virtually isomorphic.

Various distinctions among the objectives of exchange rate targeting have been considered in the literature and should be identified. One is that between targeting the *nominal* exchange rate and targeting the *real* exchange rate (see, e.g., Montiel and Ostry, 1991). A second distinction concerns targeting the *level* of the exchange rate, as opposed to targeting its *rate of change*. This policy is one of maintaining a crawling peg and has been extensively discussed in the literature (see, e.g., Mathieson 1976, and others).[2] Most of the discussion regarding the exchange rate relates to the *spot* rate. However, periodically authors have advocated targeting the *forward* rate. This view was first proposed by Spraos (1959), who argued that "the forward rate should not only be supported, as a defense against speculative attack, but should actually be pegged." In any event, whatever the objective of exchange rate policy, it does imply some underlying monetary policy. One of the potential advantages of forward market intervention is that it does not entail any changing of domestic credit conditions and may therefore eliminate certain sources of fluctuations that may otherwise be generated through an active monetary policy.

The general literature on exchange rate targeting and the associated

---

[1] Early contributions to the literature on exchange market intervention include those of Boyer (1978) and Henderson (1979).
[2] See, e.g., Mantel and Martirena-Mantel (1982).

monetary policy underlying it has grown voluminously over the past two decades. Various approaches can be identified, with the alternative analytical frameworks offering different analytic insights and leading to different policy recommendations and, in some cases, actual policy implementation. At the same time, the evolution of analytic approaches has been influenced in part by actual experiences under different exchange rate regimes and exchange rate management policies.

In this essay we discuss four relatively recent analytic approaches to the issue, discussing what we view as the merits and limitations of each. We refer to these approaches as dynamic portfolio models, new classical stochastic models, rational intertemporal models, and target zone models. Each approach addresses the issue from a different perspective, and each has developed an extensive and growing literature. In the available space, we do not attempt to be comprehensive, but rather discuss the essence of what each approach has to offer.

5.2   Dynamic portfolio models

The worldwide increase in exchange rate flexibility that took place in the 1970s led to the development of the monetary approach to exchange rate determination. The critical elements of this approach included the following:

(i)   The exchange rate is determined by the interaction between relevant stocks and flows in a general equilibrium framework.

(ii) The asset markets are central in the determination of this equilibrium.

(iii) Among the asset markets, the money market is key.

(iv) Capital mobility and expectations are of critical importance in the determination of exchange rates.

Numerous contributions embodying this approach exist, and comprehensive expositions are provided by, for example, Allen and Kenen (1980).

5.2.1   Basic portfolio model

For our purposes, a convenient starting point is the seminal Dornbusch (1976) model. This is based on the traditional macroeconomic assumption that the country produces a single commodity, part of which is consumed domestically, the remainder of which is exported. The model can be summarized by the following set of equations:

$$r = r^* + \epsilon, \tag{5.1a}$$

$$\epsilon = \theta(\overline{E} - E), \qquad \theta > 0, \tag{5.1b}$$

$$M - P = \alpha_1 Y - \alpha_2 r, \qquad \alpha_1 > 0, \alpha_2 > 0, \tag{5.1c}$$

$$\dot{P}(t) = \rho[\beta_0 + (\beta_1 - 1)Y - \beta_2 r + \beta_3(E - P)],$$
$$0 < \beta_1 < 1, \beta_2 > 0, \beta_3 > 0, \tag{5.1d}$$

where
- r^* = foreign (nominal) interest rate, taken to be exogenous,
- r = domestic (nominal) interest rate,
- ϵ = expected rate of exchange depreciation,
- E = logarithm of the current exchange rate (measured in terms of units of domestic currency per unit of foreign currency),
- $\overline{E}$ = logarithm of the equilibrium exchange rate,
- M = logarithm of the domestic nominal money supply,
- P = logarithm of the price of domestic output,
- Y = logarithm of domestic real output, taken to be fixed.

Equation (5.1a) asserts that, through arbitrage, the domestic interest rate is kept equal to the exogenous world rate, plus the expected rate of change of the domestic currency price of foreign exchange. The second equation describes the formation of exchange rate expectations, specifying them to be formed regressively. Thus, equation (5.1b) states that if the domestic currency is currently depreciated below its long-run equilibrium level, it is expected to appreciate, and vice versa. The demand for money is of the conventional type (expressed in logarithms), with the demand for money varying positively with domestic output and inversely with the domestic interest rate. Equation (5.1c) describes continuous equilibrium in the domestic money market. Finally, equation (5.1d) is a price adjustment equation, according to which the rate of domestic price adjustment is proportional to excess demand. This is described by the term in parentheses and is seen to vary inversely with domestic output and the domestic interest rate, and positively with the relative price (real exchange rate) $E - P$.

If we substitute (5.1a) and (5.1b) into (5.1c) and (5.1d), the model reduces to

$$M - P = \alpha_1 Y - \alpha_2[r^* + \theta(\overline{E} - E)], \tag{5.2a}$$

$$\dot{P} = \rho[\beta_0 + (\beta_1 - 1)Y - \beta_2[r^* + \theta(\overline{E} - E)] + \beta_3(E - P)]. \tag{5.2b}$$

From (5.2a) we see that, given the predetermined price level P, the nominal money stock M, and the long-run equilibrium exchange rate $\overline{E}$, the current exchange rate E adjusts instantaneously to clear the money market. E having thus been determined, the domestic price level P adjusts gradually to eliminate disequilibrium in the goods market.

These two equations exhibit the essence of the Dornbusch model: the contrast between rapid adjustment in the exchange rate to clear the money market and sluggish movement in the price level to eventually clear the goods market. With output fixed, this results in the celebrated "overshooting" property of the exchange rate in response to a monetary disturbance. This refers to the phenomenon that while a 1 percent increase in the money supply leads to a long-run 1 percent depreciation of the domestic exchange rate, in the short run the exchange rate will actually depreciate by more than 1 percent.

It is not our objective to provide a critique of the Dornbusch model or to examine the robustness of the overshooting result. It is testimonial to the influence of Dornbusch's contribution that, following its appearance, an industry developed doing just that. For our purposes, the point is that in the Dornbusch model monetary policy is purely passive (exogenous). That is, monetary policy is specified in the form of an exogenously set level of the money supply M or, more generally, an arbitrarily specified time path for M. The analysis of the Dornbusch model and much of the literature that it spawned focused on the consequences of exogenous monetary expansions upon the time path of the exchange rate and other macroeconomic variables of consequence.

For the record, we should note some of the variants of this type of model, which were developed in the decade or so following the appearance of Dornbusch's paper:

  (i)   Replacement of the *regressive* exchange rate expectations assumption with *rational expectations* (perfect foresight); see, for example, Gray and Turnovsky (1979) and Wilson (1979).
 (ii)   Recasting of the model so that long-run equilibrium is one of ongoing inflation (and exchange depreciation), rather than some endogenously determined stable level of the exchange rate; see, for example, Buiter and Miller (1981).
(iii)   Introduction of domestic bonds, which are imperfect substitutes for foreign bonds, with the result that asset accumulation dynamics, price dynamics, and (when combined with variant (i)) exchange rate dynamics all become interdependent; see, for example, Driskill and McCafferty (1980).
 (iv)   Introduction of wealth effects, with or without sticky prices; see, for example, Dornbusch and Fischer (1980), Driskill and McCafferty (1985), and Engel and Flood (1985).

For the purposes of considering monetary policy, the most important modification is the second, and we will discuss it further in due course.

5.2.2   *Alternative monetary rules*

Recognizing that the exchange rate responds to monetary shocks, it is natural to consider the capacity of monetary policy to influence the behavior of the exchange rate. Typical of such rules are the following, whereas in the earlier specification of the Dornbusch model, all variables are specified in logarithms:

(i)   Leaning against the wind:

$$M - \overline{M} = \mu(\overline{E} - E) \quad \text{or} \quad \dot{M}(t) = -\mu\dot{E}(t),$$
$$\mu > 0.$$

(ii)   Accommodating monetary growth:

$$M = vP \quad \text{or} \quad \dot{M}(t) = v\dot{P}(t), \quad v > 0.$$

(iii)   Constant rate of exchange depreciation (fixed crawling peg):

$$\dot{E}(t) = \overline{e}.$$

Since a monetary expansion will generally cause an exchange depreciation, the first rule, leaning against the wind, proposes responding to a depreciated or to a depreciating exchange rate with a contractionary monetary policy. An example of this type is provided in Chapter 8 by Grimes and Wong for the case of New Zealand monetary policy. Their essay determines the adjustment in the money supply necessary to maintain a fixed exchange rate target in the face of various exogenous shocks. The second rule asserts that the monetary authority responds to an increase in the price level with a monetary expansion, with the objective being to maintain the real stock of money balances. Such a policy is sometimes referred to as a "real bills" doctrine (see Sargent, 1977). The third rule is one in which the money supply is set so as to achieve a fixed target rate of exchange depreciation.[3]

It is clear that the introduction of monetary rules into a system such as specified in (5.2) will affect the dynamic adjustment. This can be seen by inserting the specified rule into (5.2) and observing the change in the eigenvalues of the corresponding dynamic system. Following this ap-

[3] For example, since 1965, when it was first adopted by Chile, some form of crawling peg has become a standard regime for Latin American countries.

proach, a literature has developed examining the implications of various rules for the dynamic characteristics of the time path of the economy. Issues such as whether the path of the exchange rate is smoothed or whether overshooting of the exchange rate is eliminated have been discussed.

While a detailed discussion of the properties of the various rules is clearly not feasible in the space available, it is worth noting some of the characteristics associated with them. First, since the models in which such rules are typically embedded assume that domestic prices are determined by a Phillips curve, they permit no long-run adjustment of output. Indeed, if these rules were introduced into the original Dornbusch formulation, in which output is fixed at all times, even transitory output responses would be ruled out. Such rules are therefore directed more toward transitional dynamics, and in particular the dynamics of nominal variables such as the exchange rate and the price level. Thus, a policy of leaning against the wind can be shown to mitigate, but not eliminate, the overshooting associated with an exogenous monetary expansion, while slowing down the subsequent dynamic adjustment. An accommodating monetary policy, specified as maintaining a fixed real stock of money, implies that all shocks originating in the monetary sector are transmitted elsewhere in the economy, essentially as in the original Poole (1970) analysis. Finally, under the often-assumed assumption of uncovered interest parity, pegging the rate of exchange depreciation is equivalent to pegging the domestic nominal interest rate. In this case, if the domestic output is fixed, any monetary shock must be absorbed by adjustment in the real money supply.

To my mind, this line of research is of limited interest. The rules considered and the underlying dynamic models are inevitably restrictive. Consequently, the dynamic characteristics of any particular analytical system are necessarily model specific and almost certainly offer at best a limited guide to the likely dynamic adjustment path of a real-world economy.

5.2.3   *Long-run constraints on policy options*

In my view, the most interesting insights into monetary policy options to emerge from these dynamic portfolio models come from a consideration of their steady-state equilibrium conditions. Many of them are obvious, but they are nevertheless important. It is most fruitful to address this in the context of an equilibrium characterized by an ongoing inflation. In this situation, the following steady-state conditions can be shown to prevail:

$$m = p = q + e,$$
$$r = r^* + e. \tag{5.3}$$

where p = equilibrium domestic rate of inflation,
 q = equilibrium foreign rate of inflation,
 e = equilibrium rate of exchange depreciation of domestic currency,
 m = domestic nominal money growth rate,
 r = domestic nominal interest rate,
 r^* = foreign nominal interest rate, taken to be fixed.

The first of these equations embodies the assumption that the steady-state stock of real money balances must be constant, so that in the absence of real growth, the domestic rate of inflation must equal the rate of nominal money growth.[4] At the same time, long-run equilibrium requires the *real* exchange rate to be constant, which implies that the long-run rate of exchange depreciation of the domestic currency must equal the difference between the domestic and foreign rates of inflation. The second equation is simply the long-run interest parity relationship.

These relationships highlight the long-run constraints facing the monetary policymaker. Suppose, for example, that the policymaker chooses to set a fixed money growth rate $m = \overline{m}$, say. This then determines an equilibrium long-run domestic rate of inflation and, given the foreign rate of inflation, a corresponding long-run rate of exchange depreciation and, therefore, the domestic nominal interest rate. If the monetary authority chooses this particular monetary growth rate, it must accept the resulting response of the exchange rate. Alternatively, if the authority targets a particular rate of exchange depreciation, this determines the equilibrium domestic interest rate and the corresponding money growth rate, which will sustain the equilibrium, as well as the corresponding inflation rate. In the case that it opts for a fixed exchange rate (i.e., sets $e = 0$), it must be willing to accept the world inflation rate. The point is that only *one* of the potential policy targets, m, p, e, r, can be chosen independently.

5.2.4   *Sterilized intervention*

Most of the dynamic portfolio models follow the assumption originally adopted by Dornbusch, namely that uncovered interest parity holds, thereby constraining all intervention to be nonsterilized. But the as-

---

[4] In an economy with real growth, the equilibrium inflation rate equals the rate of growth of the nominal money supply less the real growth rate.

sumption of uncovered interest parity is restrictive both theoretically and as an empirical and policy matter. First, at a theoretical level it implies that in the absence of any ongoing inflation, in the long run the domestic interest is tied (identically) to the foreign interest rate and is independent of the composition of domestic asset supplies. Also, the exchange rate is independent of the supply of domestic bonds. Second, the empirical evidence on uncovered interest parity is not strong; indeed, the evidence on the weaker assumption of covered interest parity is much more compelling. Furthermore, in practice several economies, including many Pacific Basin countries, sterilize extensively (see, e.g., Glick and Hutchison, Chapter 10, this volume, for a discussion of sterilized exchange market intervention policy in Japan and Kwack, Chapter 12, for a similar discussion on exchange rate policy in Korea).

Partly for analytical reasons, there are virtually no formal dynamic portfolio models analyzing exchange rate management through sterilized intervention. The problem is that the dimensionality of the dynamics is increased considerably, rendering formal analysis intractable. One relevant paper is that of Eaton and Turnovsky (1983b), who replace the assumption of uncovered interest parity in the Dornbusch model with covered interest parity, the empirical evidence for which, as we have noted, is much stronger. This leads to fundamental changes in the dynamics, with the stock of domestic bonds playing a crucial role both during the transition and in the long-run equilibrium. Several of the restrictive implications of the Dornbusch model are relaxed. For example, in the long run, the domestic interest rate now responds only partially to an increase in the foreign interest rate. It is now sensitive to the composition of domestic asset supplies, varying inversely with the domestic money stock and positively with the supply of domestic bonds. The long-run exchange rate is also dependent on the stock of domestic bonds and thereby on domestic fiscal policy.

One further aspect of this approach should be noted. The assumption of covered interest parity explicitly introduces a consideration of the risk premium into the analysis, with the equilibrium determining its evolution over time. Indeed, the model provides a framework for investigating the macroeconomic determinants of the risk premium. While Eaton and Turnovsky do not emphasize this aspect of the model, it is clear from its equilibrium structure that the steady-state risk premium responds very much like the domestic interest rate.[5] Specifically, it varies

---

[5] Being a deterministic model, the Eaton–Turnovsky analysis does not really attempt to address the question of the determination of the risk premium adequately. To do so obviously requires a stochastic model.

positively with the stock of domestic bonds and negatively with the stock of domestic money. In addition, with the domestic interest rate now responding only partially to a rise in the foreign interest rate, this requires an accompanying fall in the risk premium if covered interest parity is to be maintained.

5.2.5 *Optimal monetary policy*

Before concluding this discussion, we should note that several authors have used variants of the Dornbusch model to address issues of optimal monetary policy in a small open economy (see, e.g, Turnovsky, 1979; Driffill, 1982; Pitchford and Vousden, 1987; Stemp and Turnovsky, 1987). Many variants of this approach exist, but typically monetary policy is chosen subject to the dynamic constraints of the model, as specified in (5.2), or some similar system, with the objective being to minimize a quadratic loss function defined over, say, deviations in the price level (or the exchange rate) and output from some stationary equilibrium level. It is then possible to characterize the optimal (cost-minimizing) time path of output, the price level, and the exchange rate. Related to this literature is an early contribution by Mathieson (1976), who addresses the question of the consumption-maximizing optimal crawl (rate of exchange depreciation).

To illustrate the nature of models, we shall focus on the Stemp-Turnovsky (1987) article in more detail. This article examines the optimal output–inflation trade-off in a Dornbusch-type model, though with exchange rate expectations being characterized by perfect foresight, rather than being formed regressively. In addition to the imposition of the usual quadratic costs on output and inflation, an important feature of this model is the acknowledgment that under perfect foresight the announcement of an optimal monetary policy may potentially introduce an initial unanticipated jump in the nominal exchange rate. With the price of output being predetermined at any instant, this change in the nominal exchange rate translates into an instantaneous unanticipated jump in the real exchange rate $E - P$, which in turn causes an unanticipated jump in real output. These jumps in *real* magnitudes impose real (structural) adjustment costs on the economy, and these must be taken into account in assessing the overall benefits of the optimal stabilization policy to the economy.

Stemp and Turnovsky show how the magnitude of the initial jump in the exchange rate depends on the magnitude of the adjustment cost. In the limiting case, when this is zero, the optimal monetary policy is simply to move the economy instantaneously to the steady state. In this case the dynamic time path degenerates. In the more reasonable case where such costs exist and are significant, a well-defined optimal intertemporal adjustment path is obtained by, in effect, balancing off the initial costs associated with implementing the policy, with the subsequent improvement in the performance of the economy. This procedure for generating a gradual adjustment process is essentially analogous to early rationales for distributed lag investment functions, which could be obtained by balancing off the costs of an initial adjustment in the capital stock with the costs of being away from some optimal target level. An interesting aspect of this formulation that arises here, however, is the potential for the optimal policy to be *time inconsistent.* Whether this in fact turns out to be a problem depends crucially on the nature of the adjustment costs associated with the unanticipated jump in the exchange rate. Where the costs favor a large number of small jumps (as is the case if the cost function is quadratic), it will be optimal for the policymaker to reoptimize continually, leading to a time-inconsistent policy. If, however, the cost function penalizes these initial jumps heavily, it will be optimal for there to be at most one, and possibly no, initial jump in the exchange rate. In this case the problem of time inconsistency does not arise and following the possibly unique initial jump, the system evolves continuously over time.

Assuming time consistency, Stemp and Turnovsky express the optimal monetary rule as a linear feedback rule in which the *real* money supply is adjusted to the *real* exchange rate. In most cases, the relationship is a positive one, implying a policy of leaning *with* the wind rather than one of leaning against the wind. As we will see, this also turns out to be the form of the optimal policy in many cases in the stochastic model to be described in Section 5.3. Furthermore, the corresponding adjustments in output and price inflation can also be expressed as linear functions of the real exchange rate. Accordingly, along the optimal path the relationship between output and inflation is a linear one.

The intuition underlying this optimal path can be understood in terms of the case studied in some detail where the economy starts from a stagflation, with output below its equilibrium and a positive inflation rate. Assuming that the adjustment costs are insufficient to rule out an initial jump in the nominal exchange rate, the optimal policy calls for an initial monetary expansion, thereby generating an initial increase in output and in the *level* of prices, followed by an instantaneous reduction in its rate of inflation. Thereafter, as the economy moves along its optimal path, money growth remains positive, but declines (as the real exchange rate appreciates), so that output and inflation converge to their respective equilibria.

While these models have the advantage of tractability, being able to exploit the simplicity of linear-quadratic optimization methods, this literature suffers from two types of shortcoming. The first is the arbitrariness of the underlying macro model, and the second is the limitation of the objective function, particularly the use of the quadratic loss function. The rational intertemporal model to be discussed in Section 5.4 is clearly superior, at least from a theoretical viewpoint, and does offer a very different perspective to optimal monetary policymaking.

5.3   New classical stochastic models

We turn now to the second type of model used to study exchange rate policy. The simplest such model typically considers a small open economy, subject to various sources of stochastic disturbances of both domestic and foreign origin. The models are linear and assume rational expectations. In the simplest cases there is a single good, with purchasing power parity assumed to hold. Also, domestic and foreign assets are perfect substitutes on an uncovered basis, so that uncovered interest parity also holds. The basic model, spelled out in the following subsections, is usually some variant of a "new classical" macro model.

5.3.1   A simple stochastic model of a small open economy

In order to keep the technical details to a minimum, we shall base our discussion on the simplest generic model, which we summarize by the following set of equations:[6]

$$P_t = Q_t + E_t, \tag{5.4a}$$

$$M_t - P_t = \alpha_1 Y_t - \alpha_2 r_t + u_{1t}, \tag{5.4b}$$

$$r_t = \Omega_t + E^*_{t+1,t} - E_t, \tag{5.4c}$$

$$M_t = \overline{M} - \mu(E_t - \overline{E}), \tag{5.4d}$$

$$Y_t - \hat{Y} = \gamma(P_t - P^*_{t,t-1}) + u_{2t}, \tag{5.4e}$$

while for any variable, say X,

$$X^*_{s,t} = E_t(X_s), \tag{5.4f}$$

[6] The exposition in this section is drawn in part from Turnovsky (1984a).

where $E_t(\ )$ = conditional expectations operator, conditional on information at time t,

P_t = domestic price of traded good at time t, expressed in logarithms,

Q_t = world price of the traded good at time t, expressed in logarithms,

E_t = current exchange rate (measured in units of the domestic currency per unit of foreign currency), expressed in logarithms,

$\overline{E}$ = equilibrium (steady-state) level of E, endogenously determined,

M_t = domestic nominal money supply, expressed in logarithms,

$\overline{M}$ = fixed exogenous component of the domestic nominal money supply,

Y_t = real domestic output at time t,

$\hat{Y}$ = full employment level of output,

r_t = domestic nominal interest rate at time t,

Ω_t = foreign nominal interest rate at time t,

$E^*_{t+s,t}$ = expectation of E for time $t+s$, held at time t, $s = 1, 2, \ldots$,

$P^*_{t+s,t}$ = expectation of P for time $t+s$ held at time t, $s = 1, 2, \ldots$,

u_{1t} = stochastic disturbance in demand for domestic money at time t,

u_{2t} = stochastic disturbance in domestic output supply at time t.

The equations of the model are standard. Given purchasing power parity, the domestic price of a freely traded commodity equals the price abroad multiplied by its exchange rate. Equation (5.4a) is just a logarithmic version of this relationship. The domestic monetary sector is summarized by equations (5.4b)–(5.4d). The first of these describes the domestic LM curve, making the usual assumption that all domestic money is held by domestic residents, who also hold no foreign currency. The assumption of perfect capital market integration is embodied in the interest parity condition (5.1c). The intervention policy is described by (5.1d), which expresses the degree of intervention by the authority as a function of the observed deviation of the exchange rate from its long-run equilibrium level and which the authorities are assumed to know. The limiting cases $\mu \to \infty$, $\mu = 0$, correspond to fixed and flexible regimes, respectively, while any finite, nonzero value of μ describes a managed float. A policy of setting $\mu > 0$ implies that if the current exchange rate is above its long-run level, the monetary authority introduces a monetary contraction (sets M below $\overline{M}$), thereby reducing the pressure on the exchange rate. Such a policy was described earlier as "leaning against the wind." If $\mu < 0$, the monetary authority reacts to a depreciating exchange rate by adopting an expansionary policy, thereby adding to the pressure on the exchange rate. This may be referred to as "leaning with the wind." The optimal intervention policy is to choose μ to optimize an objective, yet to be specified, and as we shall demonstrate, an optimal policy may involve either $\mu > 0$ or $\mu < 0$, depending on the primary source of the stochastic disturbances. Note that the reaction function is expressed in terms of current values of M and E, which are therefore assumed to be instantaneously observable.

The supply of output is specified by (5.4e). This relationship postulates the deviation in output from its full employment level to depend on the unanticipated component of the current domestic price of output. It is essentially a Lucas (1973) new classical supply function. Finally, equation (5.4f) describes the rationality of expectations.

The two domestic stochastic disturbances u_{1t}, u_{2t} are assumed to have zero means and finite second moments satisfying

$$E(u_{1t}) = E(u_{2t}) = 0, \tag{5.5a}$$

$$E(u_{1t}^2) = \sigma_1^2; \qquad E(u_{2t}^2) = \sigma_2^2; \qquad E(u_{1t}u_{2t}) = \sigma_1\sigma_2\rho, \tag{5.5b}$$

where ρ is the correlation coefficient between the two variables. While we have written u_{1t} as reflecting a stochastic disturbance in demand, it can equally well be interpreted (with a sign change) as being a stochastic disturbance in the money supply. The two foreign variables in the system Ω_t, Q_t are also assumed to be random, being described by

$$\Omega_t = \overline{\Omega} + \omega_t, \tag{5.6a}$$

$$Q_t = \overline{Q} + q_t, \tag{5.6b}$$

where $\overline{\Omega}$, $\overline{Q}$ are constant and

$$E(\omega_t) = E(q_t) = 0, \tag{5.7a}$$

$$E(\omega_t^2) = \sigma_\omega^2; \qquad E(q_t^2) = \sigma_q^2; \qquad E(\omega_t q_t) = \sigma_\omega\sigma_q\eta, \tag{5.7b}$$

where η denotes the corresponding correlation coefficient. In addition, all random variables are assumed to be independently distributed over time, and for simplicity we assume that domestic and foreign variables are uncorrelated. This enables us to distinguish unambiguously between domestic and foreign stochastic influences.

But whereas ω_t and q_t are exogenous to the small country, they are themselves endogenously determined in the rest of the world, reflecting the various stochastic influences occurring abroad. To solve for these variables it is reasonable, given the small-country assumption of the domestic economy, to treat the rest of the world as a large closed economy, unaffected by the domestic economy. One can then solve for ω_t, q_t as functions of the random variables occurring abroad, and as a result the correlation between them will reflect the prevalent sources of these foreign disturbances.[7]

In order to simplify notation it is convenient to consider an initial equilibrium defined by assuming that all expectations are realized and setting all random variables equal to zero. We may then express the system in deviation form about this equilibrium as

$$p_t = q_t + e_t, \tag{5.8a}$$

$$m_t - p_t = \alpha_1 y_t - \alpha_2 [e^*_{t+1,t} - e_t] + u_{1t} - \alpha_2 \omega_t, \tag{5.8b}$$

$$m_t = -\mu e_t, \tag{5.8c}$$

$$y_t = \gamma (p_t - p^*_{t,t-1}) + u_{2t}, \tag{5.8d}$$

where lowercase letters denote variables measured in deviation form and for convenience r_t has been eliminated. Equations (5.8a)–(5.8d) yield four stochastic difference equations in domestic output y_t, the price of domestic output p_t and its expectation, the exchange rate e_t and its expectation, and the domestic nominal money supply m_t.

5.3.2   Solution of the system

Various procedures exist for solving the system (5.8). Whichever is chosen, the solution is plagued by the nonuniqueness characteristic of rational expectations equilibria, and to complete the solution some arbitrary choice must be made. For simplicity, we shall adopt the McCallum (1983) minimum state representation solution. This involves choosing the most parsimonious solution consistent with expectations being rational. Under the present assumptions of white noise disturbances, this turns out to imply a solution in which the exchange rate and price level depend only upon current disturbances, so that $e^*_{t,t-1} = p^*_{t,t-1} = 0$ for all t. That is, given the stationarity of the system, expectations are static. Both the exchange rate and the price level are always expected to equal their respective long-run equilibrium values.

[7] See, e.g., Cox (1980).

The solutions for y_t, p_t, and e_t are thus obtained by setting all expectations equal to zero in (5.8), yielding the expressions

$$y_t = \frac{\gamma(\alpha_2 + \mu)q_t + (1 + \alpha_2 + \mu)u_{2t} + \gamma(\alpha_2\omega_t - u_{1t})}{1 + \alpha_2 + \mu + \alpha_1\gamma}, \qquad (5.9a)$$

$$p_t = \frac{(\alpha_2 + \mu)q_t - \alpha_1 u_{2t} + \alpha_2\omega_t - u_{1t}}{1 + \alpha_2 + \mu + \alpha_1\gamma}, \qquad (5.9b)$$

$$e_t = \frac{-(1 + \alpha_1\gamma)q_t - \alpha_1 u_{2t} + \alpha_2\omega_t - u_{1t}}{1 + \alpha_2 + \mu + \alpha_1\gamma}. \qquad (5.9c)$$

Thus, y_t, p_t, and e_t all fluctuate statically in response to the domestic random variables, as well as the random variables of foreign origin (q_t, ω_t). Observe also that the intervention parameter μ affects the response of all three endogenous variables to all four exogenous random shocks.

Differentiating (5.9) with respect to μ, we can show that an increase in the degree of exchange market intervention, taking the form of more intensive leaning against the wind, has the following effects on the domestic economy. It reduces the impact of disturbances in the domestic monetary sector u_{1t} or in the foreign nominal interest rate ω_t on all three variables y_t, p_t, and e_t. An increase in μ raises the effect of a domestic supply shock u_{2t} on output, while lowering the effects on the domestic price level and the exchange rate. Finally, an increase in μ raises the effect of a positive foreign price disturbance q_t on y_t and p_t, but reduces the appreciation of the domestic currency.

The following intuitive explanation for the domestic disturbances may be given. An increase in the domestic demand for money tends to raise the domestic interest rate, leading to an appreciation of the domestic currency, which in turn leads to a fall in the domestic price level and a contraction in domestic output. If the monetary authority responds to the appreciating domestic exchange rate by a monetary expansion, this will generate an offsetting expansionary effect, thereby reducing the fall in y_t, p_t, and e_t. A positive supply disturbance raises income, lowering the domestic price level and causing the domestic currency to appreciate. If the monetary authority responds by increasing the money supply, output will increase further, thereby reducing the fall in the domestic price level. The foreign disturbance effects can be discussed similarly.

5.3.3   Optimal exchange market intervention

The general approach to the question of the optimal degree of intervention is to choose μ so as to minimize some objective function expressed in terms of the asymptotic variances of relevant endogenous variables in the economy. Typically, this includes the stabilization of some measure of output, and the following criteria are prevalent in the literature:

(i)   minimizing the variance of output;
(ii) minimizing a weighted average of the variances of output and the price level;
(iii) minimizing the variance of output about some frictionless equilibrium level (rather than zero).[8]

Even for the simple model just outlined, the determination of the optimal degree of intervention, $\hat{\mu}$ say, turns out to be surprisingly complicated. However, two main conclusions can be established:

(i)   While fixed and flexible exchange rates can emerge as optimal in polar cases, in general neither of these extreme regimes is optimal.
(ii) Optimal policy may involve leaning with the wind or leaning against the wind.

In general, even in the simplest possible stochastic model such as that outlined in the preceding subsection, the optimal monetary intervention rule can be almost of any form, depending on the sources of the shocks hitting the economy and their relative magnitudes.

For example, suppose that the only source of stochastic shocks is a domestic monetary disturbance u_{1t}. From the solutions (5.9a), (5.9b), it is seen that the perfectly fixed rate regime $\mu \rightarrow \infty$ has the property of stabilizing y_t and p_t perfectly. The economic explanation for this is straightforward. Given that the domestic price level is determined by purchasing power parity, it follows that if e_t is fixed and if there are no disturbances in q_t, then p_t must be fixed as well. It follows from the domestic supply function that if p_t is fixed and if, in addition, (i) price expectations are static, as the solution implies, and (ii) there are no disturbances in domestic supply, domestic output must itself also remain fixed.

The perfect stability of y_t and p_t can also be viewed as an example of the following general characteristic. The current observability of certain market variables implies information on the source of random

---

[8] The justification sometimes given for measuring the variance of output around the output level that would prevail in a frictionless economy is that under appropriate conditions it can be identified with the welfare losses resulting from the existence of rigidities, such as contracts; see, e.g., Aizenman and Frenkel (1985).

shocks in the economy. More specifically, the observability of m_t and e_t is equivalent to the observability of the linear combination of random variables $u_{1t} + \alpha_1 u_{2t} + (1 + \alpha_1\gamma)q_t - \alpha_2\omega_t$.[9] When only one random variable is present, it follows that the observability of this linear combination of disturbances reduces to the observability of the random variable itself, which may therefore be appropriately offset, thereby maintaining perfect stability of at least one random variable of the system. The result that both y_t and p_t can be stabilized perfectly in this instance follows directly from the fact that if there is only one disturbance and it is not a domestic supply shock, then domestic output and prices move proportionately.

By contrast, stabilizing in the face of a domestic supply disturbance u_{2t} gives rise to a conflict with respect to price and output stability. From (5.9a)–(5.9c) it is seen that while a fixed exchange rate $\mu \to \infty$ will stabilize the domestic price level exactly, this will maximize the instability of domestic real income. On the other hand, income will be stabilized perfectly by adopting the policy of leaning with the wind in accordance with the rule $\mu = -(1 + \alpha_2)$. It is thus impossible to stabilize both p_t and y_t exactly in the face of domestic supply disturbances, and a trade-off between the stability of the two variables must be made.

Most discussions of intervention policy limit their attention to parameters that characterize leaning against the wind. The intuitive idea is that such a policy, by alleviating fluctuations in the exchange rate, will increase stability elsewhere in the economy. The fact that an optimal policy may involve exacerbating swings in the exchange rate is therefore of interest and merits further comment. When the only disturbance is in u_{2t} equations (5.8a)–(5.8d) can be combined to yield

$$-\mu e_t = (1 + \alpha_2)e_t + \alpha_1 y_t, \tag{5.8b'}$$

$$y_t = \gamma e_t + u_{2t}. \tag{5.8d'}$$

It is evident from (5.8b') that a policy of leaning with the wind ($\mu < 0$) will tend to provide greater insulation for y_t from the random disturbance u_{2t}, forcing the shock to be absorbed more fully by the exchange rate. If, for instance, the exchange rate tends to appreciate, the domestic interest rate must take on higher values and m_t must be contracted to keep y_t from rising. If the objective puts most of the weight on the stabilization of output, this strategy is clearly appropriate.

---

[9] This can be seen by eliminating y_t and p_t from (5.8a), (5.8b), and (5.8d), setting expectations equal to zero, and writing the resulting equation as

$$m_t = (1 + \alpha_1\gamma + \alpha_2)e_t + [u_{1t} + \alpha_1 u_{2t} + (1 + \alpha_1\gamma)q_t - \alpha_2\omega_t].$$

The overall optimal policy is not clear and involves balancing off the various conflicting elements associated with the various disturbances of both domestic and foreign origin. In general, the formal expression for the actual optimal policy is not particularly informative. Rather, the main merit of this approach lies in understanding how each type of disturbance contributes to exchange market pressure and how the different policies determine how the shocks are absorbed by the economy – that is, by the adjustment in exchange rates versus reserves.[10]

A detailed, case-by-case treatment of different disturbances was carried out by Turnovsky (1984b). It is useful to conclude this discussion by considering the circumstances under which the polar regimes of perfectly fixed and perfectly flexible regimes will be optimal. As already shown, the former is optimal in stabilizing for *domestic monetary* disturbances. By contrast, the latter can be shown to stabilize the domestic income and price level perfectly in the face of *foreign monetary* disturbances. That this is so is not quite as obvious, but can be seen as follows. We have already commented on how the foreign disturbances ω_t, q_t impinging on the domestic economy will depend on the sources of the stochastic disturbances abroad. If they reflect a foreign monetary shock, a rise in the foreign price level resulting from a monetary expansion abroad will be accompanied by a fall in the foreign interest rate. Solving explicitly for ω_t and q_t in the face of such a disturbance, one can show that they are exactly offsetting, that is $\omega_t + q_t = 0$ (see, e.g., Cox, 1980). When this condition is substituted into (5.9a) and (5.9b), it immediately follows that allowing the exchange rate to be perfectly flexible (i.e., setting $\mu = 0$) permits both the domestic output and the domestic price level to be stabilized perfectly against this composite foreign shock.

5.3.4   *Extensions of this approach*

The new classical stochastic model we have outlined is a basic one used to address issues of exchange market intervention. Subsequent analysis has led to several extensions of this type of model, introducing different considerations. These include the following:

Available information set. A key aspect of this type of stabilization analysis concerns the degree to which information is available to the

---

[10] The notion of exchange market pressure was introduced by Girton and Roper (1977). It is discussed at length in the context of the present model by Turnovsky (1984a). It is also discussed by Popper and Lowell in Chapter 9, this volume.

various agents in the economy. To discuss this issue it is convenient to focus on the time period t and to partition it into the infinitesimally short subperiod $(t, t+)$.

One motivation for the supply function is that the wage at time t is determined by a contract signed at time $t - 1$ on the basis of information available at time $t - 1$. Prices and financial variables are assumed to be observed instantaneously by all agents, so that they all have complete current information on these variables when they make their respective decisions.[11] More specifically, these instantaneously observed variables include (i) the domestic and foreign interest rates, (ii) the exchange rate, and (iii) the domestic price level. Given purchasing power parity, (ii) and (iii) imply the observability of the foreign price level as well.

At time t, two sets of decisions are made. First, there is the policy decision – that is, the implementation of the monetary intervention rule. Second, there are the decisions of the private agents in the economy, which include the production, portfolio, and consumption decisions, as well as the formation of forecasts for the next period. We assume that the two sets of decisions are made in the above order, at instances we denote by $t, t+$, respectively. This means that monetary policy, which is determined at time t, is known by the time the production decision is made at the next instant of time, $t+$.

This distinction in effect differentiates the information set available to the public and private agents in the economy. It is possible to make further distinctions among the various private agents along the lines of Canzoneri, Henderson, and Rogoff (1983). For example, one can allow investors, who make predictions of the future exchange rate to have information that is different from an individual concerned with predicting prices in the determination of the wage contract. Their information may differ from that of producers as well.

The key informational issue concerns the observability of the domestic monetary disturbance u_{1t} and the domestic supply disturbance u_{2t}. Under the above-mentioned assumptions, three different informational situations exist:

(i) u_{1t} and u_{2t} are observed instantaneously at time t by both public and private agents. This full information assumption turns out to be in effect the information structure considered by Karni (1983) in his discussion of wage indexation policy.

---

[11] Information problems are also stressed by Grimes and Wong in their analysis of the role of the exchange rate in New Zealand monetary policy (Chapter 8, this volume).

(ii) u_{1t} and u_{2t} are observed in the time interval $(t, t+)$. They are therefore unobserved by the stabilization authority, but are known to private agents. This asymmetric information assumption is made throughout much of the literature and is implicit in the above analysis (see Canzoneri, 1982; Turnovsky, 1983; and several of the papers in Bhandari, 1985).

(iii) u_{1t} and u_{2t} are observed after time $t+$. They are therefore unknown to both public and private agents when decisions for time t are made. In this case, agents form estimates of the two stochastic variables at time t, as required for forecasting decisions, by utilizing information on the observed financial variables. This information is symmetric between public and private agents. This setup has been utilized by Aizenman and Frenkel (1985).

The informational issue we have been discussing pertains to the timing of the available information. The question of the role of this type of information in the conduct of optimal monetary policy is discussed at length by Turnovsky (1987a). Other authors have extended the role of differential information underlying the Lucas (1972, 1973) "islands" model to an open economy context. The essential informational asymmetry here arises from the notion that agents are trading in different local markets and observe different prices. Most of this literature does not address optimal policy, but rather focuses on the comparison of fixed versus flexible rates. For example, Kimbrough (1984) shows that the degree to which an unanticipated change in the money supply is perceived by agents, and therefore its impact on output, depends on the exchange rate regime. Under flexible exchange rates, systematic monetary policy can have an effect on real output by altering the information content of the exchange rate. This is not the case under fixed exchange rates, since under this regime the exchange rate fails to provide useful information. This argument is extended to a two-country world by Glick and Wihlborg (1990). Similarly, Flood and Hodrick (1985) show that the policy of fixed exchange rates is the worst from the standpoint of revealing information and that it will be dominated by any floating rate regime. They further show that a purely flexible system is dominated by an optimal feedback policy where the monetary authority reacts to past money supply shocks.[12]

---

[12] In relation to the Flood–Hodrick result, Turnovsky (1985) considers two types of monetary policy rules, one based on contemporaneous information concerning financial and price variables such as in (5.8c), and (5.8c′), the other a feedback rule based on past information concerning the target variable. He shows not only that the latter can

"Augmented" versus "simple rules": the design of "policy packages." The simple model that we have outlined assumes that the only piece of information used by the monetary authority in determining its intervention at time t is the current exchange rate. In so doing, the authority would seem to be disregarding a great deal of information that is likely to be available. For example, if information on other financial variables, such as domestic and foreign interest rates and domestic and foreign price levels, is available concurrently, it is reasonable that it should play a role in determining monetary policy. Assuming that purchasing power parity and uncovered interest parity hold, not all of these pieces of information are independent, but a monetary rule analogous to (5.8c) that incorporates all independent pieces of information is

$$m_t = \mu_1 e_t + \mu_2 r_t + \mu_3 \omega_t + \mu_4 q_t. \tag{5.8c'}$$

As discussed by Turnovsky (1984a, 1987a), such a rule based on more information enables the monetary authority to react to the foreign shocks directly, and this turns out to simplify the determination of the optimal policy rule.

In the early 1980s, research on international macroeconomics emphasized the interdependence between the choice of exchange rate regime and the degree of wage indexation. Such authors as Marston (1982) and Flood and Marion (1982) showed how (i) the choice between fixed and flexible exchange rates from the viewpoint of maximizing stability depends on the degree of wage indexation and (ii) the choice of the optimal degree of wage indexation depends on the exchange rate regime. Building on these contributions, Turnovsky (1983) and Aizenman and Frenkel (1985) took a more integrated approach to the question of the optimal stabilization of an open economy by analyzing general rules for both wage indexation and monetary policy. These authors focused on the trade-offs between these stabilization instruments, and their approach was directed at the design of overall, integrated, stabilization policy packages. Taking monetary policy to be in the form of exchange market intervention, Turnovsky showed how the degree of intervention impinges on the effectiveness of wage indexation and vice versa. Full indexation of wages to prices renders exchange market intervention ineffective in stabilizing output. On the other hand, exchange market intervention that results in the domestic money supply being accommodated to the extent that it precisely offsets the change in the demand for money due to movements in the exchange rate, renders wage in-

outperform the former but, rather surprisingly, that it may actually achieve perfect stabilization of output, in that its variance is reduced to zero.

dexation totally ineffective. Aizenman and Frenkel (1985) and Turnovsky (1987a) consider the joint determination of optimal indexation and optimal monetary policy among more general forms of monetary policy rules. Their analyses stress the relationship between the number of pieces of independent information regarding the sources of stochastic disturbances impinging on the economy and the number of independent policy parameters. The key contribution of this literature is to embed exchange rate policy within a broader integrated policymaking context.

Nature of disturbances. The stochastic disturbances impinging on the economy can be dichotomized in various ways: (i) real versus nominal, (ii) domestic versus foreign, (iii) temporary versus permanent, and (iv) unanticipated versus anticipated. The simple model discussed earlier includes both real and nominal disturbances, as well as disturbances of both domestic and foreign origin. Being white noise, all disturbances were assumed to be temporary and were unanticipated.

From an analytical viewpoint, distinctions (iii) and (iv) are much more important. This is because agents' perceptions of whether disturbances are temporary will affect expectations. Under the assumption of white noise disturbances, all expectations are essentially zero, so that prices and the exchange rate can be expected to remain at their respective long-run equilibrium levels. However, if a disturbance is perceived as being permanent, this will have an impact on both exchange rate and price expectations, thereby influencing the behavior of output and the determination of optimal monetary policy. The same applies with respect to an anticipated disturbance. The determination of optimal monetary policy under this more general type of disturbance is analyzed at length by Turnovsky (1984a, 1987b), where it is shown to imply forms of optimal policy that are very different from those obtained under the more familiar white noise assumption. Indeed, in the case where disturbances are perceived as being permanent, the optimal intervention rule not only is nonunique, but is actually able to replicate precisely the output of a frictionless economy, using very limited pieces of information.

Intervention in spot versus forward markets: unsterilized versus sterilized intervention. Most of the literature assumes that the intervention takes place through the spot exchange market. This involves accommodating changes in the domestic money supply, leading to potential problems of instability stemming from fluctuations in domestic credit conditions. In this case, what we have been describing can be said to be *unsterilized intervention*. Spraos (1959) was an early advocate of intervention in the forward market, arguing that the forward rate should be pegged. Formal analyses of intervention in the forward market under conditions of covered interest parity have been carried out by Eaton and Turnovsky (1984) and Turnovsky (1989). The conclusions of the latter regarding the desirability of fixing the forward rate are very much open to question, and whether such intervention in the forward market stabilizes the spot rate depends on the sources of the disturbances impinging on the economy. Eaton and Turnovsky (1983a) and Kawai (1984) consider more general models in which covered interest parity need not hold. In this case, intervention in the spot market, intervention in the domestic bond market, and intervention in the forward exchange market are all linearly independent. However, in the special case where covered interest parity prevails, intervention in the domestic bond market and in the forward exchange market become identical, in which case intervention in the forward market is equivalent to *sterilized intervention* in the spot market.

5.3.5 *Criticisms of this approach*

While the new classical approach has provided a fertile framework for analyzing monetary intervention problems, it is subject to several substantial criticisms. First, it does not yield any very strong positive conclusions with respect to how policy should be conducted and in this respect is of limited assistance to policymakers. All kinds of policies may be optimal, depending on the sources of the shocks.[13] Its greatest merit is that it helps us to understand how different shocks affect exchange market pressure and how each should be dealt with in isolation.

Second, the model is subject to the Lucas critique. With few exceptions, the literature assumes that the economic structure remains invariant with respect to changes in the exchange rate regime. Yet the changes in private behavior induced by the regime changes may be important. As originally shown by McCafferty and Driskill (1980) in a different context, this renders the solution for rational expectations equilibrium nonlinear, raising potential problems of nonexistence and nonuniqueness of equilibria. These issues are addressed in a limited way in this framework by Black (1985) and Turnovsky (1989).

Finally, the underlying model is not based on firm microeconomic underpinnings, and the variance criteria used to evaluate policy in this framework do not provide a satisfactory basis for a rigorous welfare analysis.

---

[13] Recognizing the importance of this, there is a body of empirical work that attempts to measure the relative magnitudes of domestic and foreign shocks. Moreno, in Chapter 6, this volume, provides an example.

5.4   Rational intertemporal models

As is the case with most contemporary macroeconomics, recent research on international macroeconomics is based on the intertemporal optimization of representative agents in the economy. The attractive feature of this approach is that the intertemporal welfare of the representative agent is explicit and serves as a natural criterion for assessing the welfare implications of specified policy changes. Most of the literature deals with assessing real policies, such as tariffs, taxes, and expenditure policies. Relatively little literature is devoted to assessing exchange rate policy in this type of framework, although the articles of Helpman and Razin (1979, 1987) are notable exceptions. Furthermore, most of the international macroeconomic literature analyzing policy using this approach is deterministic.

One of the general conclusions to emerge from this framework is that, in the absence of distortions, the exchange rate does not really affect the real part of the system. In effect, money is neutral, or superneutral, so that exchange rate policy – which is a form of monetary policy – does not matter. Essentially, this is a manifestation of the well-known Sidrauski (1967) analysis, which showed that in a model of capital accumulation the capital–labor ratio is independent of the monetary growth rate. In the following subsections, we outline a model – one that abstracts from capital – in which the only real effects of monetary policy occur through the interaction between the real money stock and the marginal rate of substitution between consumption and leisure. This will generate real effects.

Although money turns out to have a more limited role, the framework does highlight certain constraints on exchange rate policy and other forms of government policy, notably tax and expenditure policy. For example, the rate of monetary growth will be shown to have an impact on equilibrium real money balances. This affects the real revenues received by the government and will thereby influence fiscal policy, in order for the intertemporal government budget constraint to be met. The intertemporal solvency of the government and the nation is a very important dimension not addressed by the earlier literature.

5.4.1   Simple intertemporal optimizing model

In this section we briefly sketch a model adapted from Turnovsky (1987b). It is of an infinitely lived representative agent who supplies labor to produce a single traded good, which he also consumes. The agent holds domestic money, as well as an internationally traded bond.

Purchasing power parity and uncovered interest parity are also assumed to hold. In this respect, the model is based on assumptions virtually identical to those introduced previously.

For the present purposes, the household and production sectors of the economy may be consolidated. The agent's decisions are to choose his rate of consumption c, his supply of labor l, his holdings of real money balances m, and real stock of bonds b to maximize his intertemporal utility function

$$\int_0^\infty U(c, l, m, g)e^{-(r^*-q)t}\,dt, \qquad U_c > 0,\ U_l < 0,\ U_g > 0, \qquad (5.10a)$$

subject to the accumulation equation

$$\dot{m} + \dot{b} + c = f(l) + (r^* - q)b - (q + e)m - T \qquad (5.10b)$$

and initial conditions

$$m(o) = \frac{M_o}{P(o)} = \frac{M_o}{Q_o E(o)}; \qquad b(o) = \frac{E(o)B_o}{Q_o E(o)} = \frac{B_o}{Q_o}, \qquad (5.10c)$$

where r^* = foreign nominal interest rate,
$\quad\ q$ = foreign rate of inflation,
$\quad\ e$ = rate of exchange depreciation,
$\quad\ g$ = real government expenditure,
$\quad\ T$ = real lump-sum tax,
$\quad M$ = nominal money balances,
$\quad\ B$ = nominal stock of bonds,
$\quad\ P$ = domestic price level,
$\quad\ Q$ = foreign price level,
$\quad\ E$ = exchange rate, measured in terms of units of domestic currency per unit of foreign currency.

Several features of this specification merit comment. First, the consumer's rate of time preference is the world real rate of interest $r^* - q$. As is well known, as long as the rate of time preference is assumed to be constant, this is the only value that under perfect capital mobility is consistent with the ultimate attainment of a steady-state equilibrium. Second, the utility function is assumed to be concave in its four arguments, c, g, l, and m. Consumers are assumed to derive positive marginal utility from the consumption of both private and public goods, but positive marginal disutility from providing labor services. We shall assume that for given values of c, g, and l, the marginal utility of money is subject to a satiation level, $m = m^*$ say, where $U_m = 0$ (cf. Friedman, 1969). Third, the budget constraint is expressed in real flow terms and is standard. The initial conditions (5.10c) pertain to the initial stocks of real bonds and money held by the private agent, defined as the corresponding initial nominal stocks divided by the initial price level. In the case of the real money stock, this is endogenously determined through an appropriate initial jump in the exchange rate, $E(o)$. By contrast, the initial stock of real bonds is predetermined by past accumulation.

The other agent in the economy is the domestic government, whose decisions are subject to the real flow constraint

$$\dot{m} + \dot{a} = g + (r^* - q)a - (q + e)m - T, \qquad (5.11)$$

where a is the real stock of traded bonds issued by the government ($= A/P$, where A is the corresponding nominal stock).

Subtracting (5.11) from (5.10b) yields

$$\dot{n} = f(l) - c - g + (r^* - q)n, \qquad (5.12)$$

where $n \equiv b - a$ is the stock of net credit of the domestic economy.[14] That is, the rate of accumulation of traded bonds held by the domestic economy equals the balance of payments on current account, which in turn equals the balance of trade plus the net interest income earned on traded bonds. With a single traded commodity, the balance of trade is simply the excess of domestic production over domestic absorption.

5.4.2   *Macroeconomic equilibrium*

The macroeconomic equilibrium considered is one of perfect foresight in which all markets continuously clear. The equilibrium is obtained as follows. First, the equilibrium to the private agent's optimization problem is obtained. In addition to the usual first-order conditions, this includes the transversality conditions

$$\lim_{t \to \infty} \mu m e^{-(r^* - q)t} = \lim_{t \to \infty} \mu b e^{-(r^* - q)t} = 0. \qquad (5.13)$$

To complete the macroeconomic equilibrium, government policy must be specified. In the present analysis, the government has four policy instruments available to it, M, A, g, and T, any three of which can be chosen independently. In the absence of capital accumulation, the op-

---

[14] The economy is a net creditor or net debtor according to whether n is greater than or less than zero.

timal policies turn out to be constant over time.[15] Specifically, we shall assume that the government specifies monetary policy in terms of a constant nominal monetary growth rate, θ say. The rate of real money growth is therefore

$$\dot{m} = (\theta - q - e)m, \tag{5.14a}$$

with the corresponding change in real traded bonds being

$$\dot{a} = g + (r^* - q)a - \theta m - T. \tag{5.14b}$$

In this context, the optimal choice of exchange rate regime concerns the optimal choice of θ. In making its policy decisions, the government must meet its intertemporal budget constraint

$$\lim_{t \to \infty} ae^{-(r^* - q)t} = 0. \tag{5.15}$$

Taking account of the definition of n, this equation combined with the second transversality condition in (5.13) implies

$$\lim_{t \to \infty} ne^{-(r^* - q)t} = 0. \tag{5.16}$$

This equation is an intertemporal budget constraint on the economy, ruling out the possibility that the country can run up infinite credit or debt with the rest of the world.

With perfect capital markets, the transversality conditions can be shown to impose severe constraints on the economy. First, in order for the real money stock not to become unbounded, we require that

$$\theta = q + e,$$

so that $\dot{m} \equiv 0$. Thus, in order for the real money stock to be ultimately bounded, it must in fact remain constant at all times. Given that the money stock is predetermined, the required (constant) real money stock is attained by an appropriate initial jump in the nominal exchange rate $E(o)$.

Using standard methods, the perfect foresight equilibrium can be shown to consist of the following five equations (see Turnovsky, 1987b):

$$U_c(c, l, m, g) = \mu, \tag{5.17a}$$

$$U_l(c, l, m, g) = -f'(l)\mu, \tag{5.17b}$$

$$U_m(c, l, m, g) = (r^* + \theta - q)\mu, \tag{5.17c}$$

---

[15] The stationarity of the optimal policies is established by Turnovsky (1987b).

$$(r^* - q)b_o + f(l) - T - \theta m - c = 0, \tag{5.17d}$$

$$(r^* - q)(b_o - a_o) + f(l) - c - g = 0, \tag{5.17e}$$

where μ is the marginal utility of wealth and is constant. The first three equations are conventional first-order marginal conditions for consumers. The remaining two are budget constraints and are consequences of the transversality conditions. The equilibrium is one having the characteristic that the economy is always in steady-state equilibrium, so that no accumulation of assets occurs. Equation (5.17d) requires that the private agent's real interest income from his inherited bond holdings plus income from current production, less lump-sum taxes and inflation tax on money balances, must equal current consumption. Equation (5.17e) is the analogous constraint for the overall economy. With b_o being predetermined by previous accumulation and a_o being the initial stock of government bonds outstanding, these five equations determine equilibrium values for c, l, m, μ, together with one of the policy instruments, θ, T, or g.

We assume that with θ being chosen to optimize welfare, the necessary accommodation is undertaken by one of the fiscal parameters T or g. We shall restrict our comments to the former, treating g as given. Other forms of accommodation are also possible, as Turnovsky (1987b) discusses.

The macroeconomic equilibrium (5.17) highlights the two key points made earlier with respect to monetary policy in this rational intertemporal framework. First, if the utility function is additively separable in say c, l on the one hand and m on the other, it is clear that the equilibrium levels of consumption, employment, and output are all determined jointly through the two marginal conditions (5.17a) and (5.17b), together with the national resource constraint (5.17c), and are independent of monetary policy. Monetary policy therefore affects the real part of the system only through the interaction of real money stock with the marginal rate of substitution between consumption and labor. Second, the fact that the lump-sum tax must accommodate any chosen money growth rate in order to sustain the equilibrium emphasizes the constraints that exist between monetary and fiscal policy. The stationarity of the equilibrium in the present simple model merely serves to simplify the nature of these constraints.

5.4.3   Optimal monetary policy

We now turn to the determination of the optimal money growth rate θ. In so doing we assume that the domestic government chooses the growth rate to maximize the intertemporal utility function of the representative agent (5.10a), subject to the equilibrium constraints (5.17). Since everything is stationary, this can be accomplished by maximizing the instantaneous utility function. This problem can be formulated by expressing consumer utility as an indirect utility function in terms of government policy and then optimizing. Alternatively, it can be described in terms of a standard Lagrangian expression.

Details of the optimality conditions are provided by Turnovsky (1987b) and need not be repeated here. There it is shown how the optimal monetary growth rate depends on the form of fiscal accommodation carried out to finance the government budget. In the case where the accommodation occurs through lump-sum taxation and there is no distortionary income tax, the optimal rate of money growth turns out to be

$$\hat{\theta} = -(r^* - q) \quad \text{or equivalently} \quad \hat{r} = r^* + e = 0. \qquad (5.18)$$

This relationship asserts that the optimal rate of money growth is precisely the celebrated Friedman full liquidity rule, namely that the domestic nominal interest rate should be set to zero. Under the assumption of interest parity, this implies that the domestic exchange rate should appreciate steadily at the exogenously given world nominal interest rate r^*.

In the version of this model developed by Turnovsky, domestic income is taxed at a constant rate τ. In this case, one can show that the optimal money growth rate is given by the expression

$$\hat{\theta} = \frac{\tau f' U_c}{\Delta} \frac{\partial}{\partial m}\left(\frac{U_l}{U_c}\right) - (r^* - q); \qquad \Delta < 0. \qquad (5.18')$$

Thus, in the presence of a distortionary income tax, the optimal money growth rate will coincide with the Friedman rule if and only if the marginal rate of substitution between consumption and labor is independent of real money balances. Otherwise, if, say, $\partial(U_l/U_c)/\partial m < 0$, by reducing m below m^*, the marginal rate of substitution of labor for consumption will be increased; workers will be willing to supply more labor, output will increase, and the utility from consumption will rise correspondingly. The opposite is true if $\partial(U_l/U_c)/\partial m > 0$. In effect, the optimal monetary policy calls for balancing off the direct utility of money, on the one hand, with its indirect effects resulting from its interaction with consumption and leisure, on the other. This may be characterized as a "distorted" Friedman rule. Using the steady-state relationship $\theta = q + e$, (5.18') translates into an equivalent relationship describing the optimal crawling peg $\hat{e}$.

Turnovsky also addresses the case where the accommodation is carried out by means of the adjustment in the distortionary tax rate τ rather than through lump-sum taxation. This is shown to lead to a trade-off between the inflation tax and the distortionary income tax rate similar to that originally discussed by Phelps (1973) for a closed economy.

5.4.4   *A stochastic intertemporal model*

Turnovsky and Grinols (1992) analyze the choice of optimal monetary policy and exchange rate regime in a stochastic intertemporal optimizing model, based on the behavior of risk-averse optimizing agents. Because of the formulation of debt policy in that particular model, monetary policy is able to influence the real part of the system, and therefore welfare, through the domestic interest rate, which thus should serve as an intermediate target. Optimal monetary policy, which determines the optimal exchange rate regime, should therefore be directed at trying to attain an optimal target nominal interest rate. This rate, which maximizes the intertemporal utility of the representative agent, is determined by balancing off the marginal gains of a higher interest rate on increased growth, and the future consumption it generates, against the marginal losses stemming from a reduction in the holdings of real money balances. This optimal interest rate can always be achieved by an appropriately set mean money growth rate, which may be either positive or negative, depending on how fiscal instruments are set.

Under certain conditions, the target may also be attained by continuously adjusting the current rate of money growth in response to stochastic fluctuations in the current exchange rate. However, this form of intervention may not always be feasible, while in other circumstances it may be associated with multiple equilibria. In any event, an appropriately set money growth rate eliminates the need for continuous intervention in the exchange market. This view of exchange rate management is very different from those characterizing the simple stochastic models discussed in Section 5.3. More specifically, the latter requires the monetary authority to monitor movements in the exchange rate continuously, as they respond to the various stochastic disturbances impinging on the economy. By contrast, the Turnovsky–Grinols analysis suggests that this is unnecessary. All the monetary authority need do is to set an appropriate money growth rate and ignore current stochastic shocks as they impinge on the economy. While such shocks introduce variance into the system, this can be accommodated by an appropriately set money growth rate, without any adverse effects on economic welfare.

5.4.5   *Critique*

The rational intertemporal optimizing approach is the purest from a theoretical viewpoint, in that the underlying equilibrium is obtained from the intertemporal optimization of rational agents. But this, too, is a restrictive framework. First, the use of the representative agent, while currently embraced by macroeconomists, is viewed much more critically by economic theorists, in that only under restrictive conditions will it serve as a reasonable guide to aggregate behavior (see, e.g., Lewbel, 1989; Kirman, 1992). Second, this approach is based on market clearing and abstracts from all kinds of rigidities that may well be important in practice. It is therefore more likely to serve as a superior guide to choosing long-run monetary regimes rather than short-run stabilization. The most important general lesson to emerge from this approach is the recognition that monetary policy must be consistent with the intertemporal budget constraints facing the agents in the economy and that this will most likely require the coordination of monetary policy with fiscal policy.

5.5   Target zone models

The final type of model of exchange rate management that we shall discuss, briefly, is the target zone model. The traditional discussion of fixed versus flexible exchange rates was based on the assumption that fixed rates were fixed exactly, with only occasional discrete changes when the currency was devalued. In practice, however, fixed exchange rate regimes typically allow the exchange rate to fluctuate within specified bands. This issue has been widely discussed in the context of the European Monetary System, where until recently the bands for most exchange rates were ±2.25 percent around a central long-run parity. But within the Pacific Rim, there has also been discussion about whether Japan has been following a target zone approach to pegging the yen–dollar exchange rate, particularly between mid-1989 to mid-1992, as discussed by Watanabe in Chapter 11. However, unlike the conventional literature, which is based on an announced and credible target zone, Japanese officials have denied the existence of such a policy (see also Ito, 1989:350–5). Since one of the ways the target zone stabilizes is through its effect on expectations, this raises the question of how effective this can be in the situation suggested by Watanabe in which the policy is unannounced.

The presence of exchange rate bands has attracted much research recently regarding the behavior of the exchange rate within the band.

The seminal model for this analysis is that of Krugman (1991), and has formed the basis for much of the subsequent work. Krugman uses a minimalist monetary model specified as

$$e = m + v + \gamma E(de)/dt, \tag{5.19}$$

where e is the spot exchange rate in logarithms, m is the domestic money supply in logarithms, and v represents stochastic shocks. In this equation, the current exchange rate is driven by monetary and other shocks (the fundamentals) and the expected rate of exchange depreciation.

The Krugman analysis assumes that m is passive, it being shifted only to maintain a fixed target zone. That is, the monetary authority is willing to reduce m in order to prevent e from rising above some maximum level $\bar{e}$ and to increase m in order to prevent e from falling below some minimum level $\underline{e}$. As long as e lies within the band between these upper and lower limits, the money supply remains unchanged. Intervention therefore occurs only marginally, as the respective bands are reached.

With the money supply being determined in this way, the only exogenous source of exchange rate dynamics is due to random shocks in v, which Krugman takes to be generated by a random walk process:

$$dv = \sigma \, dz.$$

As Krugman notes, this assumption is based not on any strong compelling economic argument, but on analytic tractability.

The important contribution of Krugman was to show that the existence of exchange rate bands, assumed to be credibly defended, affects the behavior of the exchange rate within the band. At first sight this may appear surprising, in that one might expect the exchange rate to behave like a pure random variable within the band, responding to the intervention only when the band is reached. However, this is not correct. This is because, as the band is approached, the monetary authority will act to defend the target zone. Thus, as the exchange rate approaches the top of the band say, a fall in v will reduce e more than a rise in v will increase e. Since v follows a random walk, the expected rate of exchange depreciation is negative, and this will tend to reduce the exchange rate itself. The result is that the relationship between them is S-shaped rather than piecewise linear (see Krugman, 1991).

This simple model has been extended in various ways by different authors. Miller and Weller (1991) embed it into the structurally richer Dornbusch (1976) model. The assumption that all intervention occurs at the margin is clearly unrealistic, and intramarginal intervention has been considered by several authors (e.g., Pesenti, 1990; Froot and Obstfeld, 1991). For a more complete but nontechnical exposition of the model and comprehensive references to subsequent extensions, see Svensson (1992).

5.6   Conclusions

This essay has discussed four approaches to the analysis of exchange rate management that have developed since the mid-1970s. Each emphasizes different aspects and offers different insights, but each is also restrictive.

The introduction of monetary rules into dynamic portfolio models, while intended to increase our understanding of how active monetary policy influences the dynamics of the economy, achieve this in only a limited way. The underlying economic structure, and indeed the policy rules themselves, are typically arbitrary and the dynamics too simple and model-specific to offer any firm guidance to the likely dynamic adjustment of any real-world economy. The most interesting aspect of this approach is that it emphasizes the long-run constraints on the options confronting the policymaker, which long-run equilibrium considerations impose.

The second class of models we have discussed, namely the new classical stochastic models, focus on the sources and nature of the underlying stochastic disturbances as determinants of optimal monetary policy. These models also suffer from arbitrariness, and the fact that the optimality criterion is based on some form of variance minimization that at best is of limited welfare significance. In addition, the main conclusion here is a negative one, namely that all kinds of policies may turn out to be optimal, depending on the sources and properties of the underlying disturbances. But there are two positive aspects of this approach that should be highlighted. First, it helps us understand how individual disturbances affect the economy and how each should be stabilized in isolation. Indeed, it is the conflicting responses that different shocks require that lead to the ambiguity of the overall optimal policy. Second, several contributions to this approach have emphasized the interdependence and trade-offs between different forms of stabilization – in particular wage indexation and intervention – leading to the question of the design of overall policy packages.

The third type of model we have considered, namely what we have termed the rational intertemporal model, provides a very different perspective on exchange rate management. Perhaps the main insight it offers is the need to take account of the intertemporal budget constraints facing the economy and the restrictions that these impose on a consistent formulation of fiscal, monetary, and exchange rate policies. However, despite (or perhaps because of) its relative theoretical purity, it also has drawbacks. By abstracting from real-world rigidities, which surely are in conflict with the underlying assumptions of this approach, its guide to real-world practitioners of exchange rate policy is limited.

Finally, the target zone models, which are the most recent development, are based on only the very simplest model of the fundamentals. Indeed, the fundamentals component of the Krugman model is almost trivial. It will be a challenge to integrate the existence of exchange rate bands into models having a richer economic structure, and some work in this direction is beginning.

This essay has been entitled "a partial review" and indeed that is what it is. We have dealt entirely with a small open economy, yet many of the interesting issues of exchange rate management relate to large economies and their integration into monetary unions and into the world economy. There has been a growing literature dealing with problems of monetary policy coordination and issues pertaining to strategic behavior. These will be ongoing issues generating substantial research activity in the coming years.

References

Aizenman, J., and J. A. Frenkel (1985). "Optimal Wage Indexation, Foreign Exchange Market Intervention, and Monetary Policy," *American Economic Review* 75:402–23.

Allen, P. R., and P. B. Kenen (1980). *Asset Markets, Exchange Rates, and Economic Integration.* Cambridge University Press.

Bhandari, J. S., ed. (1985). *Exchange Rate Management Under Uncertainty.* Cambridge, MA: MIT Press.

Black, S. W. (1985). "The Effect of Alternative Intervention Policies on the Variability of Exchange Rates: The Harrod Effect." In J. S. Bhandari, ed., *Exchange Rate Management Under Uncertainty,* pp. 73–82. Cambridge, MA: MIT Press.

Boyer, R. (1978). "Optimal Foreign Exchange Market Intervention," *Journal of Political Economy* 86:1045–56.

Buiter, W. H., and M. H. Miller (1981). "Monetary Policy and International Competitiveness: The Problems of Adjustment," *Oxford Economic Papers* 33:143–75.

Canzoneri, M. B. (1982). "Exchange Intervention Policy in a Multiple Country World," *Journal of International Economics* 13:267–89.

Canzoneri, M. B., D. W. Henderson, and K. S. Rogoff (1983). "The Information Content of the Interest Rate and Optimal Moneary Policy," *Quarterly Journal of Economics* 98:545–66.

Cox, W. M. (1980). "Unanticipated Money, Output, and Prices in the Small Economy," *Journal of Monetary Economics* 6:359–84.

Dornbusch, R. (1976). "Expectations and Exchange Rate Dynamics," *Journal of Political Economy* 84:1161–76.

Dornbusch, R., and S. Fischer (1980). "Exchange Rates and the Current Account," *American Economic Review* 70:960–71.

Driffill, J. (1982). "Optimal Money and Exchange Rate Policies," *Greek Economic Review* 4:261–83.

Driskill, R., and S. McCafferty (1980). "Exchange Rate Variability, Real and Monetary Shocks, and the Degree of Capital Mobility Under Rational Expectations," *Quarterly Journal of Economics* 95:577–86.

  (1985). "Exchange Rate Dynamics with Wealth Effects: Some Theoretical Ambiguities," *Journal of International Economics* 19:329–40.

Eaton, J., and S. J. Turnovsky (1983a). "Exchange Risk, Political Risk, and Macroeconomic Equilibrium," *American Economic Review* 73:183–9.

  (1983b). "Covered Interest Parity, Uncovered Interest Parity, and Exchange Rate Dynamics," *Economic Journal* 93:555–75.

  (1984). "The Forward Exchange Market, Speculation, and Exchange Market Intervention," *Quarterly Journal of Economics* 99:45–69.

Engel, C. M., and R. P. Flood (1985). "Exchange Rate Dynamics, Sticky Prices, and the Current Account," *Journal of Money, Credit, and Banking* 17:312–27.

Fischer, S. (1977). "Stability and Exchange Rate Systems in a Monetarist Model of the Balance of Payments." In R. Aliber, ed., *The Political Economy of Monetary Reform*, pp. 59–73. Montclair, NJ: Allanheld, Ossum.

Flood, R. P. (1979). "Capital Mobility and the Choice of Exchange Rate System," *International Economic Review* 20:405–16.

Flood, R. P., and R. J. Hodrick (1985). "Central Bank Intervention in a Rational Open Economy: A Model with Asymmetric Information." In J. S. Bhandari, ed., *Exchange Rate Management under Uncertainty*, pp. 154–85. Cambridge, MA: MIT Press.

Flood, R. P., and N. P. Marion (1982). "The Transmission of Disturbances Under Alternative Exchange Rate Regimes with Optimal Indexing," *Quarterly Journal of Economics* 97:43–66.

Friedman, M. (1953). "The Case for Flexible Exchange Rates," *Essays in Positive Economics*, pp. 157–203. Chicago: University of Chicago Press.

  (1969). "The Optimum Quantity of Money," *The Optimum Quantity of Money and Other Essays*, pp. 1–51. Chicago: Aldine.

Froot, K. A., and M. Obstfeld (1991). "Exchange Rate Dynamics Under Stochastic Regime Shifts: A Unified Approach," *Journal of International Economics* 31:203–29.

Girton, L., and D. E. Roper (1977). "A Monetary Model of Exchange Market Pressure Applied to the Postwar Canadian Experience," *American Economic Review* 67:537–48.

Glick, R., and C. Wihlborg (1990). "Real Exchange Rate Effects of Monetary Shocks under Fixed and Flexible Exchange Rates, *Journal of International Economics* 28:267–90.

Gray, J. A. (1976). "Wage Indexation: A Macroeconomic Approach," *Journal of Monetary Economics* 2:221–35.

Gray, M. R., and S. J. Turnovsky (1979). "The Stability of Exchange Rate Dynamics under Perfect Myopic Foresight," *International Economic Review* 20:643–60.

Helpman, E., and A. Razin (1979). "Towards a Consistent Comparison of

Alternative Exchange Rate Regimes," *Canadian Journal of Economics* 12:394–409.

(1987). "Exchange Rate Management: Intertemporal Tradeoffs," *American Economic Review* 77:107–23.

Henderson, D. W. (1979). "Financial Policies in Open Economies," *American Economic Review, Papers and Proceedings* 69:232–9.

Ito, T. (1989). "Is the Bank of Japan a Closet Monetarist? Monetary Targeting in Japan, 1978–88," NBER Working Paper no. 2874. Cambridge, MA.

Johnson, H. G. (1969). "The Case for Flexible Exchange Rates, 1969," (Federal Reserve Bank of St. Louis) *Economic Review* 51:12–24.

Karni, E. (1983). "On Optimal Wage Indexation," *Journal of Political Economy* 91:282–92.

Kawai, M. (1984). "The Effect of Forward Exchange on Spot-Rate Volatility Under Risk and Rational Expectations," *Journal of International Economics* 16:155–72.

Kimbrough, K. P. (1984). "Aggregate Information and the Role of Monetary Policy in an Open Economy," *Journal of Political Economy* 92:268–85.

Kindleberger, C. P. (1969). "The Case for Fixed Exchange Rates, 1969." In *The International Adjustment Mechanism,* Federal Reserve Bank of Boston Conference Series, no. 2, pp. 93–108.

Kirman, A. P. (1992). "Whom or What Does the Representative Individual Represent?" *Journal of Economic Perspectives* 6:117–36.

Krugman, P. (1991). "Target Zones and Exchange Rate Dynamics," *Quarterly Journal of Economics* 106:669–82.

Lewbel, A. (1989). "Exact Aggregation and a Representative Consumer," *Quarterly Journal of Economics* 104:622–33.

Lucas, R. E. (1972). "Expectations and the Neutrality of Money," *Journal of Economic Theory* 4:103–24.

(1973). "Some International Evidence on Output–Inflation Tradeoffs," *American Economic Review* 63:326–34.

Mantel, R., and A. M. Martirena-Mantel (1982). "Exchange Rate Policies in a Small Economy: The Active Crawling Peg," *Journal of International Economics* 13:301–20.

Marston, R. C. (1982). "Wages, Relative Prices and Choice Between Fixed and Flexible Exchange Rates," *Canadian Journal of Economics* 15:87–103.

Mathieson, D. J. (1976). "Is There an Optimal Crawl?" *Journal of International Economics* 6:183–202.

McCafferty, S., and R. Driskill (1980). "Problems of Existence and Uniqueness in Nonlinear Rational Expectations Models," *Econometrica* 48:1313–17.

McCallum, B. T. (1983). "On Non-uniqueness in Rational Expectations Models: An Attempt at Perspective," *Journal of Monetary Economics* 11:139–68.

Meade, J. E. (1955). "The Case for Variable Exchange Rates," *Three Banks Review,* 3–27.

Miller, M. H., and P. Weller (1991). "Exchange Rate Bands with Price Inertia," *Economic Journal* 101:1380–99.

Montiel, P. J., and J. D. Ostry (1991). "Implications of Real Exchange Rate Targeting in Developing Countries," (International Monetary Fund) *Staff Papers* 38:872–900.

Pesenti, P. A. (1990). "Perforate and Imperforate Currency Bands: Exchange

Rate Management and the Term Structure of Interest Rate Differentials,"
Working paper, Yale University.

Phelps, E. S. (1973). "Inflation in the Theory of Public Finance," *Swedish Journal of Economics* 75:67–82.

Pitchford, J. D., and N. Vousden (1987). "Exchange Rates, Policy Rules, and Inflation," *Australian Economic Papers* 26:43–57.

Poole, W. (1970). "Optimal Choice of Monetary Policy Instruments in a Simple Stochastic Macro Model," *Quarterly Journal of Economics* 84:197–216.

Sargent, T. J. (1977). "The Demand for Money During Hyperinflations Under Rational Expectations: I," *International Economic Review* 18:59–82.

Sidrauski, M. (1967). "Rational Choice and Patterns of Growth in a Monetary Economy," *American Economic Review* 57:534–44.

Spraos, J. (1959). "Speculation, Arbitrage, and Sterling," *Economic Journal* 69:1–21.

Stemp, P. J., and S. J. Turnovsky (1987). "Optimal Monetary Policy in an Open Economy," *European Economic Review* 31:1113–35.

Svensson, L. E. O. (1992). "An Interpretation of Recent Research on Exchange Rate Target Zones," *Journal of Economic Perspectives* 6:119–44.

Turnovsky, S. J. (1976). "The Relative Stability of Exchange Rate Systems in the Presence of Random Disturbances," *Journal of Money, Credit, and Banking* 8:29–50.

(1979). "Optimal Monetary Policy Under Flexible Exchange Rates," *Journal of Economic Dynamics and Control* 1:85–99.

(1983). "Wage Indexation and Exchange Market Intervention in a Small Open Economy," *Canadian Journal of Economics* 16:574–92.

(1984a). "Exchange Market Intervention Under Alternative Forms of Exogenous Disturbances," *Journal of International Economics* 17:279–97.

(1984b). "Exchange Market Intervention in a Small Open Economy: An Expository Model." In P. Malgrange and P. A. Muet, eds., *Contemporary Macroeconomic Modelling*, pp. 156–73. Oxford: Basil Blackwell.

(1985). "Optimal Exchange Market Intervention: Two Alternative Classes of Rules." In J. S. Bhandari, ed., *Exchange Rate Management under Uncertainty*, pp. 55–72. Cambridge, MA: MIT Press.

(1987a). "Optimal Monetary Policy and Wage Indexation Under Alternative Disturbances and Information Structures," *Journal of Money, Credit, and Banking* 19:157–80.

(1987b). "Optimal Monetary Growth with Accommodating Fiscal Policy in a Small Open Economy," *Journal of International Money and Finance* 6:179–93.

(1989). "Risk, Exchange Market Intervention and Private Speculative Behavior in a Small Open Economy." In C. C. Stone, ed., *Financial Risk: Theory, Evidence, and Implications*, pp. 41–76. Boston: Kluwer.

Turnovsky, S. J., and E. L. Grinols (1992). "Optimal Monetary Policy and Exchange Rate Management in a Stochastically Growing Open Economy," Working paper, University of Washington.

Wilson, C. A. (1979). "Anticipated Shocks and Exchange Rate Dynamics," *Journal of Political Economy* 87:639–47.

CHAPTER 6

Exchange rate policy and insulation from external shocks: the cases of Korea and Taiwan, 1970–1990

Ramon Moreno

6.1   Introduction

In recent years, growing recognition of the various channels of transmission of external shocks has spurred interest in ascertaining whether
a country should peg its exchange rate or allow it to float in response
to such shocks. One argument offered in favor of floating is that greater
exchange rate flexibility can insulate domestic prices in a small economy
from external shocks. For example, under a floating rate regime, a small
country can offset inflationary pressures originating from abroad by
allowing its exchange rate to appreciate. In general, however, the degree
to which flexible exchange rates contribute to the insulation of prices,
output, and other domestic economic variables of interest from external
shocks cannot be determined a priori. As is apparent from the discussion
by Turnovsky in Chapter 5 of this volume, the degree of insulation
afforded by flexible exchange rates depends on at least three factors.

First, the extent of insulation under floating is affected by the type
of shock. For example, floating exchange rates do not fully insulate
against external real shocks, but they may provide complete insulation
against external monetary shocks. In the latter case, a purely monetary
foreign disturbance that does not affect real interest rates or real output
in the long run will also leave the domestic price level unaffected as
long as the exchange rate can adjust.

Second, the extent of insulation from external shocks under floating

The author thanks Phillip Cagan, Jordi Gali, Michael Gavin, Michael Hutchison, and
Bharat Trehan for useful discussions and comments, but is solely responsible for any
errors. The research assistance of Judy Wallen is gratefully acknowledged. The opinions
expressed in this essay are those of the author and do not necessarily reflect the views of
the Board of Governors of the Federal Reserve System or of the Federal Reserve Bank
of San Francisco.

exchange rates depends on the degree of openness of the economy. A smaller traded goods sector enhances insulation from external shocks due to the relative independence of the domestic economy from foreign demand and supply. A reduction in international capital mobility increases insulation from external shocks by limiting the impact of foreign disturbances on domestic prices through interest rate and asset demand effects.[1] The effects of capital mobility are very relevant in any effort to assess the insulation properties of alternative exchange rate regimes in the postwar period, since the Bretton Woods fixed exchange rate regime in place up to the early 1970s was associated with very limited capital mobility, while the period of flexible exchange rates that followed has been associated with a high degree of capital mobility.

Third, the extent of insulation from external shocks is affected by whether the government allows the exchange rate to float freely or manages the float in a manner that promotes insulation from external shocks. For example, if a non–oil producer manages its float so that the currency appreciates in response to an oil price increase, the domestic price level may be insulated from the effects of such a shock. In contrast, under a pure float, it is quite plausible that the exchange rate will depreciate in response to an oil price increase as the cost of oil imports rises, which would tend to *amplify* the impact on the domestic price level.

In order to shed light on how the choice of exchange rate regime affects insulation, this essay examines the vulnerability of Korea and Taiwan to shocks to foreign oil prices and a set of external shocks proxied by U.S. macroeconomic variables during the period 1970:1–1990:4. The experiences of these two countries are of interest for a number of reasons. First, both countries maintained adjustable pegs to the U.S. dollar for most of the 1970s and then implemented basket pegs or managed floats against the U.S. dollar in the 1980s. This shift in policy allows us to ascertain whether these two economies experienced greater insulation from external shocks when they abandoned their pegs to the U.S. dollar. Second, both economies successfully stabilized domestic prices in the 1980s, after the float was adopted. Their experiences provide a potentially instructive model for other economies that have made little progress in achieving price stability.

The empirical analysis in this essay is implemented by using the estimates from small vector autoregression (VAR) models for each economy to assess the impact of a common set of external variables on the domestic price level of each economy under alternative exchange rate regimes. The relative contribution of external shocks to the variability

---

[1] For a discussion, see Flood (1979).

of domestic prices, as well as the magnitude of the impact of external shocks on domestic prices, are compared during periods when Korea and Taiwan maintained adjustable pegs to the U.S. dollar and during periods when they did not. The analysis suggests that Korea and Taiwan became less vulnerable to external shocks after they abandoned their respective pegs to the U.S. dollar.

The essay is organized as follows. Section 6.2 briefly reviews some previous empirical studies on the relationship between exchange rate regimes and insulation that are also based on VAR models. To provide a context for the empirical analysis, Section 6.3 provides some background on Korea and Taiwan. Section 6.4 describes the VAR model. Section 6.5 describes data analysis and estimation. Section 6.6 reports the empirical results. Section 6.7 summarizes the findings.

6.2   Empirical studies based on VAR models

Since insulation under alternative exchange rate regimes depends on the type of external shock, the degree of openness, and the nature of a floating rate policy, the question of whether flexible exchange rates insulate is ultimately an empirical one. However, a full empirical analysis is difficult because the underlying sources of foreign disturbances (real or nominal, demand or supply) are generally unobservable.

In a study of Japan, Hutchison and Walsh (1992) address this difficulty directly by using long-run restrictions proposed by Blanchard and Quah (1989) in a VAR model to identify external demand and supply shocks. They then compare the effects of these shocks on Japanese GNP during the Bretton Woods period and the period of flexible exchange rates that followed. The study reveals that a U.S. monetary shock has an expansionary short-run effect on Japanese GNP under flexible rates, but a contractionary effect under fixed rates. Also, the short-run effect of U.S. monetary shocks is *larger* under flexible exchange rates. The results suggest that flexible exchange rates have not insulated Japan from foreign monetary shocks.

Other researchers also estimate VAR models to assess how foreign macroeconomic disturbances affect domestic macroeconomic variables under alternative exchange rate regimes but do not attempt to distinguish between demand and supply shocks. The evidence from these studies provides little support for the hypothesis that flexible exchange rates insulate against foreign shocks. For example, Genberg, Salemi, and Swoboda (1987) investigate economic interdependence by estimating a VAR model for Switzerland over the period 1964–81. They find no consistent evidence of greater insulation from external shocks under flexible exchange rates. Lastrapes and Koray (1990) analyze economic interdependence between the United States, the United Kingdom, France, and Germany between 1959 and 1985. They find some evidence supporting greater insulation from external shocks during the flexible rate period that followed the collapse of the Bretton Woods system in the case of the United Kingdom but not in the cases of France or Germany.

One possible reason these studies find little evidence of insulation under flexible exchange rates is that some of the countries studied did not actually allow their currencies to float freely following the collapse of Bretton Woods. For example, France and Germany currently link their currencies through the European Monetary System. There were also periods in the 1970s when the Japanese yen moved relatively little against the U.S. dollar. These studies therefore compare a regime of fixed rates to a regime of adjustable pegs under conditions of generalized floating, rather than compare purely fixed and purely flexible exchange rate regimes typically modeled in the theoretical literature.

In addition, the comparison of the period of fixed rates under Bretton Woods with the flexible exchange rate period that followed may have disguised evidence favoring insulation under flexible exchange rates in a number of ways: (i) external shocks appear to have been much larger after the early 1970s than in the 1960s, and this may have overwhelmed any insulating effects that might have resulted from the adoption of flexible rates; (ii) the relative importance of real shocks, against which flexible rates do not insulate, may have increased in the 1970s in comparison with the 1960s; (iii) greater international capital mobility in the 1970s and 1980s, in comparison with the 1960s, may have strengthened the international transmission of disturbances, also offsetting any insulation afforded by flexible rates.

6.3   Background

This section discusses several factors that are likely to have influenced Korea and Taiwan's vulnerability to external shocks in the sample period: the degree of openness and the direction of trade, policies affecting capital mobility, and exchange rate policies.

6.3.1   Openness and the direction of trade

Table 6.1 reports the degree of openness (as measured by the share of exports plus imports to GNP), and Table 6.2 reviews the direction of total trade (as measured by the share of exports and imports of a given

Table 6.1. *Openness*

Country	1975	1980	1985	1990
Korea	61.0	65.2	67.8	56.7
Taiwan	73.6	96.7	84.4	75.4

Note: Openness is defined as share of exports plus imports to GNP (percent).

country to total exports plus imports) and the composition of exports in Korea and Taiwan in selected years. It is apparent from Table 6.1 that while both economies are very open, Taiwan is more open than is Korea. For the years reported, the peak measure of openness reaches 97 percent in Taiwan and 68 percent in Korea.

Table 6.2 shows that the United States is a larger trading partner of both economies than is Japan, although the United States is relatively more important for Taiwan than it is for Korea. However, the United States is the dominant export market by far in the cases of both Taiwan and Korea, so both countries are particularly vulnerable to U.S. demand shocks.

6.3.2   *Policies affecting capital mobility*

Up to the late 1970s, Korea and Taiwan had restrictions affecting capital flows, including controls on foreign exchange availability for current account transactions, controls on capital flows, restrictions on foreign exchange market transactions (such as forward or future transactions, swaps or options), and restrictions on foreign access to the domestic financial sector.

An examination of these policies suggests that Korea's controls may have been more restrictive than Taiwan's. For example, Taiwan liberalized controls on current account transactions in 1987, whereas Korea maintained such controls to the end of the sample period. In addition, Korea traditionally limited capital inflows as well as outflows, whereas Taiwan restricted only outflows. Government approval was needed in Korea in the 1980s for any external borrowing exceeding specified limits: U.S. $200,000 before October 1982 and U.S. $1,000,000 thereafter. There was no comparable limit in Taiwan until 1987, when a surge in speculative capital inflows prompted the government to freeze external

Table 6.2. *Direction and composition of trade*

	1975	1980	1985	1990
Shares in total trade: Korea				
U.S.	27.7	23.9	28.3	27.6
Japan	30.2	22.4	19.7	25.2
Other	42.2	53.7	52.0	47.2
Shares in total trade: Taiwan				
U.S.	30.9	28.9	38.4	28.2
Japan	22.3	19.1	17.7	20.0
Other	46.9	52.0	43.9	51.9
Shares in total exports: Korea				
U.S.	30.2	26.4	35.6	31.7
Japan	25.4	17.4	15.0	20.9
Other	44.3	56.2	49.4	47.5
Shares in total exports: Taiwan				
U.S.	34.3	34.1	48.1	32.3
Japan	13.1	11.0	11.3	12.4
Other	52.6	54.9	40.6	55.3

Note: Figures are in percent terms.

bank borrowing. This ceiling on Taiwan banks' external liabilities has since been lifted gradually.[2]

6.3.3   *Exchange rate policies*

Korea maintained an adjustable peg to the U.S. dollar from the early 1970s until January 1980 and subsequently pegged to a basket of currencies comprising a trade-weighted basket and special drawing rights (SDR) basket. Neither the targets nor the weights were publicly disclosed, and the regime in place may broadly be described as a managed float. In March 1990, Korea switched to a system of smoothing daily fluctuations in the won–dollar exchange rate (or an explicit managed float against the U.S. dollar).

Taiwan maintained a peg to the U.S. dollar until January 1979. For most of the succeeding period, it maintained a central rate trading system

---

[2] A chronology of government policies affecting international capital mobility from the late 1970s up to 1990 in Korea and Taiwan is given in Moreno (1993).

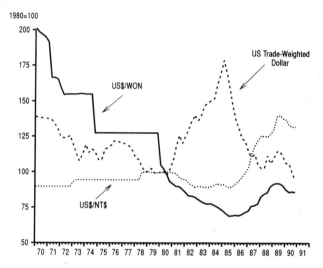

Figure 6.1. Exchange rates.

wherein fluctuations in the U.S. dollar–new Taiwan (NT) dollar spot rate were limited by the weighted average of interbank transaction rates on the previous day (2.25 percent per day for most of the 1980s). In April 1989, the NT dollar was allowed to float freely against the U.S. dollar.[3]

To illustrate the implications of these exchange rate policies, Figure 6.1 shows indices of the U.S. trade-weighted dollar (expressed in units of foreign currencies per U.S. dollar) and the U.S. dollar exchange rates of the Korean won and the NT dollar (expressed in U.S. dollars per unit of the won or the NT dollar respectively) from 1970:1 to 1990:4. It can be seen that both the won and the NT dollar were stable against the U.S. dollar for extended periods in the 1970s, although the won was subject to larger and somewhat more frequent adjustments than the NT dollar in that period. Both currencies tended to depreciate against the U.S. dollar in the first half of the 1980s, as the U.S. trade-weighted dollar appreciated, and to appreciate against the U.S. dollar in the second half of the 1980s, as the U.S. trade-weighted dollar depreciated.

In spite of these broad similarities, the trend behavior of the won and that of the NT dollar are very different. The won has tended to depreciate against the U.S. dollar over the roughly two decades shown

---

[3] Moreno (1993) provides a brief chronology of the exchange rate policies of Taiwan and Korea.

in the figure, while the NT dollar has tended to appreciate. These respective exchange rate trends are consistent with the persistent current account deficits experienced by Korea for most of the sample period, as well as the associated heavy external debt burdens it faced up to the first half of the 1980s and the large and persistent current account surpluses experienced by Taiwan since the early 1980s.

6.4 The VAR model

To analyze the effects of external shocks, very simple VAR models of Korea and Taiwan are estimated. In a VAR model, a variable is regressed on its own lagged values and the lagged values of other variables in the system. The equations in a VAR model can be interpreted as reduced-form specifications that capture the relationships among variables over time, while requiring little knowledge about the underlying structure of the economy.

The VAR models for each country consist of an external and a domestic sector. The oil price and a set of U.S. macroeconomic variables – the U.S. consumer price index (CPI), the U.S. real interest rate, and the U.S. trade-weighted dollar – are used to represent the external sector. The domestic sector is represented by the domestic CPI.

The relationships in the VAR model can be expressed compactly as

$$H(L)z_t = u_t, \tag{6.1}$$

where $H(L)$ is a matrix of polynomials in the lag operator, z_t is the vector of variables comprising the system, and u_t is the vector of disturbances.

The model is specified by defining the vector $z_t = [\text{oilp}_t, \text{usp}_t, \text{usrat}_t, \text{ustwd}_t, \text{cpi}_t]$, where oilp_t is oil price, usp_t is U.S. CPI, usrat_t is U.S. real interest rate, ustwd_t is the Federal Reserve Board index of the trade-weighted value of the U.S. dollar against currencies of ten industrial economies (this index excludes Korea or Taiwan), and cpi_t is the Korean or Taiwanese CPI. The U.S. real interest rate is constructed ex post as the difference between the three-month U.S. Treasury bill rate and the annualized quarterly U.S. CPI inflation rate.

Oilp_t, usp_t, usrat_t, and ustwd_t represent the external sector, while cpi_t represents the domestic sector.[4] The variables that represent the external sector were chosen because they seem to have had a visible impact on international economic activity over the past two decades. Shocks to oil

---

[4] The focus on the domestic price level can be motivated by thinking of an economy with nominal wage contracts where deviations of the actual price level from the expected price create a deadweight loss due to a divergence between the marginal private value

prices were a dominant feature of macroeconomic fluctuations in the 1970s. The inclusion of the U.S. price level is of particular interest, because it can shed light on the international transmission of price disturbances under alternative exchange rate regimes. In addition, changes in the U.S. price level as well as in the real rate appear to reflect dramatic changes in U.S. macroeconomic policies between the 1970s and the 1980s that are widely believed to have had a marked influence on world economic activity. Finally, sharp fluctuations in the value of the U.S. trade-weighted dollar appear to have been closely connected to the performance of Korea and Taiwan, particularly in the 1980s.

In specifying the matrix of lag polynomials, it is assumed that shocks to the domestic CPI do not affect the external sector. It is also assumed that oil prices are unaffected by the remaining variables in the system.[5]

If the elements in the vector z_t are stationary, the system (6.1) has a moving average representation,

$$z_t = C(L)u_t, \tag{6.2}$$

where $C(L) = H(L)^{-1}$. The inverse of the VAR coefficient matrix, the matrix $C(L)$, traces out the impact of the disturbances u_t on the elements of z_t. In general, the elements of u_t are contemporaneously correlated and cannot be used to distinguish between domestic and external shocks. For example, a shock to the domestic price equation u_{5t} reflects the impact of both external and domestic shocks.

In order to distinguish between external and domestic shocks, it is desirable to define a vector of disturbances ϵ_t that are mutually orthogonal or uncorrelated. Following Sims (1980), a set of mutually orthogonal disturbances from the system in equation (6.1) is identified by assuming that the economy described by the variables in equation (6.1) has a recursive structure. Under such a structure, the first variable is contemporaneously unaffected by shocks to the remaining variables, the second variable is affected by shocks to the first two variables, but is unaffected by shocks to the remaining variables, and so on. (The last variable is affected by shocks to all variables.)

The above restrictions may be imposed by picking a matrix G such that $\epsilon_t = G^{-1}u_t$ and $E\epsilon_t\epsilon_t' = G^{-1}\Sigma G'^{-1} = I$, where $\Sigma = Eu_tu_t'$. The vector moving average representation of equation (6.1) can be represented by

of labor and labor's marginal social value. Minimization of a quadratic loss function in prices is equivalent to the minimization of a quadratic loss function in output if a Phillips curve–type relationship links output and prices. For a discussion along these lines, see Flood (1979).

[5] This assumption is also adopted by Shapiro and Watson (1988).

Table 6.3. *Tests for unit roots*

	Augmented Dickey–Fuller		Phillips–Perron	
	Levels	First differences	Levels	First differences
Oil price	−1.7	−4.3***	−1.8	−6.1***
U.S. CPI	−2.6	−2.3	−1.1	−3.5**
U.S. real interest rate	−2.2	−5.0***	−4.4***	−14.2***
U.S. trade-weighted dollar	−1.9	−3.0**	−1.9	−6.1***
Taiwan CPI	−1.4	−4.6***	−0.6	−4.6***
Korea CPI	−1.2	−2.7	−0.7	−4.4***
U.S. Treasury bill rate	−2.1	−4.7***	−2.2	−7.6***

Note: Tests in levels include a linear deterministic trend, while tests in first differences do not. In the case of the U.S. real interest rate, the test statistics reported are for the case with no linear deterministic trend. Three lags are used in the augmented Dickey–Fuller test and ten lags in the Phillips–Peron test. ***Reject unit root null at 1%; **reject unit root null at 5%.

$$z_t = C(L)GG^{-1}u_t = B(L)\epsilon_t. \tag{6.3}$$

Since all the elements of the vector of disturbances ϵ_t are mutually orthogonal, it is now possible to distinguish between external and domestic shocks. A fuller discussion of this procedure and some alternatives is given in Moreno (1992).

6.5   Data analysis and estimation

Before estimating equation (6.1), it is desirable to ascertain whether the variables included in the model are stationary. For this purpose, unit root tests were performed on each of the variables in the equation. Data series and sources are described in more detail in the Appendix. Table 6.3 reports the results of augmented Dickey–Fuller (ADF) and Phillips–Perron (PP) tests for unit roots for the series in the model and, for reference, the U.S. three-month Treasury bill rate. The tests indicate that the oil price, the U.S. trade-weighted dollar, and Taiwan's CPI are difference stationary.

The results for the U.S. real interest rate, the U.S. CPI, and the Korean CPI are ambiguous. The PP test suggests that the U.S. real interest rate is stationary in levels, while the ADF test suggests that it is difference stationary. The PP test suggests that the U.S. and Korean CPIs are difference stationary, while the ADF test indicates that the inflation rates in the U.S. and Korea are nonstationary.

These ambiguities are resolved as follows. Since interest rates in the United States are market-determined, theory suggests that a stationary process in the real interest rate level (as indicated by the PP test) should be presumed in estimating the VAR model. However, this does not necessarily mean that one should also follow the PP test results in concluding that the inflation rates in both the United States and Korea are stationary.[6] In the case of the United States, there is the additional evidence from both the PP and ADF tests that the U.S. Treasury bill rate is nonstationary. Combined with the assumption that the real rate is stationary, this implies that the U.S. inflation rate is nonstationary and co-integrated with the U.S. Treasury bill rate, with co-integrating vector $(1, -1)$. It is therefore assumed in what follows that the U.S. inflation rate is nonstationary. (Shapiro and Watson, 1988, and Gali, 1992, make a similar assumption.) It is also assumed that the Korean inflation rate is nonstationary.

It is interesting that the unit root test results support the conclusion that Korean inflation is nonstationary whereas Taiwan's inflation is not. Such a conclusion is consistent with the fact that Korea has had less success than Taiwan in curbing inflation. This is particularly apparent in the more frequent adjustments required in the Korean won in the 1970s, when it was pegged to the U.S. dollar, and the marked tendency for the won to depreciate. In contrast, as noted previously, the NT dollar required fewer (and smaller) adjustments during the dollar peg period, and the NT dollar has appreciated over time.

On the basis of the preceding unit root test results, the system described by (6.1) was estimated using the level of the U.S. real interest rate and first differences of the oil price, the U.S. trade-weighted dollar, and the second difference of the U.S. CPI. The first difference of Taiwan's CPI is used in the Taiwan model, and the second difference of the Korean CPI is used in the Korea model. Three lags were used in estimation, which yielded Q-statistics that do not rule out the hypothesis that the residuals in each of the VAR equations are white noise.

In order to compare the degree of insulation under alternative exchange rate regimes, equation (6.1) was estimated for both Korea and

[6] Perron (1988) points out that the true ARMA process (which is generally unknown) governing the individual time series determines which of the two unit root tests is superior. For example, he reports Monte Carlo simulations for an IMA(1,1) that indicate that the Phillips–Perron statistic has greater power and is more robust across alternative lag specifications if the moving average coefficient is positive. However, if the moving average coefficient is negative, the Phillips–Perron statistic is inferior according to these same criteria.

Taiwan over two subsamples in the period 1970:1–1990:4.[7] In the case of Taiwan, the sample was broken in 1979:1, the quarter in which the government abandoned the peg to the U.S. dollar. In the case of Korea, the sample is broken in 1980:1, as Korea switched to a basket peg in February 1980.

6.6 Results

6.6.1 *Variance decompositions*

One way of measuring the impact of external shocks on the domestic economy is to consider the forecast of the domestic price (which represents the domestic sector in the model) at a given time horizon, say four quarters. The error in such a forecast can be expressed as a weighted average of external and domestic shocks that could not be anticipated at the time the forecast was made (the weights used reflect the dynamic effects of the respective shocks on the domestic price level). In this framework, the impact of external shocks can be gauged by measuring the contribution of these shocks to the variance of the forecast error in the domestic price level at a four-quarter horizon. If the contribution of external shocks to the variance is smaller when the exchange rate is more flexible, it can be argued that the flexible exchange rate regime is associated with a greater degree of insulation from external shocks.

Tables 6.4 and 6.5 report the variance decompositions of the orthogonal forecast errors of Korea's CPI and Taiwan's CPI, respectively, at horizons up to forty quarters (ten years). Column (6) in each table gives the sum of the contributions of the external shocks.

The tables suggest that external shocks have an important influence on price behavior in the two economies. They also suggest that, in both periods, external shocks were relatively less important in Korea than they were in Taiwan. In Korea, the contribution of external shocks

---

[7] To maximize the available degrees of freedom, the beginning date of the sample in both economies is 1970:1. Two points must be made about this date. First, the beginning of the sample predates the collapse of Bretton Woods by a number of quarters. The first major shock to Bretton Woods was Nixon's suspension of the convertibility of the dollar to gold in 1971. The switch to freely floating exchange rates occurred in March 1973. Using March 1973 as the beginning date makes estimation difficult, due to degrees of freedom problems. Second, in the case of Korea, the beginning of the sample overlaps by about two years with a period when Korea maintained a crawling peg to the U.S. dollar.

Table 6.4. *Variance decompositions, Korea price level*

Quarters ahead (1)	External shocks					Domestic shocks, subtotal (7)
	Oil price (2)	U.S. CPI (3)	U.S. real rate (4)	U.S. dollar (5)	Subtotal (6)	
U.S. dollar peg regime, 1970:1–1979:4						
1	17.9	0.4	5.8	0.0	24.1	75.9
4	21.3	0.9	7.8	12.8	42.7	57.3
8	21.7	1.9	3.0	23.2	49.7	50.2
20	11.8	1.6	0.8	33.8	47.9	52.1
40	6.4	1.2	0.3	38.9	46.9	53.1
Managed float/basket peg regime, 1980:1–1990:4						
1	1.2	8.9	4.0	1.8	16.0	84.1
4	3.6	17.2	2.8	0.5	24.1	75.9
8	1.1	19.7	3.8	2.7	27.3	72.7
20	0.1	15.8	4.0	6.3	26.2	73.8
40	0.1	9.6	3.1	7.9	20.6	79.4

Note: Totals may not sum to 100 due to rounding.

ranges from 21 to 47 percent at long horizons, whereas it ranges from 61 to 81 percent in Taiwan. This is consistent with some of the characteristics of these two economies cited earlier, namely that Taiwan is more open than is Korea, that it trades relatively more with the United States than does Korea, and that Taiwan's policies tended to restrict capital movements less than did Korea's.

The variance decompositions for Korea convey a strong impression of greater insulation from external shocks in the managed float period. In that period, the contribution of foreign shocks to the variance of the Korean price level at a forty-quarter forecast horizon is 21 percent, compared with 47 percent in the pegged period. This decline is associated with declines in the impact of all external shocks except the U.S. price. In the case of Taiwan, there is an across-the-board reduction in the contribution of external shocks to the variance of the forecast error of Taiwan's price level at horizons up to four quarters. The decline in the relative importance of external shocks in the two subsamples is relatively large. It falls from 48 percent to 15 percent at one quarter's horizon, and from 51 to 43 percent at four quarters. However, there is no evidence of greater insulation in the long run,

Table 6.5. *Variance decompositions, Taiwan price level*

Step (1)	Oil price (2)	U.S. price (3)	U.S. real rate (4)	U.S. dollar (5)	Subtotal (6)	Domestic shocks, subtotal (7)
U.S. dollar peg regime, 1970:1–1978:4						
1	19.2	4.3	2.9	20.9	47.5	52.6
4	22.9	13.3	5.6	9.2	51.1	48.9
8	27.3	23.2	15.3	3.6	69.5	30.5
20	14.8	23.0	21.9	4.0	63.7	36.3
40	8.6	23.3	25.1	3.7	60.6	39.4
Managed float/basket peg regime, 1979:1–1990:4						
1	0.0	0.7	1.2	13.0	15.0	85.0
4	6.8	3.0	10.1	22.5	42.4	57.6
8	4.9	16.8	16.6	19.7	58.0	41.9
20	11.5	38.6	20.5	5.9	76.6	23.4
40	15.0	42.5	20.4	2.9	80.8	19.2

The column headers "U.S. price", "U.S. real rate", "U.S. dollar", and "Subtotal" fall under a spanning header **External shocks**.

Note: Totals may not sum to 100 due to rounding.

largely because of an increase in the impact of shocks to the U.S. price.

6.6.2 Magnitude of shocks

The variance decomposition results reflect the values of the moving average coefficients that measure the impact of external shocks to the domestic price level, as well as the sizes of the respective external and domestic shocks. As a result, it is not entirely clear to what extent the decline in the contribution of external shocks represents changes in the transmission of external shocks or changes in the sizes of the shocks across the two subsamples. This may be clarified by investigating whether shocks in the second (managed float) period were larger than in the first (dollar peg) period. In such a case, the lower contribution of external shocks in the managed float period would reflect greater insulation.

To estimate the magnitude of the shocks during the two periods, columns (1) and (2) of Table 6.6 report the standard errors of the estimates of the regressions for the two models over the two sample

Table 6.6. *Estimated magnitudes of disturbances (percent)*

	U.S. dollar peg (1)	Managed float (2)	Percent change (3)
Korea model			
Oil price	6.3	13.6	114
U.S. CPI	0.4	0.5	36
U.S. real interest rate	1.5	2.0	31
U.S. trade-weighted dollar	2.8	4.3	51
Korea CPI	2.2	0.8	−63
Taiwan model			
Oil price	6.3	13.6	114
U.S. CPI	0.4	0.5	32
U.S. real interest rate	1.5	1.9	25
U.S. trade-weighted dollar	3.0	4.2	40
Taiwan CPI	3.6	0.9	−76

Note: The magnitudes of external shocks differ slightly in the two models because of different break dates.

periods. The percent change in the standard errors is reported in column (3).

It should be noted that Table 6.6 measures the relative volatility of *nonorthogonal* innovations. The relative volatility of orthogonal innovations is not used because the standard deviations of orthogonalized innovations in each subsample are normalized to unity by the Choleski decomposition procedure used in the paper. The volatility measures for the external sector in Table 6.6 nevertheless indicate whether external shocks (which are unaffected by domestic shocks by construction) generally increased over the two subsamples.

It is apparent from the table that the size of external shocks tended to increase (in some cases substantially) in the managed float period, while the size of domestic shocks dropped sharply in both Korea and Taiwan. Since the domestic shocks also reflect the impact of the larger external shocks (the disturbances in the domestic price equations reported in Table 6.6 are not orthogonalized, so they are correlated with the external disturbances), domestic shocks excluding these external effects must have fallen even more than indicated in Table 6.6. In view of the increase in the magnitude of external disturbances relative to domestic disturbances across the two samples, the variance decompositions do indicate an increase in insulation from external shocks in Korea and Taiwan in the second period.

6.6.3 *Impulse responses*

Additional evidence on insulation can be obtained by analyzing the impulse responses to unit shocks to the external variables over the two subsamples in Korea and Taiwan. It is worth noting that as the impulse responses reflect the responses to the combined effects of demand and supply shocks, there is no unambiguous guidance from theory on what signs we might expect for the impulse responses. It seems reasonable to expect that when a country is pegging to the U.S. dollar, shocks to the oil price (which is denominated in U.S. dollars) and shocks to the U.S. CPI will result in increases in the domestic price level. However, if a country implements a managed float, it can dampen these effects (or reverse them) by allowing its currency to appreciate against the U.S. dollar.

It is harder to predict the response of the domestic price level to shocks to the U.S. real interest rate and the U.S. trade-weighted dollar. If a rise in the U.S. real rate largely reflects an expansion in U.S. demand, it may be associated with an increase in the domestic price level. On the other hand, increases in the U.S. real rate may (temporarily) reflect tighter U.S. monetary policies, which may in turn contribute to deflationary pressures in Korea or Taiwan. Expectations may also play a role. If a rise in the U.S. real interest rate reflects an expected U.S. deflation, there may be capital outflows and a concomitant reduction in demand for domestic money, leading to increases in the domestic price level. For the same reasons, the response of the domestic price level to fluctuations in the nominal trade-weighted dollar is difficult to predict.

In spite of the uncertainty about the *sign* of the response to certain external shocks, it is still possible to ascertain whether the *size* of the responses to these shocks fell when Taiwan and Korea adopted more flexible exchange rates. In order to ascertain the magnitude of the responses to shocks, the impulse responses for inflation are illustrated in Figure 6.2 for Korea and Figure 6.3 for Taiwan. In each figure, the solid line (labeled "Period 1") refers to the response during the dollar peg period, while the dashed line (labeled "Period 2") refers to the response during the flexible exchange rate period.

Responses to oil price shocks (Figures 6.2A and 6.3A). Both Korea and Taiwan appear to have become much less vulnerable to oil price

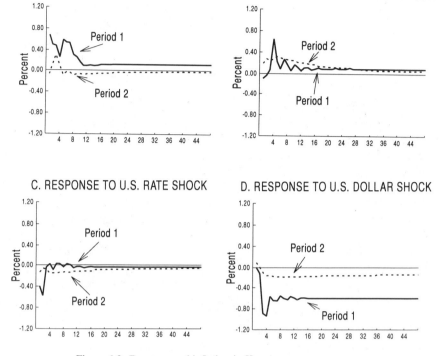

Figure 6.2. Responses of inflation in Korea.

disturbances in the managed float period. It is particularly interesting that the response of inflation to oil price shocks in Korea is permanent in the first period, whereas it appears to be temporary in the second period. Also, the response to oil price shocks in both economies appears to be negative in the managed float period over certain forecast horizons. This may reflect disinflationary policy responses or the effects of output contraction.

Responses to shocks to U.S. inflation (Figures 6.2B and 6.3B). The impulse response for Taiwan's CPI also suggests that Taiwan became less vulnerable to shocks to U.S. inflation during the managed float period. In the case of Korea, greater insulation is not as apparent, and the long-run responses in the two periods tend to converge at long horizons.

The impulse responses also show two noteworthy features. First, in the case of Korea, the impact effect of a shock to U.S. inflation during the dollar peg period appears to be negative, although the response

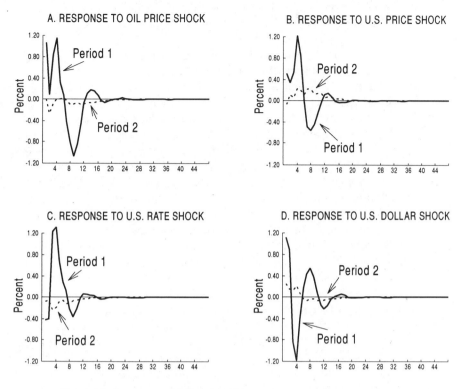

Figure 6.3. Responses of inflation in Taiwan.

turns positive after two quarters. Second, the short-run response of
Taiwan's price to a shock to the U.S. price tends to be larger than in
Korea. This finding seems consistent with the fact that Korea is a less
open economy and appears to restrict capital mobility more severely
than does Taiwan. In the long run, however, the cumulative response
of the Korean price level to U.S. price shocks exceeds that of Taiwan,
reflecting the assumption that Korean inflation is nonstationary.

Responses to shocks to the U.S. real interest rate (Figures 6.2C and
6.3C). Korean inflation declines in both periods. In the first period, the
inflation response at short horizons is much larger than in the second
period. The impulse responses of Korean inflation give the impression
that the more flexible exchange rate regime provides greater insulation
in the short run, but not in the long run. In Taiwan, the impulse responses suggest greater insulation from the managed float regime at
both short and long horizons. However, the cumulative long-run re-

sponse of Taiwan's price to a shock to the U.S. real interest rate switches signs (from positive to negative) over the two periods.

Responses to shocks to the U.S. trade-weighted dollar (Figures 6.2D and 6.3D). An appreciation of the dollar produces a sharp permanent *decline* in inflation in Korea in the first period and a much smaller decline in the second period. In the case of Taiwan, an appreciation of the dollar produces a sharp (and erratic) increase in inflation and a much smaller increase in the second period. One possible explanation for the differing signs of the responses to U.S. dollar shocks in the two economies is less capital mobility in Korea than in Taiwan. For example, suppose an appreciation of the trade-weighted dollar largely reflects expectations of deflation in the United States. Under these circumstances, a dollar appreciation could reduce the demand for Korean goods (particularly during the period when the Korean won was pegged to the dollar) and tend to deflate Korean prices. While similar effects would be present in Taiwan, a dollar appreciation could also encourage holders of NT dollars to shift to U.S. dollars (this effect would be absent in Korea if capital were not mobile). If the resulting reduction in the demand for NT dollar assets were sufficiently strong, the price level would rise.

The overall impression conveyed by the impulse responses is un-ambiguous: the short-run impact of external shocks dropped (in some cases very sharply) between the first and second sample periods for most variables. In some cases, the long-run response of inflation in Korea is larger in the second period than in the first. However, the differences are small and may reflect sampling error.

6.7   Conclusions

The preceding analysis of Korea's and Taiwan's experiences with alter-native exchange rate regimes over the past two decades offers some interesting results. First, external shocks have had an important influ-ence on long-run price level behavior in the two economies, though less so in Korea than in Taiwan. This is consistent with some of the char-acteristics of these two economies cited earlier, namely that Taiwan is more open than is Korea, that it trades more with the United States than does Korea, and that capital appears to have been more mobile internationally in Taiwan than in Korea. Second, in spite of certain contrasts in their dynamic responses to external shocks, both Korea and Taiwan became more insulated from external disturbances after they abandoned their respective pegs to the U.S. dollar.

A number of alternative explanations may be offered for the increase in insulation. First, external monetary shocks were relatively important over the sample period, and insulation from these shocks was enhanced by the switch in exchange rate regime. Second, external shocks were negatively correlated across countries, so that abandoning the peg to the U.S. dollar enhanced insulation. Third, Korea and Taiwan managed their exchange rates in the 1980s in a manner that may have contributed to insulation from external shocks.

While testing these alternative explanations is outside the scope of this essay, such tests can be implemented by modifying the model. A model that distinguishes between nominal and real shocks and that incorporates shocks from other countries may provide a test of the first two explanations. The inclusion of other countries would also clarify whether the conclusions about insulation from U.S. shocks reported in this essay can be more broadly interpreted to refer to external shocks from all sources. The model may also be usefully extended to include output, which may shed light on whether there is an empirically important trade-off between insulating output and inflation from external shocks, and how alternative exchange rate regimes affect such a trade-off. Finally, an attempt may be made to model the government's monetary policy reaction function explicitly to see whether differences in insulation under alternative exchange rate regimes reflect differences in the implementation of domestic macroeconomic policy.

Data appendix

External

Oil price: Crude petroleum component of U.S. producer price index, 1982 = 100, quarterly average of monthly figures, seasonally unadjusted. Source: Citibase PW561. Original source: U.S. Department of Labor, Bureau of Labor Statistics.

United States CPI: Consumer price index, 1982–4 = 100, quarterly average of monthly figures, seasonally adjusted. Source: Citibase PU-NEW. Original source: U.S. Department of Labor, Bureau of Labor Statistics.

United States trade-weighted dollar: Weighted average exchange rate against G-10 currencies based on 1972–6 total bilateral trade shares, 1973 = 100, quarterly average of daily figures. Source: Citibase EX-VUS. Original source: Federal Reserve Board.

U.S. three-month Treasury bill rate: Quarterly average of daily figures, secondary market, yields in percent per annum. Source: Citibase FYGM3. Original source: Federal Reserve Board.

Korea

Korea CPI: Consumer price index, 1985 = 100, quarterly average of monthly figures, seasonally adjusted. Source: *International Financial Statistics,* International Monetary Fund.

Taiwan

Taiwan CPI: Consumer price index, 1985 = 100, quarterly average of monthly figures, seasonally adjusted. Source: *Financial statistics,* Central Bank of China.

References

Blanchard, Olivier Jean, and Danny Quah (1989). "The Dynamic Effects of Aggregate Demand and Supply Disturbances," *American Economic Review* 79(September):655–73.

Flood, Robert P. (1979). "Capital Mobility and the Choice of Exchange Rate System," *International Economic Review* 20(2):405–16.

Gali, Jordi (1992). "How Well Does the IS–LM Model Fit Postwar U.S. Data?" *Quarterly Journal of Economics* 107(2):709–38.

Genberg, Hans, Michael K. Salemi, and Alexander Swoboda (1987). "The Relative Importance of Foreign and Domestic Disturbances for Aggregate Fluctuations in the Open Economy: Switzerland, 1964–1981," *Journal of Monetary Economics* 19(1):45–67.

Hutchison, Michael, and Carl Walsh (1992). "Empirical Evidence on the Insulation Properties of Fixed and Flexible Exchange Rates: The Japanese Experience," *Journal of International Economics* 32(3–4):241–63.

Lastrapes, William D., and Faik Koray (1990). "International Transmission of Aggregate Shocks under Fixed and Flexible Exchange Rate Regimes: United Kingdom, France and Germany, 1959 to 1985," *Journal of International Money and Finance* 9(4):402–23.

Moreno, Ramon (1992). "Macroeconomic Shocks and Business Cycles in Australia," (Federal Reserve Bank of San Francisco) *Economic Review* (3):34–52.

  (1993). "Exchange Rate Policy and Insulation from External Shocks: The Experiences of Taiwan and Korea – 1970–1990," Center for Pacific Basin Monetary and Economic Studies Working paper no. PB93-05. Federal Reserve Bank of San Francisco.

Perron, Pierre (1988). "Trends and Random Walks in Macroeconomic Time Series," *Journal of Economic Dynamics and Control* 12(2–3):297–332.

Shapiro, Matthew D., and Mark W. Watson (1988). "Sources of Business Cycle Fluctuations." In *NBER Macroeconomics Annual, 1988,* pp. 111–56. Cambridge, MA: MIT Press.

Sims, Christopher A (1980). "Macroeconomics and Reality," *Econometrica* 48(1):1–48.

CHAPTER 7

Trade price shocks and insulation: Australia's experience with floating rates

John Pitchford

7.1   Introduction

While many countries moved to floating exchange rate systems in the early 1970s, Australia experimented with a variety of pegged and managed regimes until the currency was floated in December 1983.[1] In particular, throughout the period of turbulent price movements associated with the early 1970s and the first oil price shock in 1974, the rate was not allowed to float freely. This essay argues that in important respects the subsequent floating rate regime has served the economy much better than it was served by the regimes of the 1970s and that a floating rate remains preferable to pegged or managed rates. The theme of the essay is that a floating rate system provides the best potential for insulation from the disparate and substantial foreign price movements to which the Australian economy is subject and that this is an extremely valuable attribute of floating rates with important implications for the level of real activity as well as for nominal variables. Further, there appears to be empirical support for the proposition that such insulation has occurred since the exchange rate was floated in Australia.

The capacity of a flexible rate regime to insulate against foreign inflation is well known.[2] If foreign inflation is uniform across commodities and steady, then the theoretical proposition is that, provided the

I am indebted to Steve Dowrick, Cesari Kapuscinski, Phillip Lowe, Adrian Pagan, and Peter Stemp for discussions on this topic. Data used in the essay are taken from Australian Bureau of Statistics and Reserve Bank databases as supplied by the Australian economic statistical facility dX. Because of space constraints, a number of graphs illustrating the behavior of the series used have been omitted. They are available from the author.

[1] Blundell-Wignall and Gregory (1990) describe the nature and timing of changes in these systems in their Table 1, p. 230.

[2] See, e.g., Turnovsky (1979) and Pitchford (1985).

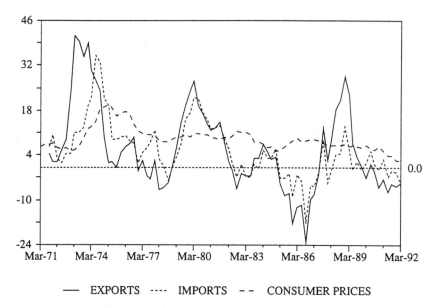

Figure 7.1. Foreign currency export and import prices and domestic consumer prices (percent change per annum).

Fisher effect works abroad, the exchange rate will appreciate at the rate of foreign inflation.[3] Consequently, domestic-currency-denominated traded goods prices will remain constant – that is, the exchange rate appreciation will insulate all other domestic nominal and real variables from the effects of foreign inflation. In practice, however, relevant foreign price movements are anything but uniform and steady. Figure 7.1, showing annual rates of change of Australian foreign-currency-denominated export and import prices and of the index of domestic consumer prices, illustrates this clearly. Hence, it is necessary to rework the inflation insulation property into a form that holds in such conditions. The reformulated proposition is that, other things being equal, nominal exchange rate movements will be a weighted average of changes in foreign currency trade prices. Thus, "on average" the exchange rate mechanism will still have an insulating role when trade price movements are diverse.

---

[3] It is important to note that this proposition is also closely associated with the capacity of flexible rates to ensure independence of monetary policy. For a small country with fixed rates, not only would the foreign price inflation be fully imported, but foreign monetary expansion would induce a commensurate rate of increase in the domestic money supply.

It is this reformulated proposition which will be expounded and tested in the present essay.

It has been claimed that the major benefit from floating has been the capacity of this system to ameliorate the effects of the considerable terms-of-trade shocks to which Australia is periodically subject.[4] However, it is argued here that the potential of a flexible rate to insulate against *nominal* foreign currency trade price shocks is possibly its most important advantage. This does not preclude the exchange rate having a role with respect to terms-of-trade changes because, as changes in export and import prices and terms-of-trade changes are definitionally related, the foreign price insulation property of floating rates applied to these trade prices implies some amelioration of the effects of terms-of-trade movements. Finally, another beneficial property of floating rates is thought to be their capacity to insulate against real shocks. This is closely related to terms-of-trade insulation and, while of considerable interest, is not separately examined here.

Section 7.2 treats the theoretical basis for insulation with respect to both nominal trade price and terms-of-trade shocks. Discussion and empirical analysis of Australia's experience with trade price shocks and insulation are undertaken in Section 7.3, and conclusions are set out in Section 7.4.

7.2   Theoretical aspects of the inflation insulation property

It can be shown that, if exchange rates are neither pegged nor managed, the monetary authorities will usually be able to control the domestic money supply. Further, under certain circumstances, the domestic inflation rate and all domestic nominal and real variables (other than the nominal exchange rate) will be independent of the foreign inflation rate. This is the standard foreign inflation insulation property of flexible exchange rates.

The essential circumstance required for this property to hold is that there is no money illusion in relevant domestic and foreign decisions so that real variables will not depend on nominal variables.[5] If this is so abroad and at home, the foreign real interest rate will be independent of the foreign inflation rate, and the domestic real money supply and real exchange rate will also be independent of the foreign rate of inflation. The independence of the real and nominal money

---

[4] See, e.g., Blundell-Wignall and Gregory (1990).

[5] The usual money demand relation is presumed, with real money demand depending on the nominal interest rate.

supply of foreign inflation ensures that the domestic inflation rate is similarly independent. The independence of the real exchange rate of foreign inflation, combined with that of the domestic inflation rate, means that the nominal exchange rate must move to offset the effects of foreign inflation.

To see these points precisely, define the real money supply l and the real exchange rate c as

$$l = m - \psi, \tag{7.1}$$

$$c = e + p^* - \psi, \tag{7.2}$$

where (all variables being measured in logarithms) m is the nominal money supply, p^* the foreign currency price of imported goods, ψ the price index, and e the price of foreign money. Differentiating with respect to time to get proportional rates of change yields

$$\dot{l} = \dot{m} - \dot{\psi}, \tag{7.3}$$

$$\dot{c} = \dot{e} + \dot{p}^* - \dot{\psi}, \tag{7.4}$$

where $\dot{x} = dx/dt$. From (7.3) the independence of $\dot{m}$ and $\dot{l}$ ensures that $\dot{\psi}$ is also independent of the foreign inflation rate. Given this, the independence of $\dot{c}$ is, from (7.4), ensured by appropriate movements in $\dot{e}$. For example, if the real exchange rate were constant,

$$\dot{e} = -\dot{p}^* + \dot{\psi}, \tag{7.5}$$

and if the domestic macro conditions were such that the domestic inflation rate was zero, the exchange rate would appreciate at the rate of foreign inflation.

Now consider the nature of insulation from foreign price shocks in a small open economy producing exportables, importables, and nontraded goods. In the case in which the foreign inflation rate is uniform across all commodities, the one-good model results carry across to the three-good model. However, it has been emphasized that in practice foreign currency traded goods price movements are very much more volatile than foreign consumer price inflation rates. The theory needs adaptation in order to deal with such circumstances.

Market clearing for the nontraded good is given by

$$y = -\gamma\rho + \mu(s - q) + \omega g \\ + \delta_X(e + s - \psi) + \delta_M(e + q - \psi), \tag{7.6}$$

where the price index ψ is

$$\psi = a_X(e + s) + a_M(e + q) + a_N p, \tag{7.7}$$

where y = output of nontraded goods,
   g = GDP measured without terms-of-trade effects,
   p = price of nontraded goods,
   s = price of exportables in foreign currency,
   q = price of importables in foreign currency,
   ψ = consumption price index,
   e = the price of foreign currency,
   E = the price of domestic currency = $-e$,
   ρ = domestic real interest rate,
   a_i = weight of good i in consumption price index, i = X, M, N,
X, M, N = exportables, importables, nontradables.

All variables other than interest rates are measured in logarithms. In (7.6) the demand for nontraded goods is assumed to be a function of the real interest rate ρ, terms-of-trade effects $s - q$, real GDP as conventionally measured without terms-of-trade effects g, the relative price of exportables $e + s - \psi$, and the relative price of importables $e + q - \psi$. Supposing goods are gross substitutes, these effects will have signs such that the elasticities μ, ω, δ_X, δ_M are all positive. The terms of trade and GDP enter this demand function through the income effects of their changes on real demand. Foreign currency tradeable prices are assumed exogenous for the economy considered. Further, the real interest rate is taken to be exogenous. From interest parity, the domestic real interest rate equals the foreign real interest rate plus the expected depreciation of the real exchange rate.[6] If now the assumption is made that the expected depreciation of the real exchange rate is zero, the domestic real interest rate can be taken to equal the foreign real interest rate, which will be treated as a parameter independent of the foreign inflation rate.[7]

To isolate the insulation question in this framework, hold other variables constant to find the nominal exchange rate responses to changes in foreign prices. These are given by

---

[6] The real exchange rate is defined in the conventional way as the domestic currency-valued foreign consumption price index divided by the domestic consumption price index.

[7] These assumptions will not be critical if the domestic real interest has an insignificant effect on real demand for the length of period considered.

$$\frac{\partial e}{\partial s} = - \frac{\delta_X + \mu}{\delta_X + \delta_M} < 0, \tag{7.8}$$

$$\frac{\partial e}{\partial q} = - \frac{\delta_M - \mu}{\delta_X + \delta_M} < 0, \tag{7.9}$$

$$\frac{\partial e}{\partial s} ds + \frac{\partial e}{\partial q} dq = - \left[\frac{\delta_X}{\delta_X + \delta_M} ds + \frac{\delta_M}{\delta_X + \delta_M} dq \right]$$

$$- \left[\frac{\mu}{\delta_X + \delta_M} \right] [ds - dq]$$

$$= - \left[\frac{\delta_X + \mu}{\delta_X + \delta_M} ds + \frac{\delta_M - \mu}{\delta_X + \delta_M} dq \right]. \tag{7.10}$$

If $ds = dq$, it follows that $de = ds = dq$, which is the standard insulation result. It is shown by Long and Pitchford (1993) that, provided goods are gross substitutes, $\delta_M - \mu$ is unambiguously positive and so the derivative (7.9) is unambiguously negative. For example, when importables prices alone rise, the nominal exchange rate appreciates, but by a smaller proportion than the rise in those prices, and the same is true for exportables prices, so the exchange rate appreciates partly to offset individual foreign currency price rises. In general, with other influences held constant, movements of the exchange rate will be a weighted average of those of exportables and importables prices.

To obtain total effects, differentiate (7.6) totally with respect to time,

$$\dot{E} = -\dot{e} = \frac{\delta_X}{\delta}\dot{q} - \dot{\psi} + \frac{\mu}{\delta}(\dot{s} - \dot{q})$$

$$- \frac{\gamma}{\delta}\dot{\rho} + \frac{\omega}{\delta}\dot{g} - \frac{1}{\delta}\dot{y}, \tag{7.11}$$

where $\delta = \delta_X + \delta_M$. Combining the terms-of-trade effect into its component price effects and labeling groups of coefficients yields

$$\dot{E} = a_s\dot{s} + a_q\dot{q} - \dot{\psi} + a_g\dot{g} + a_\rho\dot{\rho} + a_y\dot{y}. \tag{7.12}$$

Thus, the nontraded goods market equilibrium condition implies that movements in the exchange rate will depend not only on the proportional rate of change of foreign currency prices and domestic inflation, but also on real GDP, the real interest rate, and real nontraded goods output changes. Note that if the exchange rate were pegged or managed, (7.12) would not be expected to hold without significant modification to take account of the nature and extent of official intervention in spot and futures foreign exchange markets.

One way of appreciating the nature of the insulation result in the three-good model is to compare this system with the two-good, traded/nontraded goods, model. This model can be constructed from the former by averaging the prices of traded goods. Assuming the absence of money illusion and other things being equal, the standard insulation result will hold for the traded/nontraded goods system in the form that the exchange rate will appreciate at the rate of increase of the foreign currency traded goods price. This price rises at a rate determined by the average of the rates of increase of foreign currency export and import prices in the underlying three-good model. Hence, the rate of appreciation of the exchange rate is the average of the inflation rates of foreign currency export and import prices.

While the type of insulation studied here applies to prices, in practice its application is broader. Declines in product prices are liable to induce output falls, and rises in input prices, such as oil price increases, can also lead to reduced output. When inflation is imported and raises domestic prices, the monetary authority typically will increase interest rates and bring on a recession. Thus unstable prices may well mean unstable output.

Now consider the question of insulation from terms-of-trade fluctuations. From (7.12) the terms-of-trade effect is subsumed into foreign currency trade price movements. In a recent appraisal of exchange rate policy, Blundell-Wignall and Gregory (1990) conclude that because Australia is a commodity-exporting country subject to substantial swings in its terms of trade, control of inflation is greatly assisted by a floating rate regime.[8]

There would seem to be two main ways in which the terms of trade/exchange rate relationship might be expected to aid macroeconomic management. First, assuming that the real exchange rate and the terms of trade are correlated, movements in the latter require adjustments in the former and these adjustments will be "easier" in a floating rate regime.[9] This effect is subsumed in the price insulation property of flexible rates. Second, terms-of-trade changes imply move-

---

[8] In their words, "The choice of a broadly floating exchange rate is essential for low-inflation monetary policy in a commodity exporting country" (p. 268). Their argument is based partly on a theoretical model of optimal intervention to minimize the variance of inflation around a target level in the face of terms-of-trade shocks and partly on empirical results supporting the view that the real exchange rate is significantly correlated with the terms of trade.

[9] For example, if a real depreciation is required, there is less likely to be pressure on domestic real and nominal variables if the real depreciation is effected through nominal depreciation rather than through a fall in domestic prices.

ments in real income. Improvements in the terms of trade are expansionary, thus leading to price rises because they imply a rise in real income. Worsened terms of trade imply a fall in real income and so put downward pressure on prices, other things being equal.[10] Thus, terms-of-trade changes are likely to affect both prices and output in the same direction. Hence, if stabilizing output growth is an additional target of policy, arguments for a floating rate regime on the grounds of controlling inflation apply equally to the output target.

Indeed, there is theoretical justification for this in the article by Roper and Turnovsky (1980). They formulate a Keynesian-type model with fixed prices and variable output, rather than the variable price and fixed output class of model employed by Blundell-Wignall and Gregory. This is used to examine the consequences of a criterion involving the minimization of the variance of real output around a target value. Their conclusion is that floating is preferable if the source of the shocks is real demand. Terms-of-trade shifts that affect real income can be looked on as real demand shifts in their model. Reinforcing this work, Stemp (1991) has examined the consequences of including both output and price deviations in the objective function of the authorities. Again, his conclusion is that where output shocks rather than monetary shocks dominate, some form of floating is optimal.[11]

These results are subject to an important caveat. Terms-of-trade movements imply changes in real income and therefore constitute a real shock. However, if the assumption is maintained that foreign currency export and import prices are exogenous, no amount of implicit or explicit intervention can offset the relative price shift. The effects on demand of a given terms-of-trade (and hence real income) rise can be offset, say, by monetary restraint, but relative prices and *equilibrium* real income will remain affected as long as the terms-of-trade increase lasts. Presumably, the role of active or passive intervention with respect to the impact effects on real variables is to attempt to offset any tendency for these to cause *temporary* excess demand or supply.

[10] These relationships are spelled out for the exportables, importables, and nontraded goods model in Long and Pitchford (1993).

[11] These conclusions are not all that surprising, in that they are special cases of the basic Mundell–Fleming model. With perfectly mobile financial capital, pegged rates insulate an economy from domestic monetary shocks while floating rates insulate from real shocks, such as terms-of-trade changes. See Bruce and Purvis (1985) and Pitchford (1985).

7.3 An evaluation of price insulation in the floating rate regime

It has been shown in the preceding section that floating exchange rates have a price insulation attribute. The aim of the present section is to see whether and to what extent this property has operated since Australia's exchange rate was floated and to suggest why it may have been beneficial to economic management. This will be approached in Section 7.3.1 through a review of some major episodes of foreign price shocks and in Section 7.3.2 by attempting to see how well equation (7.12) performs empirically in the post- and prefloat periods.

7.3.1 *The experience of trade price shocks*

Australia's nominal exchange rate was pegged in a variety of ways before November 1971, was managed from that date to December 1983, and has floated from then to the present.[12] The float has not been entirely without intervention. Reserve Bank intervention is measured by its net market purchases of foreign exchange and is sterilized.[13] If intervention were substantial and clearly effective, it could be argued that the Australian dollar, rather than floating since December 1983, has been managed. However, there is doubt on both theoretical and empirical grounds about the effectiveness of sterilized intervention. Economic theory suggests that sterilized intervention can have a lasting impact on the exchange rate only to the extent that domestic and foreign assets are imperfect substitutes.[14] Further, empirical work, including that described in the present essay, does not support the view that sterilized intervention is particularly effective. Also, a stated purpose of intervention has been to smooth fluctuations in the nominal exchange rate, and the data show that intervention has been on both sides of the market. The other way in which the float could have been impure is if monetary

---

[12] Blundell-Wignall and Gregory (1990) describe the managed system as a crawling peg with respect to the U.S. dollar.

[13] The Reserve Bank also "intervenes" in the sense that it sells foreign exchange to the Commonwealth government to facilitate the latter's transactions needs. Some argue that this is also a form of intervention, giving results different from what would be obtained if the government had to go through the market. However, the argument against this is that the Reserve Bank is an agent purchasing foreign exchange on the government's behalf.

[14] It has been argued, however, that even if substitution is perfect, the markets may take the intervention to signal the potential for a likely change in monetary policy. For this effect to work there would need to be some form of stable relation between intervention and the subsequent monetary stance.

policy had targeted the exchange rate. There has been talk of this from time to time in Australia as an adjunct to inflation policy, but if it has been practiced it has not appeared to last for any significant length of time. Hence, it seems reasonable for present purposes to assume that the float has not been subject to excessive intervention or targeting.

I shall follow the usual convention in Australia of treating the foreign currency price of domestic currency as the exchange rate, though the reciprocal (price of foreign currency) is often a more convenient measure and is used at times. The nominal exchange rate, whether measured against the U.S. dollar, against the yen, or as a trade-weighted index (the effective exchange rate), shows considerable depreciation from the mid-1970s to the mid-1980s, particularly in 1985–6.

The behavior of traded goods prices in foreign currency terms is central to the analysis. For most Australian exports and imports, it is regarded as reasonable to assume that domestic demand and supply have little impact on world prices. Hence, the foreign currency prices of the commodities Australia exports and imports are taken to be exogenous variables. It follows that fluctuations in such prices have the potential to introduce substantial shocks into the economy. The implicit price deflators for exports and imports were converted to foreign currency units by multiplying them by the nominal trade-weighted exchange rate index (TWI).[15] Their annual rates of change (quarter this year to same quarter previous year) are compared with that of the Australian consumption price deflator in Figure 7.1 and with those of the TWI in Figure 7.2. Clearly, these trade prices were subject to large fluctuations, even in the 1980s, when inflation rates in most industrial countries were low and stable. Moreover, these fluctuations are absorbed in some fashion, in that domestic consumption price inflation is far steadier than foreign currency trade price movements. The data in Figure 7.2 suggest the hypothesis, to be tested later, that the TWI more closely followed foreign currency trade prices in the 1980s than previously. This would support the view that floating exchange rates insulate domestic prices from the effects of foreign nominal price movements.

While the traded goods prices tend to move together, there is sufficient lack of synchronization and different degrees of change to cause large swings in the terms of trade. To take only one example, Australia's

---

[15] Rather than constructing the data on foreign currency trade prices from domestic currency indexes, it would have been preferable to have had data on trade prices in foreign currencies from which to build up an index. Support for the claim that the constructed indexes measure what they purport to can be had from comparing them with the Reserve Bank of Australia's foreign currency index of commodity prices. The series show similar movement.

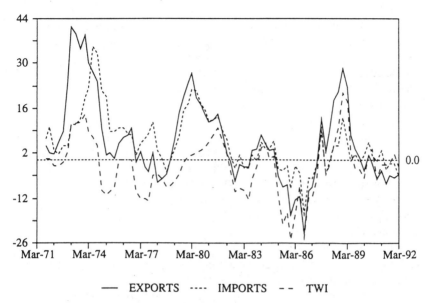

Figure 7.2. Foreign currency export and import prices and the trade-weighted exchange rate index (percent change per annum).

export prices increased rapidly in the early 1970s, while import prices rose somewhat later with the first oil price shock, producing a rise and then a fall in the terms of trade. Terms-of-trade fluctuations are a source of considerable variation in Australia's real income.[16]

Four episodes of large movements in foreign currency trade prices stand out clearly in Figure 7.1.[17] They occurred in (i) the early 1970s, (ii) 1980, (iii) the mid-1980s, and (iv) the late 1980s. The first two episodes occurred essentially before, and the last two episodes after, the floating of the Australian dollar. Consider each in turn.

(i) Export prices increased substantially in the early 1970s while import prices rose somewhat later in the mid-1970s. Foreign currency export prices rose over the year 1972 by 24 percent and over 1973 by

[16] Using a formula derived in Long and Pitchford (1993), in 1972–3 and 1988–9 terms-of-trade improvements contributed 2.6% and 2.3% to real GDP, respectively, while a deterioration in 1974–5 subtracted 1.5% from GDP. Such real income movements can be expected to give rise to significant changes in demand and hence pose problems for macroeconomic management.

[17] Each of the swings involved price rises or falls in excess of 20%. Using the criterion that an episode starts when price increases clearly accelerate or decelerate, they can be dated roughly as June 1972 to March 1975, June 1979 to December 1981, March 1985 to March 1987, and March 1988 to June 1989.

39 percent. In the year to June 1974 import prices increased at a 35 percent annual rate. With managed and pegged exchange rates, one consequence was a substantial increase in the money supply in the early 1970s and in part another was an increase in the inflation rate to 18 percent in the middle of the decade. Wage claims escalated on the basis of this and expected future inflation. The authorities treated this inflation as if it were no different from that which would originate from domestic sources in a closed economy.[18] Their response was a tightening of monetary policy in 1974–5, which helped to reduce growth and increase unemployment. The inflation rate fell somewhat, though because of the large imported inflation component it remained high through the 1970s. A floating exchange rate could have been expected to result in greater control over the money supply as well as a significant insulating appreciation of the TWI, both during the export boom of the early 1970s and the import price rise following the 1974 oil price shock. The benefit to the economy would have been less imported inflation, greater monetary autonomy, and a lessened need for con-tractionary anti-inflation policies.

(ii) The second episode, beginning in 1980, involved foreign currency traded goods prices first rising rapidly and then more slowly (e.g., in the year to March 1980 there was a 27 percent export price and 22 percent import price rise). Once more, large wage claims resulted. Mon-etary policy was again tightened. This shock was over before the floating of the rate in December 1983. It is interesting that the changes in both export and import prices were sufficiently closely synchronized in time and size that the terms of trade hardly changed. These foreign price rises could well have helped to maintain a high inflation rate through this period, despite continued tight monetary policy and the recession of 1982–3. A floating rate system might have been expected, other things being equal, to induce an appreciation of the same order of magnitude as the foreign price rises, so resulting in a lower inflation rate than a pegged rate system.

(iii) Foreign currency traded goods prices fell in the mid-1980s, with the fall in export prices (23 percent in the year to September 1986) larger than that of import prices (17 percent). From (7.12) the insulating re-sponse should be a depreciation. It turns out that this was indeed a period of substantial depreciation. The aspects of this episode that at-tracted the attention of the authorities at the time were concerns about whether the depreciation was excessive and whether the worsening of

---

[18] To complicate matters, there were also domestic inflationary pressures, particularly from increased government expenditure.

the terms of trade would result in further rises in the current account deficit.

This was a period of continuing inflation, so it might be argued that Australia could have benefited from a pegged rate regime by importing deflation. However, this would also have required downward pressure on the money supply, since the authorities would have had to sell foreign exchange to prevent the depreciating insulation response. Further, unless they had opted for fixed rates, they would have needed to be aware of the trend that traded goods prices were taking and this is no mean task. Given its potential to impose significant costs, an anti-inflation policy is probably best conducted as an explicit monetary policy exercise.

(iv) The final episode saw both import and export prices rising at about the same time, but with import prices rising at a lesser rate. For example, annual rises to December 1988 were 28.4 percent for exports and 13 percent for imports. In this period of floating, the exchange rate appreciated at a rate intermediate between the rates of increase of export and import prices. Such a response would help to insulate against imported inflation. In fact, the inflation rate came down slowly during this period. While the magnitude of these shocks was less than that of 1972–4, it is probable that with a pegged exchange rate they would have provided significant pressure on both the domestic inflation rate and the money supply. The flexible rate regime may well have reduced the capacity of these shocks to increase inflationary pressure. The interesting thing about this episode is that, apart from the terms-of-trade improvement, it attracted almost no attention from the authorities and commentators, perhaps because the exchange rate response concealed the nominal price rises.

This review of these trade price shocks strongly suggests that the exchange rate mechanism was much more insulating in the post- than in the prefloat period. Further, the advantage of floating for policy would appear to be that the import of foreign inflationary and deflationary pressures, both directly through domestic currency trade prices and indirectly through the effects on the money supply of supporting a fixed exchange rate, is lessened.

In the following subsection it is shown more rigorously that the major influences on the exchange rate are foreign currency trade price movements and the inflation rate and that movements in the TWI have tended to track trade price movements more closely in the post- than in the prefloat period. The greatest deviations occur in 1972–5 and 1979–80, episodes singled out above as times not only when trade price shocks were considerable, but also when the economy appeared to import inflation because of a policy of limiting exchange rate movements.

7.3.2   *A test for insulation*

We now turn to a test of the hypothesis that the exchange rate was insulating in the postfloat period and that the insulation it then provided was superior to that in the prefloat era.[19] Based on (7.12) the equation tested was

$$\dot{E} = a_0 + a_s\dot{s} + a_q\dot{q} + a_\psi\dot{\psi} + a_g\dot{g} + a_\rho\dot{\rho} + a_y\dot{y} + \epsilon, \quad (7.13)$$

where theory implies that

$$a_s > 0, \qquad a_q > 0, \qquad a_g > 0, \qquad a_\rho < 0, \qquad a_y < 0,$$
$$a_s + a_q = 1, \qquad a_\psi = -1.$$

While this appears to be a partial relationship, most of the variables on the right-hand side of (7.13) can be seen to have some claim to exogeneity. Foreign currency traded goods prices are often taken to be exogenous, while an argument was made earlier for treating the real interest rate in the same way. The inflation rate can be taken to represent exogenous monetary policy. Output variables cannot be so treated, but turn out not to be significant in the regressions.

Quarterly data from 1971:Q3 to 1992:Q1 were used for the tests. The TWI was taken as the measure of the nominal exchange rate and the rate of change of the consumption price deflator as the measure of inflation. Because there are no data for the output of nontraded goods, this variable was excluded from the regressions. The proportional rates of change were initially taken to be annual rates over the same quarter for the preceding year. However, better results were obtained with rates of change of variables over the previous quarter. The ordinary least squares regression results, with the dependent variable being the quarterly proportional rate of change of the TWI, are shown in Table 7.1. The top portion of the table treats the floating rate period (1983:Q4–1992:Q1), and the lower portion the prefloat period (1971:Q3–1983:Q3). Real interest variables did not perform well in any of the regressions and so were omitted from subsequent tests. When GDP growth variables were significant, they were of the wrong sign.[20] The results for the postfloat period appear to be improved by including a lag of two periods for the domestic inflation variable, though no other lags were significant. This general lack of lagged effects seems consistent with the view that

[19] It would have been preferable to test the insulation property in a macroeconometric model with at least the three relevant production sectors.

[20] Because the nontraded goods market need not clear, a variety of indicators of disequilibrium, such as the unemployment rate, were also tried, but none performed well.

Table 7.1. *Regression results for TWI change*

Regressor	Coefficient	Std. error	t-statistic
Floating rate period			
Constant	.16	1.22	.13
Export price change	.73	.16	4.65
Import price change	.48	.20	2.40
Inflation	−2.37	.59	−4.00
Inflation (−2)	1.76	.66	2.66
$R^2 = .88$ Std. error of regression = 1.96		DW^a = 1.70	
chi-sq. (4) = 2.21 (.70)		$F(4,25)$ = .44 (.78)	
DF^b = −5.23 (−4.85)		ADF(1)^c = −4.79 (−4.87)	
Prefloat period			
Constant	−.64	.76	.41
Export price change	.36	.08	4.44
Import price change	.23	.11	2.01
Inflation	−.43	.27	−1.55
$R^2 = .57$ Std. error of regression = 1.95		DW^a = 1.70	
chi-sq. (4) = 1.83 (.77)^b		$F(3,45)$ = .40 (81)	
DF^b = −5.90 (−4.33)		ADF(1)^c = −4.64 (−4.34)	

Note: Floating rate period defined as 1983:Q4–1992:Q2. Prefloat period defined as 1971:Q3–1983:Q3. Figures in parentheses denote 95% critical values of test statistics.
^{a}DW denotes Durbin–Watson statistic.
^{b}DF denotes Dickey–Fuller test of unit root for residuals.
^{c}ADF(1) denotes augmented Dickey–Fuller test of unit root for residuals with one lag.

the exchange rate is quick to adjust. The signs of the coefficients on foreign currency trade price changes are positive, as the theory would suggest, and sum to 1.21. The sign on the inflation variable with no lag is negative, and with two quarters' lag is positive. Their sum is −0.61, which accords with the theoretical proposition that higher domestic inflation depreciates the exchange rate. The lag structure suggests exchange rate overshooting with respect to an inflationary (monetary) shock. The restrictions are that the sum of coefficients on trade prices is unity and the sum of the coefficients on the inflation variable is −1. These restrictions were tested jointly, and could not be rejected.[21]

As well as the variables suggested by (7.13), an intervention variable,

---

[21] The Wald test gave a chi-square parameter of 4.37 (0.11) for the joint restriction.

net market purchases of foreign exchange as a percentage of total reserves, was included in the regressions. This intervention measure does not seem to have an important effect on the TWI in that while it was significant in a number of tests it had the wrong sign. This is consistent with the notion that sterilized intervention had no detectable effect but was put into effect when exchange rates were moving in the direction opposite to that which the intervention was meant to achieve.

The best results for the prefloat period are shown in the lower half of Table 7.1. These results are in all important respects worse than for the floating rate period. The exchange rate system would seem to have performed less well in its insulating task before the float. For instance, for the prefloat period the sum of the coefficients on trade price changes is 0.59 and on inflation is -0.43. However, when the exchange rate is pegged or managed, it is perhaps not appropriate to treat it as a dependent variable. Rather, the question then becomes one of the degree of monetary independence and of the extent to which inflation was imported.

7.4   Conclusions

It would seem reasonable to conclude that lack of flexibility in exchange rate adjustment to external price shocks in the 1970s exacerbated Australia's problems in adjusting to the substantial price instability in that decade. Further, there would appear to be much greater cap. :ity since the float for exchange rate flexibility to offset nominal trade price shocks. This presumably accounts for the fact that although trade price shocks in foreign currency terms were also considerable in the 1980s, they seem to have had little effect on the domestic economy (except through the terms-of-trade effects).

Floating is preferred if monetary independence is required. Related to this, floating has the potential to moderate the effects on the domestic economy of the considerable foreign currency nominal trade price swings to which Australia is subject. Not only does this have benefits with respect to the control of inflation, but lesser absolute price changes also will imply lesser induced real effects in a system in which wages and prices are not perfectly flexible. Testing these propositions with data on nominal exchange rate and trade price movements suggests that in the postfloat period the nominal exchange rate moved to offset foreign currency price fluctuations significantly better than before December 1983.

One conventional justification for floating rates has been that they ameliorate the effects of terms-of-trade fluctuations on the domestic economy. It has been argued that to the extent that the exchange rate mechanism can help in this matter, the insulation capacity against absolute price shocks subsumes its contribution. In any case, the exchange rate mechanism can help in this respect by producing effects on demand that assist in offsetting temporary excess demand and supply produced by terms-of-trade changes.

References

Blundell-Wignall, A., and Gregory, R. G. (1990). "Exchange Rate Policy in Advanced Commodity-Exporting Countries: Australia and New Zealand." In V. Argy and P. DeGrauwe, eds., *Choosing an Exchange Rate Regime*, pp. 224–71. Washington, DC: International Monetary Fund.

Bruce, N., and Purvis, D. D. (1985). "The Specification and Influences of Factor and Goods Markets in Open Economy Macroeconomics." In R. W. Jones and P. B. Kenen, eds., *Handbook of International Economics*, Vol. 2, pp. 307–58. Amsterdam: Elsevier.

Long, N. V., and Pitchford, J. D. (1993). "The Terms of Trade and Real Income in a Small Open Economy." In H. Herberg and N. V. Long, eds., *Trade, Welfare, and Economic Policies: Essays in Honour of Murray Kemp*, pp. 367–78. Ann Arbor: University of Michigan Press.

Pitchford, J. D. (1985). "The Insulation Capacity of a Flexible Exchange Rate System in the Context of External Inflation," *Scandinavian Journal of Economics* 87:44–65.

Roper, D. E., and Turnovsky, S. J. (1980). "Optimal Exchange Rate Intervention in a Simple Stochastic Macroeconomic Model," *Canadian Journal of Economics* 13:296–309.

Stemp, P. J. (1991). "Optimal Weights in a Check-List of Monetary Indicators," *Economic Record* 67:1–13.

Turnovsky, S. J. (1979). "On the Insulation Properties of Flexible Exchange Rates," *Revue Economique* 30:719–46.

CHAPTER 8

The role of the exchange rate in New Zealand monetary policy

Arthur Grimes and Jason Wong

8.1   Introduction

The objective of New Zealand monetary policy is clear: the Reserve Bank of New Zealand is to achieve and maintain price stability, defined as annual consumer price inflation of between 0 and 2 percent. This is perhaps the most clearly stated and single-focused objective for monetary policy of any country, but the Reserve Bank nonetheless faces the same control problem as other monetary authorities. How should it implement monetary policy to achieve its objective? Is there some intermediate target that will assist in achieving price stability – for instance, a monetary aggregate or the exchange rate?

The choice and use of such an intermediate target form the subject matter of this essay. The discussion is organized as follows. First, some background is provided concerning recent developments in New Zealand monetary policy and the existing monetary framework. Monetary policy is driven directly by the inflation target and is implemented primarily through control of the level of bank reserves via open market operations. In order to guide the setting of the target for bank reserves, inflationary influences (including the impact of monetary aggregate developments) are forecast and bank reserves are then set at a level that will yield an exchange rate band consistent with achieving the inflation target given the other inflationary influences. Thus, the exchange rate

Earlier versions of this essay were presented to seminars at the Reserve Bank of New Zealand and Stanford University. The essay was revised while the first author was a visiting scholar at the Center for Pacific Basin Monetary and Economic Studies, Federal Reserve Bank of San Francisco. We wish to thank Reuven Glick, Michael Hutchison, Sun Bae Kim, seminar participants, and colleagues for helpful comments on earlier drafts, but neither they nor the Reserve Bank of New Zealand are responsible for the views expressed.

is used as a calibration device for setting monetary policy, but neither it nor a monetary aggregate is treated as a target in its own right.

A brief theoretical section outlines why adherence to a single intermediate target – be it a monetary aggregate or the exchange rate – may be inappropriate, so providing a conceptual basis for the approach adopted in New Zealand. Ultimately, however, the appropriate regime will be determined by empirical factors. Thus, the essay tests empirically for the suitability of either a monetary aggregate or the exchange rate, as well as a combination of the two, as a guide for monetary policy in New Zealand. These tests are conducted in the context of comparing two simple rules for policy – one based on purchasing power parity, the other on the quantity theory of money. Both long-run and short-run properties of the alternative rules are examined. The concluding section relates the theoretical and empirical findings of the essay to the initial discussion of monetary policy implementation in New Zealand.

8.2   The New Zealand monetary framework

The Reserve Bank of New Zealand Act 1989 states that the Reserve Bank's monetary policy role "is to formulate and implement monetary policy directed to the economic objective of achieving and maintaining stability in the general level of prices."[1] Further, the act requires a Policy Targets Agreement to be signed between the governor of the bank and the minister of finance setting out more specific objectives for policy. This agreement has set a formal 0 to 2 percent inflation target for monetary policy.[2] The governor of the bank is accountable for achieving inflation in this range and can be dismissed if his or her performance "in ensuring that the Bank achieves the policy targets . . . has been inadequate."

Thus, the objectives for monetary policy are clear, as is the accountability mechanism. This situation contrasts with the previous environment, in which there was a multiplicity of objectives for monetary policy and the Reserve Bank implemented policy according to the directions

---

[1] The historical material in this section is based principally on two books published by the Reserve Bank of New Zealand: *Financial Policy Reform* (1986) and *Monetary Policy and the New Zealand Financial System* (3d ed., 1992).

[2] The Policy Targets Agreement signed in December 1990 allows for some temporary deviation from this band in the event of major supply shocks or other major relative price changes such as significant terms-of-trade changes, indirect tax changes, or natural disasters. In these cases, it is envisaged that the first-round effect of the shocks may flow through into the general price level, but the bank is charged with returning inflation to the 0 to 2 percent band thereafter.

of the minister of finance. Before mid-1984, objectives were rarely stated clearly, although with annual inflation averaging 13.6 percent in the decade to June 1984, price stability had not been a high priority. The election of a new government in July 1984 led, in effect, to a single focus for monetary policy toward reducing inflation, and by 1988 this focus had crystallized into targeting price stability.[3] This focus was subsequently incorporated into legislation, which took effect formally in February 1990.

Implementation mechanisms also changed radically in the mid-1980s. Before July 1984, monetary policy was implemented through an array of regulations and controls. By 1984, all interest rates in the economy were controlled, the exchange rate was fixed, banks and other financial institutions were subject to a variety of ratio controls, and capital account transactions were heavily regulated. By March 1985, all these controls (including all ratio controls) had been lifted,[4] and there was a freely floating exchange rate. With the introduction of a market-linked interest rate on bank reserves in late 1985, all interest rates set by the Reserve Bank were now priced directly off prevailing market rates. This regime has been maintained since then. Notably, with regard to the floating exchange rate, there has been no official intervention in the foreign exchange market since March 1985.

Within the post–July 1984 period, however, we can characterize three separate regimes. The first extends to March 1985, the month the exchange rate was first floated. Policy in this period concentrated on controlling the quantity of bank reserves and, in attempting to place downward pressure on inflation, forced a rise in domestic interest rates. However, the removal of capital controls and the desire to maintain a fixed exchange rate led to strong private capital inflows, which frustrated the authorities' ability to control the monetary base.

The floating of the exchange rate in March 1985 made feasible the targeting of bank reserves; thus began the second regime. In some respects – concerning the regulatory environment and the basic manner of implementing policy (through open market operations targeting a

---

[3] The adoption of this single focus for monetary policy reflected a judgment that, in the long term, monetary policy could materially affect only the price level. This judgment was in turn derived both from theory and from New Zealand's historical experience: New Zealand had the lowest economic growth rate in the post–World War II era of all OECD countries despite, or perhaps because of, having a higher than average inflation rate.

[4] Banks are subject to prudential controls, such as capital ratios and large exposure limits, but these are not used for monetary policy purposes.

daily level of bank reserves) – this regime remains in force. However, the principles guiding the setting of the bank reserves target have changed over this period.

In the period to August 1988, policy placed greater weight than subsequently on the level of bank reserves as an important target in its own right. This approach was implicitly based on a quantity theory approach relating the price level to the quantity of base money. It was increasingly recognized, however, that this relationship was not stable in the short term, and so the reserves target was varied in response to other indicators. Most important of these (especially toward the end of the period) was the slope of the yield curve, acting as a proxy for inflation expectations over time. The level of interest rates and of the exchange rate were also used as indicators but were less important, and both showed strong volatility over this period; for instance, monthly volatility in the U.S.–New Zealand exchange rate (defined as the percent difference between the high and low values of the exchange rate over the month) rose from 2.9 percent prefloat (when the exchange rate was pegged to a basket) to around 7 percent in the postfloat period up until September 1988. The broader monetary and credit aggregates grew strongly during this period, but this was principally a result of deregulation, with deposits returning to the banking system from previously unregulated fringe financial operations (e.g., lawyers), and so was not regarded as an indicator of strong inflationary pressure.

With the emergence of a clearer target for monetary policy in 1988 came a desire to have a more explicit framework to guide daily operations. In addition, there was increasing dissatisfaction with the interest rate and exchange rate volatility of the second regime. A strong fall in the exchange rate (of close to 10 percent) in August 1988 led the Reserve Bank to reevaluate its relative lack of emphasis on exchange rate movements, particularly in the light of empirical work which showed that domestic inflation was strongly influenced by traded goods prices, and hence by the exchange rate. Policy moved toward curtailing large exchange rate swings that were not consistent with the achievement of its inflation targets. Thus began the third regime, characterized by essentially the same operational mechanisms as before, but with substantially less interest rate and exchange rate volatility than in the preceding regime (monthly exchange rate volatility dropped to 4 percent in the following eighteen months, and has since declined further).

This third regime remains intact. Here we describe in more detail this approach to policy. The framework can be characterized as consisting of three steps:

(i) There is an *unambiguous objective* for monetary policy (the 0 to 2 percent inflation target).

(ii) There is a *clear reaction function* for the qualitative (but not the quantitative) response of monetary policy if *forecast* inflation deviates from the target range (i.e., tighten [loosen] policy if forecast inflation is higher [lower] than 0 to 2 percent).

(iii) There is *discretion* over how to forecast inflation and over how much to change monetary settings if forecast inflation deviates from the target range (discussed further later).

From these steps, it is clear that monetary policy in New Zealand is forward looking. It is generally accepted that actions are unlikely to have a significant effect on inflation in the contemporaneous or subsequent quarter; instead, the major impact of a monetary policy action on inflation is likely to occur over a period of two to about eight quarters ahead.[5] The Reserve Bank forecasts inflation three years ahead. These forecasts are based on an econometric equation for the consumer price index (CPI), which in turn is a function of the producer price index (PPI) for both inputs and outputs. The format of these equations is such that the CPI, in the long run, can be interpreted predominantly as a markup on normal costs, together with the additional influence of house prices. The inflation rate in any quarter responds to deviations of the CPI from its equilibrium level and responds also to changes in other prices, wages, and productivity. The semireduced form for CPI inflation after solving out for the PPI variables (and omitting the effects of indirect taxes, for simplicity) can be written as

$$\Delta CPI_t = f(\Delta TWI_t, \Delta PXGW_t, \Delta PMGW_t, \Delta NPROD_t, \Delta W_t, \\ \Delta PH_t, CPI_{t-1} - CPI^*_{t-1}), \qquad (8.1)$$

where the equilibrium price level CPI* is given by

$$CPI^*_t = g(TWI_t, PXGW_t, PMGW_t, NPROD_t, W_t, PH_t) \qquad (8.2)$$

and where TWI   = trade-weighted exchange rate,
            PXG   = New Zealand dollar price of exports of goods,
            PXGW = PXG × TWI (the "world" price of exports),
            PMG   = New Zealand dollar price of imports of goods,
            PMGW = PMG × TWI (the "world" price of imports),
            NPROD = "normal" productivity,

[5] See, e.g., the evidence in Brooks and Gibbs (1991).

W = hourly wage rate,
PH = price of existing dwellings.

Given that New Zealand is a small open economy, PXGW and PMGW are taken to be independent of domestic monetary policy actions and are forecast on the basis of information about likely price developments in the relevant commodities comprising the country's exports and imports. Normal productivity is proxied by a moving average of actual labor productivity. Ideally, wages and house prices should be expressed as a function of foreign price movements, real influences, and the monetary policy control variable. In practice, however, no reliable empirical forecasting equations have been obtained for these two variables. They are therefore forecast judgmentally (albeit using econometric evidence as one input), with these forecasts entered into the CPI forecast framework. In addition, while it has been difficult to estimate reliable margin effects arising from demand changes, some allowance is made for changes in margins based on evidence from leading indicator relationships.

Given these forecasts, a range for the exchange rate path over time can be derived that is consistent with the maintenance of 0 to 2 percent inflation. Thus, there is a conditional range for the exchange rate that is consistent with forecast price stability, and this range will vary as forecasts of other inflationary influences vary. In practice, forecasts of these other influences generally do not change sharply, and hence the conditional range for the exchange rate tends to move smoothly over time.

Monetary policy is generally implemented with the desire to keep the exchange rate consistent with the conditional range. The monetary aggregates do not have a formal role in this framework. They are not completely ignored, however. They serve as an input into judgments on house prices (where some empirical linkages have in the past been shown) and on profit margins.[6] Thus, while there is a clear objective for policy and a clear implementation framework, no simple rule for implementing policy has been adopted. Rather, given all other influences (including developments in monetary aggregates), the exchange rate acts as the principal guide for calibrating how much monetary settings should be changed when forecast inflation deviates from the target range. This is not because significance is attached to the exchange rate level per se, but because it is considered to be a strong influence on the future

---

[6] The yield gap between short- and long-dated government paper is also used as an indicator in this sense, as are surveyed inflationary expectations and real sector developments.

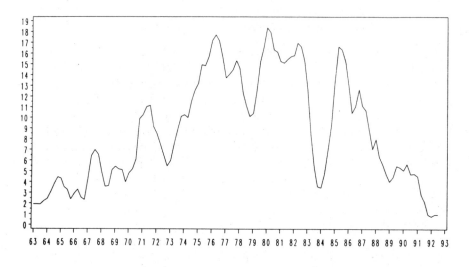

March Years

Figure 8.1. Annual consumer price inflation.

price level and it has the additional advantage that it can be monitored continuously.

This framework for policy appears to be well understood within the financial markets. The result has been to establish a self-equilibrating mechanism within the money and foreign exchange markets. If the Reserve Bank revises down its forecasts of inflationary influences (or if financial market participants expect this to occur), interest rates and the exchange rate tend to weaken (frequently obviating the need for an explicit monetary policy action) so as to keep CPI inflation within the 0 to 2 percent band.

The success of the structure cannot be measured solely in terms of market acceptance; the structure must also succeed in achieving its objectives. Figure 8.1 graphs the annual CPI inflation rate since 1963. (The CPI series used in the figure excludes the estimated price impact of the imposition of a 10 percent value added tax – called the goods and services tax [GST] – in October 1986 and of its subsequent increase to 12.5 percent in July 1989.) The figure documents the steady rise in inflation through the 1960s and early 1970s, with a plateau of around 14 to 18 percent through the mid-1980s. (The sharp fall in inflation in 1983–4 corresponds to a period of strict wage and price controls, the lifting of which contributed to the rebound in inflation in 1985.) The inflation rate

has fallen steadily since the mid-1980s to stand at 1 percent in the year
to September 1992.

This fall cannot be attributed solely to monetary policy. Fiscal policy,
which may have an impact on wages, profit margins, and house prices
through demand channels, has generally become tighter over this period,
with the primary surplus averaging 3.5 percent of GDP from 1987–8 to
1990–1 compared with an average primary deficit of 1.6 percent of GDP
from 1981–2 to 1984–5. In addition, a major liberalization of the economy has occurred at the same time as the disinflationary program has
been undertaken. In particular, a reduction in trade protection has contributed directly to a fall in prices of imported goods and has placed
indirect downward pressure on prices by increasing competition. Further, labor laws were changed substantially with the Employment Contracts Act, which took effect in May 1991. This act significantly reduced
the prevalence of centralized wage deals and appears to have placed (at
least temporary) downward pressure on wage settlements.

These factors are likely to have aided the transition to price stability,
but ultimately the task of maintaining stable prices rests with monetary
policy. The next two sections therefore examine theoretical and empirical arguments as to how this might best be achieved, and the final
section compares the resulting insights with the actual practice of monetary policy as described here.

8.3   Theoretical framework

A modified version of Dornbusch's (1976) model is adopted to illustrate
the role of the exchange rate versus a monetary aggregate in the conduct
of monetary policy.[7] The model is based on the existence of a stable
demand for money (with allowance, however, for shocks to money
demand); demand-determined output in the short run, responding to
both the real exchange rate and the real interest rate as well as to other
real shocks; sticky prices, with inflation responding to excess demand;
and perfect capital mobility, with rational exchange rate expectations
implying that uncovered interest parity always holds, although again
subject to shocks. While output is demand-determined in the short run,
in the long run it tends toward the natural rate, which is assumed to
remain unaffected by any of the shocks.

Formally, the model is as follows (where all variables are measured
as deviations from means and are in logarithmic form except for [the

[7] The modification is that output responds to real, rather than nominal, interest rates.

Arthur Grimes and Jason Wong

level of] the interest rate; a prime after a variable denotes a time derivative; all coefficients are positive):

$$m = -\lambda i + \phi y + p + z1, \tag{8.3}$$

$$y = \delta(e - p) - \gamma(i - p') + z2, \tag{8.4}$$

$$p' = \pi y, \tag{8.5}$$

$$i = e' + z3, \tag{8.6}$$

where m = money supply,
i = nominal interest rate,
y = output,
p = price level,
e = exchange rate (an increase in e is a depreciation),
$z1$ = permanent money demand shock,
$z2$ = permanent real aggregate demand shock,
$z3$ = permanent risk premium shock to domestic interest rates.

Equation (8.3) is the LM curve in which real money balances are a negative function of the nominal interest rate and a positive function of output; allowance is made for step changes in money demand (i.e., a nominal shock) through the variable $z1$. Equation (8.4) is the IS curve in which output is a function of the real interest rate (with inflation assumed to be perfectly anticipated) and of the real exchange rate (with the foreign price level assumed constant). The variable $z2$ represents a shock to real aggregate demand – for instance, as a result of increased world demand for the country's exports.

Equation (8.5) has inflation (p') responding to excess demand (with $y = 0$ being the natural rate of output). Equation (8.6) is the uncovered interest parity condition in which the domestic interest rate increases in line with the (perfectly anticipated) rate of exchange rate depreciation (e'). The variable $z3$ represents a shock to the risk premium required on domestic assets (i.e., it is a form of real shock); an increase in $z3$ requires the exchange-rate-adjusted domestic return to be greater than that on equivalent foreign assets. (Alternatively, $z3$ can be interpreted as a shock to the foreign real interest rate.)

The model can be manipulated so that the authorities can choose either the money base or the exchange rate as a (controllable) intermediate target.[8] (It is assumed that the authorities have no information

[8] Grimes (1989) demonstrates that, within this model, use of the interest rate as an intermediate target results in price indeterminacy. It can, however, be used as an op-

regarding the various shocks, and hence are not in a position to target the price level directly.) In the case of a money base target, the steady-state values for p and e are given by (8.7);[9] with an exchange rate target, the steady state equations for p and m are given by (8.8):

$$\begin{bmatrix} p \\ e \end{bmatrix} = \begin{bmatrix} -1 & 0 & \lambda \\ -1 & -1/\delta & (\gamma + \lambda\delta)/\delta \end{bmatrix} \begin{bmatrix} z1 \\ z2 \\ z3 \end{bmatrix}, \tag{8.7}$$

$$\begin{bmatrix} p \\ m \end{bmatrix} = \begin{bmatrix} 0 & -1/\delta & -\gamma/\delta \\ 1 & 1/\delta & -(\gamma + \lambda\delta)/\delta \end{bmatrix} \begin{bmatrix} z1 \\ z2 \\ z3 \end{bmatrix}. \tag{8.8}$$

Denote the steady-state variance of p under an exchange rate target and a money target as σ_{pe}^2 and σ_{pm}^2, respectively, and the variance of shock zi by σ_{zi}^2. Assuming that the shocks are uncorrelated, equations (8.7) and (8.8) then imply

$$\sigma_{pe}^2 = \sigma_{z1}^2 + \lambda^2\sigma_{z3}^2 , \tag{8.9a}$$

$$\sigma_{pm}^2 = (1/\delta)^2\sigma_{z2}^2 + (\lambda/\delta)^2\sigma_{z3}^2 . \tag{8.9b}$$

Given an objective of minimizing the variance of the steady-state price level, the choice between a pure exchange rate target and a pure money base target will be determined by the relevant parameters and variances of the shocks appearing in (8.9). Leaving aside the interest rate shock, an exchange rate target will generally be preferable when nominal ($z1$) shocks predominate, while a money base target will be preferable when real ($z2$) shocks predominate. The reason for the former is that under an exchange rate target, the money supply is allowed to accommodate a change in money demand, so leaving the price level unaffected by such a shock, whereas the price level must adjust in these circumstances with a money supply target. The reason for the latter result is that the nominal exchange rate is free to vary to offset the effect of a real shock under a money base target, whereas the price level must adjust to enable the required real exchange rate change under a nominal exchange rate target. Neither regime stabilizes the price level in response to interest rate shocks, and indeed the price level moves in opposite directions in response to this shock under the two regimes.

erating target that responds to movements in some nominal variable (the price level, the money base, or the exchange rate).

[9] The dynamic paths of p and e in this case, and of p and m in the case of an exchange rate target, are detailed in Grimes (1989), together with a fuller discussion of the effects of the various shocks under the alternative regimes. Glick and Hutchison (1989) use a similar model to address these and related issues.

In the presence of a range of shocks, it is clear that neither a pure exchange rate target nor a pure money target (i.e., a pure float) will be optimal (Glick and Hutchison, 1989). Instead, the optimal regime will generally be characterized by a convex combination of the two rules, with the weights being chosen so as to minimize the variance of the price level. For instance, in circumstances where the variance of nominal shocks is high but there is also some exposure to real shocks, the optimal policy will be to place a large weight on targeting the exchange rate but with some exchange rate flexibility driven by developments in the monetary aggregates. Accordingly, the choice of optimal monetary and exchange rate regime is primarily an empirical matter depending on the structure of the economy, including the nature of shocks.

8.4   Empirical evidence

Since the choice of optimal regime is ultimately an empirical matter, we undertake a number of tests to ascertain whether an exchange rate or a monetary aggregate target would have delivered the better inflation performance historically in New Zealand.[10] We also examine whether some combination of the approaches would have yielded a superior performance than either of the two pure approaches.

The first test aims to assess which of the two approaches would have been the more effective guide for achieving price stability in the long run. The theoretical framework of the preceding section was presented in terms of a noninflationary international environment. Hence, the two natural rules to adopt in targeting price stability are maintaining a fixed money base and a fixed exchange rate. It is simple to reinterpret the model variables as representing deviations from trend rates of growth and the shocks as representing level shifts from these trend rates of growth. In this case the corollary of the previous simple rules are ones based on purchasing power parity (PPP) and on a simple specification of money demand, such as the quantity theory of money. In the former case, the exchange rate is targeted to appreciate at a rate equal to the forecast foreign inflation rate in order to deliver price stability. In the latter case, the money supply is targeted to increase at a rate equal to the growth rate of real output.

The empirical analysis of the long-run relationship is based on co-

---

[10] Without conducting formal tests of this issue, it is difficult to judge the superiority of the alternative targets, since New Zealand has been subject to both major real shocks (particularly via the terms of trade) and major nominal shocks (particularly after financial liberalization).

integration methodology (Engle and Granger, 1987). The variables under consideration are tested for their order of integration using the tests of Perron (1988) and Phillips and Perron (1988). We then analyze long-run relationships among the variables of interest and test for co-integration using the Phillips $Z(t)$ test.[11]

For policy purposes, it is also important to assess the usefulness of alternative targets as guides for short-run price developments, since monetary policy attempts to keep inflation within the 0 to 2 percent target at all times (excluding periods corresponding to the types of shocks indicated in note 2). Our second set of empirical tests therefore aims to assess the comparative merits of each approach, and of a combination of approaches, in the short run.

Seasonally unadjusted quarterly data are used for the empirical study. The sample period chosen is June 1963 to March 1991.[12] All variables used in the study are expressed as logarithms, and all are found to be nonstationary $[I(1)]$.[13] The variables are as described in Section 8.2, with the addition of

PC   =   New Zealand consumer price index,
PCE =   PC adjusted for the effect of GST,
PW   =   trade-weighted "world" consumer price index,
M3   =   nominal M3 monetary aggregate,
QX   =   real GDP.

8.4.1   Long-run evidence

Our long-run test is based on a comparison of two simple models. The first is a PPP relationship (Model A) in which the domestic price level (PCE) is explained by the "world" CPI, adjusted for the exchange rate. The second model is a money demand function based on the quantity theory of money (Model B). Figure 8.2 graphs the domestic price level (PCE) relative to the influences of the two competing models, (PW − TWI) in the case of Model A, and (M3 − QX) in the case of Model B (the latter variable is deseasonalized in Figure 8.2). Both tracked PCE fairly closely over the twenty-eight-year period, albeit with significant periods of one-sided deviations in both cases.

Because of these deviations, co-integration among the variables in the very simple framework of Model A would not be found. Previous studies have shown that New Zealand's equilibrium real exchange rate

[11] See Phillips and Ouliaris (1990).
[12] The source of the data is the Reserve Bank of New Zealand database.
[13] Further details are available in Grimes and Wong (1992).

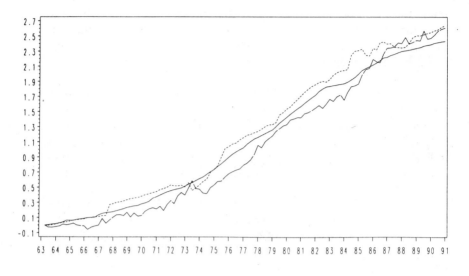

March Years

Figure 8.2. Long-run price and monetary trends. PCE, ——; PW–TWI, ---;
M3–QX, – –.

is influenced by the terms of trade, which is a nonstationary variable.
Hence, its omission is likely to have contributed to the rejection of the
pure PPP model. In order to account for this, we also include in the
model a proxy for the terms of trade – the difference between the (logs
of) export prices and world consumer prices, denominated in New Zealand dollars.[14] As expected, the introduction of GST, proxied by the
inclusion of PC − PCE, was found to have no significant effect within
this model.

Given the evidence of previous New Zealand studies (summarized
in Wong and Grimes, 1991), a broad monetary aggregate, M3, was
chosen for the analysis in Model B, since this has been the only monetary
aggregate to yield consistent co-integration results for the type of model
examined here. No interest rate term is included (or required) in the
quantity theory relationship since almost all of M3 bears a market interest rate that varies along with movements in competing interest rates.
We do, however, include a dummy variable taking the value of zero
until 1984 second quarter and unity thereafter to proxy for a step shift
in money demand consequent on the extensive financial sector dere-

---

[14] This proxy for the terms of trade performs better than the standard measure of the
terms of trade – the difference between export and import prices.

gulation that began in July 1984. The use of this variable is in keeping with its use by Orden and Fisher (1993). We include seasonal dummies in Model B because of the seasonal nature of both the M3 and QX variables. Further, since the relevant price variable in the quantity theory model is PC rather than PCE, we include (PC − PCE) as an independent variable with coefficient restricted to −1. (As expected, the inclusion of this variable improves the equation's performance.)[15] For the sake of exposition, in what follows we suppress further mention of these dummy variables.

The two models, each embodying restrictions implied by theory,[16] are given as

$$PCE = \alpha_0 + \alpha_1(PW - TWI) + \alpha_2(PXG - PW \qquad (A)$$
$$+ TWI) + \epsilon_A, \quad \text{with restriction } \alpha_1 = 1,$$

$$PCE = \beta_0 + \beta_1 M3 + \beta_2 QX + \epsilon_B, \qquad (B)$$
$$\text{with restrictions } \beta_1 = 1, \beta_2 = -1.$$

Since all variables in the models are $I(1)$, it is straightforward to apply co-integration methodology. Ordinary least squares (OLS) is applied to the models, and the residuals from these two regressions are each tested for a unit root. Models A and B represent co-integrating relationships if and only if the residuals of the OLS regressions, $\hat{\epsilon}_A$ and $\hat{\epsilon}_B$, respectively, are found to be stationary. In Model A, if the OLS residuals are stationary, then PPP, modified for the effect of terms of trade, can be said to hold. In Model B, if the OLS residuals are stationary, then the quantity theory of money, modified for the impact of financial deregulation, is statistically valid. The co-integration results are:

Model A: $\alpha_2 = 0.39,$
$$Z(t) = -3.53 \text{ (critical value} = -3.37 \text{ [5 percent])},$$

Model B: $Z(t) = -5.83 \text{ (critical value} = -3.37 \text{ [5 percent])}.$

The results imply that in the long run the modified versions of both PPP and the quantity theory are valid at the 5 percent level.[17] These two

[15] Because the PCE and (PW − TWI) series both appeared to contain a drift component, initially a time trend was included in both models. However, it was later dropped because it did not have a significant effect on the results. Indeed, its unrestricted inclusion led to the rejection of co-integration in the two models.

[16] Model B was also estimated without the second restriction, $\beta_2 = -1$, since not all money demand theories require this restriction. However, since the restriction was easily upheld, it was retained.

[17] When only the nominal homogeneity restriction is imposed in Model B, the estimate for β_2 is -0.65 with $Z(t) = -5.97$. When Model B (with restrictions) is estimated

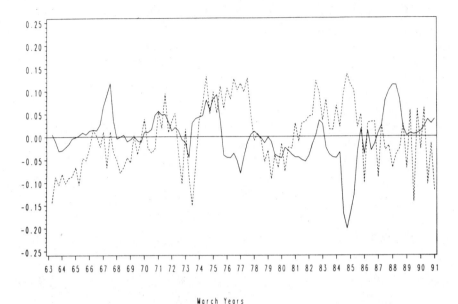

Figure 8.3. Co-integrating residuals. Model A, ———; Model B, ---.

simple models reveal that, potentially, exchange rate targeting and monetary aggregate targeting could each be used to achieve a stable price level in the long run. Shocks, apart from terms-of-trade and financial deregulation shocks, have in each case been transitory.

Figure 8.3 plots the residuals from both models. At times the residuals from the two models behave quite differently. This is consistent with the theoretical framework, which demonstrates the superiority of the alternative targets under different types of shocks. For instance, in late 1984 the actual price level was considerably below the estimated equilibrium price level from Model A (following an exchange rate devaluation in July 1984), but was considerably above the estimated equilibrium price level from Model B. Thus, a focus on the exchange rate at that time (through the PPP model) would have implied the danger of an ensuing burst of inflation, whereas a focus on M3 (through the quantity theory model) would have implied the danger of an ensuing deflation. (In fact, as revealed in Figure 8.1, a strong inflation did ensue, in keeping with the indicated response from Model A.) While the shocks

without the financial deregulation dummy variable, the $Z(t)$ statistic is -2.93. When Model A (with restriction) is estimated without the terms-of-trade variable, the $Z(t)$ statistic is -2.39.

Table 8.1. *Model A VECM significance levels*

	ZA_{-1}	$\Sigma \Delta PCE$	$\Sigma \Delta PW$	$\Sigma \Delta TWI$	$\Sigma \Delta PXG$	$\bar{R}^2$
ΔPCE	.00	.00	.00	.02	.21	.68
ΔPW	.32	.92	.00	.87	.41	.38
ΔTWI	.56	.46	.03	.29	.08	.20
ΔPXG	.14	.32	.15	.33	.00	.30

Table 8.2. *Model B VECM significance levels*

	ZB_{-1}	$\Sigma \Delta PCE$	$\Sigma \Delta M3$	$\Sigma \Delta QX$	$\bar{R}^2$
ΔPCE	.55	.00	.40	.77	.55
$\Delta M3$	.00	.23	.00	.07	.88
ΔQX	.01	.98	.14	.02	.74

exhibited in the residuals have been transitory, and so have not affected the long-run relationships, the differing nature of the shocks implies that it is important for policy purposes to analyze the short-run predictive power of the two models.

8.4.2 *Short-run evidence*

In order to examine the capacity of the two models to predict short-run inflation trends, we estimate a vector error correction model (VECM) for each system. Within each system, there will exist an ECM by Granger's representation theorem[18] – that is, each system will include at least one equation with an error correction term, being the lagged residual from the relevant co-integrating vector. For each system, a VECM containing the relevant error correction term and a lag structure of four quarters of all variables in that system is estimated.

Tables 8.1 and 8.2 present the results of the two VECMs in terms of the significance levels of the variables. ZA and ZB are the lagged residuals from the co-integrating vectors in Models A and B respectively, while the remaining terms represent the sum of the four lags on the relevant variables.

In the Model A VECM, the error correction term from the PPP equation enters significantly into the PCE equation, indicating that a

[18] Engle and Granger (1987).

Table 8.3. *Encompassing VECM significance levels*

	ZA_{-1}	ZB_{-1}	$\Sigma \Delta PW$	$\Sigma \Delta TWI$	$\Sigma \Delta QX$	$\bar{R}^2$
ΔPCE	.01		.00			.68
ΔPW						.36
ΔTWI			.03			.16
ΔPXG	.02		.04			.32
$\Delta M3$	.04	.00	.08	.07	.08	.89
ΔQX	.03	.04				.75

Note: Only variables significant at 10% (excluding own lags) are reported.

deviation from PPP causes a domestic inflation response. The domestic inflation rate is also affected significantly by changes in world prices and the exchange rate. Not surprisingly, there is little evidence that domestic variables cause changes in world prices, export prices, or the exchange rate.

In the case of Model B, the error correction term does not have a significant influence on PCE. Instead, a disequilibrium from the quantity equation causes adjustments in the growth rates of M3 and GDP. Indeed, inflation is not explained significantly by any of the variables in the system (except by its own lags), and the explanatory power of this equation is considerably below that of the PCE equation in the PPP VECM. Thus, for the period being considered, it appears that inflation has been affected predominantly by international factors adjusted for the exchange rate and that M3 has adjusted endogenously to changes in the domestic price level.

We can compare the two models of inflation more formally in two ways. First, we conduct a non-nested test of the PCE equations from the two models using the Davidson–MacKinnon *J*-test. Using this test, we can reject (at the 1 percent level) the null hypothesis that the quantity theory model is the appropriate specification by the alternative hypothesis that the PPP model is the correct specification. But we cannot reject (at the 5 percent level) the null hypothesis that the PPP model is the correct specification by the alternative that the quantity theory explanation holds. Thus, the Davidson–MacKinnon test unambiguously favors the PPP model.

The second test is to estimate an encompassing VECM including all variables in the two models. Table 8.3 reports the variables in this model that are significant at less than the 10 percent level with their associated significance levels. (Own lags are excluded for reporting purposes; PCE,

Table 8.4. *Parsimonious ECM*

Explanatory variable	Coefficient	t-value	Significance level
Intercept	0.0039	2.26	.0257
ZA_{-1}	-0.06	4.04	.0001
ΔPCE_{-1}	0.55	8.50	.0001
ΔPW	0.30	4.13	.0001
ΔTWI	-0.05	2.47	.0153
$\Delta M3_{-4}$	0.03	2.15	.0337

Diagnostics (significance levels in brackets)

LM test for autocorrelation   Jarque-Bera test for normality
  $LM(1) = 1.70\ (.19)$ $\chi^2(2) = 8.07\ (.02)$
  $LM(4) = 3.41\ (.49)$ White test for heteroskedasticity
ARCH test for heteroskedasticity $White(21) = 12.5\ (.93)$
  $ARCH(1) = 0.12\ (.73)$
  $ARCH(4) = 2.36\ (.67)$

Note: Dependent variable is ΔPCE. Sample: 1963:2–1991:1; $\overline{R}^2 = .65$; DW = 2.213; $h = 1.55$.

PXG, and M3 do not appear as explanatory variables in the table, since they are not significant at the 10 percent level in any of the equations, although all equations are estimated with these variables included.)

The results are generally in keeping with the results of the previous VECMs and with the Davidson–MacKinnon test. Domestic inflation is influenced significantly only by the PPP error correction term and by world prices; the explanatory power is the same as in the PPP VECM. M3 and QX are each influenced by both error correction terms. Also of interest is the recursive structure revealed in the model. No variable that appears in the PPP model is influenced significantly by any of the variables that appear in the quantity theory model, whereas some of the PPP variables significantly influence the quantity theory variables.

Not surprisingly, the encompassing model again reveals that the dominant influence on inflation in New Zealand has come from the exchange rate and international price variables. But this system contains a large number of variables that could potentially hide some relationships. In order to check whether this is the case, we estimate a parsimonious version of the encompassing PCE equation, retaining just those variables that are significant at the 10 percent level.

The resulting equation is presented in Table 8.4, together with diagnostic statistics. Again, the PPP error correction term is significant, while the error correction term from the quantity theory equation is not. The relatively small adjustment coefficient on the PPP error correction term implies fairly slow adjustment of domestic prices to their equilibrium level following a shock, although the adjustment dynamics are supplemented by the inclusion of the lagged inflation rate and of current changes in the exchange rate and world prices. The relatively slow adjustment is consistent with findings of long-term deviations from PPP in many countries. Contrary to the previous results, however, there is some indication of an effect of monetary growth on inflation, with the four-quarter lagged change in M3 being significant. But it has only a small elasticity of 0.03, so the PPP variables remain the major explanatory variables for inflation.

The diagnostic statistics of the equation are generally favorable, although the residuals from the short-run ECM are seen to be non-normal (possibly as a result of one outlier).[19] A CUSUM plot is well within the bounds throughout the sample period,[20] and a Chow test for structural stability at the time of the floating of the exchange rate (March 1985) suggests no sign of parameter instability.

This body of results is, of course, sample specific and may reflect no more than the monetary regime in place over the estimation period. In order to check how robust the results are over different regimes, we reestimate the four price equations presented here over the fixed exchange rate period of 1963(2) to 1985(1). We then generate a dynamic forecast until 1991(1) for each equation, given the actual values of the other explanatory variables. We examine the root mean squared error (RMSE) and the mean error (ME) for each of the four equations over the full forecast period and over the two subperiods, 1985:2–1988:2 and 1988:3–1991:1; these two subperiods correspond to the second and third regimes discussed in Section 8.2. The results of the first subperiod are particularly important given that this was a period when the (floating) exchange rate was not being used as a major indicator for monetary policy. The RMSE and ME of the four equations over these periods are reported in Table 8.5.

In each of the subperiods, the pure PPP model is preferred to the quantity theory model according to both criteria, although it is interesting that the PPP model underpredicts inflation in each subperiod,

---

[19] Including a single dummy variable at the sample point associated with the largest residual of the ECM (March 1967) results in a Jarque-Bera normality test statistic of 1.77 (sig. = 0.49). All other diagnostic tests are also passed at the 10% level. Moreover, the intercept term is no longer significant at the 5% level once this dummy variable is included.

[20] Reported in Grimes and Wong (1992).

Table 8.5. *Forecasting performance*

Sample	Statistic	Model A	Model B	Encompassing	Parsimonious
1985:2–91:1	ME	.0054	− .0083	.0002	.0021
	RMSE	.0091	.0137	.0105	.0076
1985:2–88:2	ME	.0089	− .0126	.0002	.0035
	RMSE	.0114	.0163	.0108	.0095
1988:3–91:1	ME	.0013	− .0032	.0002	.0004
	RMSE	.0052	.0097	.0101	.0047

Note: ME denotes mean error; RMSE denotes root mean square error.

while the quantity theory model overpredicts inflation in both cases. As a result, and in accordance with the theoretical discussion, the two combined models perform the best. The encompassing model has the lowest ME in both subperiods, while the parsimonious model has the lowest RMSE in each. These two models are dominated by PPP influences but also allow for some influence of monetary aggregates on inflation.

8.5   Assessment

Theory indicates that a monetary policy aimed at achieving price stability should generally adopt neither a pure exchange rate nor a pure monetary aggregate target. Instead, some combination of the two approaches will generally be optimal, with the weighting on each approach being determined empirically according to the nature of the economy. Our empirical work supports this finding. The two pure approaches are dominated by combined approaches in explaining inflation across a range of historical regimes in New Zealand. But the empirical work also indicates that the exchange rate (within a PPP context) has been a substantially better guide for monetary policy than the monetary aggregate (within a quantity theory framework). Hence, for New Zealand, any combined approach should weight the exchange rate considerably more heavily than monetary aggregates in guiding monetary policy.

These findings mirror current policy practice in New Zealand. Policy is aimed explicitly at the objective of maintaining price stability, and no formal intermediate targets are adopted. The exchange rate is used, however, as a calibration device to determine appropriate monetary settings (the level of bank reserves) to deliver the inflation target given other forecast inflation influences. The process of forecasting other inflation influences means that the influence of monetary aggregates on inflation can be taken into account through channels such as the impact of monetary growth on house prices.

The process also forces an explicit assessment to be made of real developments that (under an exchange rate target) would have an impact on the price level and hence, temporarily, on measured inflation. For instance, changes in labor practices in 1990 and 1992 led to downward revisions in forecast real wage growth and hence, given other short-run inflationary influences, to temporary downward shifts in forecast inflation. As a result, the range for the exchange rate that was consistent with the inflation target was also revised downward on these occasions. This example demonstrates that while the exchange rate is used as a guide for monetary policy, there is no formal exchange rate intermediate target. One can characterize this framework as being equivalent to the combined approach analyzed earlier in this essay.

The key challenge for this approach is the necessity to forecast both other inflationary influences and the impact of exchange rate changes on inflation. It will be the success of this process that will determine the ability of monetary policy to keep inflation within the 0 to 2 percent target range.

References

Brooks, R., and D. T. Gibbs (1991). "The Reserve Bank Econometric Model of the New Zealand Economy: Model XII," Reserve Bank of New Zealand Research Paper no. 42. Wellington.

Dornbusch, R. (1976). "Expectations and Exchange Rate Dynamics," *Journal of Political Economy* 84:1161–76.

Engle, R. F., and C. W. J. Granger (1987). "Cointegration and Error Correction: Representation, Estimation and Testing," *Econometrica* 55:251–76.

Glick, R., and M. Hutchison (1989). "Exchange Rates and Monetary Policy," (Federal Reserve Bank of San Francisco) *Economic Review* (Spring):17–29.

Grimes, A. (1989). "The Choice of Intermediate and Operating Targets for Monetary Policy," Reserve Bank of New Zealand Discussion Paper G89/3. Wellington.

Grimes, A., and J. Wong (1992). "The Role of Monetary Aggregates and the Exchange Rate in Monetary Policy," Reserve Bank of New Zealand Working Paper W92/4. Wellington.

Orden, D., and L. A. Fisher (1993). "Financial Deregulation and the Dynamics of Money, Prices and Output in New Zealand and Australia," *Journal of Money, Credit and Banking,* 25:273–92.

Perron, P. (1988). "Trends and Random Walks in Macroeconomic Time Series: Further Evidence from a New Approach," *Journal of Economic Dynamics and Control* 12:297–332.

Phillips, P. C. B., and S. Ouliaris (1990). "Asymptotic Properties of Residual Based Tests for Cointegration," *Econometrica* 58:165–93.
Phillips, P. C. B., and P. Perron (1988). "Testing for a Unit Root in Time Series Regression," *Biometrika* 75:335–46.
Reserve Bank of New Zealand (1986). *Financial Policy Reform.* Wellington.
Reserve Bank of New Zealand (1992). *Monetary Policy and the New Zealand Financial System,* 3d ed. Wellington.
Wong, A., and A. Grimes (1991). "The New Zealand Monetary Aggregates," (Reserve Bank of New Zealand) *Bulletin* 54:330–40. Reprinted in *Monetary Policy and the New Zealand Financial System,* 3d ed., Reserve Bank of New Zealand, Wellington, 1992.

CHAPTER 9

Officially floating, implicitly targeted exchange rates: examples from the Pacific Basin

Helen Popper and Julia Lowell

9.1 Introduction

According to the International Monetary Fund (IMF), as of December 1991, only 29 of its 156 members had exchange rate arrangements that could be described as "independently floating." Forty-two member countries had arrangements described as "managed floats," "adjusted according to a set of indicators," or "cooperative arrangements."[1] More than one-half of the IMF membership had either official pegs to a single currency or currency basket, or arrangements that were described as "flexibility limited vis-à-vis a single currency." While the collapse of Bretton Woods meant the end of that particular fixed rate system, almost twenty years later a majority of countries still choose to impose some sort of constraint on the free movement of the value of their currencies.

Even those countries that claim to adhere to an independently floating exchange rate regime typically manage their exchange rates to some extent. Most central banks have policies of intervening to stabilize the prices of their currencies when the foreign exchange markets become "disorderly," as, for example, after the U.S. stock market crash in October 1987. In addition, some central banks with an official policy of freely floating rates also have implicit exchange rate targets that affect the conduct of monetary policy.[2] Sometimes these targets are part of

We are grateful for helpful discussions with Bruce Kasman, Mike Leahy, John Morton, and especially Michael Hutchison. All errors are, of course, our own. Financial support was provided through the Presidential Research Grant awarded by Santa Clara University.
[1] This description refers to those currencies that make up the European Monetary System.
[2] Theoretically, exchange rate targets may affect fiscal policy as well as monetary policy. In fact, the frequent call for a reduction in U.S. budget deficits by its trading partners may be interpreted as a call for the United States to use contractionary fiscal policy to put downward pressure on the dollar. We restrict our discussion to monetary policy

198

international agreements, such as the Plaza Agreement of 1985 and the Louvre Accord of 1987. Both agreements stressed that "exchange rates should better reflect fundamental economic conditions," and the Louvre Accord actually proposed specific targets for the dollar, mark, and yen exchange rates.[3]

What makes one country's monetary authority more likely to actively pursue an exchange rate target than another? Economists have suggested that the optimal choice of exchange rate regime depends on the structure of the economy in question. The openness of the economy's goods and capital markets, the level of wage indexation, the nature and pattern of disturbances, and the capacity of domestic markets to absorb those disturbances are all factors in determining the best exchange regime for a particular country. Most important are national priorities regarding output fluctuations, domestic price stability, and the stability of the terms of trade.

In this essay we explore to what extent (if at all) the governments of four Pacific Basin countries have implicitly targeted their exchange rates. We consider the exchange rate policies of Australia, Canada, Japan, and the United States.[4] All four of these countries are developed and have relatively open capital markets, and all four officially describe their exchange rate regimes as floating. The countries differ in terms of their size and their major exports. Australia and Canada have small economies relative to the other two and are primarily commodity producers, while Japan produces mostly manufactured goods, and the United States is an important producer of both types of goods. Because of their size and their greater reliance on commodity exports, we might expect the governments of Australia and Canada to be more apt to control exchange rate movements than the governments of Japan and the United States.[5]

Simple correlations among key economic variables across countries

---

both because it is the operating method for exchange rate intervention and because institutional factors generally make fiscal policy an awkward instrument for influencing exchange rate movements.

[3] See Obstfeld (1990) and Funabashi (1988).

[4] Unfortunately, a lack of data prevented us in this study from including New Zealand, the only other Pacific Rim country with an official policy of floating exchange rates and with relatively open capital markets. See Grimes and Wong (Chapter 8, this volume).

[5] The optimal degree of exchange rate management for commodity exporters depends on the objectives of policymakers. Blundell-Wignall and Gregory (1990) argue that a flexible exchange rate regime is preferable when the object of policy is to stabilize the price of nontradable goods, and Carmichael (1990) points out that active exchange rate management is desirable if the objective is to stabilize a broader measure of prices, such as a consumer price index.

may give some indication of the extent of exchange rate management. For example, consider the correlations between the interest rates and prices of the United States and those of Australia, Canada, and Japan.[6] The Canadian correlations with U.S. variables were about 0.7 to 0.9, while the Japanese correlations were somewhat lower, about 0.5 to 0.6, and the Australian correlations were much lower, about 0.2 to 0.4. These correlations might be interpreted as evidence that Canada follows U.S. monetary policy most assiduously, but that Japan, not Australia, is next in line. However, while the correlations are interesting and could suggest an ordering of exchange rate targeting, they may simply indicate common shocks rather than monetary policy synchronization.

In this essay, we examine two forms of exchange rate targeting. First, we examine foreign exchange market intervention by the central banks of the four countries. This measures the degree to which exchange market pressure in each country is absorbed by the exchange rate as opposed to being absorbed by movements in official foreign reserves. Next, since exchange rates may be targeted using domestic instruments, we examine the extent to which monetary policy in general is formed on the basis of exchange rate concerns. We do this by modeling the objective function of a central bank in the context of a small open economy. Finally, we draw some tentative conclusions regarding the extent of exchange rate targeting in the four countries.

9.2   A cross-country comparison of foreign exchange market intervention

According to monetary models of exchange rate determination, a bilateral exchange rate is simply the relative price of two currencies. In order to fix this price, the central bank must be able to influence the relative supplies of the two currencies concerned. For example, suppose that the demand for the domestic currency in the foreign exchange market declines. To resist a depreciation of the exchange rate, the central bank may take one of three actions: first, it may increase the supply of foreign currency to the market, without affecting the supply of domestic currency; second, it may both increase the supply of foreign currency and decrease the supply of domestic currency; or, third, it may reduce the supply of the domestic currency. The first two options, ster-

---

[6] These bilateral correlations suggest the degree to which Australia, Canada, and Japan may have tied their monetary policies to that of the United States. Since such correlations are not the focus of this essay, we do not extend the analysis to multilateral correlations here. Prices and interest rates used in calculating the correlations are described in the appendix.

ilized and unsterilized foreign exchange market intervention, require that the monetary authority hold foreign exchange reserves.

Theoretically, under a regime of pure floating, the central bank can reduce its official net foreign asset position to zero. Any intergovernmental transfer of funds across borders (such as foreign aid provided in the case of a war or natural disaster) simply requires conversion to the currency of the receiving country through transactions in the private foreign exchange market. Neither government needs to hold the currency of its counterpart to the transaction. Similarly, governments' foreign purchases that require conversion into the currency of invoicing can also be accommodated in the private market. In this idealized world, all foreign exchange transactions take place in private markets, and both net foreign asset holdings and official intervention are zero.[7]

In practice, all governments keep at least some minimum level of official reserves and many governments actively intervene in the foreign exchange markets.[8] Even those countries that classify their systems as floating rate regimes do not relinquish the ability to intervene in disorderly markets, and some reserve growth is desired simply to keep pace with the size of the market. However, abnormal changes in reserves should be considered active intervention with the intent to manage exchange rates.[9] To operationalize the term "abnormal" and to facilitate comparisons across countries, in the discussion to follow we deflate each central bank's net foreign asset position by its monetary base.[10]

The four countries' normalized official foreign reserves at the end of

---

[7] We use the terms "net foreign assets" and "foreign reserves" interchangeably in this essay, and we define them to be the net foreign assets on the balance sheet of the central bank and other government authorities responsible for exchange rate management.

[8] Funabashi (1988) vividly describes the evolution of exchange rate management in Japan and the United States during the 1980s. A more general description of the G-7 coordination process, including activist exchange rate policies on the part of Canada, Japan, and the United States, is given by Dobson (1991). A discussion of Australian exchange rate management is found in Blundell-Wignall and Gregory (1990). In addition, exchange market intervention is discussed in this volume by Glick and Hutchison (Chapter 10) and by Watanabe (Chapter 11) for Japan and by Pitchford (Chapter 7) for Australia.

[9] In their discussion of the proper measurement of official exchange intervention, Adams and Henderson (1983) argue convincingly that exchange transactions between private agents and a central bank – whether the bank acts on its own account or on behalf of the Treasury or Ministry of Finance – should be included in comprehensive measures of intervention. Similarly, interest payments on foreign reserves that are kept as additions to reserves should also be considered intervention. These types of intervention are captured by the measures of net foreign assets used later.

[10] Strictly speaking, intervention to achieve the stabilization of disorderly markets is as much exchange rate management as is intervention to achieve an exchange rate tar-

each quarter from 1974 through 1991 are presented in Figure 9.1. The pattern of foreign reserve holdings relative to the monetary base differs both across countries and over time. For instance, Australian net foreign assets were never less than 30 percent of base money and in the late 1980s reached well over 100 percent; its foreign reserves increased rapidly before the Australian dollar was allowed to float in December 1983, and remained high thereafter. Canadian net foreign assets grew more slowly than the monetary base until 1986, when reserves rose abruptly, nearly doubling their earlier levels. The Japanese pattern consists of two large bumps, one between 1977 and 1979 and another between 1987 and 1989. U.S. foreign reserves were the lowest of the four countries, at no point rising above 30 percent of the monetary base. Still, like Canada and Australia, U.S. reserves also ratcheted up over the period, taking one large step in 1980 and another at the end of 1988.

Periods of significant intervention are more apparent when *changes* in normalized foreign reserve holdings are considered.[11] By this measure, Australia has intervened the most of the four countries; quarterly changes in net foreign assets reach as much as 35 percent of the monetary base. U.S. intervention has been smallest; its maximum intervention, in mid-1989, did not quite reach 4 percent of the U.S. monetary base. On average, all four countries increased their normalized net foreign assets from 1974 to 1991, suggesting that they were more concerned with resisting domestic currency appreciation than with defending against depreciation.[12]

Since countries that officially subscribe to floating rate regimes do not explicitly target particular bilateral exchange rates or exchange rate baskets, the exact goal of intervention is typically unclear. In fact, it is likely that the authorities have different objectives at different times. However, since the U.S. dollar is an official currency of intervention for most countries and is a key currency for Australia, Canada, and Japan, in particular, one obvious candidate for targeting by these coun-

---

get. Some "abnormal" intervention may be undertaken precisely with the intent to stabilize markets, and we interpret this as exchange rate management.

The intervention patterns described later are similar when net foreign assets are not deflated by the monetary base.

[11] Specifically, intervention is defined to be the change in foreign reserve holdings over the quarter as a fraction of the monetary base at the end of the previous quarter.

[12] There may be an upward bias to this measure of intervention: governments may wish to hold reserves as a precaution in the event that they have to enter into the foreign exchange market to support their currencies, yet the incentive for reducing their holdings is not symmetric since they use their own currency should they wish to do the opposite.

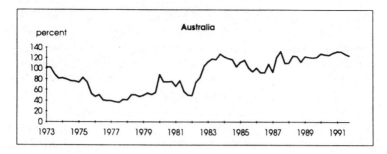

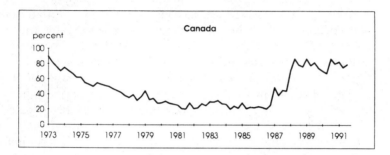

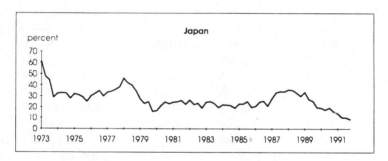

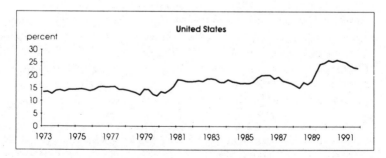

Figure 9.1. Official net foreign assets as percentage of monetary base.

tries is their respective bilateral exchange rate against the U.S. dollar.[13] For the United States, however, possible targets of exchange rate management are less obvious. In this section we consider the target of U.S. policy to be the price of U.S. dollars in terms of special drawing rights (SDRs).

The combination of normalized intervention plus exchange rate movements provides a measure of the exchange market pressure facing a particular currency.[14] While the magnitude of exchange market pressure will naturally differ across currencies and across periods, the composition of exchange market pressure, that is, changes in foreign reserves as opposed to changes in the exchange rate, is an important indicator of the degree to which the authorities target exchange rates using foreign reserves. The larger the component represented by intervention, the farther away from a true float. One measure of the composition is given by the ratio of normalized intervention to currency appreciation, shown in Figure 9.2.[15] Positive values of the ratio represent periods when official intervention was used to counteract undesirable exchange rate movements; negative values imply that the intervention and the exchange rate were both pushing in the same direction. Spikes indicate that large changes in official reserves were not accompanied by comparable changes in exchange rates, while values close to zero indicate minimal foreign reserve movements and/or very large exchange rate changes.

All four countries are characterized by a few large spikes that dominate smaller fluctuations. However, it is difficult to associate these spikes with known (or at least presumed) instances of exchange market intervention. For example, there are large spikes in the Australian, Japanese, and U.S. measures in 1987, but all are too early to reflect the U.S. stock market crash in October of that year, which put strong downward pressure on the foreign currency value of the U.S. dollar. In the fourth quarter of 1987, the U.S. dollar depreciated sharply against the yen, and to a lesser extent against the Canadian dollar. Both the Bank of Canada and the Bank of Japan also intervened quite heavily over the quarter. Another large spike in the U.S. intervention–appreciation ratio occurred in the fourth quarter of 1979. Largely reflecting the marked contraction in the U.S. monetary base of that quarter, the spike may also reflect a change in the Federal Reserve's views about the importance of holding foreign reserves. In particular, it may reflect

[13] While the United States is a primary trading partner for each of the three countries, it is somewhat less important for Australia than for the other two.
[14] Girton and Roper (1977) provide an explicit model of exchange market pressure.
[15] Appreciation is measured as the annualized rate of change in the exchange rate over its level at the end of the preceding quarter.

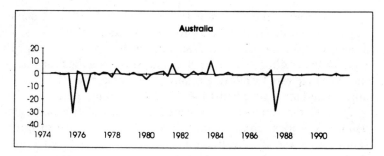

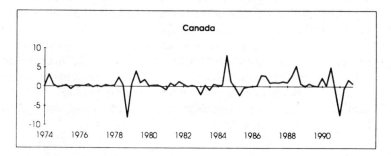

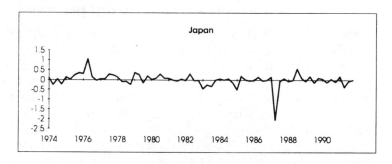

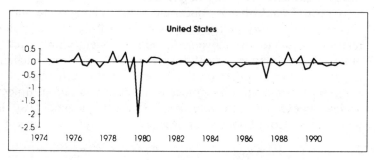

Figure 9.2. Official normalized intervention as ratio to currency appreciation.

a recognition of the potential for political difficulties associated with relying on swap arrangements for intervention. While it is generally argued that the monetary contraction was designed to manage the U.S. inflation rate rather than the U.S. dollar, shrinking the base does support the exchange rate by altering relative money supplies.[16] The U.S. dollar appreciated strongly against the SDR in the same period.

Despite the difficulties associated with identifying particular intervention episodes, cross-country differences in the use of intervention stand out. Over all, Australia and Canada appear to have intervened in the foreign exchange markets to a much greater extent than either Japan or the United States. In particular, Australia's maximum intervention was 33 percent of its monetary base. For Canada the maximum was 20 percent, for Japan 10 percent, and for the United States only 4 percent. The average flows tell the same story: the average absolute value of normalized Australian intervention, 7.6 percent of the monetary base, is ten times as large as the corresponding values for U.S. intervention, three times as large as Japanese intervention, and almost twice as large as Canadian intervention.

9.3   A model of domestic prices with exchange rate targeting

While changes in foreign reserves give an indication of the extent to which exchange rate pressure is allowed to affect exchange rates, they do not show how the central bank uses other instruments to prevent the pressure in the first place. When exchange rate targeting occurs through the use of domestic instruments, it may never show itself through changes in reserves. Therefore, to assess the extent of exchange rate targeting, it is necessary to examine the use of monetary policy in affecting exchange rates. This section considers the targeting of exchange rates using monetary policy in any form.

A central bank that is concerned with exchange rate stability will choose its monetary policy at least partly in response to potential or realized exchange rate movements. Since monetary policy also affects other macroeconomic variables, utilizing it to reach an exchange rate target will have an effect on those variables. In particular, the central bank must compromise its domestic inflation and output objectives to achieve an exchange rate objective. Using a simple model, we illustrate that the behavior of domestic prices, especially their observed response

---

[16] Targeting the exchange rate through domestic instruments will be discussed in the next section.

to exchange rate movements, ultimately depends on the extent of exchange rate targeting.[17]

The model employs a familiar description of the central bank. Monetary policy is chosen to minimize fluctuations in output, inflation, and the exchange rate. Specifically, the central bank minimizes the following loss function:

$$L = ap^2 + (y - by_n)^2 + ce^2,$$ (9.1)

where p represents the log change in the domestic price level, y the log change in real output, y_n an underlying "natural" rate of growth, and e the log change in the exchange rate. The three parameters a, b, and c describe the importance of each of these objectives of monetary policy.

The importance of exchange rate stability as an independent objective of monetary policy is reflected by the parameter c. A positive value of c implies that the exchange rate has some importance that is distinct from whatever role it plays in determining prices or output.[18] If c is zero, the exchange rate is allowed to float freely. In the extreme case of a fixed exchange rate, the parameters a and b both equal zero, while c is positive, indicating that the exchange rate target supersedes all others for the conduct of monetary policy.

The model's characterization of the central bank's objectives implies a particular definition of exchange rate targeting.[19] Namely, this definition requires that the central bank value exchange rate stability for its own sake. The treatment of the exchange rate as an objective of policy as opposed to an instrument of policy distinguishes this essay from much of the literature on optimal exchange rate regimes.[20] That literature focuses on the central bank's optimal choice of instruments, given various patterns of disturbances. Here, we attempt to identify the actual objectives of policy rather than the ideal instruments used to obtain those objectives.

The central bank may view a stable exchange rate as an objective for a number of reasons. First, the central bank may want to eliminate

---

[17] We focus on the behavior of prices in this essay, but the model has implications for the behavior of output as well.

[18] If the exchange rate matters to the central bank only because its value affects the price level (however broadly defined), this concern is reflected in the parameter a, not in c. Even if the exchange rate is used as the instrument of monetary policy, it will not enter the objective function with c unless the central bank has an independent exchange rate target.

[19] This characterization of central bank behavior follows Frankel (1990).

[20] For discussions of the central bank's choice between the exchange rate, money, and the interest rate as the optimal instrument see, e.g., Argy and Porter (1972), Boyer (1978), Frenkel and Aizenman (1982), and Glick and Hutchison (1989).

exchange rate movements that are perceived to have deleterious effects on the composition of output. The Plaza and Louvre Accords of the 1980s are examples of worldwide efforts to limit big swings in exchange rates, in part because they were perceived to have undesirable consequences for the manufacturing sector of the United States. Second, a stable exchange rate may lend inflation-fighting credibility to the central bank. For example, it is often argued that the European Exchange Rate Mechanism is an attempt by inflation-prone countries to borrow the anti-inflation reputation of the German central bank.

The loss function given by equation (9.1) describes the role of the central bank. The remainder of the model describes the behavior of output, the exchange rate, and the interest rate.[21] Output growth in this • model depends on the underlying growth rate, on unexpected changes in prices, and on an unexpected supply shock u_s:

$$y = y_n + d(p - p^e) - u_s, \tag{9.2}$$

where p^e is the expected price change.[22]

Nominal exchange rate appreciation depends on domestic and foreign price changes and on unexpected real appreciation u_e:

$$e = (p_f - p) + u_e, \tag{9.3}$$

where, as throughout the essay, the subscript f denotes a foreign variable. In this specification, monetary policy affects the exchange rate through prices.

The model equates domestic and foreign expected real interest rates. So the nominal interest rate i equals the foreign interest rate i_f, less the expected difference between domestic and foreign price changes:

$$i = (i_f - p_f^e) + p^e. \tag{9.4}$$

Equations (9.1)–(9.4) describe the basic model. Deriving its implications for domestic prices entails three steps. First, we solve for optimal prices. Second, we determine expected prices on the basis of optimal prices. Third, we characterize prices in terms of observable variables.

Minimizing the objective function gives an expression for optimal price changes:

---

[21] The model does not include a description of the money market. Instead, it treats the central bank as choosing prices rather than money, following Barro and Gordon (1983). Relaxing this assumption to include a simple (albeit restrictive) description of the money market of the form $m = p + u_m$, where $E(u_m \mid u_e, u_s) = 0$, does not affect the results.

[22] This description of output is fairly general. It can be derived either from nominal rigidities, as in Gray (1976) and Taylor (1980), or from imperfect information, as in Lucas (1972).

$$p = \frac{d^2 p^e + c p_f + c u_e + d u_s + (bd - d) y_n}{a + c + d^2}. \tag{9.5}$$

Next, we use equation (9.5) to find expected prices by assuming rational expectations:

$$p^e = \frac{c p_f + (bd - d) y_n}{a + c}. \tag{9.6}$$

Substituting expected prices back into equation (9.5) gives domestic prices in terms of foreign prices, the underlying growth rate, and shocks to output and the exchange rate:

$$p = \frac{c}{a + c} p_f + \frac{bd - d}{a + c} y_n + \frac{d}{a + c + d^2} u_s + \frac{c}{a + c + d^2} u_e.$$

Finally, we use the equations for output, exchange rate appreciation, and the interest rate to substitute for the price expression's unobservable variables: the shocks to output, the exchange rate, and expected foreign prices.[23] This gives a more useful expression for prices:

$$p = \left[\frac{db}{a} + \frac{d^2 c(b - 1)}{a(a + c)} \right] y_n - \frac{d}{a} y + \frac{dc}{a(a + c)} p_f$$
$$+ \frac{d^2 c}{a^2} (i - i_f) + \frac{c}{a} e. \tag{9.7}$$

This price equation expresses the price changes in terms of the underlying growth rate and observable variables: output, foreign prices, the interest rate differential, and the exchange rate.[24] Note that the coefficients on foreign prices, the interest rate differential, and the exchange rate all depend on the parameter c, which reflects the importance of exchange rate stability. When the exchange rate floats freely, c equals zero and these coefficients also equal zero.

When the exchange rate is targeted ($c > 0$), its coefficient is positive. That is, an exchange rate depreciation results in a price decline. This price response contrasts with the common assertion that exchange rate depreciation is passed through into higher prices. The present, opposite, price response arises entirely from the role of the central bank: choosing

---

[23] The expected foreign price level is found by combining the interest rate equation with the expression for the expected price level.

[24] Output can be similarly expressed:

$$y = \left(\frac{d^2 - db}{a + c} - b \right) y_n + a p + \frac{ad}{a + c} p_f + d(i - i_f) - \frac{c}{d} e.$$

to target the exchange rate, the central bank will attempt to offset depreciation. In this model, it offsets a depreciation with a decline in prices. While the positive coefficient is inconsistent with the intuition offered by pass-through, it is surprising only when monetary policy is ignored. The extent of exchange rate pass-through depends on the extent of exchange rate targeting.[25]

While the model is too simple to capture all of the important aspects of the economy, it underscores a basic point: the behavior of prices depends on monetary policy. If monetary policy is altered to address exchange rate concerns, price behavior will be altered also. By showing how the behavior of prices depends on the extent of exchange rate targeting, the model's price equation provides another avenue for examining the extent of targeting of exchange rates. Moreover, in the context of the model, the assessment of targeting can be made irrespective of the central bank's policy with regard to foreign reserve holdings. The next section presents an empirical examination of the model's price equation and draws some tentative conclusions regarding the extent of targeting.

9.4   Price equation estimation

The model of the preceding section characterized prices as depending in part on the extent of exchange rate targeting. Moreover, the dependence is not affected by the particular channels that the central bank uses to manipulate the exchange rate. In this section we empirically examine the model's characterization of prices by estimating the price equation for Australia, Canada, Japan, and the United States. Since the model implies that some of the coefficients in the equation depend on the importance of the exchange rate to the central bank, an examination of the estimated coefficients may provide some information regarding the extent of exchange rate targeting in each country. Specifically, positive coefficients on the exchange rate, on foreign prices, and on the interest rate differential provide evidence that the central bank has an exchange rate target. By contrast, if the central bank targets

---

[25] Notice that when the central bank optimally targets only output and prices (a pure float), there also is no observed pass-through since, as already described, prices do not depend on the exchange rate when c equals zero. So the coefficient on the exchange rate is zero, not negative. Again, this is an outcome of central bank policy. When the central bank targets only prices and output, it reacts to exchange rate changes so that output and prices will not react to them. The central bank insulates output and prices from changes in the exchange rate.

only prices and output, and in the process insulates them from exchange rate changes, these coefficients should be insignificant. In neither case will the coefficients be negative, as would be predicted by simple pass-through arguments.[26] Thus, an important implication of the model is that pass-through parameters are not invariant to the policies of the central bank.

The estimated equations differ in three ways from the price specification implied by equation (9.7). First, the estimated equations constrain the underlying growth rate y_n to be constant. Second, the estimated equations include lags of all of the variables, and an error term. For each country, we estimate the coefficients $\beta = (\beta_{y_n}, \beta_{p,L}, \beta_{p_fL}, \beta_{i,L}, \beta_{e,L})$ in the following equation:

$$
p_t = \beta_{y_n} y_n + \sum_{L=1}^{2} \beta_{p,L} p_{t-L} + \sum_{L=0}^{2} \beta_{y,L} y_{t-L} + \sum_{L=0}^{2} \beta_{p_f,L} p_{f,t-L}
$$
$$
+ \sum_{L=0}^{2} \beta_{i,L} (i - i_f)_{t-L} + \sum_{L=0}^{2} \beta_{e,L} e_{t-L} + u_t.
$$

Lagged price changes are included as regressors, since evidence elsewhere indicates that past inflation is an important determinant of current inflation, and excluding past prices here would result in strong serial correlation of the errors. Two lags ($L = 2$) of each variable are included in the equation; this is the smallest number for which the mis-specification tests described later are not rejected for any of the four countries. Finally, since some shocks are likely to be common to many of the variables, the equations are estimated using lagged variables and seasonal dummies as instruments for the contemporaneous variables. To correct for any possible remaining serial correlation, a serial correlation consistent covariance matrix is estimated using Hansen's (1982) method of moments estimator.[27]

We estimate the equations using quarterly data from the International Monetary Fund's *International Financial Statistics*, with the exception of Australian GDP, which comes from the Organization for Economic Cooperation and Development's *Main Economic Indicators*. Output is represented by seasonally adjusted real GDP or real GNP, prices are the corresponding implicit deflators, and interest rates are short-term

---

[26] Central bank targeting implies non-negative pass-through coefficients when measured by an aggregate price index. Pass-through coefficients on individual price indexes, that is, on a micro level, could still be negative.

[27] A correction to force the estimated covariance matrix to be positive is required. The technique follows Newey and West (1987).

market rates.[28] A data appendix provides more detail. The sample period extends from the third quarter of 1975 through the third quarter of 1990, again with the exception of Australia, for which the estimation begins in 1984. Because it is not possible to identify the exact exchange rate targets of countries that officially subscribe to floating rate regimes, we estimate the price equations first using trade-weighted targets, then using bilateral targets.

The trade-weighted exchange rates are measured against the currencies of each country's five major trading partners. We choose the five major trading partners as those countries with the highest average value of total bilateral trade from 1974 to 1990. The currency of each trading partner is weighted by the ratio of that partner's trade to the trade of all five partners. These same weights are also used to construct corresponding weighted average measures of foreign prices and interest rates. The trade weights themselves are provided in the Appendix.

The estimated price equations for the four countries are reported in Table 9.1. The top panel of the table presents statistics testing for serially correlated errors and for the significance of sums of subsets of regressors that reflect the relevance of the exchange rate to the central bank. The bottom panel of the table provides the equations' estimated coefficients and their standard errors.

The first statistics reported in the top panel of the table test for serially correlated errors with a fairly general test for mis-specification, the Breusch–Godfrey test.[29] The statistics are not significant for any of the equations.

The table's next two rows present the results that are of primary interest: the statistics that test the implications of the model for a country whose exchange rate floats freely. In this case, prices should not depend on exchange rates, on foreign prices, or on the interest rate differential. In the case of exchange rate targeting, we should find positive coefficients. At the same time, a negative coefficient on the exchange rate is consistent with a central bank that neither targets the exchange rate nor acts to achieve a price objective by insulating prices from exchange rate changes. We examine the signs and significance of the coefficients in two separate tests for each country. First, in the test labeled H_0^1, we

---

[28] We also estimate the price equations using consumer price indices in lieu of the implicit price deflators.

[29] This test is derived in Breusch (1978) and Godfrey (1978). The statistic equals the number of observations less the number of lags tested multiplied by the R^2 from a regression of the estimated residuals on their lags and on the independent regressors. The statistic is distributed χ^2 with degrees of freedom equal to the number of lags, in this case 16.

Table 9.1. *Trade-weighted price equation estimates*

$$p_t = \beta_{y_n} y_n + \sum_{L=1}^{2} \beta_{p,L} p_{t-L} + \sum_{L=0}^{2} \beta_{y,L} y_{t-L} + \sum_{L=0}^{2} \beta_{p_f,L} p_{f,t-L}$$

$$+ \sum_{L=0}^{2} \beta_{i,L} (i - i_f)_{t-L} + \sum_{L=0}^{2} \beta_{e,L} e_{t-L} + u_t$$

		Hypothesis tests			
		Australia	Canada	Japan	U.S.
Breusch-Godfrey test, $\chi^{2(16)}$		16.60	18.89	21.29	18.68
$H_0^1: \sum_{L=0}^{2} \beta_{e,L} = 0$		−2.6284**	1.6702	−0.6548	−0.9903
$H_0^2: \sum_{L=0}^{2} \beta_{p_f,L} + \sum_{L=0}^{2} \beta_{i,L}$ $+ \sum_{L=0}^{2} \beta_{e,L} = 0$		−3.8047**	3.3287**	1.7491	1.3714
		Coefficient estimates[a]			
Constant	y_n	.2986** (.0838)	.0523 (.0340)	.0057 (.0190)	.0225* (.0100)
Price	p_{t-1}	−1.3626 (.4136)	.2190 (.2420)	.0234 (.2551)	.6593** (.1581)
	p_{t-2}	−.3892 (.3427)	−.2688 (.1270)	−.2323 (.1542)	−.4667 (.1170)
Output	y	.6298** (.0932)	−.6160 (.2861)	−.3041 (.1626)	−.1855 (.0806)
	y_{t-1}	−.1139 (.1712)	.1711 (.1642)	.1381 (.1454)	.1027 (.0903)
	y_{t-2}	.3666** (.0908)	−.0557 (.0748)	.1814 (.1715)	−.0736 (.0727)
Foreign price	p_f	5.0217* (2.0438)	.3606 (.8961)	.6868 (.5969)	.2763 (.3770)
	$p_{f,t-1}$	−4.1252 (1.3109)	.3205 (.5015)	−.3435 (.4548)	.1389 (.1674)
	$p_{f,t-2}$	−7.7621 (2.5692)	.4460 (.3235)	.5807 (.4098)	.0657 (.2904)

Table 9.1 (*continued*)

		Coefficient estimates[a]			
Interest rate differential	$i - i_f$	$-.0064$ (.0086)	$-.0156$ (.0059)	.0096* (.0039)	.0145 (.0085)
	$(i - i_f)_{t-1}$	.0285* (.0111)	.0020 (.0063)	$-.0062$ (.0039)	$-.0124$ (.0093)
	$(i - i_f)_{t-2}$	$-.0113$ (.0026)	.0004 (.0052)	.0072** (.0032)	.0052 (.0040)
Exchange rate	e	$-.1048$ (.0141)	.1145 (.0582)	$-.0174$ (.0483)	$-.0117$ (.0343)
	e_{t-1}	.0984** (.0075)	.0120 (.0609)	.0041 (.0129)	.0572* (.0243)
	e_{t-2}	$-.0536$ (.0184)	.0250 (.0649)	$-.0216$ (.0230)	$-.0399$ (.0200)

Note: Observations are taken quarterly from 1975:3 to 1990:3, except for Australia, for which the sample begins at 1984:1. A single asterisk denotes a value significant at the 5% level, and a double asterisk represents a value significant at the 1% level. Instruments were used for contemporaneous regressors. Hansen's (1982) generalized method of moments estimator is used to correct for serial correlation.
[a]Standard errors in parentheses.

examine the sum of the coefficients on exchange rate and its lags. Next, in the test labeled H_0^2, we examine the sum of the coefficients on exchange rates, foreign prices, and interest rate differentials.

   Considered alone, the exchange rate coefficients do not support the hypothesis of exchange rate targeting in any of the four countries. On the contrary, as shown in the first row of the table, the only country for which the sum of exchange rate coefficients is significant is Australia, but the sign is negative.[30] When all of the foreign variables are considered, evidence of targeting appears in the behavior of Canadian prices: the sum of the coefficients on the Canadian price equation is significantly positive.[31] However, even by this measure, Japanese and U.S. prices still show no evidence of exchange rate targeting.

[30] The finding of Australia's significant negative sum is not robust. It disappears both when bilateral exchange rates are considered and when prices are represented by the consumer price index instead of the implicit price deflator. The smaller period during which the Australian dollar has floated may be a problem here since it diminishes the degrees of freedom.

[31] Recall that, in the model described in the preceding section, mimicking foreign monetary policy is equivalent, ex ante, to targeting the exchange rate.

While these trade-weighted estimates are preliminary indicators of the extent to which exchange rate targeting may have played a role in the ultimate determination of prices in the four countries, some might argue that the United States is a more appropriate "foreign" entity than is a weighted average of trading partners. Much trade is invoiced in dollars, and the dollar is an important reserve currency for Australia, Canada, and Japan.[32] To consider this possibility, we have also estimated the price equations using the U.S. dollar as the exchange rate target for Australia, Canada, and Japan. To estimate the U.S. price equation, we have used the yen as the targeted currency. These bilateral estimates are reported in Table 9.2.

As shown in the first panel of the table, the hypothesis that the bilateral exchange rate is unimportant in the price equation cannot be rejected for any of the countries, including Australia. However, the broader hypothesis that all the foreign variables together affect prices is supported by the behavior of prices in both Canada and the United States. Thus, the response of Canadian prices to changes in foreign variables is even stronger when "foreign" is defined as "U.S." In turn, U.S. prices appear more sensitive to Japanese variables than to the broader trade-weighted measures in which Canada weighs heavily. To the extent that the U.S. dollar is targeted, it appears to be its value against the yen that is of most concern to the monetary authorities. The yen's prominent role in U.S. exchange rate policy is suggested by the "aggressive bilateralism" described by Funabashi (1988).[33]

Our estimations are based on the assumption that the measure of prices targeted by the central banks in our sample is an implicit price deflator, which reflects only the prices of domestically produce goods. However, the central banks instead may target a broader price index, such as a consumer price index, which is directly affected by movements in the exchange rate. Consumer prices may be a particularly plausible target of policy in smaller open economies such as Australia and Canada.

If the true target of policy is a consumer price index, the coefficient estimates for the exchange rate in the equations presented in Tables 9.1 and 9.2 will be upwardly biased. To examine this possibility, we also estimate the equations using the consumer price index in lieu of the implicit price deflator. The estimates are largely unchanged from the previous trade-weighted estimates; the only noticeable difference is in

[32] Of course, holding large dollar reserves does not indicate that a central bank is most concerned with its exchange rate against the dollar. It may simply reflect the ease of converting U.S. dollars into other currencies of concern.

[33] See pp. 151–75, especially the section discussing the "Baker–Miyazawa Accord."

Table 9.2. *Bilateral price equation estimates*

$$p_t = \beta_{y_n} y_n + \sum_{L=1}^{2} \beta_{p,L} p_{t-L} + \sum_{L=0}^{2} \beta_{y,L} y_{t-L} + \sum_{L=0}^{2} \beta_{p_f,L} p_{f,t-L}$$

$$+ \sum_{L=0}^{2} \beta_{i,L} (i - i_f)_{t-L} + \sum_{L=0}^{2} \beta_{e,L} e_{t-L} + u_t$$

		Hypothesis tests			
		Australia	Canada	Japan	U.S.
Breusch–Godfrey test, $\chi^{2(16)}$		16.60	18.89	21.29	18.68
$H_0^1: \sum_{L=0}^{2} \beta_{e,L} = 0$		0.3193	0.3565	−0.6607	−0.1970
$H_0^2: \sum_{L=0}^{2} \beta_{p_f,L} + \sum_{L=0}^{2} \beta_{i,L} + \sum_{L=0}^{2} \beta_{e,L} = 0$		0.1798	5.403**	1.6377	2.9178**

		Coefficient estimates[a]			
Constant	y_n	.0742 (.0583)	−.0141 (.0591)	.0397 (.0498)	.0652 (.0405)
Price	p_{t-1}	−.3074 (.4311)	−.0920 (.2566)	−.2560 (.2103)	−.1997 (.1924)
	p_{t-2}	.1633 (.1049)	−.0019 (.2505)	−.2849 (.4024)	−.3373 (.2307)
Output	y	.3592** (.1051)	−.4037 (.3893)	−.9266 (.5733)	.0324 (.3581)
	y_{t-1}	−.0459 (.1774)	.1013 (.1057)	−.2676 (.2229)	−.5081 (.2299)
	y_{t-2}	−.0445 (.1522)	.2157 (.1887)	.2841 (.1928)	.3679 (.5695)
Foreign price	p_f	1.7705 (1.2887)	1.6297 (.7717)	3.7757* (1.5144)	.0085 (1.0288)
	$p_{f,t-1}$	−1.2334 (.2816)	.3081 (.5585)	−1.2771 (.8043)	.2454 (.4177)
	$p_{f,t-2}$	−.3941 (.7027)	−.4345 (.3679)	−1.0531 (.7194)	1.3786 (1.2640)

Table 9.2 (*continued*)

		Coefficient estimates[a]			
Interest rate differential	$i - i_f$	−.0083 (.0062)	.00006 (.0246)	.0160 (.0138)	−.0341 (.0221)
	$(i - i_f)_{t-1}$	.0082* (.0037)	−.0040 (.0106)	−.0116 (.0122)	.0413 (.0206)
	$(i - i_f)_{t-2}$	−.0011 (.0031)	.0074 (.0066)	.0068 (.0043)	−.0171 (.0099)
Exchange rate	e	−.0092 (.0329)	−.0440 (.1930)	−.0459 (.1081)	−.0003 (.0010)
	e_{t-1}	.0537** (.0165)	−.0335 (.0558)	.0051 (.0207)	.00002 (.0001)
	e_{t-2}	−.0163 (.0633)	.0037 (.0405)	−.0282 (.0677)	.00007 (.0001)

Note: Observations are taken quarterly from 1975:3 to 1990:3, except for Australia, for which the sample begins at 1984:1. A single asterisk denotes a value significant at the 5% level, and a double asterisk represents a value significant at the 1% level. Lags of remaining regressors were used as instruments for prices. Hansen's (1982) generalized method of moments estimator is used to correct for serial correlation.
[a]Standard errors in parentheses.

the Australian coefficient estimates, which are no longer significantly negative.

9.5 Conclusions

This essay has examined the exchange rate regimes of four Pacific Basin countries: Australia, Canada, Japan, and the United States. While over much of the period all of these countries have had relatively open capital markets, they differ tremendously in terms of the openness of their goods markets, the extent of their economic dependence on their trading partners, and the sources of the economic disturbances they experience. Yet, officially, they all have the same exchange rate policy – floating rates. In light of much of the theoretical analysis of the choice of an optimal exchange rate regime, it would be remarkable for the same exchange rate policy to be optimal for this diverse group of countries. In this essay, we have argued that while the governments of these countries share the same official exchange rate policy, they do not share the same de facto policy. Although they have in common an official policy of floating their exchange rates, they respond to their individual circumstances by implicitly targeting their exchange rates to varying degrees.

Changes in foreign reserve holdings are one measure of the extent of exchange rate targeting. We observed that the central banks' holdings of foreign assets varied substantially throughout the period and inferred that these changes were largely in response to exchange rate concerns. Occasionally, that inference was confirmed by official statements regarding foreign exchange market intervention. Normalized by their respective monetary bases, the foreign reserve holdings of the central banks of Australia and Canada were the largest and exhibited the biggest fluctuations, while the central banks of Japan and the United States had smaller overall holdings of foreign reserves with smaller fluctuations.

Of course, regardless of central banks' stated intentions, altering foreign asset holdings alone may affect exchange rates very little. Other instruments of monetary policy are more powerful determinants of exchange rates. Thus, ascertaining the extent of exchange rate targeting requires examining monetary policy more broadly. When monetary policy is altered by exchange rate concerns, the behavior of other macroeconomic variables influenced by monetary policy also changes. This suggests that the behavior of other macroeconomic variables might provide an indication of the importance of exchange rates in determining monetary policy. We focused here on the behavior of domestic prices.

The simple model presented in Section 9.3 showed how the behavior of prices can depend on the extent of exchange rate targeting. The model clarified the intuition that a central bank caring strongly about exchange rate stability will offset a depreciation, for example, with tighter monetary policy, hence lowering prices or inflation. Thus, the behavior of prices in response to exchange rate changes ultimately depends on the extent to which the central bank targets the exchange rate. In our examination of the behavior of the prices of the four countries, we found that, in the context of the model, the behavior of Canadian prices indicated exchange rate targeting, while the behavior of Japanese prices did not. The estimates for Australia suggest that not only did the central bank refrain from targeting exchange rates, but it also refrained from insulating prices from exchange rate changes. The behavior of U.S. prices showed some evidence of targeting, but only vis-à-vis the yen.

In attempting to ascertain the extent of exchange rate targeting, this essay has also provided an example of how important it is that historical examinations of macroeconomic variables recognize the dependence of macroeconomic variables on monetary policy. Estimates of exchange rate pass-through to domestic prices are sensitive to exchange rate targeting. Similarly, recognizing the extent to which these and other countries have targeted their exchange rates is important in evaluating the appropriateness and performance of alternative exchange rate regimes. Comparing alternative regimes requires that the regimes be characterized correctly. The outcome of an official policy of floating exchange rates coupled with a strong implicit target should not be used as an example of a floating exchange rate regime. Given that floating exchange rates are often targeted in practice, it should not be surprising that they have failed to insulate some countries from external shocks.

Data appendix

All data are quarterly and with one exception are taken from the IMF's *International Financial Statistics* (*IFS*). The exception is Australian GDP, which comes from the OECD's *Main Economic Indicators*.

Output and prices

Real output consists of GNP for Canada, Japan, and the United States, and GDP for Australia, all with a base year of 1985 = 100. All series are seasonally adjusted. The price series is constructed by deflating the nominal GNP and GDP series by the real output series.

Money and interest rates

The monetary base is taken from line 14 of *IFS*. All are end-of-period values. The interest rate series are taken from *IFS* line 60, which consists of representative short-term interest rates prevailing in the private market.

Exchange rates

All exchange rates are end-of-quarter rates, measured as the foreign currency price of the domestic currency.

Net foreign assets

Net foreign assets are calculated from line 11 of *IFS*, foreign assets of the monetary authorities (which includes relevant holdings by other official participants in the foreign exchange markets that are not central banks). We subtract line 16d, foreign liabilities of the monetary authorities, where relevant. All are end-of-quarter values.

Trade weights

		Trade share			Trade share
Australia:	Japan	43.5	Japan:	United States	64.0
	United States	28.2		Australia	12.3
	United Kingdom	12.6		Germany	8.7
	New Zealand	7.9		Canada	8.5
	Germany	7.8		United Kingdom	6.5
Canada:	United States	85.3	United States:	Canada	43.5
	Japan	6.9		Japan	28.9
	United Kingdom	4.1		Germany	11.1
	Germany	2.3		United Kingdom	10.1
	France	1.4		France	6.0

References

Adams, D., and Henderson, D. (1983). "Definition and Measurement of Exchange Market Intervention," Board of Governors of the Federal Reserve System Staff Study no. 126. Washington, DC.

Argy, V., and Porter, M. (1972). "The Forward Exchange Market and the Effects of Domestic and External Disturbances Under Alternative Exchange Rate Systems," (International Monetary Fund) *Staff Papers* 19:503–78.

Barro, R., and Gordon, D. (1983). "A Positive Theory of Monetary Policy in a Natural Rate Model," *Journal of Political Economy* 91:589–610.

Blundell-Wignall, A., and Gregory, R. (1990). "Exchange Rate Policy in Advanced Commodity Exporting Countries: Australia and New Zealand." In V. Argy and P. DeGrauwe, eds., *Choosing an Exchange Rate Regime: The Challenge for Smaller Industrial Countries,* pp. 224–71. Washington, DC: International Monetary Fund.

Boyer, R. (1978). "Optimal Foreign Exchange Intervention," *Journal of Political Economy* 86:1045–55.

Breusch, T. (1978). "Testing for Autocorrelation in Dynamic Linear Models," *Australian Economic Papers* 17:334–55.

Carmichael, J. (1990). "Comment on Exchange Rate Policy in Advanced Commodity Exporting Countries: Australia and New Zealand." In V. Argy and P. DeGrauwe, eds., *Choosing an Exchange Rate Regime: The Challenge for Smaller Industrial Countries,* pp. 272–76. Washington, DC: International Monetary Fund.

Dobson, W. (1991). *Economic Policy Coordination: Requiem or Prologue?* Washington, DC: Institute for International Economics.

Frankel, J. (1990). "Obstacles to Coordination and a Consideration of Two Proposals to Overcome Them: International Nominal Targeting (INT) and the Hosomi Fund." In W. Branson, J. Frenkel, and M. Goldstein, eds., *International Policy Coordination and Exchange Rate Fluctuations,* pp. 109–58. Chicago: University of Chicago Press.

Frenkel, J., and Aizenman, J. (1982). "Aspects of the Optimal Management of Exchange Rates," *Journal of International Economics* 13:231–56.

Funabashi, Y. (1988). *Managing the Dollar: From the Plaza to the Louvre.* Washington, DC: Institute for International Economics.

Girton, L., and Roper, D. (1977). "A Monetary Model of Exchange Market Pressure Applied to the Postwar Canadian Experience," *American Economic Review* 67:537–48.

Glick, R., and Hutchison, M. (1989). "Exchange Rates and Monetary Policy," (Federal Reserve Bank of San Francisco) *Economic Review* (Spring):17–29.

Godfrey, L. (1978). "Testing Against General Autoregressive and Moving Average Error Models When the Regressors Include Lagged Dependent Variables," *Econometrica* 46:1293–1302.

Gray, J. (1976). "Wage Indexation: A Macroeconomic Approach," *Journal of Monetary Economics* 2:221–35.

Hansen, L. (1982). "Large Sample Properties of Generalized Methods of Moments Estimators," *Econometrica* 50:1269–86.

Lucas, R. (1972). "Expectations and the Neutrality of Money," *Journal of Economic Theory* 4:103–24.

Newey, W., and West K. (1987). "A Simple, Positive Definite, Heteroskedasticity and Autocorrelation Consistent Covariance Matrix," *Econometrica* 55:703–8.

Obstfeld, M. (1990). "The Effectiveness of Foreign Exchange Intervention: Recent Experience, 1985–88." In W. Branson, J. Frenkel, and M. Goldstein, eds., *International Policy Coordination and Exchange Rate Fluctuations,* pp. 197–246. Chicago: University of Chicago Press.

Taylor, J. (1980). "Aggregate Dynamics and Staggered Contracts," *Journal of Political Economy* 88:1–23.

PART III
INTERVENTION AND STERILIZATION
POLICIES

CHAPTER 10

Monetary policy, intervention, and exchange rates in Japan

Reuven Glick and Michael M. Hutchison

10.1 Introduction

Until the end of the Bretton Woods system in the early 1970s, Japanese monetary policy was driven by concern about maintaining the international value of the yen fixed. The need to maintain fixed exchange rate parities limited the degree of discretion by the Bank of Japan in its conduct of monetary policy. Balance-of-payments deficits and downward pressure on the yen necessitated contractionary policy and a growth slowdown; surpluses and upward yen pressure required expansionary policy.

With the exchange rate anchor for monetary policy eliminated at the end of the Bretton Woods era, the Bank of Japan (BOJ) switched to domestic price stability as the main target of policy, with the strategic aim of reducing the inflation rate. The BOJ's success in maintaining the lowest rate of price inflation among industrial countries since the late 1970s has been attributed to a so-called money-focused monetary policy (Suzuki, 1985; Fukui, 1986). The conventional wisdom is that this money-focused approach has resulted in the placing of relatively little weight on the state of the economy when determining monetary policy (e.g., Friedman 1985).

However, Hamada and Hayashi (1985), Ito (1989), and Bryant (1991) express doubt that the BOJ places much weight on limiting deviations of any given money aggregate from targeted values and assert that the BOJ does not focus on any single target. A number of recent papers

Helpful comments by Tsutomu Watanabe and research assistance by Robert Marquez are gratefully acknowledged. The views presented are the authors' alone and do not reflect those of the Federal Reserve Bank of San Francisco or the Board of Governors of the Federal Reserve System.

have focused on the role of external considerations in the determination of BOJ monetary policy. Hutchison (1988), for example, finds that during the period from August 1978 to September 1985 Japanese monetary policy was sensitive to exchange rate changes. These results support the view that the BOJ has pursued a flexible monetary policy since the mid-1970s and has not attempted rigid short-term control of money aggregates.

The inclusion of exchange rate or balance-of-payments considerations in a central bank's objective function generates the potential for conflict with domestic policy targets. Such a conflict surfaced strikingly in the case of the BOJ when the yen began a sharp appreciation against the dollar in early 1985. Initially welcomed as a long-overdue correction to the overvalued dollar, and sanctioned by the G-5 Plaza Agreement in September 1985, the yen appreciation was aided by dollar sales in the foreign exchange market in late September and October (Figure 10.1). As the yen appreciation accelerated in early 1986, however, a marked shift in Japanese intervention policy led to the rapid accumulation of foreign exchange reserves in support of the dollar. During the period 1986–8 Japan's foreign exchange reserves jumped more than fourfold, from $22 billion to $90 billion. The accumulation of reserves was accompanied by an increase in monetary base growth from 5 percent to nearly 15 percent, and a subsequent rise in consumer price inflation from nearly zero between early 1986 and mid-1988 to almost 4 percent by December 1990. The BOJ reacted to these developments by sharply raising money market interest rates and tightening monetary conditions from mid-1988 through 1990.

With this recent experience of Japan in mind, Poole (1992), Tschoegl (1989), and others have argued that exchange rate targeting has tended to exacerbate business cycles in Japan. While on average Japanese monetary policy has successfully constrained inflation, periodic efforts to limit yen appreciations, as in the period after the Plaza Agreement, have resulted in excessive monetary expansions followed by the need for undue monetary contraction. Takagi (1991), by contrast, argues that domestic monetary control in Japan has not been seriously compromised by external considerations.

To shed light on these issues, in this essay we investigate the pattern of official Japanese exchange market intervention and the extent to which the BOJ has been able to insulate domestic monetary control from exchange rate considerations since the early 1970s. The objective is to identify and explain possible sources of conflict between domestic monetary control and exchange rate policy in Japan.

Three broad findings emerge from our study of Japanese monetary

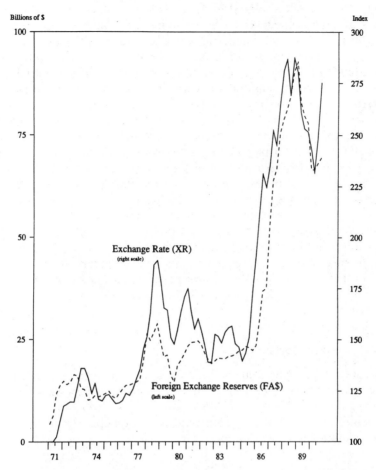

Figure 10.1. Exchange rate and foreign exchange reserves. Reserves in billions of U.S. dollars; exchange rate in $/Yen (1970:Q1 = 100).

policy. First, we find evidence that the intervention and sterilization policy responses of Japanese monetary authorities have varied across different time periods and particular episodes of strong yen appreciation and depreciation. We attribute this finding to policy preference shifts, external developments, and financial market liberalization in Japan that have influenced the timing and magnitude of foreign exchange intervention, sterilization, and their ultimate impact on monetary conditions.

Second, we identify differences between the contemporaneous and longer-term influence of foreign reserves on money aggregates. This suggests a possible trade-off in the pursuit of conflicting short-run and long-run policy objectives by Japanese monetary authorities.

Third, we find an asymmetric response pattern in Japanese foreign exchange market intervention policy: Japanese monetary authorities have tended to resist yen depreciations more strongly than yen appreciations. A pattern of asymmetry exists in sterilization behavior as well: foreign currency purchases (sales) in response to yen appreciation (depreciation) have generally been met with greater (less) offsetting domestic credit operations. We argue that this behavior is consistent with monetary control in pursuit of general price stability in the face of a long-term trend appreciation of the yen.

The essay is organized as follows. Section 10.2 presents stylized facts relevant to Japanese monetary and exchange rate policy and looks at monetary developments during episodes of sharp yen appreciation and depreciation. Sections 10.3 and 10.4 present empirical analyses of intervention and sterilization policies, respectively. Section 10.5 considers the linkages between foreign reserves, the monetary base, and the money supply. Section 10.6 draws policy implications. An appendix describes the institutional mechanics of foreign exchange market intervention in Japan.

10.2   Stylized facts

This section presents some stylized facts about movements in Japan's money aggregates, the value of the yen, and Japanese official reserve holdings over the period 1971–90. Attention is also drawn to macroeconomic and monetary developments in several episodes of sharp yen appreciation and depreciation.

10.2.1   *General developments*

Figure 10.2 plots quarterly growth rates of Japan's broad money supply (BM) and monetary base (MB) over the period 1971–90. Broad money is defined as M2 before May 1979 and as M2 + CDs afterward. Growth rates are calculated as the percent change over four quarters.[1]

Movements in broad money and monetary base growth display the

---

[1] Broad money and monetary base stocks each quarter are constructed as the average of end-of-month stock figures. Broad money figures were obtained in seasonally adjusted form from the Bank of Japan, *Economics Statistics Monthly;* monetary base figures are from the International Monetary Fund (IMF), *International Finance Statistics* (*IFS*), line 14 ("Monetary Authorities, Reserve Money"), and were seasonally adjusted using the X-11 procedure in SAS.

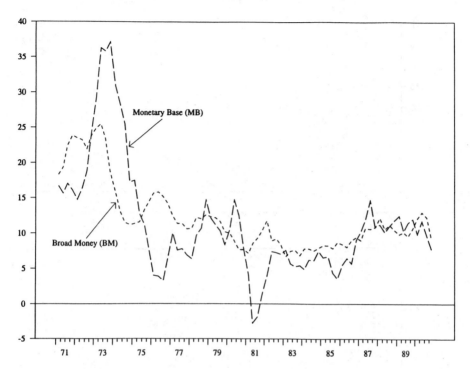

Figure 10.2. Broad money and monetary base aggregates. Percent change over four quarters.

same secular trend, although the contemporaneous covariation between the two series is generally low, particularly through the late 1970s. The BOJ's decisive action in the mid-1970s to reduce trend money growth is the most striking feature of the behavior of both money aggregates. After a decade of trend decline, however, the rate of growth of broad money picked up in late 1983, gradually increased, and then jumped almost 4 percentage points to double-digit levels in 1987.[2]

Figure 10.3 plots growth rates of the nominal dollar value of the yen (XR) and of the dollar-denominated (FA$, in the top panel) and yen-denominated (FA, in the bottom panel) value of official net foreign exchange reserve assets held by Japanese monetary authorities over the

[2] The rise in consumer price inflation was preceded by bursts of financial asset and real estate inflation. Broad money and monetary base stocks each quarter are constructed as the average of end-of-month stock figures.

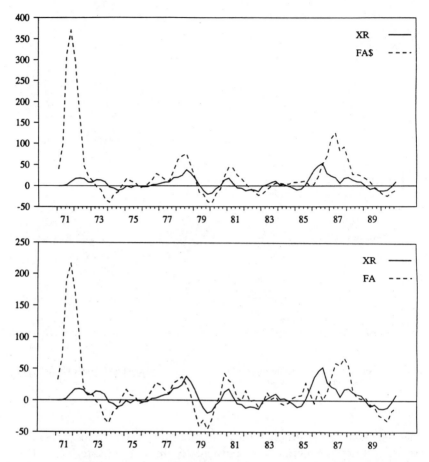

Figure 10.3. Exchange rate and foreign exchange reserves in dollars (top) and yen (bottom). Percent change over four quarters. Exchange rate in $/yen; positive values imply a yen appreciation.

period 1971–90.[3] We focus on the nominal U.S. dollar value of the yen, since the U.S. dollar is dominant in any measure of the effective exchange rate index of the yen. Positive values indicate a rise in the dollar value of

---

[3] The exchange rate series are averages of monthly period average figures, from the *IFS*, line rf. Foreign exchange reserve stocks each quarter are constructed as the average of end-of-month stock figures. Figures in dollars were obtained from *IFS*, line 1d.d ("Foreign Exchange"); figures in yen are from *IFS*, line 11 ("Monetary Authorities, Foreign Assets"). Both monthly series were seasonally adjusted using the X-11 procedure in SAS.

the yen and a yen appreciation. We examine net official assets, since the Japanese authorities do not make gross intervention data public.

Movements in the yen exchange rate and Japanese foreign reserves are positively correlated during most periods in the sample. Yen appreciation (depreciation) tends to be accompanied by increases (decreases) in foreign reserves. This is also clear from Figure 10.1, where dollar-denominated reserves are expressed in level terms (rather than in percent changes). Thus, Japanese monetary authorities have generally sold (bought) yen and bought (sold) foreign reserves when the value of the yen appreciates (depreciates), seeking to dampen or slow exchange rate fluctuations.

Particularly significant increases in reserves can be observed following the periods of sharp yen appreciation accompanying the breakup of Bretton Woods in the early 1970s and the decline of the dollar in the mid-1980s; large declines in the stock of official reserves occurred following the oil price hikes and depreciations of the yen in 1973–4 and 1978–9. The two most evident episodes of high money growth identified in Figure 10.2, one in the early 1970s and the second in the late 1980s, followed periods of rapid yen appreciation, substantial foreign exchange intervention, and the accumulation of international reserves. This suggests a link between rapid money growth during periods of sharp yen appreciation and unsterilized dollar-support foreign exchange market intervention.

Turning to the linkage between intervention and the monetary base, the foreign exchange reserve data most useful in this regard are the yen value of official foreign asset acquisitions by the BOJ. The yen-denominated foreign asset changes presented in Figure 10.3, FA, include, along with changes in BOJ reserve holdings, changes in the net foreign claims of other government agencies that transact in foreign exchange markets through the Foreign Exchange Fund Special Account (FEFSA). In addition, because they value reserve assets at the current exchange rate, FA includes the effects of exchange-rate-induced fluctuations in the yen value of existing foreign reserves as well as reinvested interest earnings on foreign assets.[4] These valuation changes enter the capital component, rather than the bank reserves component, of the liability side of the consolidated balance sheet of the monetary authorities.

Following the approach of Takagi (1991), we construct an estimate (FABOJ) of the yen value of the BOJ's official foreign assets that is independent of these exchange rate valuation effects. This measure, obtained by subtracting available information on the consolidated credit balance of

---

[4] The figures exclude foreign assets other than those classified by the IMF as foreign exchange reserves, such as special drawing rights and the IMF reserve position.

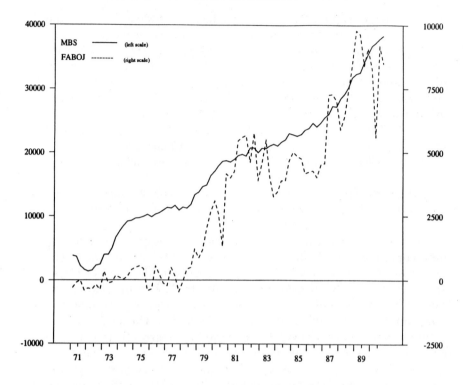

Figure 10.4. Monetary base and Bank of Japan foreign exchange reserves. Billions of yen.

the BOJ and the FEFSA to the central government from the BOJ's out-standing credit to the central government, represents an estimate of the outstanding value of the BOJ's credit to the FEFSA.[5] It may be inter-preted as the cumulative sum of all purchases (and sales) of foreign ex-change bills by the BOJ from the FEFSA, valued at *historical* exchange rates. It thus provides a measure of the yen value of official foreign assets that is independent of valuation effects. Changes in FABOJ measure the effect of intervention on the monetary base at the exchange rate prevail-ing at the time foreign exchange transactions were made.

Figure 10.4 plots FABOJ and a liability sources-side measure of the BOJ's monetary base, MBS, both in yen levels.[6] The latter is defined

[5] The balance sheet of Japanese monetary authorities is defined as the consolidated ac-count of the BOJ and the FEFSA. See the Appendix.

[6] Quarterly observations of both series were constructed as the average of end-of-month stock figures obtained from the BOJ *Economics Statistics Monthly*. The monthly data were seasonally adjusted using the X-11 procedure of SAS.

as the sum of bills discounted, loans, bills purchases, and government bonds held by the BOJ. Other components are excluded because they are relatively minor and/or stable.

Relative to movements in the monetary base, the foreign exchange reserves series exhibits substantial variability. However, in a number of periods, particularly in the early to mid-1970s, some positive covariation in the series is observable. This suggests a shift over time since the 1970s in either the desire or ability of the Bank of Japan to sterilize fully the effects of its intervention operations and consequent reserve movements on the monetary base.

10.2.2 *Focal episodes*

Clear patterns in the data over the full period since the end of the Bretton Woods era may be difficult to discern if policy responses tend to vary with episodes of sharp movements in the exchange rate. In this case, looking at particular focal episodes may provide more information on the extent to which monetary control has been influenced by external considerations. To this end, we examine the policy response of Japanese monetary authorities during specific episodes of yen appreciation and depreciation. We focus on three periods of appreciation beginning with (i) 1971:Q3, when the yen appreciated with the unraveling of the Bretton Woods system; (ii) 1976:Q1, when the yen strengthened with Japan's recovery from the effects of earlier oil price rises and recession; and (iii) 1985:Q4, following the Plaza Agreement. We also examine two periods of depreciation associated with oil price shocks in 1973:Q4 and 1978:Q4.

Episodes of appreciation. The six panels of Figure 10.5 show various monetary policy indicators before and after the beginning of the three yen appreciation episodes. Time 0 indicates the beginning of each episode. Points to the right (left) refer to variable values in subsequent (preceding) quarters. Indicators of change in the exchange rate, foreign exchange reserves, monetary base, broad money (M2 + CDs), and the consumer price index (CPI), as well as the call money rate level, are shown. All variables are measured as four quarter rates of change, except the call money rate, which is in percent levels.[7]

---

[7] The series for the exchange rate, foreign exchange reserves denominated in yen, the monetary base, and broad money (M2 + CDs) are represented by the variables XR, FA, MB, and BM defined and discussed previously. The CPI is obtained from the *IFS*, line 64.

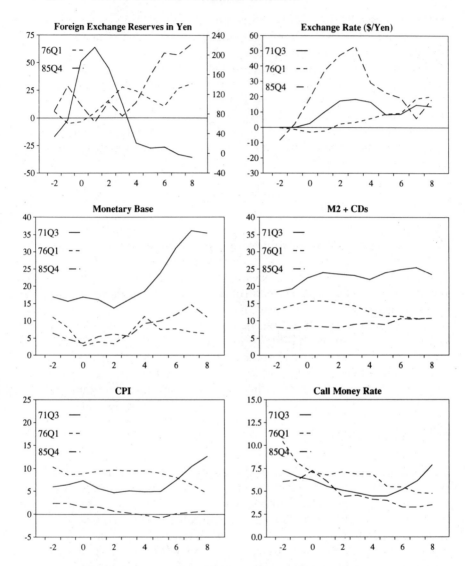

Figure 10.5. Yen appreciation episodes. Percent change over four quarters, except the call money rate, which is in percent levels.

(i) Breakup of Bretton Woods: Existing exchange rate parities came under increasing pressure in 1971, with the overvaluation of the dollar at Y/$ 360 forcing the Japanese authorities to intervene heavily to maintain the exchange rate peg. As a consequence, Japanese foreign ex-

change reserves grew rapidly in the months before August 1971, when the U.S. finally closed the "gold window" and the yen was subsequently revalued. Pressures on the dollar continued in the following months, however, and the yen appreciated further despite large-scale intervention by the Japanese monetary authorities. Even the new realignments sanctioned by the Smithsonian Agreement in December 1971 ceased to halt the rise in the yen against the dollar in early 1972.

Against this background, monetary base growth began to accelerate sharply in 1972 and peaked at more than 35 percent in early 1973. The broad money supply, which had been growing at almost 20 percent per year before the initial appreciation of the yen, rose even faster, at almost 25 percent per year, through the latter part of 1971 and into 1973. Loose monetary conditions were also reflected in call money interest rate declines through most of 1971–2. Japanese inflation rose to double-digit levels at the beginning of 1973, in response to the monetary stimulus. Japan completely abandoned its fixed parity with the dollar in early 1973 and, together with most other industrial countries, moved to the present system of managed floating.

(ii) Mid-1970s: Beginning in early 1976, the yen experienced a second period of sustained appreciation. During this episode, the Japanese monetary authorities again engaged in substantial intervention operations designed to moderate yen appreciation by dollar purchases in the foreign exchange market. The authorities intervened particularly heavily when yen appreciation accelerated in late 1977 and early 1978. This intervention was accompanied by increased growth in the monetary base through 1976 and into the first half of 1977. However, money supply growth declined somewhat in 1976–7. Money market interest rates and inflation also fell gradually during this episode.

(iii) Post–Plaza Agreement: After a moderate appreciation in early 1985, the yen began a sharp and sustained appreciation following the agreement of the G-5 countries held in September 1985 at the Plaza Hotel in New York. The Japanese monetary authorities joined other central banks in selling dollars in coordinated intervention from late September through the end of October and immediately tightened monetary conditions somewhat by raising interest rates. From the spring of 1986 through the end of 1988, however, the stance of intervention policy abruptly changed to limiting yen appreciation by buying dollars, particularly in 1987 after the February Louvre Accord.

Monetary base growth increased through 1986 and 1987 from 5 percent to nearly 15 percent per year. Japanese broad money supply growth initially remained steady at around 8 percent, but then rose to around 10 percent by mid-1987. The generally accommodative stance of policy during this time was also marked by successive declines in interest rates. Nonetheless, virtual price stability was maintained during much of this period, as import price declines helped to offset some increases in the domestic component of the overall CPI index. Inflation began to accelerate toward the end of 1988, however, and peaked at almost 4 percent two years later.

A comparison of these three episodes of yen appreciation indicates that all were generally characterized by the accumulation of foreign exchange reserves and rising monetary base growth, indicating less than complete sterilization, at least in the short run. However, only in the first episode, at the time of the breakdown of the Bretton Woods system, was the increase in monetary base growth immediately followed by a sharp rise in the broad money supply. This may indicate that structural shifts in the relationship between the monetary base and the broad money supply since then, perhaps attributable to financial market developments in Japan, have lessened the impact of base money changes on the broad money supply. We discuss this issue in Section 10.5.

Episodes of depreciation. Figure 10.6 illustrates the two episodes of yen depreciation associated with sharp oil price increases.[8] In both cases the monetary authorities intervened by selling foreign exchange reserves to strengthen the yen.

(i) First oil price rise: In the case of the first oil price rise at the end of 1973, monetary base growth fell sharply in response to the monetary tightening already begun early in the year in response to building inflationary pressures. Broad money growth, which had also been declining several quarters before the depreciation of the yen, fell further as well. Money market rates rose again after the oil shock, further tightening monetary conditions. Thus, foreign exchange sales during this episode were unsterilized and contributed to the overall restrictive monetary policy stance.[9]

(ii) Second oil price rise: Monetary conditions were quite different before the second oil price shock at the end of 1978. Inflation pressure

---

[8] See Hutchison (1991) for an international comparison of macroeconomic developments and policy responses at the time of oil price shocks in the 1970s and 1990.

[9] Broad money growth declined from more than 25 percent in early 1973 to about 11 percent in mid-1974, and short-term interest rates more than doubled from 6 percent to 13 percent.

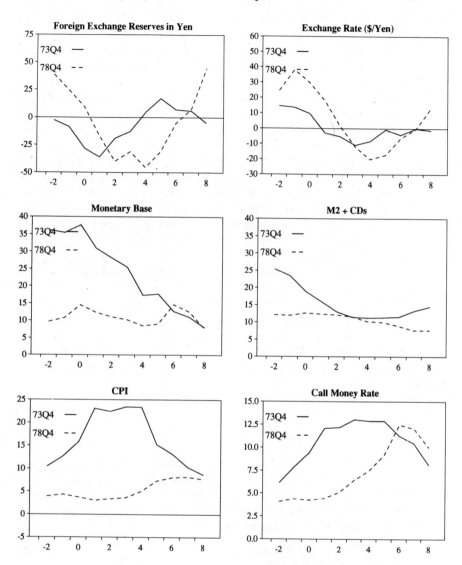

Figure 10.6. Yen depreciation episodes. Percent change over four quarters, except the call money rate, which is in percent levels.

was not evident, money aggregate growth rates were fairly stable, and interest rates had been steady for some time. In the year and a half following the oil shock, the yen depreciated by more than 25 percent against the dollar; substantial foreign exchange market dollar sales to support the yen led to a sharp drop in international reserves. Base money growth declined substantially as the yen depreciated, reflecting unsterilized intervention operations and a sharp discretionary rise in short-term interest rates. Broad money also declined, albeit gradually, during this episode.

In both cases the depreciation of the yen was accompanied by declining foreign exchange reserves, declining monetary base growth, and monetary policy tightening. Substantial unsterilized foreign exchange market intervention is clearly evident, perhaps more so than in the episodes of yen appreciation in 1976–7 and after the Plaza Agreement. It is not clear, however, how to separate the policy response to yen depreciation from the oil price hikes themselves or, in the 1973 case, from prior concerns and policy actions about inflation. Nevertheless, the comparison of episodes suggests some possible asymmetries in the behavior of Japanese monetary authorities during depreciations and appreciations of the yen.

The preliminary examination of the data in this section indicates some linkage of money growth performance in Japan with foreign exchange intervention activity. Attempting to discern the impact of foreign exchange operations on money growth from simple bivariate relationships may be misleading, however. The linkages between foreign exchange operations and monetary growth are potentially complex. Controlling for other variables that may affect the foreign exchange–money link is also essential. To this end, we now turn to more formal statistical analysis.

10.3   Intervention policy

To assess the extent of the association of foreign exchange intervention by Japanese monetary authorities and movements in the nominal value of the yen, we estimate a standard central bank intervention function, with the magnitude of intervention assumed to be linearly related to the percent change in the exchange rate:[10]

$$I_t = \alpha + \beta \, \Delta XR_t + \epsilon_t, \tag{10.1}$$

where I is the amount of intervention and ΔXR is the (log) percent change in the average monthly exchange rate (with an increase defined as an appreciation of the yen against the dollar). We employ seasonally

[10] Earlier studies of Japanese intervention policy testing a similar equation include Quirk (1977), Hutchison (1984), and Takagi (1991).

adjusted monthly data over the managed floating exchange rate period 1973:3–1990:12.[11] We consider three different measures of intervention. ΔFA denotes the change in the yen-denominated value of (net) official foreign asset holdings of the FEFSA; ΔFA\$ denotes the equivalent in dollar terms. Some argue that interest earnings should be excluded from measures of reserve holdings. However, such reinvestment may be properly thought of as intervention, since the Japanese monetary authorities could have used the dollar interest earnings to reduce the flow of yen-denominated assets into private portfolios, simultaneously leaving more dollar assets for the private market to hold. Nevertheless, we consider a third, interest-rate-adjusted measure of intervention defined as

$$\Delta FA\$ADJ_t = \Delta FA\$_t - R_t[(FA\$_t + FA\$_{t-1})/2],$$

where R is the average U.S. Treasury bill rate. All intervention measures are expressed in percent change form by means of scaling by the level of foreign asset holdings at the end of time t.

To the extent that intervention affects the contemporaneous level of the exchange rate, estimating equation (10.1) by ordinary least squares (OLS) is subject to simultaneity bias. Estimation results were also obtained by instrumenting out the current exchange rate change with three lags each of the Japanese call money rate, the Federal Reserve funds rate, and logarithmic changes in the Japanese CPI and the exchange rate.

The estimation results for (10.1) with the alternative measures of intervention are reported in the top part of Table 10.1 with a time trend and with and without a lag of the dependent variable. (The constant and trend terms are not reported.) Observe that the sign of the estimated coefficient of the exchange rate variable is positive and generally significant, indicating that the monetary authorities tended to sell (buy) foreign exchange when the yen depreciated (appreciated). This is consistent with an intervention policy of leaning against the wind. The inclusion of lagged dependent variables reduces the degree of serial correlation, but it and the method of estimation do not generally affect the significance of the estimated coefficients.

The dollar-based measures of reserves indicate that during the whole of the post–Bretton Woods period the Japanese authorities have responded to a 1 percent appreciation of the yen by increasing international reserves by about ½ to 1 percent on average. The yen-based

---

[11] Data were seasonally adjusted using the X-11 procedure in SAS. The results are unaffected using seasonally unadjusted data with seasonal dummies.

Table 10.1. *Response of official foreign exchange reserves, 1973:3–1990:12*

Dependent variable	Exchange rate	Lagged dependent variable	Q-msl	Adj. R^2	OLS/ INST
ΔFA/FA	0.65 (.03)	—	.35	.11	OLS
	0.60 (.00)	0.13 (.04)	.42	.12	OLS
	0.51 (.08)	—	.31	.10	INST
	0.30 (.36)	0.16 (.02)	.34	.10	INST
ΔFA$/FA$	0.74 (.00)	—	.00	.22	OLS
	0.61 (.00)	0.28 (.00)	.36	.29	OLS
	0.96 (.00)	—	.00	.20	INST
	0.52 (.05)	0.30 (.00)	.37	.28	INST
ΔFAADJ/FA	0.76 (.00)	—	.00	.22	OLS
	0.62 (.00)	0.29 (.00)	.36	.30	OLS
	1.04 (.00)	—	.00	.19	INST
	0.58 (.03)	0.30 (.00)	.36	.30	INST

Dependent variable	Exchange rate appreciation	Exchange rate depreciation	Lagged dependent variable	Q-msl	Adj. R^2
ΔFA/FA	0.26 (.19)	1.19 (.00)	.12 (.08)	.54	.13
ΔFA$/FA$	0.37 (.01)	1.02 (.00)	.26 (.00)	.20	.30
ΔFAADJ/FA	0.37 (.01)	1.05 (.00)	.27 (.00)	.20	.20

Note: Dependent variables are defined as the monthly change in the end-of-period stocks scaled by the end-of-period level. The stock series were seasonally adjusted. The exchange rate is defined as the logarithmic change in the average monthly exchange rate of the U.S. dollar against the yen; an increase in the exchange rate denotes an appreciation of the yen. Numbers in parentheses denote marginal significance levels; Q-msl refers to the marginal significance level of the Ljung–Box Q-statistic for serial correlation.

measure of reserves gives a somewhat lower response in the ⅓ to ⅔ percent range.[12] The lagged dependent variables are highly significant, ranging from .13 to .30, and indicate that the longer-run intervention response exceeds the initial impact effects. The adjusted R^2 statistics

[12] The estimated exchange rate coefficients using the yen-denominated measure of intervention tend to be smaller than the dollar-denominated measures. This is because of the valuation effects of exchange rate changes on the yen value of foreign reserve

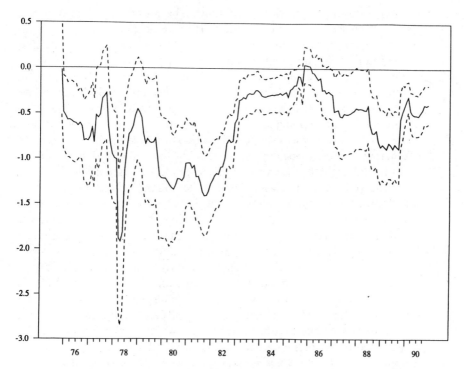

Figure 10.7. Response of foreign exchange reserves to exchange rate. Rolling 33-month sample periods (30 degrees of freedom).

indicate that substantial variation in international reserves remains unexplained by the model (about 90 percent when using the yen-based international reserves measure), reflecting the simplicity of the empirical formulation.

In order to investigate the stability of the degree of intervention, we employ a series of thirty-three-month rolling OLS regressions using the $\Delta FA\$$ measure of intervention and a lagged dependent variable (i.e., the first estimation period covers 1973:3–1975:12, the second covers 1973:4–1976:1, and so on, until the last period, covering 1988:4–1990:12). Each regression has thirty degrees of freedom. The results are summarized in Figure 10.7, where the coefficient on the exchange rate

holdings. As the monetary authorities sell dollar reserves and buy yen in order to limit depreciation of the yen (a rise in the yen price of the dollar), the depreciation of the yen renders the value of remaining dollar reserve holdings larger in yen terms. Hence, yen-denominated reserve holdings decline less in response to a given exchange rate change.

(β) in the rolling regressions is plotted. The identifying date noted in the chart represents the end of the thirty-three-observation sample period for each of the rolling regressions. A 10 percent statistical confidence interval for the point estimates is also plotted.

Observe that the intervention coefficient tended to be highest (in absolute value) for sample periods ending with observations in the late 1970s and early 1980s, when the yen was generally depreciating. This is consistent with a policy of greater sales of dollar reserves (and purchases of yen) in order to support the value of the yen. The intervention coefficient tended to be lowest, indicating less sale of dollars, in the periods ending with observations in the middle to late 1980s, roughly when the yen was appreciating against the dollar.[13] Thus, when the yen was depreciating, the monetary authorities sold relatively more dollar reserves, while when the yen was appreciating, they sold relatively fewer dollar reserves. This is consistent with a policy of moderating exchange rate movements in both periods – that is, leaning against the wind – but with a stronger response on average attempting to limit yen depreciation.

This finding is confirmed with a regression that reestimates (10.1) with separate variables for ΔXR when the yen is appreciating and when it is depreciating. (The first variable is constructed by multiplying ΔXR by a dummy variable that has a value of 1 when ΔXR is positive and a value of 0 otherwise; the second variable is constructed analogously with a dummy variable that has a value of 1 when ΔXR is negative.) The results, reported in the bottom panel of Table 10.1, show that the Japanese monetary authorities indeed tended to intervene roughly three times more in response to a depreciation than to an appreciation.[14] They are consistent with Takagi's (1991) estimates of intervention activity by the Japanese authorities.[15]

At first glance it appears odd that a bias by policymakers toward foreign exchange sales (against yen depreciation) is consistent with the large accumulation of foreign exchange reserves by Japan over the last two decades, as shown in Figure 10.1. However, given the relatively

---

[13] The finding of limited intervention and sales of dollars in 1983 and 1984, even though the value of the yen was then low, indicates that the BOJ was refraining from much active intervention during this period. From late 1985 through mid-1988, as the yen appreciated rapidly, the stance of intervention became more active. The BOJ clearly sought to limit further yen appreciation by buying dollars, particularly in 1987 after the February Louvre Accord and the October stock market crash.

[14] An F-test indicates that this difference is statistically significant.

[15] This finding is not consistent with Hutchison (1984), however, perhaps because of the earlier and more limited sample period (March 1973 to November 1981) employed in his study.

high longer-term productivity growth and other factors contributing to rising international competitiveness in Japan, the yen has appreciated against the dollar over most of the managed floating rate period. Under these circumstances, a symmetric leaning-against-the-wind policy would have led to an even greater accumulation of foreign exchange reserves and subsequent problems for monetary control.[16] From this perspective, greater resistance to currency depreciation than to appreciation may be interpreted as an effort by the BOJ to limit the potentially excessive monetary stimulus associated with the trend accumulation of foreign reserves.

10.4   Sterilization policy

An activist intervention policy does not necessarily impede a central bank's ability to control monetary targets and pursue domestic policy targets. The authorities may sterilize most or all of the effects of foreign exchange reserve changes on money aggregates by systematically adjusting the level of domestic credit. Under this circumstance, monetary control would be insulated from exchange intervention operations, at least in the short run.[17] To explore this aspect of policy, we estimate the degree of sterilization of foreign exchange intervention by the BOJ over the managed floating rate period.

10.4.1 *Sterilization regressions*

The change in the monetary base, ΔMB, can be expressed as

$$\Delta\text{MB}_t = \Delta\text{FA}_t + \Delta\text{DC}_t, \tag{10.2}$$

where ΔFA and ΔDC denote the change in the official foreign reserve and domestic credit components of the monetary base, respectively, all valued in yen. We assume that domestic credit changes depend on current and lagged interventions ΔFA_{t-j}, as well as autoregressive lags,

$$\Delta\text{DC}_t = \sum_{j=0}^{m} \gamma_j \, \Delta\text{FA}_{t-j} + \sum_{j=1}^{n} \alpha_j \, \Delta\text{DC}_{t-j} + \nu_t, \tag{10.3}$$

---

[16] This assumes that intervention operations per se have not changed the long-term trend in the yen–dollar exchange rate.

[17] The extent to which sterilization is possible, and, more generally, the ability to insulate domestic policy objectives from external considerations, is dependent on the degree of capital mobility and other factors. See Herring and Marston (1977) for an exposition of this point within the context of a portfolio balance model.

where v_t is a random variable that represents other changes. The lag pattern of the individual γ_j coefficients reflects how sterilization is distributed over time. The long-run multiplier response of domestic credit to foreign asset changes is given by $\Sigma_{j=0}^{m} \gamma_j / (1 - \Sigma_{j=1}^{n} \alpha_j)$. If $\gamma_0 > -1$, intervention is less than fully sterilized in the current period and there is an initial effect on the monetary base. Whether or not foreign exchange interventions are sterilized completely in the long run depends on the lagged pattern of intervention.

The effect of intervention in period t and in earlier periods on base monetary growth in the current period can be expressed as

$$\Delta MB_t = \sum_{j=1}^{n} \alpha_j \, \Delta MB_{t-j} + (1 + \gamma_0) \, \Delta FA_t + \sum_{j=1}^{n} (\gamma_j - \alpha_j) \, \Delta FA_{t-j}$$
$$+ \sum_{j=m}^{m-n} \gamma_j \, \Delta FA_{t-j} + v_t, \tag{10.4}$$

assuming $m > n$. Observe that the coefficients on lagged intervention terms are linear combinations of lagged sterilization (γ_j) and lagged adjustment (α_j) coefficients. This points to the difficulty of interpreting coefficients in dynamic monetary base equations.[18] In order to analyze the behavior of Japanese monetary authorities, we estimate equation (10.3) empirically with seasonally adjusted monthly data over the managed floating rate period.

We measure ΔMB by the change in the source side of the monetary base, ΔMBS, discussed in Section 10.2. ΔFA is measured by changes in FABOJ, also discussed earlier. It reflects the incipient addition to domestic base money resulting from the BOJ's acquisition of foreign exchange and excludes exchange rate valuation effects that should not be reflected as changes in the monetary base. Changes in domestic credit, ΔDC, are defined as the difference between the changes in the monetary base and foreign reserves. All estimates of (10.3) included two lags of domestic credit ($n = 2$), contemporaneous and three lags of foreign assets ($m = 3$), a constant, and a trend term. This specification appeared to capture suitably the dynamics of domestic credit adjustment.

One potential econometric problem with estimating (10.3) (or 10.4)) by OLS arises from the possible simultaneity of ΔMB and ΔDC, on the

---

[18] Von Hagen (1989), for example, estimates a monetary base equation like (10.4) for Germany over the period 1979–88 and finds that the sum of the coefficients on ΔFA terms is significantly different from zero. He also finds, however, that the sum of coefficients in a regression like (10.3), of domestic credit on contemporaneous and lagged changes of international reserves, is insignificantly different from -1 (see also Obstfeld, 1983).

one hand, and ΔFA, on the other. In the presence of a systematic foreign exchange intervention rule, the change in reserves valued at a constant exchange rate may be correlated with the disturbance to the monetary base and domestic credit equations. If such a correlation exists, then OLS estimates are inconsistent. To take account of this possibility, we estimate (10.3) with instrumental variables (INST) as well as OLS.

Table 10.2 presents results of the estimates for the contemporaneous coefficient (γ_0) as well as the long-run multiplier ($\Sigma_{j=0}^{3} \gamma_j / (1 - \Sigma_{j=1}^{2} \alpha_j)$) of foreign asset changes on domestic credit. We consider the full managed floating period 1973:5–1990:12, as well as various subperiods corresponding to possible policy regime shifts by the BOJ in 1978:7 with the announced adoption of official monetary growth targets, and in 1985:9 following the Plaza Agreement by the G-5 countries to coordinate intervention.[19] We also test for asymmetry in the sterilization response between episodes of yen appreciation and depreciation.

Focusing on the OLS results, observe that over the full period the contemporaneous coefficient on foreign exchange reserves of $-.75$ is significantly different from -1 at better than 1 percent; the long-run multiplier of $-.88$ is significantly different from -1 only at the 13 percent level. Thus, in the long run it cannot be rejected that foreign asset changes were fully offset by domestic credit changes, leaving the monetary base unchanged. For the period 1973:5–1978:6, the offset was less than one for one, both in the short run ($-.47$) and in the long run ($-.64$). This implies that, during this period, foreign intervention had some positive effect on the monetary base. A one-for-one long-run offset, leaving the monetary base unchanged, cannot be rejected during either the period 1978:7–1985:8 or the period 1985:9–1990:12.[20] The results using instrumental variables suggest a similar shift in the extent of sterilization between the 1973:5–1978:6 period and afterward.

[19] See Takagi (1991) for a characterization of different monetary and exchange rate policy regimes in Japan since 1973.

[20] These results contrast somewhat with those of Takagi (1991), who estimates an equation for the monetary base that assumes only contemporaneous intervention, using quarterly data over the period 1973:Q1–1989:Q2. (His specification also includes the call money rate, the percent change in the wholesale price index, and the lagged change in the monetary base.) He finds that the coefficient on contemporaneous foreign asset changes was insignificant for the full period, but was negative and significant for the period 1973:Q2–1978:Q2 (indicating oversterilization), insignificant for the period 1978:Q3–1985:Q3, and positive and significant for the period 1985:Q4–1989:Q2 (indicating partial sterilization). He interprets this as implying that the BOJ has become more accommodative over time in the sense that it allowed an increasingly larger part of changes in the foreign asset component of the monetary base to affect the overall monetary base.

Table 10.2. *Response of domestic credit to foreign asset changes*

Sample period	Contemporaneous	Long-run multiplier	Q-msl	Adj. R^2	Regression technique
1973:5–1990:12	−0.75 (.00)	−0.88 (.13)	.01	.52	OLS
	−0.90 (.74)	−1.02 (.95)	.01	.50	INST
1973:5–1978:6	−0.47 (.00)	−0.64 (.13)	.90	.30	OLS
	−0.20 (.03)	−0.35 (.16)	.96	.23	INST
1978:7–1985:8	−0.85 (.08)	−0.99 (.94)	.02	.53	OLS
	−0.80 (.46)	−0.95 (.86)	.01	.53	INST
1985:9–1990:12	−0.76 (.00)	−0.90 (.27)	.45	.66	OLS
	−0.84 (.55)	−0.95 (.79)	.48	.65	INST
1978:7–1990:12	−0.79 (.00)	−0.90 (.24)	.02	.58	OLS
	−0.84 (.55)	−0.95 (.81)	.02	.57	INST

Sample period	Exchange rate appreciation		Exchange rate depreciation		Adj. R^2
	Contemporaneous	Long-run multiplier	Contemporaneous	Long-run multiplier	
1973:5–1990:12	−0.74 (.00)	−0.96 (.75)	−0.73 (.00)	−0.78 (.04)	.53
1978:7–1990:12	−0.78 (.02)	−0.95 (.69)	−0.77 (.00)	−0.83 (.14)	.58

Note: All equations included contemporaneous and three lags of foreign asset changes, two lags of the dependent variable, a constant, and a time trend. Numbers in parentheses for the contemporaneous effect denote marginal significance levels of t-statistic against −1; numbers in parentheses for the long-run multiplier effect denote marginal significance levels of F-test against −1; Q-msl refers to the marginal significance level of the Ljung–Box Q-statistic for serial correlation.

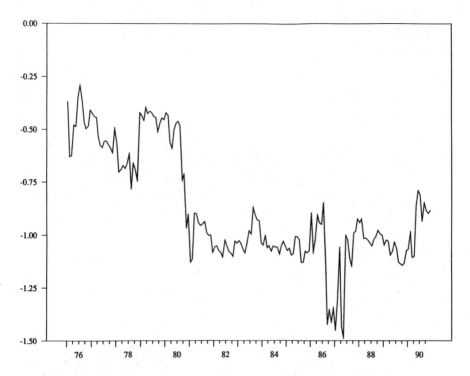

Figure 10.8. Long-run response of domestic credit to foreign exchange reserves. Rolling 33-month sample periods (25 degrees of freedom).

Figure 10.8 reports the rolling OLS regression results for the long-run multiplier response of domestic credit to foreign exchange asset changes, based on thirty-three-month rolling regressions. Each regression has twenty-five degrees of freedom. The identifying date noted in the chart represents the end of the thirty-three-month sample period for each of the rolling regressions. The figure confirms the earlier finding of a less than one-for-one degree of long-run sterilization of foreign asset changes in the mid-1970s to late 1970s, in contrast to nearly complete sterilization in subsequent periods.[21] This suggests a shift in the ability or desire of Japanese monetary authorities to sterilize the effects of foreign asset changes on the monetary base.

OLS tests of sterilization asymmetry across periods of yen appreciation and depreciation are reported in the lower panel of Table 10.2.

---

[21] There is some evidence at the end of 1980 of "oversterilization," i.e., a greater than proportionate change in domestic credit in response to foreign asset changes.

Observe that the initial response appears to be virtually identical irrespective of whether the yen is appreciating or depreciating. The contemporaneous sterilization coefficient estimate for the full sample period 1973:5–1990:12 is $-.74$ for intervention when the yen is appreciating and $-.73$ when it is depreciating. But estimates of subsequent sterilization, indicated by the long-run multipliers in the table, suggest that the BOJ sought more vigorously to insulate the monetary base during intervention episodes associated with yen appreciation. In particular, the estimated long-run sterilization coefficient is $-.96$ for episodes of yen appreciation and $-.78$ for episodes of yen depreciation. Thus, the sterilization coefficient estimates indicate that Japanese policymakers appear more reluctant to allow intervention activity to influence the monetary base during periods of yen appreciation – that is, when it is likely to prove expansionary.

10.4.2   VECM analysis

The sterilization coefficient estimates derived earlier were obtained from estimation of a single "structural" equation – the policy reaction function (10.3) – in the context of a broader, simultaneously determined system of equations representing the macroeconomy. As such, these estimates represent a partial equilibrium effect, as opposed to the full reduced-form effect, of official reserve changes on domestic credit. The full reduced-form effect in principle depends both on the policy response itself and on feedback effects of the private sector – for example, bank portfolio adjustments to sterilization and intervention operations. Hence, the ultimate effects of intervention operations on monetary control are not adequately described by policy reaction function estimates alone. This suggests the desirability of reduced-form estimates from a broader simultaneous equation system.

To address this issue we specify a simultaneous equation time series model using a vector error correction modeling strategy (VECM). This technique allows us to evaluate reduced-form effects without explicitly modeling the structural linkages in the system. It permits evaluation of the full reduced-form effects of a change ("impulse") in foreign exchange reserves on domestic credit, while controlling for the short-term dynamic interactions of these and other variables in the system.

Our VECM model is specified as

$$\Delta X_t = \Gamma_1 \Delta X_{t-1} + \cdots + \Gamma_{k-1} \Delta X_{t-k+1}$$
$$+ \alpha(\beta' X_{t-1}) + u + \epsilon_t, \tag{10.5}$$

where X is a four-variable vector consisting of DC, FA, Japanese industrial production (IP), and Japan's consumer price level (P). DC and FA are specified in trillions of yen, and IP and P are in natural log levels. The vector of error correction terms (with one lag) are denoted by $\beta'X$; α is the parameter vector indicating the speed of adjustment to an eventual equilibrium; $\Gamma_1 \ldots \Gamma_{k-1}$ are parameter vectors reflecting short-run dynamics. u is a vector of constants, and ϵ is a vector of Gaussian error terms. IP and P are included in the model to control for other factors that may influence the timing and magnitude of the domestic credit response to foreign asset changes. The model allows for the possibility of (but does not assume) an "equilibrium" (co-integrating) relationship among all of the variables in X – that is, a tendency for the variables to move together over longer periods of time. Such a constant long-run relationship implies that policy reaction functions and other structural features of the economy linking these variables are stable.

We estimate the model over the 1978:7–1990:12 period when the BOJ is generally viewed as having focused more on money aggregate targeting.[22] We restrict estimation to a six-month lag autoregressive system ($k = 7$). The empirical analysis proceeds in four steps:[23] (i) estimation of the longer-term relationships (co-integration) in the data using the Johansen methodology (Johansen, 1991); (ii) estimation of the VECM with the error correction terms implied by the co-integrating relationships; (iii) calculation of the moving average representation (MAR) of the model from the VECM estimates (using the Choleski decomposition to identify contemporaneous shocks); and (iv) calculation of the impulse response functions from the MAR.

Omitting details,[24] we focus on the impulse response function results,

[22] FA and DC are measured, as in the sterilization regressions, by the BOJ foreign asset proxy, FABOJ, and by the difference between the source-side measure of the monetary base, MBS, and FABOJ, respectively. Both of these series were seasonally adjusted using the X-11 procedure of SAS. The CPI is obtained from *IFS*, line 64; the industrial production index is from the *IFS*, line 66 . . c.

[23] Before testing for co-integrating relationships, we determined the order of integration of each variable individually using augmented Dickey–Fuller tests. We could not reject a unit root in levels, but could reject a unit root in first differences, for all of the variables of interest. The variables were therefore modeled as $I(1)$ processes, i.e., first-difference stationary. For the sake of brevity, these results are not reported in the text, but are available from the authors upon request.

[24] Using the two maximum likelihood ratio tests suggested by Johansen (1991) and the critical values tabulated in Johansen and Juselius (1991), we cannot reject the existence of one, and possibly two, co-integrating vectors in our four-variable system. The trace statistic values were 59.18 for $r = 0$, 30.88 for $r \leq 1$, 9.03 for $r \leq 2$, and 2.10 for $r \leq 3$. The maximum eigenvalue statistics were 28.30 for $r = 0$, 21.86 for $r = 1$, 6.93 for $r = 2$, and 2.10 for $r = 3$. At the .05 critical values, the trace statistic suggests at most

Table 10.3. *Effect of one unit foreign asset shock on domestic credit (cumulative impulse response from VECM)*

Months ahead	Response
1	− .80
2	− .72
3	− .68
4	− .48
5	− .39
6	− .36
9	− .45
12	− .45
15	− .38
18	− .41
21	− .38
24	− .37

Note: Results estimated from a VECM containing foreign assets, domestic credit, consumer prices, and industrial production.

reflecting the cumulative effect on domestic credit from a one-unit shock in foreign assets. These results are shown in Table 10.3. The initial impact effect estimated is −0.80, indicating that the combination of BOJ sterilization operations and private sector portfolio shifts cause domestic credit changes to offset 80 percent of the monetary-base impact of foreign exchange market intervention. This estimate is strikingly similar to the contemporaneous partial equilibrium OLS estimates shown in Table 10.2 for this sample period.

The effect of the initial sterilization operations is apparently offset by private sector portfolio adjustment, however, and the estimated cumulative effect gradually declines (in absolute value) until reaching −0.37 after about twenty-four months. This indicates that more than 60 percent of a rise in foreign assets eventually filters through to an increase in the monetary base. Thus, when the more complicated dy-

one co-integrating vector ($r = 0$ is rejected, but $r \leq 1$ is not rejected), while the maximum eigenvalue statistics indicate either one or two co-integrating vectors; i.e., $r = 0$ is rejected and $r = 1$ is close to rejection. The model is specified more completely, with a more comprehensive set of results for Japan and Germany, in Glick and Hutchison (1994).

namic structure of a simultaneous system is taken into account, we find that international reserve changes eventually have affected the growth of Japan's monetary base; foreign exchange intervention is not fully sterilized in the long run.

10.5 Monetary control

Unsterilized intervention directly affects base money and, through this link, influences broader money aggregates and monetary conditions generally. This raises two questions. First, how strong is the link between monetary base and broad money growth in the case of Japan? This is important because unsterilized intervention operations may not materially affect monetary conditions if the broad money–monetary base ratio (or money multiplier) moves in an offsetting direction (e.g., declines concurrently with unsterilized purchases of foreign exchange). Second, are there episodes when particularly rapid money growth can be considered compatible with price stability due, for example, to financial market and regulatory changes that increased money demand? In such circumstances intervention and the unsterilized accumulation of foreign exchange inflows may have limited inflationary impact.

To help us address these questions, Figure 10.9 plots the money multiplier as the ratio of broad money (M2 + CDs) to the monetary base over the managed floating exchange rate period.[25] Significant short-term swings in the multiplier are evident, suggesting that, at least in the short run, unsterilized intervention operations may not have a predictable influence on broad money growth. Observe, in particular, the significant decline in the ratio during the period 1972–5, attributable in part to the raising of bank reserve requirements and tightening of "window guidance" as instruments of tighter monetary policy during this period.[26]

Observe also in Figure 10.9 the significant long-term rise in the multiplier from the mid-1970s. The multiplier climbed from roughly 8.5 in early 1975 before leveling off at almost 12 in the late 1980s, a 50 percent increase. It is beyond the scope of this essay to analyze the factors underlying this development. The important point for our purposes is that the rise in the multiplier implies that a given amount of unsterilized

---

[25] The series for broad money and the monetary base are represented by BM and MB, respectively.

[26] See Organization for Economic Cooperation and Development, *Economic Surveys* (1975), for a description of how window guidance was extended to cover a range of financial institutions beyond the city banks and how selective credit controls were adopted beginning in 1973.

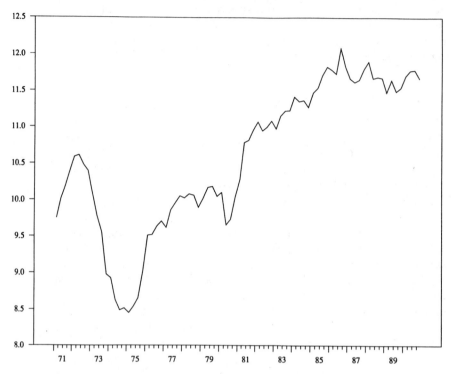

Figure 10.9. Ratio of broad money (M2 + CDs) to monetary base.

intervention operations in the 1980s should have a larger impact on broad money growth and hence greater potential inflationary impact than previously.

Our analysis in Section 10.2 of focal episodes of sharp yen appreciation in 1971–3, during the end of Bretton Woods, and in 1985–7, following the Plaza Agreement, suggested that the accumulation of foreign reserves did, in fact, contribute to rapid monetary base and broad money growth. Was money growth during these periods "excessive"?

Figure 10.10 shows the cumulative percent differences between actual broad money (M2 + CDs) growth and forecasts of broad money growth during these two episodes. The forecasts are derived from out-of-sample dynamic predictions of a simple twenty-four-lag autoregressive money growth equation, with a constant and time trend, estimated over the period 1971:1–1990:12. The horizontal scale in Figure 10.10 measures the number of months after the beginning of each episode – dated as 1971:8 in the first case and 1985:9 in the second. Positive (negative)

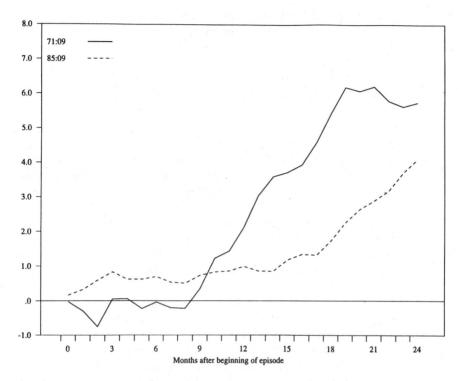

Figure 10.10. Cumulative broad money forecast errors.

values indicate the underprediction (overprediction) of actual money growth.

The figure shows that in both episodes actual money growth was much more rapid than forecast: the cumulative forecast error was more than 6 percent by early 1973 and almost 4 percent in mid-1987. Thus, based on past autoregressive patterns and trends in money growth, growth rates in both episodes of yen appreciation were unusually high. The fact that, in contrast to the experience of the early 1970s, the second episode did not result in immediately explosive consumer price inflation may be attributed in part to a favorable shift of money demand associated with financial liberalization that accommodated the excessive money growth.[27] Nonetheless, the intervention efforts and accumulation of foreign reserves to limit yen appreciation after the Plaza Agreement clearly created the potential for additional inflation that eventually

---

[27] Takagi (1991) makes this point as well. He also emphasizes the role of declining interest rates in raising money demand during this period. Also see Yoshida and Rasche (1990).

emerged in the late 1980s. In this case external considerations created problems for domestic monetary control.

10.6   Conclusion

This essay has explored the linkages between foreign exchange market intervention policy and monetary policy in Japan in order to determine whether attempts to influence the exchange rate have forced the Bank of Japan to compromise on its commitment to monetary control. Although the intervention and sterilization policies of the Japanese monetary authorities have varied across time periods and particular episodes of sharp change in the value of the yen, a number of broad findings emerge from our analysis.

Our empirical work indicates that Japan generally has followed an active foreign exchange intervention policy for most of the post–Bretton Woods period, driven in large part by a desire to dampen exchange rate fluctuations against the U.S. dollar ("leaning against the wind"). We find evidence that Japanese intervention policy has been asymmetric in the sense that the magnitude of foreign exchange reserves expended to restrain yen depreciation has generally been larger than that of reserve purchases to limit yen appreciation.

Estimates of the sterilization coefficients of a domestic credit equation indicate that the BOJ has attempted to offset a large part of the monetary effects of foreign exchange intervention operations. We also find, however, that when a more complicated dynamic system structure is taken into account, international reserve changes eventually do influence monetary base growth. Thus, in the long run, foreign exchange intervention in Japan is not fully sterilized.

Consistent with the pattern of intervention policy, we found that sterilization policy has also been asymmetric. Specifically, sterilization has generally been less during episodes of yen depreciation when the BOJ is losing foreign exchange reserves. This has tended to dampen monetary base growth and tighten monetary conditions precisely when the yen weakens. Conversely, Japanese sterilization policy has been more reluctant to allow intervention activity to influence the monetary base during periods of yen appreciation – that is, when it is likely to prove expansionary in nature.

Has domestic monetary control in Japan been affected as a consequence of its activist intervention policy? By international standards, Japan has certainly displayed successful inflation performance. The asymmetric nature of intervention and sterilization in the BOJ's operations, against a background of trend yen appreciation, may have played a role in this success. Resisting yen depreciation more vigorously than yen appreciation, and allowing foreign exchange sales to have a larger impact than foreign exchange purchases on base money, helps limit the overall accumulation of international reserves and dampens upward pressure on money growth. A symmetric activist policy would have led to a much larger accumulation of foreign exchange reserves and problems for monetary control. By implementing monetary policy in this way, the BOJ has reconciled somewhat the tension in policymaking that often arises when central banks attempt to balance internal and external objectives.

Nevertheless, while on average monetary policy in Japan has worked well, actions to limit sharp appreciations of the yen have resulted in money growth being somewhat higher than it would otherwise have been and have exacerbated the problems of monetary control. This is most apparent with the experience of the early 1970s. However, the more recent 1985–8 episode suggests the same conclusion. Intervention against the rise in the yen undoubtedly contributed to an expansion of the monetary aggegates. It can be argued that only an offsetting increase in the demand for money associated with financial liberalization limited the inflationary impact of this monetary stimulus. Thus, efforts to influence the exchange rate have had an impact on domestic monetary control in Japan.

Appendix: the mechanics of intervention and sterilization in Japan

The link between exchange rate policies and monetary control arises from the central bank's balance sheet. Domestic monetary control is achieved primarily by controlling the growth rate of the monetary base – commercial bank deposits at the central bank plus currency in circulation. The monetary base, on the sources side, consists of domestic assets and international reserves held by the central bank. Exchange rate control requires purchases and sales of foreign assets, which change the international reserves component of the base. Only if such foreign exchange interventions are "sterilized" completely, that is, have no effect on monetary base growth, will exchange rate policies not impede domestic monetary control. Otherwise, foreign exchange market interventions have some impact on the growth of the monetary base and, consequently, on domestic monetary control.

The mechanics of intervention and sterilization in Japan are similar to those in other industrial countries and work as follows. When intervening in the foreign exchange market, the BOJ acts as the agent of the

Ministry of Finance through the FEFSA of the central government. Foreign exchange market intervention involves a funds transfer between the FEFSA and the commercial banking sector and thereby directly affects the monetary base. When the FEFSA buys dollars through the BOJ, the yen funds necessary to finance the transaction are usually raised by issuing foreign exchange bills, all of which are purchased by the BOJ. In the consolidated account of the BOJ and FEFSA, the amount of foreign exchange bills issued by the FEFSA and bought by the BOJ will cancel out. The BOJ therefore needs to sell securities (e.g., government bonds, financing bills, Treasury bills) in order to absorb yen funds if it is to "sterilize" the impact of dollar purchases on the monetary base.

References

Bryant, Ralph (1991). "Model Representations of Japanese Money Policy," (Bank of Japan) *Monetary and Economic Studies* 9:11–61.

Friedman, Milton (1985). "Monetarism in Rhetoric and Practice." In A. Ando, H. Eguchi, R. Farmer, and Y. Suzuki, eds., *Monetary Policy in Our Times,* pp. 15–28. Cambridge, MA: MIT Press, 1985.

Fukui, Toshiko (1986). "The Recent Development of the Short-Term Money Market in Japan and Changes in the Techniques and Procedures of Monetary Control Used by the Bank of Japan." In *Changes in Money Market Instruments and Procedures: Objectives and Implications,* pp. 94–126. Basel: Bank for International Settlements.

Glick, Reuven, and Michael Hutchison, (1994). "Foreign Exchange Reserves and Money Dynamics in Germany and Japan." Unpublished manuscript, Federal Reserve Bank of San Francisco.

Hamada, Koichi, and Fumio Hayashi (1985). "Monetary Policy in Postwar Japan." In A. Ando, H. Eguchi, R. Farmer, and Y. Suzuki, eds., *Monetary Policy in Our Times,* pp. 83–121. Cambridge, MA: MIT Press.

Herring, Richard, and Richard Marston (1977). "Sterilization Policy: The Tradeoff between Monetary Autonomy and Control over Foreign Exchange Reserves," *European Economic Review* 10:225–343.

Hutchison, Michael (1984). "Official Japanese Intervention in the Foreign Exchange Market: Leaning Against the Wind?" *Economics Letters* 15:115–20.

(1988). "Monetary Control with an Exchange Rate Objective: The Bank of Japan, 1973–86," *Journal of International Money and Finance* 7:261–71.

(1991). *Aggregate Demand, Uncertainty, and Oil Prices: The 1990 Oil Shock in Comparative Perspective,* BIS Economic Papers no. 31. Basel.

Ito, Takatoshi (1989). "Is the Bank of Japan a Closet Monetarist? Monetary Targeting in Japan, 1978–1988," NBER Working Paper no. 2874. Cambridge, MA.

Johansen, Søren (1991). "Estimation and Hypothesis Testing of Cointegrating Vectors in Gaussian Autoregression Models," *Econometrica* 59:1551–80.

Johansen, Søren, and Katarina Juselius (1991). "Maximum Likelihood Estimation and Inference on Cointegration with Applications for the Demand for Money," *Oxford Bulletin of Economics and Statistics* 52:169–210.

Obstfeld, Maurice (1983). "Exchange Rates, Inflation, and the Sterilization Problem: Germany 1975–81," *European Economic Review* 21:161–89.

Poole, William (1992). "Exchange-Rate Management and Monetary-Policy Mismanagement: A Study of Germany, Japan, United Kingdom, and United States after Plaza," *Carnegie Rochester Conference Series on Public Policy* 36:57–92.

Quirk, Peter (1977). "Exchange Rate Policy in Japan: Leaning Against the Wind," (International Monetary Fund) *Staff Papers* 24:642–64.

Suzuki, Yoshio (1985). "Japan's Monetary Policy over the Past 10 Years," (Bank of Japan) *Monetary and Economic Studies* 3:1–18.

Takagi, Shinji (1991). "Foreign Exchange Market Intervention and Domestic Monetary Control in Japan, 1973–89," *Japan and the World Economy* 3:147–80.

Tschoegl, Adrian (1989). "Money Supply, Forex Intervention and the Stock Market." SBCI Securities (Asia), Tokyo.

von Hagen, Jürgen (1989). "Monetary Targeting with Exchange Rate Constraints: The Bundesbank in the 1980s," (Federal Reserve Bank of St. Louis) *Economic Review* (September–October):53–69.

Yoshida, Tomoo, and Robert Rasche (1990). "The M2 Demand in Japan: Shifted and Unstable?" (Bank of Japan) *Monetary and Economic Studies* 8:9–30.

CHAPTER 11

The signaling effect of foreign exchange intervention: the case of Japan

Tsutomu Watanabe

11.1 Introduction

Large-scale foreign exchange intervention by the central banks of major industrial countries since the Plaza Agreement has revived discussion concerning the effectiveness of official intervention.[1] One of the common findings in the recent literature is the importance of the signaling channel of official intervention: market participants observing official intervention revise their expectations of future monetary policy, which induces a change in the current level of the exchange rate. For example, according to Dominguez and Frankel (1990), a $100 million of official intervention had an estimated effect of 4 percent on the exchange rate through the signaling channel, while the effect through the portfolio balance channel was less than 0.1 percent. Also, in a comparative discussion of the Carter administration's dollar support operations of late 1978 and the Plaza Agreement of 1985, Marston (1988) points out that the effectiveness of sterilized intervention depends crucially on the ex-

I thank Reuven Glick, Michael Hutchison, and Shinji Takagi for helpful comments. The views presented are the author's alone and do not reflect those of the Institute for Monetary and Economic Studies or the Bank of Japan.

[1] For example, Dominguez and Frankel (1990), using the dollar–mark data of October 1984 to December 1987, estimate a two-equation simultaneous system that considers both the signaling and portfolio balance channels and find that official intervention had a statistically significant effect on the movement of the exchange rate. The same method is applied by Dominguez (1990) to the dollar–yen exchange rate from January 1985 to December 1988. Humpage (1988) examines U.S. intervention from August 1984 to August 1987 and finds that there were three instances when intervention clearly affected the exchange rates. Klein and Rosengren (1991), looking at intervention in the United States and Germany from September 1985 to October 1989, report that coordinated intervention had a statistically significant impact on daily exchange rate changes.

tent to which the intervention changes the market's expectations about future monetary policy.

In the context of an incomplete-information game between market participants and a central bank with inside information about future monetary policy, the signaling hypothesis can be broken down into two parts.[2] The first relates to the optimizing behavior of the central bank. Given a functional relationship between intervention signals and market expectations about future monetary policy, the central bank minimizes some well-specified loss function by choosing the amount of intervention. The second relates to the formation of market expectations about future monetary policy. Given a functional relationship between inside information and intervention signals, market participants use Bayesian methods of inference to form expectations about future monetary policy conditional on intervention signals. A perfect Bayesian equilibrium is defined as the functional relationship between inside information and intervention signals that is compatible with both the central bank's optimizing behavior and the market's Bayesian inference.

Corresponding to such a decomposition of the signaling hypothesis, there are two methods of empirically testing the hypothesis. The first is to examine the behavior of a central bank by focusing on the link between intervention signals and future monetary policy. In the context of Japan, we can test whether the Bank of Japan's sale of dollars tends to be followed by monetary tightening. The second method is to examine the market's expectations about future monetary policy. A testable implication is that market participants tend to expect tight monetary policy in the future when they observe the Bank of Japan selling dollars.

From a viewpoint of studying the signaling effect of intervention on the current exchange rate, the second approach appears to be simple, straightforward, and therefore more attractive. If the market's expectations about future monetary policy were observable, we could directly test the signaling hypothesis. Unfortunately, however, no such data are available. For this reason, the first approach will be adopted in this essay. In particular, we will empirically examine in Section 11.3 the behavior of the Bank of Japan by looking at the correlation between intervention and monetary policy.[3]

[2] For a game-theoretic framework to deal with intervention signaling, see Watanabe (1991).
[3] It is important to note that we deal only with a necessary condition of the signaling hypothesis. It is true that if there exists no link between intervention and monetary policy, market participants who are rational in the Bayesian sense would never revise their expectations about future monetary policy when observing official interven-

The core mechanism of the signaling hypothesis is that inside information about future monetary policy flows from a central bank to market participants through intervention. Since the role of intervention is to provide "news" for market participants, intervention should not be fully anticipated if it were to have any effect on the exchange rate. Fully anticipated intervention gives no surprise to the market, and would thus never influence the current exchange rate. Section 11.3 empirically examines the extent to which interventions of the Bank of Japan were anticipated.

This essay is organized as follows. Section 11.2 presents a simple theoretical model to deal with the signaling channel of official intervention and derives two testable implications of the model: (i) intervention should precede monetary policy changes in a predictable manner; (ii) effective intervention should not be anticipated by market participants. The first implication is examined empirically in Section 11.3 and the second in Section 11.4. Section 11.5 concludes the essay.

11.2   Implications of the signaling hypothesis

11.2.1   *A simple model*

Let us begin the analysis with the assumption that the current spot exchange rate is determined by a scalar measure of exchange rate fundamentals and the expected change in the exchange rate. That is,

$$s_t = f_t + \beta E(s_{t+1} - s_t \mid \Omega_t), \tag{11.1}$$

where s_t is the logarithm of the yen–dollar rate, f_t the factor representing fundamentals, Ω_t the set of information currently available to market participants, and β the elasticity of the current exchange rate with respect to expectations. In the target zone model of Krugman (1991), where equation (11.1) is derived in a simple flexible-price monetary model, f_t is a linear function of variables that enter money market equilibrium, including the logarithm of the money supply.

Assuming away the possibility of bubble solutions, the solution of this difference equation is given by

---

tion. In this sense, it is meaningful to check this link empirically. This is essentially what we will pursue in Section 11.3. But the existence of a link between intervention and monetary policy does not guarantee that a link exists between intervention and the market's expectations about future monetary policy, and there appears to be a large gap between the two. Examination of the latter link would be the next step.

$$s_t = (1 + \beta)^{-1} \sum_{j=0}^{\infty} [\beta(1 + \beta)^{-1}]^j E(f_{t+j} \mid \Omega_t), \qquad (11.2)$$

which simply says that the current exchange rate is essentially determined by market expectations about the future values of fundamentals conditional on currently available information.

Suppose market participants observe the Bank of Japan intervening in the foreign exchange market at time t. Let x_t denote the yen value of the net purchase of foreign currencies. Because the focus of this essay is on the signaling effect of official intervention, we assume that (i) official intervention is completely sterilized, and (ii) sterilized intervention is ineffective through the portfolio balance channel. These assumptions, which are introduced mainly for simplification, seem realistic to some extent. For example, Takagi (1991) finds that foreign exchange intervention by the Bank of Japan had no significant effect on the monetary base during the period 1973–89. As for the second assumption, Dominguez and Frankel (1990), among others, report that the effect of sterilized intervention through the portfolio balance channel is trivial. Unless otherwise mentioned, these two assumptions will be maintained throughout this essay.

The sole consequence of central bank intervention under these assumptions is to alter the information set Ω. Denoting the information set *before* and *after* the observation of the intervention by Ω and Ω', respectively, we can express the change in the exchange rate at time t induced by the official intervention, Δs, as

$$\Delta s = (1 + \beta)^{-1} \sum_{j=0}^{\infty} [\beta(1 + \beta)^{-1}]^j$$
$$\times E(f_{t+j} \mid \Omega_t') - E(f_{t+j} \mid \Omega_t)]. \qquad (11.3)$$

According to equation (11.3), sterilized intervention is effective to the extent that it influences market expectations about the future values of exchange rate fundamentals.

To extract further implications from equation (11.3), we add some assumptions. First, we specify the information set as follows. Let Y_t denote an n-vector of random variables that are observable to market participants at time t. Assuming, for simplicity, that Y has a Markov property, the state of the economy at time t is represented by $\{Y_t\}$. Then the information sets Ω and Ω' are expressed as

$$\Omega = \{Y_t\}; \qquad \Omega' = \{Y_t, x_t\}.$$

Second, we assume that $Z_{jt} \equiv (f_{t+j}, Y_t, x_t)$, which is an $(n + 2)$-vector of random variables and obeys a multivariate normal distribution, and we denote the expectation of Z_{jt} by μ_j and the variance–covariance matrix of Z_{jt} by Σ_j, which is partitioned as

$$\Sigma_j \equiv \begin{pmatrix} \Sigma_{j11} & \Sigma_{j12} & \Sigma_{j13} \\ \Sigma_{j21} & \Sigma_{j22} & \Sigma_{j23} \\ \Sigma_{j31} & \Sigma_{j32} & \Sigma_{j33} \end{pmatrix}, \tag{11.4}$$

where Σ_{j11}, Σ_{j13}, Σ_{j31}, and Σ_{j33} are scalars, Σ_{j21} and Σ_{j23} are $(n \times 1)$-vectors, Σ_{j12} and Σ_{j32} are $(1 \times n)$-vectors, and Σ_{j22} is an $(n \times n)$-matrix. For simplicity, we assume that Σ_{j22} is a diagonal matrix. Third, we assume that market participants know the distribution of Z_j.

Under this setting, we may explicitly calculate Δs in equation (11.3). In particular, we are interested in the coefficient associated with x_t, which shows how Δs would respond to a change in the amount of intervention. The coefficient of x_t in $E(f_{t+j} \mid \{Y_t, x_t\})$ turns out to be[4]

$$(\Sigma_{j13} - \Sigma_{j12}\Sigma_{j22}^{-1}\Sigma_{j23})/k_j, \qquad j > 0, \tag{11.5}$$

where $k_j \equiv \Sigma_{j33} - \Sigma_{j32}\Sigma_{j22}^{-1}\Sigma_{j23} > 0$ is a positive scalar. As long as this term is nonzero, sterilized intervention at time t affects expectations about the value of fundamentals at time $t + j$. In order to study the effectiveness of sterilized intervention through the signaling channel, therefore, it is necessary to check empirically whether this term is significantly different from zero. This is essentially how we will proceed in the empirical section of the essay.

11.2.2   *Covariance between intervention and future monetary policy*

The first term in the parentheses of equation (11.5), Σ_{j13}, represents the covariance between intervention at time t, x_t and the scalar measure of exchange rate fundamentals at time $t + j$, f_{t+j}, where $j > 0$. If this covariance is positive, the net sale of dollars by the Bank of Japan on a sterilized basis induces an appreciation of the yen.

It might seem reasonable to expect positive covariance. Since both current intervention policy and future monetary policy are determined by a single agent (the Bank of Japan), it might be reasonable to expect the two policies to be consistent. For instance, when desiring an appreciation of the yen, the Bank of Japan would sell dollars today and adopt

---

[4] For the derivation of the conditional expectation of the multivariate normal distribution, see, e.g., Hoel (1962).

a tight monetary policy at future dates (see, e.g., Mussa, 1981; Klein and Rosengren, 1991).

Although the idea that multiple decisions made by a single agent should be consistent with one another seems persuasive at first sight, there is a serious theoretical problem arising from the fact that decisions concerning intervention and monetary policy are made at different points of time. That is, "once the government has persuaded people [through intervention signaling] to expect that it will follow a future monetary policy that assists in achieving its current objectives, there is nothing to insure that the government will actually follow the future policy that people expect" (Mussa, 1981: 16). If this kind of dynamic inconsistency exists, market participants, realizing the absence of a positive correlation between intervention policy and future monetary policy, would ignore intervention signals sent by a central bank and never revise their expectations about the future values of fundamentals. As a consequence, central bank intervention would have no effect on the current exchange rate.

Several hypotheses have been offered to explain the mechanism through which central banks could send credible intervention signals. Mussa (1981) proposes the idea that intervention provides concrete evidence of the seriousness of a central bank's future policy intentions by staking its capital in support of them. For example, consider a central bank that acquires a short position in the foreign currency and a long position in the domestic currency through intervention. The central bank, paying attention to profits or losses associated with intervention, then has an incentive to adopt consistently a tight monetary policy following sales of the foreign currency.

To explain the signaling mechanism, Watanabe (1991: ch. 2) uses a foreign exchange intervention game between market participants and a central bank with inside information about future monetary policy. He argues that an important necessary condition for an intervention signal to be credible is that sending the signal is costly for the central bank. For example, if sterilized intervention disturbs domestic financial markets in the sense that intervention, even if sterilized, affects domestic interest rates, intervention signals become costly for the central bank to transmit. The unique equilibrium obtained there is characterized by full revelation of the central bank's inside information and a monotonic relationship between the amount of intervention and future money supply.[5]

---

[5] Another explanation is suggested by Dominguez (1990). On the basis of the "reputation" story of the Barro–Gordon type, Dominguez argues that the central bank has the in-

11.2.3   *Covariance between intervention and state variables*

As the second term in the parentheses of equation (11.5) indicates, a positive covariance between intervention and future monetary policy alone does not guarantee the effectiveness of intervention through the signaling channel. To understand the meaning of the second term, suppose that the realized value of Y at time t is the sole determinant of both intervention policy and future monetary policy; that is, x_t and f_{t+j} are functions only of Y_t. Although the covariance between x_t and f_{t+j} in this case would be nonzero, this does not mean that Δs is also nonzero. Since intervention itself gives no additional information to market participants, there is no difference between the two information sets Ω and Ω'. Therefore, intervention has no influence on the current level of the spot exchange rate ($\Delta s = 0$).

As this simple example suggests, it is important to distinguish the direct relationship between x_t and f_{t+j} from the indirect relationship between the two through Y_t. Since the indirect correlation reflects the backward-looking policy response of a central bank, intervention gives no surprise to market participants. On the other hand, the direct correlation implies that the central bank owns information that is not available to market participants. In this case, as private information flows from the central bank to market participants through intervention, the current exchange rate responds to central bank intervention. Equation (11.5) shows that in order to evaluate the signaling effect of intervention, it is necessary to subtract the indirect covariance between x_t and f_{t+j} through Y_t (the second term in parentheses) from the overall covariance (the first term in parentheses).

Past studies of the Bank of Japan's policy response function such as those of Hutchison (1984), Takagi (1991), and Glick and Hutchison (Chapter 10, this volume) suggest that the behavior of the Bank of Japan in the foreign exchange market is characterized by a leaning-against-the-wind policy: the Bank of Japan buys (sells) foreign currencies when the yen is appreciating (depreciating). An important aspect of this type of intervention policy is that the direction and scale of intervention depend exclusively on the direction and speed of a change in the exchange rate that occurred just before the intervention. In our terminology, an element of Y_t, which represents a change in the exchange rate between $t - 1$ and t, is the sole determinant of x_t.

---

centive to reveal information truthfully about the future course of monetary policy in order to avoid the collapse of its reputation.

If the Bank of Japan faithfully follows this type of intervention policy, intervention itself would never surprise market participants. Thus, there would be no room for the signaling channel to be effective.

11.3   Consistency of intervention policy with monetary policy

11.3.1   *Intervention and discount rate policy*

The direction of the Bank of Japan's monetary policy can be ascertained from the official discount rate. Therefore, it is important to examine the temporal relationship between intervention and changes in the discount rate.

Table 11.1 shows the relationship between discount rate changes and the direction of past intervention during the period from April 1973 to April 1992. The first two columns of the table summarize discount rate changes during this period, and the third (fourth) column reports the amount of intervention during the month (three months) before each discount rate change.[6] Monthly intervention data used in the table, which are taken from the "Supply and Demand of Funds in Money Markets" statistics published by the Bank of Japan, represent the yen value of net purchases of foreign currencies. Throughout the essay, we will use the same data for the Bank of Japan's foreign exchange intervention.

Because a reduction in the discount rate induces a depreciation of the yen through a change in exchange rate fundamentals, a necessary condition for the effectiveness of the signaling channel is that a change in the discount rate be negatively correlated with the amount of intervention defined above.

A comparison of the second column with the third or fourth column clearly indicates that a reduction (increase) in the discount rate was consistently preceded by purchases (sales) of foreign currencies. Moreover, a turning point of monetary policy where tight (loose) policy changes into loose (tight) policy tends to coincide with a turning point of intervention policy where intervention changes from sales (purchases) of dollars to purchases (sales) of dollars. There are five such turning points of monetary policy during this period: April 1975, April 1979, August 1980, May 1989, and July 1991. In four of these five, the direction of intervention policy changed simultaneously, clearly indicating that a

---

[6] See the note to Table 11.1 for details on the figures in the third and fourth columns.

Table 11.1. Discount rate policy and intervention in Japan

Date of discount rate change	Change in discount rate (%)	Amount of intervention in past (trillions of yen)		Factors cited in statements by the chairman of the policy board of the Bank of Japan announcing changes in the discount rate				
		1 month	3 months	Effective demand	Inflation	Balance of payments	Exchange rate	Money supply
04/02/73	+0.75	+0.05	+0.42		○			
05/30/73	+0.50	−0.26	−0.48		○			
07/02/73	+0.50	−0.21	−0.75		○			
08/29/73	+1.00	−0.04	−0.48		○			
12/22/73	+2.00	−0.26	−1.17		○			
04/16/75	−0.50	+0.01	+0.15	○				
06/07/75	−0.50	+0.02	+0.06	○				
08/13/75	−0.50	−0.21	−0.21	○				
10/24/75	−1.00	−0.07	−0.54	○				
03/12/77	−0.50	+0.03	+0.12	○		○		
04/19/77	−1.00	+0.09	+0.18	○		○		
09/05/77	−0.75	+0.02	+0.12	○		○		
03/16/78	−0.75	+1.33	+1.83	○		○	○	
04/17/79	+0.75	−0.72	−1.44		○	○	○	
07/24/79	+1.00	+0.13	−0.03		○		○	
11/02/79	+1.00	−0.53	−0.48		○		○	
02/19/80	+1.00	−0.12	−0.06		○		○	○
03/19/80	+1.75	−0.89	−0.93		○		○	○
08/20/80	−0.75	+0.01	+0.27	○				

Date				Interventions
11/06/80	−1.00	+0.22	+0.42	○
03/18/81	−1.00	+0.00	+0.30	○
12/11/81	−0.75	−0.13	−0.15	○
10/22/83	−0.50	+0.03	−0.12	○
01/30/86	−0.50	+0.00	−0.06	○
03/10/86	−0.50	+0.06	+0.09	○
04/21/86	−0.50	+0.49	+0.57	○
11/01/86	−0.50	+0.01	+0.48	○ ○ ○
02/23/87	−0.50	+0.01	+1.38	○ ○ ○ ○ ○
05/31/89	+0.75	−0.68	−0.69	○ ○ ○
10/11/89	+0.50	−0.36	−0.90	○ ○ ○ ○
12/25/89	+0.50	−0.06	−0.48	○ ○ ○ ○ ○ ○ ○
03/20/90	+1.00	−1.11	−1.80	○ ○ ○ ○ ○ ○ ○ ○
08/30/90	+0.75	+0.00	+0.01	○ ○ ○ ○
07/01/91	−0.50	−0.04	−0.09	○
11/14/91	−0.50	+0.00	+0.01	○ ○
12/30/91	−0.50	0.00	+0.00	○
04/01/92	−0.75	−0.03	−0.12	○

Note: Monthly intervention data are used. For discount rate changes occurring between the first and the ninth of each month, the number listed in the third column (amount of intervention in past 1 month) represents the amount of intervention in the previous month. Otherwise, it represents the amount of intervention in the present month. The same applies to the fourth column (amount of intervention in past 3 months).

Source: Economic Statistics Monthly, Research and Statistics Department of the Bank of Japan, various issues.

consistent link existed between the Bank of Japan's intervention policy and its discount rate policy during the sample period.[7]

According to Table 11.1, there were nine instances in which a change in the discount rate was *not* consistent with the direction of intervention in the three preceding months.[8] As shown in the columns of Table 11.1 presenting "factors cited in statements by the chairman of the policy board of the Bank of Japan announcing changes in the discount rate," a common characteristic almost always observed in these instances is that the Bank of Japan faced an urgent need to stimulate extremely weak economic activity caused by various shocks. Put differently, when the stability of the foreign exchange rate becomes relatively less important as a policy objective, the Bank of Japan's monetary policy tends to deviate from the course implied by preceding interventions.

11.3.2 *Intervention and the control of money supply*

A casual comparison between the time series of the amount of intervention and the time series of broad money (M2 + CDs) divided by the GNP deflator indicates that there is a close correlation between the two time series.[9]

Figure 11.1 compares the monthly amount of intervention with the growth rate of real M2 + CDs from the previous quarter. It is clearly observed in the period of 1976–92 that changes in intervention tended to precede changes in the growth rate of real M2 + CDs in a consistent manner, although no systematic relationship can be seen in the period 1973–5. More surprisingly, there is a tendency such that the more the

---

[7] A single exception is July 1991, when monetary policy changed from tightening to loosening with a view to stimulating weak economic activity, while the sale of dollars was continued in order to prevent a depreciation of the yen. This contrasts sharply with the finding of Klein and Rosengren (1991) that indicated the absence of such a link for the United States and Germany during the period between the Plaza meeting of September 1985 and the stock market crash of October 1987.

[8] Discount rate policy and intervention were inconsistent on April 2, 1973, August 13, 1975, October 24, 1975, December 11, 1981, October 22, 1983, January 30, 1986, August 30, 1990, July 1, 1991, and April 1, 1992.

[9] From the theoretical perspective, it might appear inconsistent to compare the *nominal* amount of intervention and the *real* money supply. From the practical point of view, however, the Bank of Japan pays attention not to the real amount of intervention but to the nominal amount of intervention. As far as the signaling effect of the Bank of Japan intervention is concerned, therefore, the nominal amount of intervention is probably an appropriate measure.

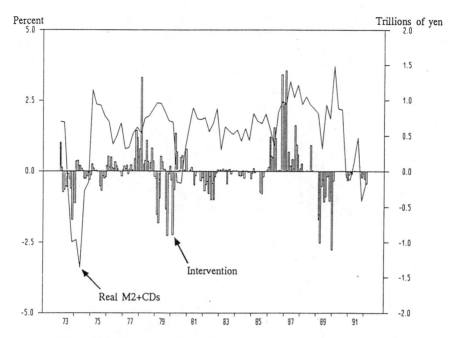

Figure 11.1. Monetary policy and intervention policy in Japan. *Line*: Growth rate of the quarterly average balance of M2 + CDs divided by GNP deflator, percent changes over the previous quarter (left scale). *Bar*: Net purchases of foreign currencies by the Foreign Exchange Funds Special Account of the National Budget, yen value (right scale). From *Economic Statistics Monthly*, Research and Statistics Department of the Bank of Japan, various issues, and *Annual Report on National Accounts*, Economic Planning Agency, various issues.

Bank of Japan purchases foreign currencies, the higher is the growth rate of real M2 + CDs.

Table 11.2 reports coefficients of correlation between the growth rate of the money supply and intervention based on quarterly data. It is observed that intervention is positively correlated with the future growth rates of money supply but is uncorrelated or negatively correlated with the past growth rates, clearly indicating that intervention tended to precede changes in the money supply. This observation depends neither on the choice of the sample period (before or after the Plaza Agreement) nor on the definition of the money supply (real or nominal).

To capture the dynamic relationship between intervention and real M2 + CDs, we estimate a two-variable vector autoregressive model composed of the yen value of net purchases of foreign currencies, the

Table 11.2. *Correlations between intervention and M2 + CDs*

Growth rate of quarterly money supply at time 0	Intervention at time										
	−Q5	−Q4	−Q3	−Q2	−Q1	0	+Q1	+Q2	+Q3	+Q4	+Q5
Real money supply											
1973:Q2–1992:Q1	0.38	0.41	0.38	0.34	0.21	0.09	0.07	−0.02	−0.04	−0.02	0.03
1973:Q2–1985:Q2	0.32	0.44	0.43	0.44	0.21	0.01	−0.03	−0.16	−0.14	0.00	0.07
1985:Q3–1992:Q1	0.41	0.37	0.32	0.19	0.18	0.15	0.16	0.12	0.01	−0.18	−0.14
Nominal money supply											
1973:Q2–1992:Q1	0.26	0.26	0.22	0.14	0.02	−0.02	−0.02	−0.10	−0.07	−0.04	−0.02
1973:Q2–1985:Q2	0.15	0.20	0.37	0.27	0.09	−0.02	0.01	−0.16	−0.07	0.08	0.09
1985:Q3–1992:Q1	0.43	0.37	0.20	0.11	0.04	0.04	0.00	0.00	−0.04	−0.15	−0.14

Note: Real money supply is defined as M2 + CDs divided by GNP deflator.
Source: Economic Statistics Monthly, Research and Statistics Department of the Bank of Japan, various issues; *Annual Report on National Accounts*, Economic Planning Agency, various issues.

Percent

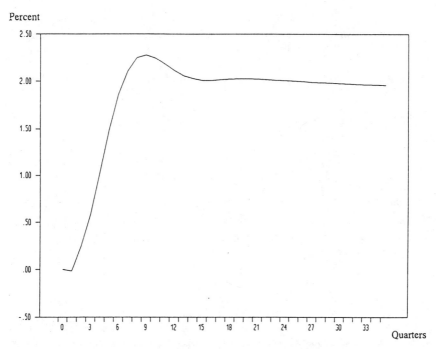

Figure 11.2. Responses of M2 + CDs to a 1-trillion-yen shock in intervention. Based on the vector autoregression model composed of the amount of intervention, the logarithm of M2 + CDs divided by the implicit deflator for GNP, and constants. It is estimated with quarterly data from the first quarter of 1974 to the first quarter of 1992. The number of lags is set at four quarters.

logarithm of M2 + CDs divided by the implicit GNP deflator, and constants.[10] It is estimated with quarterly data from the period 1974:Q1–1992:Q1. The number of lags is set at four quarters.

Figure 11.2 depicts the dynamic response of M2 + CDs to a 1-trillion-yen shock in intervention. Several points are noteworthy. First, the money supply does not respond at the moment of intervention. In other words, intervention by the Bank of Japan was completely sterilized. This is consistent with the finding of Takagi (1991), who concludes from a regression analysis that there was almost complete sterilization in Japan in the period 1973:Q2–1989:Q2. Second, M2 + CDs monotonically increases in response to a shock in intervention until it deviates 2.2 percent from the original level nine quarters later. This means that the initial

[10] An alternative specification is to use the growth rate of real M2 + CDs instead of the logarithm of real M2 + CDs. In this case, we obtain responses of the growth rate of real M2 + CDs. Taking its integral, we obtain a graph similar to Figure 11.2.

Table 11.3. *Historical decomposition of the growth rate of M2 + CDs*

Year	Forecast errors in growth rate of real M2 + CDs (%)	Explained by innovation in	
		Intervention	M2 + CDs
1985	0.48	−0.14	+0.62
1986	0.56	−0.57	+1.13
1987	3.89	+1.45	+2.44
1988	4.33	+4.60	−0.27
1989	1.64	+1.49	+0.15
1990	3.00	−2.45	+5.45
1991	−4.24	−2.61	−1.63

Note: The same quarterly vector autoregression model as in Figure 11.2 is used. The decomposition is based on the following partition of the moving average representation:

$$z_{T+j} - \sum_{s=j}^{\infty} A_s u_{T+j-s} = \sum_{s=0}^{j-1} A_s u_{T+j-s},$$

where z is the vector composed of the amount of intervention and the growth rate of real M2 + CDs, and u is the corresponding innovation vector. The left-hand side of the equation represents the forecast error: the actual value of z at $T + j$ minus the forecast of z_{T+j} based on information at time T. It is decomposed into innovations in the two variables. T is set at 1980:Q1.
Source: Economic Statistics Monthly, Research and Statistics Department of the Bank of Japan, various issues; *Annual Report on National Accounts,* Economic Planning Agency, various issues.

net purchase of foreign currencies is gradually accommodated over time after it is sterilized at the moment of intervention. Since the average balance of M2 + CDs during the sample period is 270 trillion yen, the deviation of 2.2 percent is equivalent to 5.9 trillion yen. Taking the average money multiplier of 10.7 into consideration, 55 percent of the initial net purchase of foreign currencies is accommodated over time.

An interesting question related to this point concerns how much of the fluctuation in real M2 + CDs during the post-Plaza period can be explained by innovations in intervention. Based on the estimation of the same vector autoregressive model, Table 11.3 reports the historical decomposition of the growth rate of M2 + CDs.[11] We can read from

[11] For details on the method of historical decomposition, see the note to Table 11.3.

the table that (i) the forecast errors in the (positive) growth rate of real M2 + CDs from 1987 to 1989 are mostly explained by innovations in intervention; (ii) the negative forecast error in 1991 is also explained by innovations in intervention. Put differently, a market participant observing innovations in intervention could predict a loose monetary policy in the period 1987–9 as well as a tight policy in 1991.[12]

11.4   Unanticipated component of intervention

The positive correlation between monetary policy and intervention that we found in the preceding section implies that there is a common factor governing both the determination of monetary policy and that of intervention policy. As discussed in Section 11.2, a point to be checked next is whether that common factor is observable to market participants. If the common factor is fully observable, intervention would provide no new information for market participants, so that the current exchange rate would never respond to intervention. Only when the conduct of both intervention policy and monetary policy is based on a common factor that is not observable to market participants does intervention influence the current exchange rate. The purpose of this section is to examine to what extent intervention by the Bank of Japan was anticipated during the sample period. More specifically, we will investigate the type of correlation between intervention and a vector of variables that are observable to market participants, Y, by specifying the Bank of Japan's policy response function regarding foreign exchange intervention.

---

[12] On the basis of the fact that the Treasury or the Ministry of Finance partly controls foreign exchange intervention in most countries, Humpage (1991) points out the possibility that intervention could signal changes in future fiscal policy. In the case of Japan, the institution in charge of foreign exchange intervention is the Foreign Exchange Funds Special Account of the National Budget. Accordingly, foreign exchange intervention is ultimately controlled by the Japanese Ministry of Finance, which is also responsible for fiscal policy. Therefore, it is plausible that the Japanese Ministry of Finance with a target yen rate higher than the current spot rate urges the Bank of Japan to sell dollars today and controls government expenditures at future dates with a view to maintaining the strong yen. Since typical models used in discussion among economists seem to indicate that an increase in government expenditure causes an appreciation of the domestic currency, the hypothesis that intervention serves as a signal to future fiscal policy predicts a negative correlation between the net purchase of foreign currencies and changes in government expenditure. A tentative examination of the Japanese data, however, shows a strong positive correlation between the two time series, suggesting the possibility that Humpage's hypothesis does not hold in Japan.

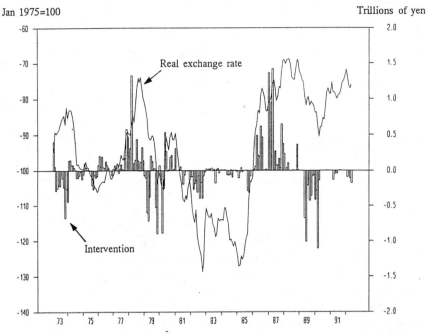

Figure 11.3. Movement of the real exchange rate and official foreign exchange market intervention in Japan. *Line*: Logarithm of real exchange rate (yen per dollar, Jan. 1975 = 100, left scale, reversed scale) ≡ log of spot yen–dollar rate (closing rate in Tokyo market) + log of U.S. WPI (industrial commodities) − log of Japan WPI (manufacturing industry products). *Bar*: Net purchases of foreign currencies by the Foreign Exchange Funds Special Account of the National Budget, yen value (right scale). From *Economic Statistics Monthly*, Research and Statistics Department of the Bank of Japan, various issues.

11.4.1   *Asymmetric leaning-against-the-wind policy*

Hutchison (1984) and Takagi (1991), among others, point out that the Bank of Japan's intervention policy can be characterized as "leaning against the wind," which implies that its intervention is predictable to some extent from the past movement of the exchange rate.

If the Bank of Japan follows a leaning-against-the-wind policy, we should systematically observe that it purchases (sells) foreign currencies when the yen appreciates (depreciates). We call this type of intervention rule a symmetric leaning-against-the-wind policy. In Figure 11.3, such a policy is observed on a monthly basis during the period from 1973 to early 1980.[13] For the rest of the sample period, however, a close ex-

---

[13] For the definition of the real exchange rate, see the note to Table 11.3.

amination of the monthly intervention data in Figure 11.3 indicates that the Bank of Japan's intervention deviated from the above rule. First, a "leaning-*with*-the-wind" policy was employed from late 1985 to early 1986 in that the Bank of Japan consistently sold dollars while the yen was appreciating.

Second, even when the Bank of Japan intervened in a leaning-against-the-wind fashion, the intervention behavior was not a symmetric leaning-against-the-wind policy as defined above. More specifically, there are two types of periods: (i) periods in which the Bank of Japan purchases foreign currencies during the month when the yen appreciates but does not intervene during the month when the yen depreciates; (ii) periods in which the Bank of Japan sells foreign currencies during the month when the yen depreciates but does not intervene during the month when the yen appreciates. In other words, on a monthly basis, the Bank of Japan responds only to an appreciation of the yen in the first case, while it responds only to a depreciation of the yen in the second case. We call this an "asymmetric leaning-against-the-wind policy."

To look more closely at the asymmetric leaning-against-the-wind policy, we divide the whole sample period into the following six subperiods depending on whether the Bank of Japan responded on a monthly basis mainly to an appreciation of the yen or to a depreciation of the yen: (i) March 1973 to April 1980; (ii) May 1980 to May 1981; (iii) June 1981 to August 1985; (iv) September 1985 to March 1986; (v) April 1986 to March 1989; (vi) April 1989 to May 1992. According to Table 11.4, the Bank of Japan responded evenly both to an appreciation of the yen and to a depreciation of the yen during the first subperiod. But during the second and fifth subperiods, the bank mainly responded only to an appreciation of the yen. For example, during the fifth subperiod, the bank never sold foreign currencies, although its purchase of foreign exchange amounted to more than 8 trillion yen. In contrast, during the third, fourth, and sixth subperiods, the bank responded mainly to a depreciation of the yen.

To characterize types of leaning-against-the-wind policies, we describe the response function of the Bank of Japan as

$$x_t = a\,\Delta q_{t-1} + v_t \quad \text{if } \Delta q_{t-1} \geq 0;$$
$$x_t = b\,\Delta q_{t-1} + v_t \quad \text{if } \Delta q_{t-1} < 0, \tag{11.6}$$

where x represents the net purchase of foreign currencies, Δq is a change in the real yen–dollar rate, a and b are nonpositive parameters, and v is a disturbance term. In words, the amount of intervention, which is determined after observing a change in the real yen–dollar rate, might

Table 11.4. *Foreign exchange market intervention policy*

From	To	Sales of yen			Purchases of yen			Estimated value of a	
		Number of months	Total (trillions of yen)	Monthly average (trillions of yen)	Number of months	Total (trillions of yen)	Monthly average (trillions of yen)	a	b
Mar. 73	Apr. 80	47	6.84	0.15	39	8.73	0.22	−0.0636** (4.216)	−0.0465** (2.811)
May 80	May 81	12	1.65	0.14	1	0.01	0.01	0.0039 (1.444)	−0.0579** (6.094)
June 81	Aug. 85	19	0.28	0.01	32	3.32	0.10	−0.0439** (5.613)	0.0041 (1.081)
Sept. 85	Mar. 86	4	0.09	0.02	3	0.69	0.23	—	0.0145 (1.232)
Apr. 86	Mar. 89	36	8.27	0.23	0	0.00	0.00	0.0143 (1.997)	−0.1297** (4.651)
Apr. 89	May 92	13	0.04	0.00	22	5.51	0.25	−0.1198** (5.363)	0.0121 (1.052)

Note: a and b in each period are estimated as follows. Divide the sample in each period into two groups depending on whether the percent change of the real exchange rate from the previous month is positive or negative. Regress in each group the amount of intervention on the percent change of the real exchange rate from the previous month. a and b represent, respectively, the estimated parameters for the positive group and the negative group.

[a] Numbers in parentheses are t-statistics.

** indicates that the parameter value is significant at the .01 level.

Source: Economic Statistics Monthly, Research and Statistics Department of the Bank of Japan, various issues.

respond differently to an appreciation of the yen and to a depreciation of the yen.

The first type, which is called a symmetric leaning-against-the-wind policy, or SLAW policy, is characterized as

$$a = b < 0. \tag{11.7a}$$

As seen in Figure 11.4, which plots the monthly amount of intervention against the percent change of the real exchange rate from the previous month, the policy adopted during the first subperiod appeared to be of this type.[14] In fact, ordinary least squares estimation indicates that $a = -0.0636$ and $b = -0.0465$ (see the last two columns of Table 11.4): on average, the Bank of Japan sold 63.6 billion yen of foreign currencies when the yen depreciated by 1 percent, and bought 46.5 billion yen of foreign currencies when the yen appreciated by 1 percent.

The second type, which is called the asymmetric leaning-against-the-wind policy of type 1, or ALAW$_1$ policy, is characterized as

$$b < a \leq 0. \tag{11.7b}$$

This policy was adopted in the second and fifth subperiods (see Figure 11.4). More formally, Table 11.4 shows that the estimated values of a are not significantly different from zero in both periods, while the estimated values of b are negative and significantly different from zero.

The third type, which is called the asymmetric leaning-against-the-wind policy of type 2, or ALAW$_2$ policy, is characterized as

$$a < b \leq 0. \tag{11.7c}$$

The Bank of Japan's intervention policy in the third and sixth subperiods appears to fall into this category (see Figure 11.4). Indeed, the estimated values of b are not significantly different from zero in both periods, and the estimated values of a are negative and significantly different from zero (Table 11.4).

11.4.2 The target exchange rate hypothesis

Having identified three kinds of leaning-against-the-wind policies based on a careful examination of the monthly intervention data, we must

[14] We must be careful in interpreting this fact, because we are discussing a contemporaneous correlation between intervention and the real exchange rate, so that simultaneity between the two variables might be a serious problem. Causality running from intervention to the real exchange rate implies a negative correlation between the two. Therefore, the observed positive correlation may well be weaker than the true correlation.

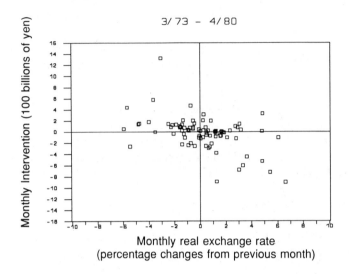

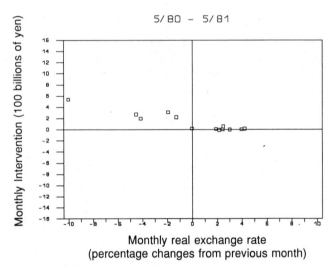

Figure 11.4. Leaning-against-the-wind intervention. From *Economic Statistics Monthly*, Research and Statistics Department of the Bank of Japan, various issues.

next ask what elements were important for the Bank of Japan in choosing among the three.

To answer this question, it is important to note that central banks often pay attention to *levels* of exchange rates as well as *changes* in exchange rates. On the basis of this understanding, we denote the Bank

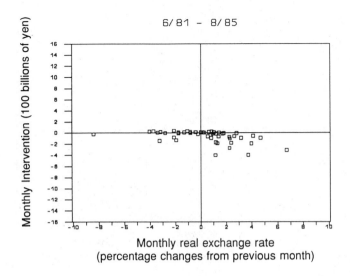

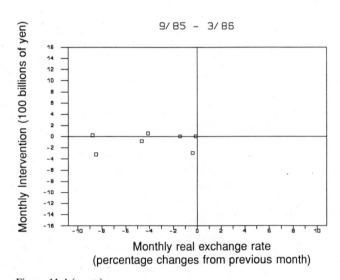

Figure 11.4 (*cont.*)

of Japan's target exchange rate at time t by T_t, which is assumed to be time variant. Then our hypothesis is that the Bank of Japan adopts at time t

$$
\begin{aligned}
\text{ALAW}_1 \quad &\text{if } q_{t-1} < T_{t-1}; \\
\text{ALAW}_2 \quad &\text{if } q_{t-1} \geq T_{t-1}.
\end{aligned}
\tag{11.8}
$$

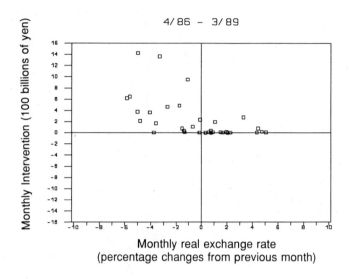

Monthly real exchange rate
(percentage changes from previous month)

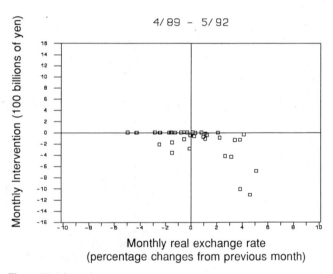

Monthly real exchange rate
(percentage changes from previous month)

Figure 11.4 (*cont.*)

In words, the Bank of Japan responds only to an appreciation of the yen when the current level of the yen is above the target level; on the other hand, it responds only to a depreciation of the yen when the current level of the yen is below the target level. Put differently, when the deviation of the exchange rate from the target level shrinks in absolute value, the Bank of Japan does not intervene, signaling its judgment that the direction of the movement of the exchange rate is desirable. By contrast, when the deviation of the exchange rate from the target level becomes larger in absolute value, the Bank of Japan sends a message through nonzero intervention that the direction of the movement of the exchange rate is undesirable.[15] In terms of the target exchange rate hypothesis, the levels of the yen were above target levels in the second and fifth subperiods and the opposite held in the third and sixth subperiods.

An important implication of the target exchange rate hypothesis is that the amount of intervention at t depends on the level of the target exchange rate at $t - 1$ as well as the percent change in the real exchange rate at $t - 1$. Therefore, market participants need to know the target exchange rate in order to infer the amount of intervention on the next day. If the target exchange rate is observable to market participants, they could know the precise time at which the Bank of Japan switches its intervention policy from one to another. If this is the case, there exists no uncertainty with respect to the timing of policy switching. But if the target exchange rate is unobservable, the timing of policy switching is uncertain for market participants. In this case, even after observing the current level of the exchange rate, market participants do not necessarily know which intervention policy will be adopted on the next day.

This suggests that the observability of target exchange rates is crucial in allowing market participants to compute the unanticipated component of intervention. In what follows, we first compute the unanticipated component of intervention under the assumption that the target exchange rate is observable to market participants, and then discuss the issue of surprise intervention in a more general setting in which the target exchange rate may not be observable.

11.4.3 *Estimation of unanticipated intervention: the case of observable target rates*

Under the hypothesis described in equation (11.8), if the target exchange rate is observable, the Bank of Japan's intervention can surprise market participants only when the disturbance term v in equation (11.6) becomes significantly different from zero. In order to assess the extent to which intervention was unanticipated, therefore, we need to compute

[15] Note that SLAW policy does not have this signaling function. Intervention policy described by equation (11.8) is quite similar to the target zone model of Lewis (1990), which generalizes the Krugman-type target zone model to allow for intramarginal intervention.

the time series of the disturbance term by estimating equation (11.6) separately in each period. This procedure is equivalent to assuming that market participants know the sample breakpoints and the Bank of Japan's response function in each subperiod ex ante.[16]

A problem we encounter in estimating the disturbance term is that, because the leaning-against-the-wind policy was *not* employed in the fourth subperiod, it is not obvious whether the policy switching in this subperiod had been predicted by market participants who had complete knowledge of the target rate. It should be noticed, however, that since the yen was consistently below the target level during the third and fourth subperiods, market participants believing that the intervention policy is characterized by equation (11.8) had no reason to predict that the Bank of Japan would deviate from $ALAW_2$ throughout the third and fourth subperiods. On the basis of this reasoning, we estimate equation (11.6) over the combined period of the third and fourth subperiods (i.e., June 1981 to March 1986).

Figure 11.5 depicts the time series of actual and anticipated intervention from 1984 to 1992. The difference between the two corresponds to the disturbance term. A casual comparison of the actual and the anticipated intervention shows that there were several instances in which the disturbance term was significantly different from zero, including the fourth quarter of 1985, when the Bank of Japan sold dollars jointly with the central banks of the other G-5 countries.[17] However, these were exceptional cases. In fact, we can observe in Figure 11.5 a striking correlation between the actual and the anticipated intervention. Therefore, we may reasonably conclude from this simple regression analysis that the Bank of Japan's intervention was mostly anticipated by market participants during this sample period.[18]

---

[16] The estimation procedure of the disturbance term is based on the assumption that the Bank of Japan's response function is stable. If its response function were not stable, it would be quite difficult to distinguish changes in the target exchange rate from changes in the reaction function.

[17] Other instances in which the disturbance term was significantly different from zero include (i) early 1987, when the massive purchases of foreign currencies were underpredicted; (ii) June 1989 and March 1990, when the massive sales of foreign currencies were underpredicted. However, these two cases differ from the intervention that occurred immediately after the Plaza meeting, because the direction of intervention was correctly anticipated in these two cases, whereas the scale of intervention was not correctly predicted.

[18] The anticipated component of intervention in other subperiods has been computed in the same way, although the figures are not shown because of space limitations. As the close correlation in each subperiod shown in Figure 11.5 suggests, we have reached the same conclusion in these cases.

Trillions of yen

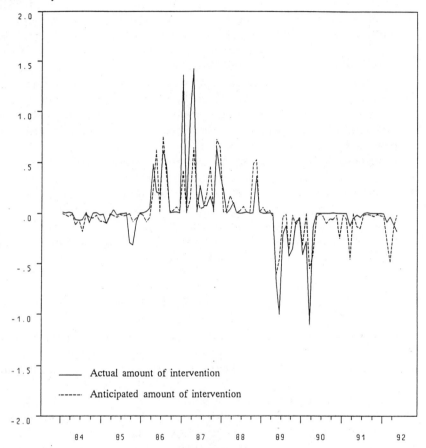

Figure 11.5. Anticipated intervention in 1984–92.

11.4.4 *Unobservable target rates*

Although the assumption that the target rate is observable is crucial in the computation of the anticipated component of intervention, the problem is that the assumption is not necessarily realistic. If the target rate is unobservable to market participants, they do not know whether $ALAW_1$ or $ALAW_2$ will be adopted, so they cannot make a precise inference on the direction and amount of intervention on the next day. In this sense, the extent to which intervention is anticipated crucially depends on the degree of observability of the target exchange rate.

Although it is quite difficult to assess the degree of observability of the Bank of Japan's target exchange rate without any formal analysis, it seems safe to rule out the possibility that the target rate was consistently known to market participants during the sample period. First, the Bank of Japan has never announced explicit target rates or target zones since it adopted the flexible exchange rate system in 1973. Second, there does not seem to have existed a systematic link between the realization of variables observable to the market and the policy switches between ALAW$_1$ and ALAW$_2$ during the sample period. This means that the target rate was determined by the Bank of Japan at least partly depending on inside information.

In sum, we have shown in this section that (i) intervention tended to be highly correlated with percent changes in the exchange rate, but (ii) the functional relationship changed several times in an unpredictable way; accordingly, (iii) the past movements of the exchange rate by themselves were not sufficient to predict future intervention accurately; therefore, (iv) the Bank of Japan could surprise market participants through intervention at least several times during the sample period 1973–92.

11.5   Conclusion

On the basis of a simple theoretical model, we have obtained two intuitive implications of the signaling hypothesis of foreign exchange intervention: intervention policy should be correlated with future monetary policy, and intervention should not be fully anticipated. Otherwise, sterilized intervention would not be effective.

To examine the first implication empirically, we have compared the Bank of Japan's intervention policy with its monetary policy in the period 1973–92. We found that (i) the purchase (sale) of foreign currencies consistently preceded a reduction (increase) in the Bank of Japan discount rate; and (ii) the purchase (sale) of foreign currencies tended to precede an increase (decrease) in the growth rate of broad money. These two findings are consistent with the signaling hypothesis.

The second implication has been investigated by specifying the Bank of Japan's policy response function regarding foreign exchange intervention. As past studies indicated, we have found that the Bank of Japan's intervention policy was dependent to some extent on the past movement of the exchange rate. At the same time, however, we have also found that the functional relationship changed several times during the period 1973–92. Between April 1986 and March 1989, for example, as the yen appreciated, the Bank of Japan intervened by buying foreign currencies in a leaning-against-the-wind fashion but did not intervene when the yen depreciated. In contrast, between April 1989 and May 1992, the Bank of Japan intervened in a leaning-against-the-wind fashion when the yen depreciated, while it did not intervene when the yen appreciated. One possible interpretation of such policy switches is that the Bank of Japan had a target exchange rate that might change over time, and intervention occurred only when the exchange rate tended to deviate greatly from the target level. If this is the case, intervention policy depended not only on the past movement of the exchange rate but also on the movement of the target exchange rate. Because it is only reasonable to assume that the target rate was unobservable to market participants during the sample period, the possibility that interventions were fully anticipated should be ruled out. We may thus conclude that the Bank of Japan's intervention data were consistent with the two implications of the signaling hypothesis.

References

Dominguez, Kathryn M. (1990). "Have Recent Central Bank Foreign Exchange Intervention Operations Influenced the Yen?" Unpublished manuscript, Harvard University.

Dominguez, Kathryn M., and Jeffrey Frankel (1990). "Does Foreign Exchange Market Intervention Matter? Disentangling the Portfolio and Expectations Effects for the Mark," NBER Working Paper no. 3299. Cambridge, MA.

Hoel, P. G. (1962). *Introduction to Mathematical Statistics*. New York: Wiley.

Humpage, Owen F. (1988). "Intervention and the Dollar's Decline," (Federal Reserve Bank of Cleveland) *Economic Review* 24 (no. 2):2–16.

(1991). "Central-Bank Intervention: Recent Literature, Continuing Controversy," (Federal Reserve Bank of Cleveland) *Economic Review* 27 (no. 2):12–26.

Hutchison, Michael M. (1984). "Official Japanese Intervention in Foreign Exchange Markets: Leaning against the Wind?" *Economics Letters* 15:115–20.

Klein, Michael W., and Eric Rosengren (1991). "Foreign Exchange Intervention as a Signal of Monetary Policy," (Federal Reserve Bank of Boston) *New England Economic Review* (May–June):39–50.

Krugman, Paul (1991). "Target Zones and Exchange Rate Dynamics," *Quarterly Journal of Economics* 106:669–82.

Lewis, Karen K. (1990). "Occasional Interventions to Target Rates," NBER Working Paper no. 3398. Cambridge, MA.

Marston, Richard C. (1988). "Exchange Rate Policy Reconsidered," In Martin Feldstein, ed., *International Economic Cooperation*, pp. 79–136. Chicago: University of Chicago Press.

Mussa, Michael (1981). *The Role of Official Intervention*. Occasional Paper no. 6. New York: Group of Thirty.

Takagi, Shinji (1991). "Foreign Exchange Market Intervention and Domestic

Monetary Control in Japan, 1973–1989," *Japan and the World Economy* 3:147–80.

Watanabe, Tsutomu (1991). "Essays on the Sterilized Intervention Signaling and the Currency Composition of Government Debt." Ph.D. dissertation, Harvard University.

CHAPTER 12

Sterilization of the monetary effects of current account surpluses and its consequences: Korea, 1986–1990

Sung Y. Kwack

12.1 Introduction

Whether the central bank of an open economy under a pegged exchange rate regime can keep its money supply under control is relevant both to balance-of-payments adjustment and to domestic stabilization policy. Regardless of the degree of capital mobility with a pegged rate, a restrictive monetary policy will induce reserves to accumulate, perhaps to an unmanageable size. This well-known result in the monetary theory of the balance of payments (e.g., Mundell, 1968; Johnson, 1973) illustrates the difficulty of achieving both domestic policy and external balance objectives by monetary policy.[1]

Korea's current account surpluses from 1986 to 1989 had a strong expansionary effect on the money supply. To maintain the money supply within the target levels, monetary policy during the second half of the 1980s focused on absorbing the monetary effects of these current account surpluses. This essay undertakes a detailed examination of the monetary effects of a current account shock and the implications of efforts to sterilize such effects. In particular, it examines whether the Bank of Korea undertook policies to neutralize the monetary impacts of the

I would like to express my appreciation to Kiesuk Byun, Yangkoo Byun, Jungho Chung, Peter B. Clark, Sungmin Kim, Paul W. Kuznets, Deborah Lindner, and Samjin Whang for their aid during this study. I thank Ramon Moreno, Reuven Glick, and Michael Hutchison for their very helpful comments and suggestions. I also thank participants of the conference "Exchange Rate Policy in Pacific Basin Countries," at the Center for Pacific Basin Studies, Federal Reserve Bank of San Francisco, September 16–18, 1992. No one but the author is responsible for the analysis and errors in this essay.

[1] For instance, Kouri (1975) examined the relationship between monetary policy and capital flows in Germany in the period 1960–72 and showed that measures of monetary policy were offset to a large extent by capital inflows.

current account surplus in 1986–9. Further, it assesses empirically the consequences of policy instruments utilized to curb the monetization of current account surpluses. It also asks what would have happened had Korea adopted a freely floating exchange rate system. The first question is answered by empirical examination of the domestic credit reaction function of the Bank of Korea. The assessment of sterilization and other policy efforts is made with simulations of an empirically estimated monthly structural model of the Korean economy that includes financial markets, as well as real domestic and foreign transactions.[2]

The essay is organized as follows. Section 12.2 briefly discusses institutional aspects of the conduct of monetary policy in Korea. Section 12.3 discusses the effects of current account shocks on monetary policy, while Section 12.4 quantitatively evaluates the extent to which the Bank of Korea sterilized these effects. Section 12.5 presents a monthly structural model of the Korean economy. The model of the Korean economy is used to estimate the effects of sterilization and other policy instruments. Section 12.6 concludes with a summary of the major findings of the analysis.

12.2   Targets and instruments of monetary policy

As in most countries, the fiscal and monetary policies of Korea seek to promote economic growth, price stability, and balance-of-payments equilibrium. The charter that established the Bank of Korea describes the objectives of the monetary authorities as stabilizing the value of money in order to achieve economic growth and directing efficient use of financial resources to promote long-term economic development. Since price stability encourages efficient utilization of financial resources, however, monetary policy is more directly concerned with controlling inflation than with economic growth or attaining external equilibrium.

The second oil shock in 1979 and the large depreciations of the won in 1980 and 1981 exerted strong inflationary pressures in the Korean economy. Consequently, monetary policy shifted sharply toward achieving price stability in the early 1980s, with top priority given to reducing inflation.

In Korea the monetary authorities use M2 as an intermediate target

[2] Central banks generally want to adopt policies to isolate their domestic markets from the disturbances generated from the balance of payments. Central banks attempt to attain their international balance objective by neutralizing the monetary impacts of international reserve flows. The effectiveness of sterilized foreign intervention remains an unresolved issue. See Girton and Henderson (1976) and Obstfeld (1988).

to achieve their macroeconomic goals.[3] The targeted rate of monetary growth is set at the same time as the goals of real growth, inflation, and balance of payments equilibrium. Interest rates and exchange rates are not explicitly targeted, but are taken into account in setting the monetary target.

Instruments of monetary policy available in Korea include discount rates on commercial bills, commercial bill rediscounting, reserve ratio requirements, and open market operations. However, with excess demand for bank credit, discount rates have not been effective in managing the volume of credit. The Korean authorities have relied more on changes in eligibility conditions for rediscounting commercial bills and required reserve ratios to control the supply of credit to banks. In addition, the Bank of Korea has provided credit to banks through policy loans mainly to small firms and to the export sector.

Open market operations have not been actively used in Korea as a means of controlling the money supply, because the market for government securities has remained underdeveloped. However, the Bank of Korea has performed open market operations with its own interest-bearing liabilities, called Monetary Stabilization Bonds (MSBs). MSBs are issued with maturities of 63 days, 91 days, 364 days, and 2 years on a discount basis, at rates below the free market, to banks and nonbank financial institutions which hold the bulk of the issues. Interest rates on the MSBs offered to the public carry interest rates that reflect market conditions.

In 1986, the Ministry of Finance began issuing Foreign Exchange Stabilization Fund Bonds as a means to absorb excess liquidity in financial markets. The maturities and interest rates of Foreign Exchange Stabilization Bonds are the same as those of MSBs. Although the Foreign Exchange Stabilization Fund Bonds issued by the Ministry of Finance are not liabilities of the Bank of Korea, the funds collected by the sale of these bonds are used mainly to decrease net claims of the Bank of Korea on the government. MSBs and Foreign Exchange Stabilization Fund Bonds are thus identical with respect to the role of

---

[3] As defined in other countries, the money supply (M2) comprises currency in circulation and demand and savings deposits of deposit money banks. M2 does not cover the deposits of nonbank financial institutions, whose share in total deposits has been rapidly growing. The shares of nonbank financial institutions were 21% in 1975, 30% in 1980, 46% in 1985, 54% in 1988, and 59% in 1990. The trend of the share of nonbank financial institutions in loans and discounts is similar to the trend of the deposit share: 27% in 1975, 41% in 1985, and 50% in 1990. The decreasing shares of deposit money banks in deposits, as well as loans and discounts, raises an issue regarding the appropriateness of M2 as the intermediate monetary target variable.

reducing domestic credit creation. In fact, the balance of Foreign Exchange Stabilization Fund Bonds is treated as a liability item of the monetary authorities in the official monetary statistics.

12.3   External shocks and monetary policy

The Korean economy was subject to a number of external shocks during the second half of the 1980s. The U.S. dollar began to depreciate in March 1985 against the currencies of major industrial countries and continued to depreciate at an accelerated rate after the meeting of the G-5 finance ministers in September 1985. The depreciation of the U.S. dollar, together with low world interest rates and the decline in crude oil world prices, triggered an export boom and decreased the imported oil bill. As shown by the macroeconomic indicators reported in Table 12.1, these developments had three major effects. First, Korean GNP growth accelerated sharply from an already robust 6.4 percent per year in 1980–5 to an exceptional 10.9 percent in 1986–90. Second, inflation, which stood at 2.8 percent in 1986–7, well below the average of 10.9 percent in 1980–5, accelerated to nearly 9 percent in 1990. Third, Korea's current account balance shifted from deficits averaging $2.7 billion ($-4.2$ percent of nominal GNP) in 1980–5 to surpluses averaging $6.3 billion (4.8 percent of nominal GNP) in 1986–90. In line with the changes in inflation and the current account, the Korean currency, the won, appreciated substantially in 1988–9 but began to depreciate in 1990, in both real and nominal effective terms.

Although Korea was by and large successful in meeting its macroeconomic targets, efforts to cool the overheated economy proved to be complicated, because current account surpluses injected large amounts of liquidity into the economy.[4] The monetary effects of current account surpluses may be illustrated by recalling that, in an open economy, the balance sheet identity of the central bank implies that the change in the monetary base or reserve money (H) equals the sum of changes in net foreign assets (NFA) and in net domestic credit (NDC), that is, $\Delta H = \Delta NFA + \Delta NDC$. In the second half of the 1980s, Korean current account surpluses tended to increase net foreign assets, and consequently the monetary base, because of the requirement that foreign exchange earnings be surrendered to the Bank of Korea in exchange for domestic

[4] The targets for output growth and inflation were largely met in the second half of the 1980s. There was less success in meeting current account targets. In the years of rising current account surplus, actual levels exceeded the targets. The reverse was true in the years of falling current account deficits. In Korea, targets of macroeconomic performance are set every year by the Economic Planning Board.

Table 12.1. *Macroeconomic performance*

	1980	1981	1982	1983	1984	1985	1986	1987	1988	1989	1990
Real GNP	-3.7	5.9	7.2	12.6	9.3	7.0	12.9	13.0	12.4	6.8	9.3
Inflation (CPI)	28.8	21.5	7.1	3.4	2.3	2.4	2.7	3.0	7.1	5.7	8.6
Current account	-5.3	-4.6	-2.6	-1.6	-1.3	-0.8	4.6	9.8	14.1	5.1	-2.2
(ratio to GNP, %)[a]	(9)	(7)	(4)	(2)	(2)	(1)	(5)	(8)	(8)	(2)	(1)
Effective exchange rate[b]	24.1	8.9	1.4	6.9	1.8	7.1	21.2	2.0	-6.7	-11.7	6.4
Real exchange rate[c]	5.9	-3.3	-1.0	6.3	2.8	7.4	19.2	0.8	-11.1	-13.3	2.0
Against yen	1.4	-0.1	-8.9	9.5	3.9	7.0	40.3	5.6	-5.6	-17.5	-4.7
Against dollar	10.6	2.1	6.2	6.0	5.9	9.0	0.4	-6.0	-13.7	-8.9	2.3

Note: Figures express rates of change as percentages, except the current account balance, which is in billions of U.S. dollars.
[a]Ratio to GNP is the ratio to the nominal value of Korean GNP.
[b]Effective exchange rate of won is an average exchange rate against the currencies of Japanese yen, German mark, and U.S. dollar, weighted by the relative trade shares (0.36, 0.18, 0.46), respectively.
[c]Real exchange rate is nominal exchange rate multiplied by foreign consumer prices relative to Korean consumer prices. A positive change indicates won depreciation.
Source: Bank of Korea, *Monthly Bulletin*; International Monetary Fund, *International Financial Statistics.*

currency. The monetary base increased by 851 billion won and net foreign assets decreased by 81 billion won from 1980 to 1985. From 1986 to 1990, the monetary base increased by 9.5 trillion won and net foreign assets grew by 9.3 trillion won. This shows that the rapid expansion in the monetary base during the second half of the 1980s was largely attributable to the expansion of net foreign assets.

The monetary authorities responded to the acceleration in money growth from the current account surpluses in part by raising the money target from 9.5 percent in 1985 to 15 to 18 percent in 1986–90. This was intended to accommodate a rise in the transaction demand for money resulting from higher targets of output growth. In addition, the Bank of Korea implemented several measures to curb the tendency toward accelerating money growth (see Table 12.2).[5]

First, it reduced the money multiplier, the ratio of broad money stock to reserve money, by raising the cost of funds. The discount rate on commercial bills was raised from 5 to 7 percent in July 1986, and then to 8 percent in September 1988. The required reserve ratios were raised on three occasions during 1985–90, reaching 11.5 percent on demand deposits and time-and-savings deposits in February 1990. A high marginal reserve requirement ratio (about 30 percent) was applied to the increment of monthly average deposits compared with monthly deposits of April 1989.

Second, the authorities tried to reduce the rate of net foreign asset accumulation by decreasing current account surpluses and encouraging capital outflows. To reduce current account surpluses, Korea took measures to open domestic markets to foreign goods and services. Korea's import-liberalization ratios increased markedly, from 88 percent in 1985 to 96 percent in 1990.[6] At the same time, average tariff rates were cut from 21 percent in 1985 to 11 percent in 1990.

As a further measure to decrease the current account surplus, the authorities allowed the exchange rate to appreciate in 1987. By 1989, the won had appreciated 26 percent on a cumulative basis, thus offsetting the depreciation of the real exchange rate during the preceding period, 1985–6.

To encourage capital outflows, the government took measures to relax the restrictions on overseas direct investments beginning in 1986. Further, the government promoted early repayments of external debt. Re-

---

[5] See Lindner (in press) and Kang (1992).
[6] Since most of the import-restricted items are agricultural, almost all manufactured items were imported without severe difficulty in 1990.

payments for public and commercial loans rose from $1.8 billion in 1985 to an annual average $4 billion in 1986–9. Because Korea's interest rates were higher than foreign interest rates and won appreciations were anticipated, however, the government's efforts generated only modest amounts of capital outflow.

Third, the monetary authorities reduced domestic credit creation to offset the expansionary monetary effects of net foreign asset accumulation. The Bank of Korea lowered the amount of local currency loans given to exporters in advance per the dollar amount of exports contracted. The ratio of loans to the contracted amount of exports decreased from 82.5 percent in 1985 to 51.3 percent during 1986–90. However, this measure had only minimal effects. The Bank of Korea drained liquidity from the system with greater success by issuing MSBs.[7] The outstanding balance of MSBs rose nearly ten times, from 1.9 trillion won in 1985 (7 percent of M2) to a peak of 18 trillion won (31 percent of M2) at the end of 1989. The large volume of MSBs complicated the task of monetary control, however, because interest payments on the outstanding MSB balance became a source of increase in credit creation. Interest payments rose from 61.5 billion won (0.2 percent of M2) in 1985 to 1.97 trillion won (3.5 percent of M2) in 1989.

Following three consecutive years of current account surpluses, in the latter months of 1989 growth in real exports declined and the economy began showing palpable signs of slowing down. To stimulate growth, the authorities lowered the discount rate to 7 percent in November 1989. In addition, open market sales of MSBs were substantially reduced so as to ease monetary conditions. The exchange rate depreciated as the current account turned into a deficit in 1990. With the end of the current account surpluses, the concern over how to contain monetary growth within target ranges diminished.

12.4 Sterilization by the Bank of Korea

In the preceding section, it was argued that domestic credit creation by the Bank of Korea was heavily influenced by the desire of the central bank to sterilize net foreign asset accumulation and follow an independent monetary policy. In this section, statistical tests are used to determine whether sterilization in fact occurred and, if so, to quantify the

[7] The sales of Foreign Exchange Stabilization Fund Bonds issued by the Ministry of Finance were also effective in reducing the net domestic asset position of the monetary authorities.

Table 12.2. *Monetary aggregates and main monetary policy instruments*

	1980	1981	1982	1983	1984	1985	1986	1987	1988	1989	1990
Money stock (M2)[a]	26.9	25.0	27.0	15.2	7.7	15.6	18.4	19.1	21.5	19.8	17.2
(ratio to GNP, %)	(34)	(35)	(38)	(37)	(35)	(37)	(37)	(38)	(39)	(41)	(40)
Reserve money[a]	−6.5	−13.6	36.5	7.1	3.7	1.7	16.2	48.9	30.2	31.8	7.7
Effective required reserve ratio[b]	11.7	7.3	4.7	5.3	4.9	4.3	4.1	4.6	6.7	9.7	10.6
Official required reserve ratio[b]	13.2	8.0	4.8	5.5	4.8	4.5	4.5	7.0	10.0	10.0	11.5
Discount rate (average)[b]	19.3	15.6	5.4	5.0	5.0	5.0	6.0	7.0	7.3	7.8	7.0
Monetary Stabilization Bonds[c]	530	1,660	927	3,360	4,459	1,900	4,285	9,006	16,297	18,003	15,611
(ratio to M2, %)	(4)	(12)	(5)	(15)	(18)	(7)	(13)	(22)	(33)	(31)	(22)
Foreign Exchange Stabilization Fund Bonds[c]	na	na	na	na	na	0.0	0.0	1,500	989	1,400	3,000

Long-term capital balance[d]	1.9	2.8	1.2	1.3	2.1	1.1	-2.0	-5.8	-2.7	-3.4	0.6
Increase in liabilities	2.2	2.8	1.7	2.1	2.0	2.6	-0.3	-5.5	-2.4	-2.0	1.3
Increase in assets	0.3	0.0	0.5	0.8	-0.1	1.5	1.6	0.3	0.4	1.4	0.7
Exchange rate (average)[a]	25.5	12.1	7.3	6.1	3.9	7.9	1.3	-6.7	-11.1	-8.2	5.4

[a] Money stock (end of period), reserve money (end of period), and exchange rate (won/$) are expressed as rates of change.
[b] Required reserve ratios and discount rate are average values as percentages during the year. Effective required reserve ratios are the average values of daily reserves divided by the deposits of deposit money banks subject to reserve requirements. Implicit is the assumption of no excess reserves. Official required reserve ratios are the average ratios of the official required ratios on time-and-savings deposits and on demand deposits, weighted by relative value shares.
[c] Monetary Stabilization Bonds and Foreign Exchange Stabilization Bonds are the outstanding balance at end of year in billions of Korean won.
[d] Long-term capital balance is in billions of U.S. dollars.
Source: Bank of Korea, *Monthly Bulletin.*

extent of sterilization by modeling the Bank of Korea's domestic credit reaction function.[8]

A domestic credit creation policy is influenced by a number of factors such as the balance of payments, inflation, real output, credit supply, and seasonal events. The main concern here is to isolate the impact of net foreign asset accumulation on domestic credit creation by the Bank of Korea, while controlling for these other factors. The measure of domestic credit creation relevant in estimating the reaction function excludes changes in credit creations due to changes in other policy instruments, such as changes in required reserve ratios. Accordingly, the following reaction function was specified and estimated:

$$\Delta\text{NDA} = a + b\,\Delta\text{NFA} + c\text{RRR}(-12) \times \text{PHI}(-1)$$
$$+ d\,\Delta\text{IP} + e\,\Delta\text{CL}, \tag{12.1}$$

where ΔNDA is the change in the net claims of the Bank of Korea on the government and banking sectors minus changes in the required reserve ratio multiplied by the sum of demand deposits and time-and-savings deposits at the end of the same month in the preceding year, ΔNFA is the change in the net foreign assets of the Bank of Korea, PHI is consumer price inflation, ΔIP is the change in real output, ΔCL is the change in claims on the private sector by deposit money banks, and RRR is the effective required reserve ratio, that is, average reserves of deposit money banks divided by average balance of demand and time deposits subject to reserves. A change in variable x, Δx, is defined here as a change of x from the same month in the preceding year in order to avoid seasonality factors. Figures in parentheses denote time lags.

If the sterilization coefficient b is negative, the Bank of Korea sterilizes the monetary effects of changes in its net foreign asset holdings through offsetting adjustments in domestic credit. If $b = -1$, the sterilization is complete and the monetary effects of net foreign asset accumulation are fully offset. If b is positive, the Bank of Korea amplifies the monetary effects of changes in its net foreign asset holdings, leading to larger increases in the money supply. During the period when the won is appreciating, a positive b coefficient estimate would be consistent with a desire to stabilize the exchange rate in order to prevent adverse effects on the traded goods sector or to achieve a certain current account balance objective.

---

[8] For domestic credit policy reaction functions, see Herring and Marston (1977), Obstfelt (1983), and Obstfeld and Cumby (1981).

Table 12.3. *The Bank of Korea's reaction function, 1980:1–1990:12,*
$\Delta NDA = a + b \Delta NFA + cRRR(-12) \times PHI(-1) + d \Delta IP + e \Delta CL$

Period	a	b	c	d	e	$R2$	DW
1980:1–1990:12	148.4	−0.80	−41.4	12.17	0.06	.92	1.55
	(1.3)	(38.8)	(1.5)	(2.4)	(5.6)		
1980:1–1985:9	−188.7	−0.63	−36.4	12.8	0.14	.71	1.58
	(0.6)	(7.1)	(1.7)	(1.8)	(2.2)		
1985:10–1990:12	736.7	−0.86	1,333.4	6.64	−0.04	.92	1.66
	(1.7)	(20)	(1.9)	(0.6)	(0.7)		

Note: Figures in parentheses are *t*-statistics, $R2$ is the coefficient of determination corrected for the degrees of freedom, and DW is the Durbin–Watson statistic. *Abbreviations:* NDA, reserve money base − net foreign assets (NFA) + net worth − RRR(−12) × (demand and time deposits); RRR, effective reserve required ratio, i.e., reserves divided by deposits subject to reserve requirements; PHI, inflation (consumer prices as percentages); CL, claims of deposit money banks on private sector; Δ, a change for a given month from the month in the preceding year.

The expected sign of c is negative, as higher inflation in the preceding month would call for a contraction in domestic credit. Both coefficients d and e are expected to be positive; that is, a rise in real output and bank credit leads to a rise in the supply of monetary base in order to accommodate the demand for liquidity.

Table 12.3 reports the estimated reaction function using monthly data over the period 1980:1–1990:12 and two subperiods 1980:1–1985:9 and 1985:10–1990:12.[9] For the entire sample period, the coefficient estimate of inflation c is not significant. However, the sterilization coefficient estimate b is statistically significant with a negative value of around −0.8. This indicates that the Bank of Korea attempted to offset a large proportion of its net foreign asset accumulation. Furthermore, the estimated absolute value of b rises from 0.6 in the first subperiod to 0.86 in the second subperiod, 1985:10–1990:12. This rise in the sterilization coefficient estimates suggests that the sterilization efforts were intensified to control rapid money growth in the face of growing current account

[9] The source of data is the *Monthly Bulletin* of the Bank of Korea.

surpluses in the second half of the 1980s. The sterilization coefficient estimate of less than 1 indicates that control of the monetary base was possible.

12.5   Consequences of policy measures

In this section, the consequences of sterilization and other policies designed to curb the monetary effects of current account surpluses are evaluated by simulating a monthly structural open macroeconomic model of Korea. This model is composed of (i) a financial sector and (ii) a real sector. The model specification follows existing theoretical open economy models (see Branson and Henderson, 1985; Fleming, 1962, Stevens et al., 1984). However, three points are worth making with regard to the specification. First, the model assumes that the financial sector clears instantaneously, while the real sector adjusts gradually over time. For this reason, lagged effects are allowed on real output, prices, exports, and imports, but not on the demand for assets. Second, an effort is made to incorporate the main characteristics of the Korean financial sector. In particular, recognizing that exchange rates were adjusted occasionally by policy considerations during the 1980s, the decision function of policymakers for determining exchange rates is modeled.[10] External capital inflows were modeled to reflect the fact that they financed the gap between desired international reserve accumulation and the current account balance. Third, it is well known that spurious correlations and simultaneity may affect the estimates when coefficients are estimated by ordinary least squares. However, it is believed that the model nevertheless conveys a reasonably accurate representation of the Korean economy.

12.5.1   The macroeconomic model

The financial sector. The financial sector model seeks to capture the key features of the Korean financial system in sufficient detail to meet the main objective of analyzing the effect of sterilization and other policies. The sector consists of two representative agents – the Bank of Korea and a private household. In the background, these two agents

---

[10] Although the exchange rate system that Korea adopted in March 1980 is a managed float system, exchange rate policy focuses mainly on supporting export competitiveness in order to achieve a target level of the current account. To promote flexibility in the

deal with deposit money banks, nonbank financial institutions, and the government, but the behavior of these last three entities is not explicitly modeled. The equations of the financial sector model are reported in Table 12.4.

The Bank of Korea holds net claims on the government and banks and net foreign assets. The total asset position equals its liabilities and net worth. The liabilities of the Bank of Korea consist of the monetary base (currency and reserve deposits) and the balance of MSBs inclusive of Foreign Exchange Stabilization Fund Bonds. Reserve deposits of banks are required by law and equal the reserve required ratios times the outstanding balance of demand and time deposits held by the public. No significant excess reserves are held by banks. The monetary base and the required reserve ratios, together with reserve deposits and public holding of currency, determine the money supply M2.

The private sector can hold wealth in the form of currency, deposits at the money deposit banks, MSBs, corporate bonds, government bonds, stocks, and deposit liabilities of nonbank financial institutions. Nonbank financial institutions use their deposit liabilities to invest mostly in MSBs, corporate bonds, government bonds, and stocks. To simplify the analysis without much loss of generality, it is assumed that the financial assets owned by the private sector include the money stock M2 (currency, demand deposits, and time-and-savings deposits), MSBs of the Bank of Korea and bonds of the Foreign Exchange Stabilization Fund, and total outstanding corporate bonds. The allocation of total wealth among the five types of assets is described by a portfolio balance model of the Tobin (1969) variety:

$$A(i)/\text{WLTH} = a(i) + b(i)(\text{IP} \times \text{CPI}/\text{WLTH})$$
$$+ c(i)\text{RMSB} + d(i)\text{RDNMD},$$
$$\text{WLTH} = \text{CUR} + \text{DD} + \text{TD} + (\text{BMSB} + \text{BFES}) + \text{HCB}, \quad (12.2)$$

where $A(i)$ stands for the value of asset i, $i =$ CUR, DD, TD, BMSB + BFES, and HCB; CUR is currency in circulation; DD is demand deposits; TD is time-and-savings deposits; BMSB is Monetary Stabilization Bonds; BFES is Foreign Exchange Stabilization Fund Bonds; HCB is corporate bonds; WLTH is financial wealth; IP is industrial production; CPI is consumer prices; RMSB is interest rate on

determination of the external value of the won, a market average exchange rate system was introduced on March 2, 1990, with allowance for a greater role for market conditions. Under the new exchange rate system, the exchange rate was initially allowed to float daily in the interbank market within 0.4 percent against the previous day's weighted-average exchange rate of the U.S. dollar. For further discussion of Korea's exchange rate system, see Kwack (1988) and Kwag (1989).

Table 12.4. *Empirical model of the financial sector, 1983:1–1990:12*

I. Portfolio demand

A(i)/WLTH = a(i) + b(i)(IP × CPI/WLTH) + c(i)RMSB + d(i)RDNMD

WLTH = CUR + DD + TD + (BMSB + BFES) + HCB

A(i)	a(i)	b(i)	c(i)	d(i)	R2	DW	WLTH	IP × CPI	RMSB	RDNMD
								Elasticity with respect to		
CUR	0.04 (5.8)	0.11 (2.8)	−0.001 (5.9)	−0.001 (3.7)	0.84	0.56	0.61	0.39	−0.40	−0.37
DD	0.05 (5.3)	0.2 (3.5)	−0.001 (5.7)	−0.002 (4.3)	0.86	1.03	0.36	0.64	−0.44	−0.35
TD	0.17 (10.0)	0.78 (8.6)	−0.003 (7.8)	−0.002 (2.8)	0.92	0.61	0.58	0.42	−0.15	−0.07
BMSB + BFES	−0.05 (1.5)	0.43 (2.3)	0.013 (19)	−0.008 (5.7)	0.83	0.38	0.86	0.14	3.26	−2.85
HCB	0.78 (17)	−1.49 (6.1)	−0.008 (9.5)	0.013 (7.1)	0.75	0.31	1.20	−0.20	−0.14	0.24

II. Money supply

$M2 = CUR + DD + TD$

$M2 = CUR + (RB - CUR - ERDT) / RRR$

$RB = RBNFA + RBNDL + RBNDG + RBNDG - (BMSB + BFES) - RBNW$

$\Delta RBNFA = 31.4 + 0.73 \times 0.001 \times BOP, R2 = 0.57, DW = 2.83$
$\qquad (1.1) \qquad (11)$

III. Policy reaction function for won–dollar exchange rate adjustment

$\log(E) = 6.6 - 0.08 \times 0.001 \times CA, R2 = 0.45, DW = 0.13$
$\qquad (803) \quad (5.8)$
$\qquad\qquad PDL<12,2>$

Note: Figures in parentheses are *t*-statistics, *R2* is the coefficient of determination corrected for the degrees of freedom, and DW is the Durbin–Watson statistic.

Abbreviations: BMSB, outstanding stock of Monetary Stabilization Bonds; BFES, outstanding stock of Foreign Exchange Stabilization Fund Bonds; CA, the current account; CPI, consumer price index; CUR, currency in circulation; DD, demand deposits; E, won–dollar exchange rate; ERDT, discrepancy in reserve identity; HCB, value of corporate bonds; IP, industrial production index; M2, money supply; RDNMD, deposit rate of nondeposit money banks; RMSB, discount rate on MSBs; RB, reserve money base; RBNFA, net foreign assets of the Bank of Korea, BOK; RBNDG, net claims on government of BOK; BNDL, net claims on banks of BOK; RBNW, net worth of BOK; TD, time deposits; WLTH, financial wealth. PDL<*a,b*> indicates *a* distributed lags with the constraint of *b* degrees.

MSBs (and BFES); and RDNMD is interest rate on deposits of non-money financial institutions and on corporate bonds.[11]

The industrial production variable IP captures the transaction motive for asset demands. Private wealth holders regard the five assets they hold as imperfect substitutes. Further, it is assumed that the five assets are strictly gross substitutes, so that a rise in the price of one asset causes its demand to decline and the demand for all other assets to rise. The balance sheet constraint for wealth holders requires that the sum of the nominal demands for the five assets must equal their nominal wealth. This implies that the sum of $a(i)$ equals 1 and that the sum of $b(i)$, the sum of $c(i)$, and the sum of $d(i)$ each equal zero. Given the money supply, wealth, income, and prices in the short run, the wealth constraint, money supply definition, and four asset demands simultaneously determine two interest rates, two components of the money supply, MSBs (and BFES), and holding of corporate bonds.

The estimated equations using monthly data over 1983:1–1990:12 are presented in Table 12.4. The estimated coefficients satisfy the balance sheet condition that the sum of the nominal demands for the five assets must equal the total wealth. All the estimated coefficients have the expected sign and size. One interesting finding is that, other things being equal, a rise in income increases the transaction demand for money and reduces the demand for corporate bonds. Demand for corporate bonds is elastic with respect to a change in wealth, and the higher the wealth, the higher is the demand for corporate bonds. Money demands and corporate bond demand are interest-inelastic, whereas the demand for BMSB and BFES is highly interest-elastic.

The foreign asset component of the money supply depends positively

[11] Sources of data used for empirical estimation are *Monthly Bulletin* of the Bank of Korea and *International Financial Statistics* of the International Monetary Fund. Several of the data series are from the internal database of the Bank of Korea. I constructed historical monthly series of Korea's net external liability (FD), interest rate on MSBs (RMSB), and non–money market interest rate (RDNMD): (1) FD is constructed by defining a benchmark figure of $15,174 million at the end of 1988; (2) RMSBs are published data for the period 1987–91 and interest rate of time deposits of one year maturity for the period 1977–86; (3) RDNMD represents interest rates on deposits of nonbank financial institutions and interest rates on corporate bond market. I attempted to take into account the importance of different forms of deposits over time and changes in regulations on interest rates on deposits at nonbank financial institutions and yields on corporate bonds. On the basis of the information available to me, I defined RDNMD as 0.28 RDOFI $+ 0.72$ RDFIM, where the weights reflect relative market size, RDOFI is the rate on bills (60–90 days) resold with recourse by Investment & Finance Co., and RDFIM is the rate on general nonspecific Money in Trust for the period 1977–84 and yields of corporate bonds (composite guaranteed and floating rate) for the period 1985–91.

on the balance of payments. Under the managed float system adopted on February 1980, the nominal value of the won against the U.S. dollar was adjusted to reflect changes in the value of the U.S. dollar against the currencies of the other major industrial countries in order to achieve target levels of the current account or external debt (see Kwack, 1988). It is estimated that the won–dollar exchange rate is negatively affected by present and lagged levels of the current account.

The real sector. The real sector of the model endogenously determines Korean income, prices, exports, imports, net investment income, and the current and capital accounts of the balance of payments. The model and estimated equations are reported in Table 12.5. As described in Kwack and Lee (1991), the demand for real exports of goods and services excluding investment income receipts depends on real foreign income and relative prices. The demand for real imports depends on real income and relative prices. Foreign income elasticity of export demand, estimated at 1.7, is higher than the U.S. income elasticity of import demand, estimated at 0.7. Long-run price elasticities of real exports and imports are 1.4 and 1.1, respectively. Net investment income is related to the U.S. Treasury bill rate times external liabilities. Since private capital transactions generally require the approval of the authorities, it is assumed that the government controls international capital flows according to the need to finance current account transactions. Hence, the capital account balance (net capital inflows into Korea) is residually determined by the balance of payments minus the current account balance.

As a reduced-form equation, aggregate demand for real output depends on real exports, including net investment income and international transfer receipts, relative prices, and the real money balance. Higher crude oil world prices reduce real aggregate demand. Consumer price inflation is affected by wage cost inflation, import price inflation, and growth in the money stock. The wage rate is treated as exogenously determined.[12] Consequently, a change in output influences prices not through its effect on the wage rate, but through changes in the exchange rates and the money supply induced by income changes. Export prices are affected by changes in the exchange rate, consumer prices, and import prices.

The open economy macroeconomic model of Korea links the real sector model to the financial model presented earlier. The model is simulated dynamically from 1985:1 to 1990:12 to test its predictive power. The root mean squared percent error statistics for the money supply,

---

[12] No systematic relationship was found between the wage rate, on the one hand, and inflation, output growth, excess capacity ratio, and other factors, on the other.

Table 12.5. *Empirical model of the real sector*

I. Current account and balance of payments

$\log(\text{XGSV/PXD}) = -4.25 + 1.66 \log(\text{FIP}) + 1.38 \log(\text{FCPI/PXD}), R2 = 0.88, \text{DW} = 1.63$
$\qquad\qquad\qquad\quad (5.7)\quad (10.4)$
$\qquad\qquad\qquad\qquad\qquad\qquad (11)$
$\qquad\qquad\qquad\qquad\qquad\qquad \text{PDL}{<}18{,}2{>}$

$\log((\text{MGSNV} + \text{MGCPV})/\text{PMD}) = 6.69 + 0.74 \log(\text{IP}) - 1.06 \log(\text{PMD} \times \text{E/CPI}), R2 = 0.94, \text{DW} = 1.91$
$\qquad\qquad\qquad\qquad\qquad\qquad\qquad (5.0)\quad (9.6)\qquad\qquad (7.5)$
$\qquad\qquad\qquad\qquad\qquad\qquad\qquad\qquad\qquad\qquad\qquad \text{PDL}{<}8{,}2{>}$

$\text{NFY} = -54.36 - 0.00038\ \text{USRTB}(-1) \times \text{FD}(-1) + 0.28\ \text{NFY}(-1), R2 = 0.51, \text{DW} = 1.92$
$\qquad\quad (3.2)\quad (5.22)\qquad\qquad\qquad\qquad\qquad\qquad (3.0)$

$\text{CA} = \text{XGSV} - \text{MGSNV} - \text{MGCPV} + \text{NFY} + \text{NTR}$

$\text{BOP} = \text{CA} + \text{DKA}$

$\Delta \text{FD} = -\text{CA}$

II. Output and prices

$\log(\text{IP}) = -0.78 + 0.29 \log((\text{XGSV} + \text{NFY} + \text{NTR})/\text{PDX}) + 0.15 \log(\text{E} \times \text{FCPI/CPI}) - 0.04 \log(\text{E} \times \text{WPCP/CPI})$
$\qquad\quad (2.6)\quad (8.1)\qquad\qquad\qquad\qquad\qquad\qquad\qquad\qquad (5.4)\qquad\qquad\qquad\qquad\qquad (3.4)$
$\qquad\qquad\qquad \text{PDL}{<}12{,}2{>}$

$\qquad\quad + 0.66 \log(\text{M2/CPI}), R2 = 0.99, \text{DW} = 1.45$
$\qquad\qquad\quad (17)$
$\qquad\qquad\quad \text{PDL}{<}24{,}2{>}$

$$\Delta \text{CPI/CPI}(-12) = -0.02 + 0.34\ \Delta \text{WRM/WRM}(-12) + 0.17\ \Delta(\text{PMD} \times \text{E})/(\text{PMD}(-12) \times \text{E}(-12))$$
$$(4.8) \qquad (14) \qquad\qquad\qquad (17.5)$$
$$\text{PDL}{<}18{,}2{>} \qquad\qquad \text{PD}{<}6{,}2{>}$$
$$+\ 0.10\ \Delta \text{M2/M2}(-12),\ R2 = 0.80,\ \text{DW} = 0.35$$
$$(3.2)$$

$$\Delta \text{PXD/PXD}(-12) = 0.02 - 0.49\ \Delta \text{E/E}(-12) + 0.22\ \text{CPI/CPI}(-12) + 0.23\ \text{PMD/PMD}(-12),\ R2 = 0.94,\ \text{DW} = 0.22$$
$$(5.8) \quad (16) \qquad\qquad (3.6) \qquad\qquad (9.9)$$

Note: Figures in parentheses are *t*-statistics, *R2* is the coefficient of determination corrected for the degrees of freedom, and DW is the Durbin–Watson statistic.

Abbreviations: BOP, the balance of payments defined as the change in international reserve assets; DKA, the capital account of the balance of payments; FCPI, foreign (U.S., Japanese, and German) consumer prices in U.S. dollars; FIP, foreign (U.S., Japanese, and German) industrial production index; FD, net external liabilities; MGCPV, imports of crude oil; MGSNV, imports of goods and services, excluding oil and interest payments; NFY, net factor incomes abroad; NTR, net transfer receipts from abroad; PMD, dollar prices of imports; PXD, dollar prices of exports; USRTB, U.S. Treasury bill rate; WPCP, dollar price of crude oil per barrel; WRM, wage rate in Korean manufacturing sector; XGSV, exports of goods and services, excluding interest receipts; PDL$<a,b>$ indicates a distributed lags with the constraint of b degrees.

interest rate on MSBs, exchange rate, consumer prices, industrial production, export value, and import value are 1.9, 6.8, 6.5, 1.5, 2.9, 9.8, and 10.5, respectively. These error statistics are relatively low and justify the use of the model as a tool for policy evaluation.

12.5.2 *Estimating the effects of major policy instruments and floating exchange rate*

The open economy macroeconomic model of Korea is used to assess the effects of three sets of major policy actions designed to curb money growth, namely changes in required reserve ratios, MSB levels, and the won–dollar exchange rate. In addition, an attempt is made to quantify the effects of these policies on the economy that would have been expected under a system of free floating.

Estimates of the effects of shifts in a policy instrument are the solutions of the model obtained by simulating it with actual values of all exogenous variables minus the solutions obtained by simulating with actual values of all exogenous variables other than the policy variable in question. The first set of simulations is called the "baseline solution," while the second set of simulations is called the "alternative policy solution." Estimates of the effects of the policy shifts are expressed as a percentage of the baseline solutions of the model. The residual errors of the estimated equations in the model are included when the simulations are undertaken for the baseline and alternative solutions. Thus, the baseline solution values are equal to or very close to actual values of the endogenous variables in the economy.

The alternative solutions of the model are what would have happened if no changes in the policy variable in question had been undertaken in 1987:1–1990:12 or if Korea had kept the values of the policy variable during 1987:1–1990:12 at the level existing during December 1986. (The values of the required reserve ratio, MSB volume, and the won–dollar exchange rate (E) in December 1986 are 0.042694, 4285.23 billion won, and 864.49 won per U.S. dollar, respectively.) The estimated effects so calculated reflect not only the size of a policy shock, but also the estimated coefficients and structure of time lags in the model. The size of changes in each of the policy instruments that are of concern here varies over time, and thus the effects are not the same as the multipliers obtained for the change of a constant amount in an exogenous variable during the entire simulation period.

Simulations were undertaken from 1987:1 to 1990:12 for the baseline solution and the three alternative solutions of the model outlined earlier. The estimated effects for key variables in Table 12.6 have the signs

Table 12.6. *Effects of changes in monetary policy instruments*

	Sample period	M2	RMSB	IP	CPI	XGSV	MGSV	CA	E	RB
Changes in RRR										
0.02	87:12	−8.8	1.8	−0.3	−1.0	−0.01	−0.03	0.02	0.1	0
0.04	88:12	−15.0	3.0	−3.7	−1.6	0.0	−0.24	0.25	0.4	0
0.07	89:12	−28.4	4.9	−9.7	−3.2	0.03	−0.58	0.64	−1.0	0
0.06	90:12	−26.9	3.6	−14.3	−3.8	0.03	−0.64	0.72	−5.2	0
Changes in BMSB										
52.4	87:12	−48.2	11.0	−9.9	−5.1	−0.04	−0.80	0.76	4.3	−63
73.7	88:12	−98.4	21.5	−34.9	−9.8	0.16	−1.97	2.20	−4.2	−123
76.2	89:12	−89.7	16.4	−51.1	−12.7	0.24	−1.73	2.16	−22.1	−107
72.6	90:12	−67.2	9.8	−44.6	−11.3	−0.48	−1.62	1.38	−15.7	−82
Changes in E										
−8.8	87:12	−0.5	0.0	−1.0	−1.5	0.04	0.27	−0.22		0
−26.1	88:12	−1.1	−0.3	−3.2	−3.7	0.03	0.68	−0.67		0
−28.0	89:12	−1.1	−0.3	−4.4	−4.6	−0.25	0.99	−1.31		0
−20.7	90:12	−1.0	−0.2	−3.9	−3.5	−0.30	0.84	−1.26		0

Note: Figures for all variables except RRR, XGSV, MGSV, and CA are percent changes evaluated from baseline solution values. Figures for XGSV, MGSV, and CA are in billions of U.S. dollars, and RRR is unadjusted. No changes in RRR, BMSB, and E mean that the required reserve ratio, the outstanding balance of MSBs, and the won–dollar exchange rate are kept at the level of 0.042694, 4285.23 billion won outstanding at the end of December 1986 and 864.49 won per dollar during December 1986, respectively.

Abbreviations: M2, money supply; RMSB, interest rate on MSBs; E, won–dollar exchange rate; RB, reserve money base; CA, the current account; BMSB, stock of MSBs; RRR, required reserve ratio; CPI, consumer prices; IP, industrial production; XGSV, export value of goods and services, excluding interest receipts; MGSV, import value of goods and services, excluding interest payments.

expected from theory. A notable exception is the sign of the variation of the exchange rate in the short run; namely, in the first year after policy changes the exchange rate does not exhibit the negative sign expected, that is the won does not immediately appreciate when the current account improves. This is because the estimated change of the current account is initially small.

We first consider the effects of an increase in the required reserve ratio during 1987 to 1990 by 0.063 (an approximately 160 percent rise from the end of 1986). This change is estimated to have caused the money supply to decline by 27 percent in 1990, as compared with the case of no policy change. The resulting monetary contraction resulted in a 14 percent decrease in real output and a 3.8 percent decrease in domestic prices. The decline in real income and prices improved the current account by $0.72 billion, primarily through a decrease in imports. The increase in the current account over time appreciates the won by 5 percent and generates the need for further rises in the reserve ratio in order to offset the current account improvement.

We consider next the effects of open market sales of MSBs, which rose 52 percent from 1986 to 1987 and by 73 percent in 1990. The domestic credit contraction effect of this policy reduced the monetary base by 82 percent in 1990, thereby decreasing the money supply by 67 percent. The decreases in the money supply led to a cumulative 44 percent fall in real output and an 11 percent decrease in prices. Because the money supply reduction was greater than the decline in money demand induced by the income and price falls, interest rates rose by 10 percentage points. The decreases in both income and domestic prices caused real imports to fall, thereby increasing the current account balance by $1.4 billion. The rise in the current balance led to a 16 percent appreciation of the exchange rate. The issuance of additional MSBs is called for to offset the liquidity effects generated by the additional current account surpluses.

We now examine the effects of exchange rate changes, by treating the exchange rate as an exogenous variable. The amount of the won's appreciation over 1987:1–1990:12 is 21 percent. This appreciation is estimated to have increased imports by $0.84 billion. The corresponding rise in export prices reduced the value of exports by $0.3 billion, thus reducing the current account balance by $1.2 billion. The currency appreciation and reduction in real exports induced real output and domestic prices to fall by 3.9 and 3.5 percent, respectively. However, the money supply was affected little by the currency appreciation. Decreases in both income and prices caused a fall in interest rates by reducing the transaction demand for money.

To summarize the results thus far, all three policy shocks reduced real output and prices, as well as the money supply. The policy of shifting the monetary base by the sale of MSBs had the most effective and largest impact on money supply, output, and prices, followed by the policy of changing the money multiplier through changes in required reserve ratios. However, these monetary policies both led the nominal interest rate to rise, whereas the exchange rate policy reduced the interest rate slightly.

The differences among the three policy instruments are very clear with respect to their effects on the current account surplus. Contractionary use of MSB operations and reserve requirements produced an increase in the current account surplus, which in turn necessitated the further use of such policies if the central bank wanted to control the money supply. This implies that these policies were effective in attaining money supply targets in the short run but not effective in keeping the money supply under control in the long run. By contrast, the policy of exchange rate adjustments was successful in reducing the current account surplus, thereby reducing the monetary effects of external money inflows. These results are in accordance with the expectation that monetary policies have the comparative advantage in controlling the money supply and interest rates, while exchange rate policies have the relative advantage in affecting the current account.

The adoption of a freely floating exchange rate by the government was improbable in the late 1980s, given the existence of severe regulations on financial markets. Nevertheless, it is interesting to speculate what might have happened had the monetary authorities allowed the exchange rate to float freely. Estimating the effects of a free float requires assumptions regarding the determination of exchange rate and capital flows. Three alternative cases are considered. In the first case ("interest rate case") the exchange rate is affected by interest rate differentials between the United States and Korea in addition to the current account variables in the exchange rate equation in the model. The exchange rate in this case is derived from the uncovered interest parity condition: $\log(E) = \log(EE) + 0.01/12(USRTB - RMSB)$ and $\log(EE) = f(CA)$, where EE is the expected exchange rate, and the coefficient $0.01/12$ is a monthly conversion factor needed because interest rates are percentages at an annual rate.

The second case ("accommodating monetary rule") includes the first case and also presumes the central bank desires to prevent the exchange rate from overshooting in response to capital inflows that take place due to the widening differential between Korean and U.S. interest rates. This is captured by assuming that the desired level of foreign reserves by the central bank is raised by $100 million.

The third case ("inflation rate rule") posits that the rate of change in the exchange rate depends on inflation rate and real interest rate differentials. The third case is thus a combination of the relative purchasing parity condition and of the real interest rate differential hypothesis (Frankel, 1979): $\Delta\log(E) = -\Delta\log(FCPI/CPI) + 0.01/12(USRTB - RMSB - FPHI + PHI)$, where FPHI and PHI stand for expected foreign and Korean inflation, respectively, and expected inflation is defined as a two-year moving average of consumer price inflation.

Models incorporating each of the three cases outlined were simulated from 1987:1 to 1990:12, and the results are reported in Table 12.7. The interest rate case produces less than a 1 percent currency appreciation over the full simulation period. This is not unexpected, because nominal interest rate differentials were in the range of 8 to 10 percentage points. Hence, no significant effects are expected on the economy. The second case yields a 1 percent appreciation of the won in 1987. As time passes, the effects of monetary expansions resulting from the rise in net foreign asset holdings of the Bank of Korea dominate the conditions of the economy. As a result, higher inflation, large capital inflows (due to the current account deficit financing and reserve increase by $100 million), and a large currency depreciation occur. The exchange rate depreciated by 1.3 percent in 1990.

The third case causes the currency to appreciate by 19 percent in 1987, and 21 percent by 1990. The currency appreciation reduced both output and prices and adversely affected the current account balance, triggering capital inflows into Korea. The effects of nominal interest rate differentials are small, as in the first case. Hence, the large exchange rate appreciation is due to a 31 percent inflation abroad in 1987, associated with the large depreciation of the U.S. dollar. Although the three cases are illustrative, the results suggest that the adoption of freely floating exchange rates would have made the won stronger, unless monetary authorities undertook accommodating monetary policy measures to stabilize the exchange rate.

12.6   Conclusions

This essay has examined the effectiveness of the policies utilized in Korea to mitigate the monetary effects of current account surpluses and to control the growth of monetary aggregates during the period 1986–90. The estimated domestic credit reaction function of the Bank of Korea indicates that a sterilization policy was followed. The sterilization coefficient estimate of -0.8 indicates that the central bank was able to

Table 12.7. *Effects of exchange rate floating, 1987:1–1990:12*

Sample period	M2	RMSB	IP	CPI	XGSV	MGSV	CA	E	RB
Interest rate case									
87:12	-0.0	0	-0.1	-0.1	0	0.02	-0.02	-0.7	0
88:12	0	0	-0.1	-0.1	0	0.02	-0.02	-0.2	0
89:12	0	0	-0.1	-0.1	0	0.02	-0.02	-0.5	0
90:12	0	0	-0.1	-0.1	0	0.04	-0.04	-0.8	0
Accommodating case									
87:12	7.2	-1.4	1.4	0.7	0	0.13	-0.13	-1.1	9.6
88:12	11.1	-2.0	4.7	1.2	-0.03	0.26	-0.30	0.2	13.4
89:12	12.4	-1.9	6.8	1.7	-0.01	0.31	-0.35	1.7	15.1
90:12	14.5	-1.9	7.6	1.8	0.04	0.41	-0.41	1.3	18.5
Inflation rate rule									
87:12	-0.9	-0.2	-2.0	-2.6	0.14	0.58	-0.45	-18.7	0
88:12	-0.9	-0.2	-2.7	-3.0	-0.21	0.69	-0.94	-15.6	0
89:12	-0.5	-0.1	-2.3	-1.9	-1.05	0.47	-0.65	-12.1	0
90:12	-0.9	-0.2	-3.3	-3.7	0.09	1.23	-1.24	-21.8	0

Note: Figures for all variables except XGSV, MGSV, and CA are in percent rates of change, evaluated from baseline solution values. Figures for XGSV, MGSV, and CA are in billions of U.S. dollars. "Interest rate case" refers to the case where 0.01 × (USRTB − RMSB)/12 is added to the equation for exchange rate adjustment. "Accommodating monetary case" is the case where the balance of payments is increased by $100 million and the interest rate case is also included. "Inflation rate rule" refers to the case where Δlog(E) = − Δlog(FCPI/CPI) + 0.01/12 × (USRTB − RMSB − FPHI + PHI) replaces the equation of exchange rate adjustment. FPHI and PHI are simple moving averages of foreign and Korean consumer price inflation, Δlog(FCPI) and Δlog(CPI), over the current and past two years.

Abbreviations: RMSB, interest rate on MSBs; E, won–dollar exchange rate; RB, reserve money base; CA, the current account; BMSB, stock of MSB; M2, money supply; RRR, required reserve ratio; CPI, consumer prices; IP, industrial production; XGSV, export value of goods and services, excluding interest receipts; MGSV, import value of goods and services, excluding interest payments.

sterilize a significant fraction of external reserve flows and to achieve its money supply goals. The simulations with a monthly open economy macro model of Korea suggest that the use of monetary policy instruments such as MSBs and required reserve ratios contributed to controlling the monetary aggregates. But surpluses in the current account balance generated by such monetary policies necessitated continuing sterilization operations and a reserve-tightening monetary policy. Thus, it can be concluded that sterilization is effective over a short period but is not effective in the long run. In contrast, the policy of exchange rate appreciations reduced the surplus in the current account and thus greatly assisted in reducing the injections of external liquidity into the economy. Although the results of the three cases we considered are illustrative, they show that if Korea had adopted a floating exchange rate system in the second half of the 1980s, an appreciation of the exchange rate and large capital inflows would have occurred.

Money supply targets were achieved despite large monetary injections from abroad through the use of a wide variety of policy measures. While some measures such as quantitative controls on loans imposed costs, other measures benefited the economy. The latter included deregulation of interest rates, opening of the home market, allowance of some flexibility in exchange rates, and relaxation of restrictions on international capital transactions.[13] While large external monetary inflows into Korea posed significant challenges for Korean policymakers, they also demonstrated that exchange rate changes are more effective than sterilized intervention in controlling money aggregates.

References

Ahn, Byungchan, Insup Kim, and Sungyoon Kang (1990). "Improvement on Reserve Requirement System," *Monthly Bulletin of the Bank of Korea,* May, 19–40.

Branson, William H., and Dale W. Henderson (1985). "The Specification and Influence of Asset Markets." In Ronald W. Jones and Peter B. Kenen, eds., *Handbook of International Economics,* Vol. 2., pp. 748–805. Amsterdam: Elsevier.

Fleming, J. M. (1962). "Domestic Financial Policies under Fixed and under Floating Exchange Rates" (International Monetary Fund) *Staff Papers* 9:369–79.

Frankel, Jeffrey A. (1979). "On the Mark: A Theory of Floating Exchange Rates Based on Real Interest Rate Differentials," *American Economic Review* 69:610–22.

Girton, L., and D. Henderson (1976). "Financial Capital Movements and Cen-

---

[13] See Kim (1988) and Ahn, Kim, and Kang (1990) for discussion of interest rate deregulation and financial development in Korea.

tral Bank Behavior in a Two-Country, Short-run Portfolio Balance Model," *Journal of Monetary Economics* 2:33–61.

Herring, Richard J., and Richard Marston (1977). "Sterilization Policy: The Trade-Off between Monetary Autonomy and Control over Foreign Exchange Reserves," *European Economic Review* 10:325–43.

International Monetary Fund. *International Financial Statistics*, various issues.

Johnson, Harry G. (1973). "The Monetary Approach to Balance of Payment Theory," *Further Essays in Monetary Economics*, pp. 229–49. Cambridge, MA: Harvard University Press. Reprinted in Jacob A. Frenkel and H. G. Johnson, eds., *The Monetary Approach to the Balance of Payments*, pp. 147–66. Toronto: University of Toronto Press.

Kang, Moonsoo (1992). "Financial Liberalization and Monetary Policy in Korea," Unpublished paper, Korea Development Institute, Seoul.

Kim, Wang-Woong (1988). "Recent Interest Liberalization in Korea," *Monthly Review of Korea Exchange Bank* 22:3–13.

Kouri, P. J. K. (1975). "The Hypothesis of Offsetting Capital Flows: A Case Study of Germany," *Journal of Monetary Economics* 1:21–39.

Kwack, Sung Y. (1988). "Korea's Exchange Rate Policy in a Changing Economic Environment," *World Development* 16:169–83.

Kwack, Sung Y., and Young Sun Lee (1991). "Is the Korean Currency Won Strong or Weak?" *International Economic Journal* 5:87–105.

Kwag, Dae-Hwan (1989). "Foreign Exchange Market in Korea," *Monthly Review of Foreign Exchange Bank* (September):3–13.

Lindner, Deborah J. (in press). "Foreign Exchange Rate Policy, Monetary Policy, and Capital Market Liberalization in Korea." In Sung Y. Kwack, ed., *The Korean Economy at a Cross Road: Development Prospects, Liberalization and South-North Economic Integration*. Westport, CT: Praeger.

Montiel, Peter (1990). "The Transmission Mechanism for Monetary Policy in Developing Countries," International Monetary Fund Working Paper no. WP/90/47, May. Washington, DC.

Mundell, Robert A. (1963). "Capital Mobility and Stabilization Policy under Fixed and Flexible Exchange Rates," *Canadian Journal of Economics and Political Sciences* 12:413–31.

Obstfeld, Maurice (1983). "Exchange Rates, Inflation, and the Sterilization Problem: Germany, 1975–1981," *European Economic Review* 21:161–89.

(1988). "The Effectiveness of Foreign-Exchange Intervention: Recent Experience," NBER Working Paper Series no. 2796, December. Cambridge, MA.

Obstfeld, Maurice, and Robert E. Cumby (1981). "Capital Mobility and the Scope for Sterilization: Mexico in the 1970s," Discussion Paper Series no. 105. Columbia University, Department of Economics.

Stevens, Guy V. G., Richard B. Berner, Peter B. Clark, Ernesto Hernandez-Cata, Howard J. Howe, and Sung Y. Kwack (1984). *The U.S. Economy in an Interdependent World: A Multicountry Model*. Washington, DC: Board of Governors of the Federal Reserve System.

Tobin, James (1969). "A General Equilibrium Approach to Monetary Theory," *Journal of Money, Credit, and Banking* 1:15–29.

PART IV
PROSPECTS FOR A YEN BLOC

CHAPTER 13

On the possibility of a yen bloc

Takatoshi Ito

13.1 Introduction

As regional economic and financial integration appears to proceed in the European Community (EC) and in North America, many wonder whether a similar economic bloc might form in Asia.[1] Most speculate that Japan would become a dominant player in such a bloc owing to its strong economic position compared with that of other countries in the region. This essay considers whether it is possible or probable that a so-called yen bloc will emerge in Asia.

The term "yen bloc" has different interpretations. Some economists and policymakers think of a yen bloc as an area where the yen is used extensively in transactions outside the legal national boundary of Japan as an invoice or vehicle currency. The larger the number of international transactions denominated in the yen, the greater the political incentive to form a currency area in which other currencies are pegged to the yen. The yen bloc in this view typically means an Asian version of the

The author acknowledges the helpful comments of Jeffrey Frankel, Reuven Glick, and Michael Hutchison.

[1] Dornbusch (1989) states such a view: "Japan will be driven to develop her own trade and finance zone in Asia. Japan is a high saving country, in part for demographic reasons, and the investment opportunities in Japan are falling short of saving potential. Capital export, therefore, is inevitable. In the past, the chief concentration of Japanese assets was in securities and direct investment in the United States. This will not stop, but a deteriorating climate will make Japan focus increasingly on alternative markets. It is difficult to avoid the conclusion that Japan's energies will increasingly focus on developing the Asian region rather than trying to own and operate Wall Street.

"The way *Japan, Inc.* operates also facilitates the formation of an Asian co-prosperity zone: government and business work hand-in-glove and business moves jointly. They move together as a group, because they are so keenly aware of vulnerability on their own. The decision will be made by consensus, and the rest is routine" (270).

317

European Monetary System (EMS) with the yen playing the role of the deutsche mark as the anchor currency.

Others use the term "yen bloc" more broadly to refer to an economic bloc, such as a free trade zone or a tariff union, where intraregional transactions are preferentially treated in terms of inspections, tariffs, and quotas. In this view Asian countries have an incentive to form such a bloc to counterbalance the increasing regionalization of trade and finance in the EC and in North America in the 1990s. The yen bloc in this interpretation more closely resembles an Asian trading bloc, similar to the EC or the North American Free Trade Area (NAFTA), with Japan as the economic and political leader.[2]

This essay investigates several questions regarding the yen bloc in its various interpretations. Is a yen bloc actually emerging? If not, is it likely to emerge? Section 13.2 discusses whether the yen is likely to become an international currency. Section 13.3 examines co-movements among Asian exchange rates and the extent to which countries in Asia have pegged their currencies against the yen. Section 13.4 analyzes the structure of trade and capital flows in Asia. Section 13.5 discusses the qualifications of an Asian country grouping for constituting an optimal currency area. Section 13.6 presents conclusions.

13.2   Yen as an international currency

This section examines evidence concerning the use of the yen as an international currency. This evidence suggests that although many indicators show the increased use of the yen, a yen bloc is not evident.

---

[2] The Association of Southeast Asian Nations (ASEAN) and the Asia Pacific Economic Cooperation (APEC) are two other Asian trade groups. APEC was established in 1989, with its founding members including Australia, Brunei, Canada, Indonesia, Japan, Korea, Malaysia, New Zealand, the Philippines, Singapore, Thailand, and the United States; China, Taiwan, and Hong Kong joined in 1991. Its objectives include technical cooperation and information exchange. Recently, discussions have focused on turning APEC into a more formal organization that would provide a forum for regional trade and fiinance negotiations.

Prime Minister Mahatir of Malaysia proposed an organization called the East Asian Economic Group in late 1990, consisting of Japan, the Newly Industrialized Economies, China, and the ASEAN countries, but excluding Australia, New Zealand, and the United States. It was originally interpreted as an organization intended to create a trading area rivaling the EC and NAFTA. Opposition from the United States and hesitant support by Japan forced Mahatir to agree to work more within APEC and to change the name of his proposed organization from "Group" to "Caucus."

Table 13.1. *Roles of an international currency*

	Private sector	Official sector
Medium of exchange	Vehicle currency	Intervention currency
Unit of account	Invoice currency	Currency peg
Store of value	Portfolio asset	Reserve currency

13.2.1 *Roles of an international currency*

The uses of a currency in international and financial markets closely parallel the three classic roles of domestic money as a unit of account, as a means of payment, and as a store of value. Table 13.1 summarizes the roles of an international currency, differentiating between its use in the private and official sectors.[3]

An invoice currency is the currency used to denominate export or import values in export and import contracts. A vehicle currency is a currency used as payment in transactions, whether between nonfinancial institutions, between banks, or between a bank and nonfinancial customers. Usually the invoice currency and the vehicle currency in a transaction are the same, but they might conceivably be different.[4] Domestic residents and governments may also hold foreign-currency-denominated assets as stores of value and/or to finance the future payment of imports.

Whether a particular national currency is utilized by the residents and government of other countries depends on the benefits and costs of its use. Invoice and currency decisions depend on concerns about the exchange rate and the relative market power of exporters and importers when entering into international transactions. The decision by private investors about which foreign currencies to hold in their portfolios is determined by the return and risk associated with the financial markets of different countries. The parallel decision by central banks about which foreign currencies to hold in their portfolio of foreign reserves depends on similar considerations and in turn influences the choice of intervention currency. Perhaps most important, the benefits of using a particular currency depend on the extent of its use by others. Because of scale

---

[3] The table is well known in the literature. See, e.g., Krugman (1984), who credits B. J. Cohen (1971).

[4] "In the European snake in the mid-1970s the currencies were pegged to one another, yet the dollar was used as a reserve and intervention currency" (Krugman, 1984: 263–4).

320   **Takatoshi Ito**

economies, the more everyone else uses a currency, the more advantageous it is to receive and hold on to that currency for use in subsequent transactions.

So far, the U.S. dollar seems to have maintained its special role as the central, or key, international currency. The dollar is the dominant currency by most of the above-mentioned criteria. It is the main vehicle currency, invoice currency, and reserve currency of the world. Many countries, particularly smaller ones, peg their currencies to the dollar. The remainder of this section investigates whether the role of the yen as an international currency has expanded as the Japanese economy has grown.

13.2.2 Yen as an invoice currency

First, we look at the long-term historical trend in the use of the yen for Japan's exports and imports. Table 13.2 shows that the use of the yen for invoicing Japanese exports and imports has been increasing. The yen-invoiced proportion of total Japanese exports increased from 1 percent in 1970 to about 30 percent in 1980 and to about 40 percent in 1990. The yen-invoiced proportion of total imports has increased more slowly. It rose from nearly zero in 1970 to about 2 percent in 1980 and 15 percent in 1991.

Table 13.3, adapted from Black (1991), shows that the yen-invoiced proportions of Japan's exports and imports in 1987 remain lower than the national currency proportions (shown in diagonal cells) of other advanced countries.[5] The United States predominantly uses U.S. dollars for both its exports and imports. This is unusual. Most other countries tend to use their national currency for the major share of their exports, but much less so for their imports.[6] The level of national currency use by Japan is clearly lower than for Germany, France, the United Kingdom, and Italy.

The literature usually points to two reasons for the relatively low degree of yen invoicing in Japan. First, given that the United States uses the U.S. dollar for its imports, a country that exports to the United States extensively, like Japan, will have a lower export yen-invoicing ratio. Second, the U.S. dollar is the transaction currency in international commodity markets, such as for crude oil and metals. Any country that imports a large quantity of raw materials will record a higher proportion

[5] These results have also been cited by Kawai (1992) and Taguchi (1994).
[6] This point has also been made by Krugman (1984:269). Bilson (1983) provides a formal analysis of the invoicing decision.

Table 13.2. *Invoice currencies of Japan's exports and imports, 1970–91*

	Exports		Imports	
Year	Yen-denominated	Dollar-denominated	Yen-denominated	Dollar-denominated
1970	0.9	90.4	0.3	80.0
1975	17.5	78.0	0.9	89.9
1980	28.9	66.3	2.4	93.1
1981	31.8	62.8	na	na
1982	33.8	60.9	na	na
1983	42.0	50.2	3.0	na
1984	39.5	53.1	na	na
1985	39.3	52.2	7.3	na
1986	36.5	53.5	9.7	na
1987	33.4	55.2	10.6	81.7
1988	34.3	53.2	13.3	78.5
1989	34.7	52.4	14.1	77.3
1990	37.5	48.8	14.5	75.5
1991	39.4	46.7	15.6	75.4

Note: Imports, 1985 and 1986, are figures for fiscal year (April to March).
Source: Kawai (1992). Original sources: Exports, through 1982, Bank of Japan; after 1982, MITI, *Export Confirmation Statistics*, 1991. Imports, until 1980, MITI; through 1985, Ministry of Finance; after 1985, MITI, *Import Reporting Statistics*, 1991.

of dollar-denominated imports. These explanations are briefly examined here.

Japan's exports and imports decomposed by destination and invoice currency ratios for each category are shown in Table 13.4. Only 16 percent of Japan's exports to the United States are invoiced in the yen. This contrasts with the higher yen-invoice share ratios of Japan's exports to other regions – 42 percent to the EC and 50 percent to Asian countries. However, even these levels are lower than the proportion of exports of European countries invoiced in national currencies, as shown in Table 13.3. Hence, the U.S. connection alone does not explain the low yen-invoicing ratio of Japanese exports. It is remarkable that about half of the exports to Asian countries from Japan are denominated in the U.S. dollar, a third-country currency. In Section 13.3, we will see that Asian currencies are de facto pegged to the U.S. dollar and that this may be

Table 13.3. *National currency and yen invoicing among six major countries, 1980 and 1987*

	1980 (share, %)						1987 (share, %)					
	Dollar	DM	Yen	Pound	FFr	Lira	Dollar	DM	Yen	Pound	FFr	Lira
Exports												
U.S.	97.0	1.0	—	1.0	1.0	—	94.0	2.0	1.0	1.0	1.0	1.0
Germany	7.2	82.3	—	1.5	2.8	—	7.4	81.6	0.5	1.8	2.5	1.7
Japan	65.7	1.9	29.4	1.1	—	—	63.6	2.0	33.4	1.0	—	—
U.K.	17.0	3.0	—	76.0	2.0	—	17.0	3.0	—	76.0	2.0	—
France	13.2	9.4	—	3.2	62.5	—	11.8	10.2	0.4	3.6	61.5	3.9
Italy	30.0	14.0	—	—	8.0	36.0	20.0	18.0	—	—	9.0	38.0
OPEC	96.0	1.0	—	1.0	1.0	1.0	92.0	0.2	—	0.2	2.0	2.0
Imports												
U.S.	85.0	4.1	1.0	1.5	1.0	1.0	80.0	8.0	0.2	3.0	2.0	2.0
Germany	33.1	42.8	1.5	3.1	3.3	—	22.0	52.4	2.5	2.6	3.9	1.6
Japan	93.1	1.4	2.4	0.9	—	—	84.0	0.2	10.6	1.0	1.0	—
U.K.	29.0	9.0	—	38.0	5.0	—	20.0	15.0	0.2	38.0	8.0	2.0
France	33.1	12.8	1.0	3.8	34.1	3.0	18.7	15.3	1.2	2.8	46.5	4.4
Italy	45.0	14.0	—	5.0	9.0	18.0	28.0	19.0	—	0.5	9.0	27.0
OPEC	50.0	10.0	—	8.0	7.0	—	40.0	20.0	10.0	0.8	7.0	—

Source: Black (1991, tables A.1–A.4).

Table 13.4. *Japan's trade by invoice currency and region, 1991*

	World			U.S.			EC			Asia		
	Amount ($ mil)	Dollar (%)	Yen (%)	Amount ($ mil)	Dollar (%)	Yen (%)	Amount ($ mil)	Dollar (%)	Yen (%)	Amount ($ mil)	Dollar (%)	Yen (%)
Exports	294,790	46.8	39.4	87,923	83.4	16.5	57,238	6.8	42.0	85,162	45.9	50.8
Imports	201,045	75.4	15.6	44,824	88.7	11.2	24,324	15.9	31.4	56,412	76.5	21.6

Source: MITI, *Export Confirmation Statistics*, 1991; *Import Reporting Statistics*, 1991.

Table 13.5. *Japan's trade by invoice currency and by commodity, 1991*

	Amount ($ mil)	Dollars (%)	Yen (%)
Exports			
All commodities	294,790	46.8	39.4
Foodstuffs	1,639	55.6	41.2
Textiles	6,102	63.0	32.5
Chemicals	15,544	63.0	26.2
Nonmetals	2,918	53.5	40.5
Metal products	18,864	76.8	19.5
Steel	13,013	87.7	9.4
Machines	230,091	42.2	42.8
Generators	7,067	40.7	48.8
TVs	2,184	35.0	56.6
VCRs	5,822	42.1	39.7
Autos	57,342	44.2	35.3
Ships	5,333	13.7	86.2
Heavy	3,207	41.0	51.5
Miscellaneous	18,467	52.7	30.4
Imports			
All commodities	201,045	75.4	15.6
Foodstuffs	32,605	72.4	22.2
Raw materials	72,442	97.2	1.9
Textiles	2,357	77.4	12.5
Ore and scrap metals	7,058	98.1	1.2
Others	13,688	91.8	5.9
Minerals	49,338	99.5	0.3
Crude oil	26,079	100.0	0.0
Manufactured goods	95,997	60.0	23.7
Chemicals	14,270	51.7	32.5
Machinery	30,984	52.5	22.5
Others	50,742	66.9	21.9

Note: "Nonmetals" include nonmetal mineral manufactured goods, such as cement and ceramics. "Machines" include generators, machine tools, computers, microprocessors, bearings, TVs, tape recorders, VCRs, semiconductors, autos, ships, cameras, copiers, and watches. "Generators" include generators and motors. "Heavy" refers to heavy electric machinery. "Miscellaneous" refers to tire tubes, musical instruments, and toys. "Raw materials, Textiles" includes wool, cotton, silk, etc. "Raw materials, Others" includes rawhide, soybean, lumber, and pulp. "Raw materials, Minerals" includes crude oil, coal, and a reason that the Asian countries prefer invoicing their imports in U.S. dollars.

Table 13.5 shows the yen-invoicing shares of Japanese exports by commodity. Ships, TVs, and industrial electronic goods recorded more than 50 percent of their exports denominated in the yen. This appears to suggest that those goods where Japan has a strong competitive edge are denominated in the yen. However, there are significant differences in the currency denomination of Japanese exports of these goods by region (not shown in the table). For example, TV and VCR exports to the United States are mostly (more than 90 percent) denominated in dollars, about two-thirds of TV and VCR exports to Southeast Asian countries are denominated in yen, and exports to EC countries are in between. Certainly, Japanese TVs and VCRs have a competitive edge worldwide, particularly in the United States.[7] This evidence suggests that competitiveness is not the only factor determining the choice of invoice currency.

The second explanation given for the low yen-invoice share of Japanese exports is associated with Japan's role as major importer of raw materials and oil. In fact, almost all raw material and oil imports to Japan are invoiced in U.S. dollars, reflecting the role of the dollar as the central international transaction currency. However, the import share of raw materials of Japan is now less than 40 percent. Therefore, raw materials and oil imports alone do not explain the low national currency ratio of import invoicing of Japan, compared with that of other European countries.

In summary, there is little evidence that a bloc based on the use of the yen as an invoice currency is emerging among Southeast Asian countries. Factors such as extensive trading with the United States or a higher dependence on imported raw materials cannot explain why yen-invoiced exports from and imports to Japan are relatively limited.

[7] To the extent that Japanese products are in competition with other Asian products in the United States and exports of the latter to the United States are invoiced in dollars, Japanese products may be similarly invoiced to protect market share.

Notes to Table 13.5 (*continued*)
natural gas. "Chemicals" includes chemical compounds, pharmaceutical goods, medical products, and cosmetics. "Machinery" includes motors, electric machines, aircrafts, and autos. "Manufactured, Others" includes wood and textile products, various alloys, and precision instruments.
Source: MITI, *Export Confirmation Statistics*, 1991; *Import Reporting Statistics*, 1991.

13.2.3   *Yen as a banking and reserve currency*

Table 13.6 shows the currency denominations of foreign exchange transactions in the three largest foreign exchange markets in 1986, 1989, and
1992. In the Tokyo market, yen–dollar exchanges were the predominant
transactions in all three years. In New York about one-third of the
transactions were deutsche mark–dollar exchanges and one-fourth were
yen–dollar exchanges. (The share of yen–dollar exchanges was a mere
10 percent in New York in 1980; see Black, 1991: 522). In 1992 U.K.
pound–dollar transactions accounted for less than 20 percent of the
London market, while deutsche mark–dollar exchanges accounted for
23 percent of transactions; yen–dollar exchanges were only 13 percent.
One notable development from 1989 to 1992 is the growth of "cross"
transactions (nondollar-to-nondollar transactions). However, in 1992
deutsche mark–yen transactions amounted to only 3 percent in London
and New York and 4 percent in Tokyo. Thus, yen-involved transactions
outside Japan are dominated by other currencies.

Table 13.7, taken from Tavlas and Ozeki (1992), shows how official
foreign reserves in central banks around the world (Panel A) and in
selected Asian countries (Panel B) are broken down by currency denomination. In 1990, yen-denominated reserves accounted for less than
10 percent of total international reserves held by central banks in the
world and 17 percent in Asia. This is much less than the share in foreign
exchange market transactions shown in the preceding table. Although
there was a jump in the yen-denominated assets of central banks in 1985,
this is attributable to passive capital gains associated with the sharp yen
appreciation against the dollar. Yen-denominated assets accounted for
as much as 30 percent of Asian central banks' international reserves in
1987. However, it is remarkable that Asian central banks seem to have
decreased their yen-denominated assets from 1987 to 1990, offsetting
almost all their capital gains in yen from 1984 to 1987. Again, we have
little evidence that the yen is gaining an increased role as a reserve
currency in the world.

Table 13.8, also taken from Tavlas and Ozeki (1992), shows that the
share of yen-denominated debt has significantly increased in most Asian
countries, most notably in Indonesia, Thailand, and Malaysia during
the 1980s. These countries are recipients of Japan's yen-denominated
loans (as part of official assistance), as shown in Table 13.9. Even though
some of the increases were due to yen appreciation (as evident in the
sharp increase from 1984 to 1986), foreign borrowing from Japan by
these countries seems to have outpaced borrowing in dollars.

Although Korea received a large volume of yen loans in the past,

Table 13.6. *Currency composition of foreign exchange market transactions, 1986, 1989, and 1992*

	London		New York		Tokyo	
April 1986						
Transactions per day ($ bil)	90.0		58.5		48.0	
Currency composition (%)	UK/$	30.0	DM/$	34.2	Yen/$	81.6
	DM/$	28.0	Yen/$	23.0	DM/$	7.7
	Yen/$	14.0	UK/$	18.6	UK/$	2.6
	SFr/$	9.0	SFr/$	9.7	SFr/$	4.0
	*/$	16.0	*/$	14.5	*/$	2.6
	Cross	3.0	Cross	na	Cross	1.5
April 1989						
Transactions per day ($ bil)	187.0		128.9		115.2	
Currency composition (%)	UK/$	27.0	DM/$	32.9	Yen/$	72.3
	DM/$	22.0	Yen/$	25.2	DM/$	9.7
	Yen/$	15.0	UK/$	14.6	UK/$	4.3
	SFr/$	10.0	SFr/$	11.8	SFr/$	4.3
	FFr/$	2.0	CAN/$	4.0	na	
	*/$	15.0	*/$	11.5	*/$	3.3
	Cross	9.0	Cross	3.6	Cross	6.1
	DM/yen	2.0	DM/yen	na	DM/yen	1.0
April 1992						
Transactions per day ($ bil)	303.0		192.3		128.0	
Currency composition (%)	DM/$	23.0	DM/$	33.7	Yen/$	67.3
	UK/$	19.0	Yen/$	22.8	DM/$	14.1
	Yen/$	13.0	UK/$	9.3	UK/$	3.8
	SFr/$	6.0	SFr/$	7.9	SFr/$	1.7
	*/$	22.0	*/$	15.0	*/$	5.3
	Cross	17.0	Cross	11.3	Cross	7.8
	DM/yen	3.0	DM/yen	2.8	DM/yen	3.9

Note: Transactions include interbank and retail customers, spot trades, futures, and options. In Tokyo, interbank transactions represent three-fourths of total transactions. "Cross" means the exchange between nondollar currencies. "*/$" means other currencies/dollar transactions.
Source: Bank of Japan, *Monthly Bulletin* [in Japanese], December 1992.

Table 13.7. *Official foreign reserves, 1980–90*

Currency	1980	1981	1982	1983	1984	1985	1986	1987	1988	1989	1990
A. All countries' central banks											
Yen	4.4	4.2	4.7	5.0	5.8	8.0	7.9	7.5	7.7	7.9	9.1
U.S. $	68.6	71.5	70.5	71.4	70.1	64.9	67.1	67.2	64.9	60.2	56.4
U.K. £	2.9	2.1	2.3	2.5	2.9	3.0	2.6	2.4	2.8	2.7	3.2
DM	14.9	12.3	12.4	11.8	12.7	15.2	14.6	14.4	15.7	19.3	19.7
FFr	1.7	1.3	1.0	0.8	0.8	0.9	0.8	0.8	1.0	1.3	2.1
SFr	3.2	2.7	2.7	2.4	2.0	2.3	2.0	2.0	1.9	1.7	1.5
NGu	1.3	1.1	1.1	0.8	0.7	1.0	1.1	1.2	1.1	1.1	1.2
B. Selected Asian countries' central banks											
Yen	13.9	15.5	17.6	15.5	16.3	26.9	22.8	30.0	26.7	17.5	17.1
U.S. $	48.6	54.4	53.2	55.7	58.2	44.8	48.4	41.2	46.7	56.4	62.7
U.K. £	3.0	2.5	2.7	2.9	3.5	4.1	3.6	3.9	4.2	6.4	4.9
DM	20.6	18.9	17.6	16.7	14.6	16.4	16.7	16.7	17.4	15.2	14.2
FFr	0.6	0.6	0.7	0.8	0.6	0.9	1.1	1.0	0.5	0.5	0.2
SFr	10.6	5.1	5.6	6.6	4.9	4.9	5.1	5.7	3.4	3.0	0.5
NGu	2.8	3.1	2.6	1.8	1.9	2.1	2.2	1.5	1.0	0.9	0.5

Note: The definition of "selected Asian countries" is not given in the source. DM refers to deutsche marks, FFr to French francs, SFr to Swiss francs, and NGu to Netherlands guilders.
Source: Tavlas and Ozeki (1992, table 25).

these loans were largely repaid in the 1980s. The Philippines received a large amount of Japanese yen-denominated assistance, but they also received large amounts of dollar-denominated assistance from the United States. Thus in both Korea and the Philippines, the dollar-denominated stock of debt still exceeds yen debt.

13.2.4   *A historical perspective*

Just as the dollar gradually replaced the pound as a key currency, many believe the yen will replace the dollar. The evidence presented in the preceding sections, however, does not indicate any likelihood of this occurring in the near future. Nevertheless, a historical perspective suggests that if the relative economic position of Japan continues to improve, there remains a possibility that the yen may become a key currency in the medium to far future.

At the end of the nineteenth century, the United Kingdom was the world's preeminent economic power, and the pound served as a key

Table 13.8. *External debt of Asian countries by currency denomination, 1980–89*

	1980	1981	1982	1983	1984	1985	1986	1987	1988	1989
Indonesia ($ bil)	15.0	15.9	18.5	21.6	22.3	26.8	32.5	41.4	41.2	40.8
Yen (%)	20.0	19.3	21.0	23.3	25.0	31.7	33.9	39.4	39.3	35.2
U.S. $ (%)	43.5	44.4	43.1	42.3	41.4	30.7	26.0	19.2	18.5	19.5
Thailand ($ bil)	3.9	5.0	6.0	6.9	7.2	9.8	11.5	14.0	13.3	12.4
Yen (%)	25.5	23.2	24.0	27.3	29.2	36.1	39.9	43.1	43.5	40.9
U.S. $ (%)	39.7	40.5	38.0	32.5	29.9	25.5	20.6	17.8	20.8	23.6
Korea ($ bil)	15.9	18.4	20.2	22.2	23.8	28.3	29.3	24.5	21.3	17.3
Yen (%)	16.6	14.1	12.3	12.5	12.8	16.7	22.0	27.2	29.5	26.6
U.S. $ (%)	53.5	60.2	63.7	64.4	66.0	60.3	49.4	33.8	32.4	35.1
Malaysia ($ bil)	4.0	5.7	8.2	11.9	13.2	14.7	16.6	18.0	16.1	14.5
Yen (%)	19.0	16.9	13.3	14.2	21.2	26.4	30.4	35.7	37.1	36.6
U.S. $ (%)	38.0	51.5	62.3	65.8	61.5	50.6	45.0	36.3	35.6	34.2
Philippines ($ bil)	6.4	7.5	8.8	10.5	11.2	13.8	19.2	23.5	23.5	23.0
Yen (%)	22.0	20.6	19.2	20.0	20.0	24.9	25.5	35.2	40.5	32.6
U.S. $ (%)	51.6	51.1	53.9	51.2	52.7	47.8	48.1	42.4	34.7	36.9
Total of above ($ bil)	45.2	52.4	61.7	73.0	77.8	93.5	109.7	121.5	115.5	108.1
Yen (%)	19.5	17.8	17.2	18.5	20.3	25.8	29.3	36.0	37.9	35.7
U.S. $ (%)	47.3	51.3	53.4	53.2	52.9	44.7	38.5	29.0	27.0	28.1

Source: Tavlas and Ozeki (1992, table 24); original source: World Bank.

Table 13.9. *Japan's yen-denominated loans in Official Development Assistance*

Recipient	Amount (million yen)	Share (%)
Indonesia	1,974,927	17.4
India	1,151,832	10.2
Philippines	1,053,113	9.3
China	993,424	8.8
Thailand	833,011	7.4
Korea	645,527	5.7
Pakistan	590,996	5.2
Malaysia	468,018	4.1
All countries	11,326,140	—

Note: Figures represent accumulated amounts up to 1990. "Share" denotes individual recipient's proportion of loans to all countries.
Source: MITI, Official Development Assistance *White Paper*, 1991.

currency for much of the first half of the twentieth century. Many currencies were pegged to the pound, and many international transactions were invoiced in the pound. International use of the dollar increased during the interwar period. However, the dollar did not attain the status of sole key currency until after World War II, well after the United States had overtaken the United Kingdom as a world economic power. Thus, even if the underlying economic fundamentals that initially pushed a currency into a key currency role have eroded, a currency may still survive in that role because of the scale economy advantages to its continued use.

As was the case for the United Kingdom and the pound, inertia associated with scale economies may preserve the key currency status of the dollar for a long time even if the U.S. economy loses its dominant world status. This suggests that the continued expansion of Japan's economy and its international trade may yet lead to an expanded role for the yen as a key currency, though not for some time.

13.3   Exchange rate co-movements

The extent to which countries peg their currencies against the yen also provides evidence about the international importance of the yen. Many Asian countries have adopted a "basket" currency system, where the exchange rate is determined as a weighted average of the values of other currencies. However, the particular currencies in the basket or their weights are usually not announced by the policymakers. Although the content of the basket is not announced, it is theoretically possible to infer the basket from historical data (presuming that the content of the basket has not changed too often).

Frankel and Wei (1994) examined the weekly exchange rate movements of nine Asian currencies: Korean won, Singapore dollar, Hong Kong dollar, Taiwan dollar, Malaysian ringgit, Indonesian rupiah, Philippine peso, Thai baht, and Chinese yuan. The weekly changes of each Asian currency (in terms of the Swiss franc) were regressed on changes of the U.S. dollar, Japanese yen, deutsche mark, Australian dollar, and New Zealand dollar (all in terms of the Swiss franc) for the sample period from January 1979 to May 1992 and several subperiods. They found high weights, .90 to 1.00, on the U.S. dollar for all nine currencies for the full period and all subperiods in the sample. In general, the yen did not have a statistically significant effect on any of the Asian currencies. The exception was the Singapore dollar, which showed statistically significant coefficients for the yen for all of the subperiods. However, the weight on the yen is less than .15, while the weight on the dollar is about .80. The Thai baht and Indonesian rupiah also showed some significant coefficients for the yen for some subperiods, but they are small in magnitude. Thus, most Asian countries implicitly limit the movements of their currencies against the U.S. dollar; there is not much evidence that they peg against the yen.

13.4   Trade and capital flows

13.4.1 *Japan's trade structure*

The difficulties of reaching multilateral trade agreements through organizations, such as the General Agreement on Tariffs and Trade (GATT), have prompted groups of countries with common interests to reach trade agreements through regional blocs. This movement toward regionalism has gained momentum in the EC and North America through the Single Market Program in Europe and NAFTA. As a defensive action, some Asian countries have pushed for a free trade zone and other kinds of trading bloc arrangements centered around Japan. For example, the idea of an East Asian economic group (EAEG) has been raised by Malaysian Prime Minister Mahatir. The EAEG, as originally proposed, would include Japan as a key member, but exclude the United States, Australia, and New Zealand. With strong opposition from the United States, Japan so far has been hesitant to endorse the EAEG proposal.

Table 13.10. *Japan's trade by region, 1981, 1986, and 1991*

	1981	1986	1991
Exports ($ mil)			
U.S.	38,609	80,456	91,538
Canada	3,399	5,526	7,251
West Europe	23,748	37,483	59,158
Southeast Asia	34,426	41,788	96,176
Korea	5,658	10,475	20,068
Taiwan	5,405	7,852	18,255
Hong Kong	5,311	7,161	16,315
Singapore	4,468	4,577	12,213
Thailand	2,251	2,030	9,431
Malaysia	2,424	1,708	7,635
Philippines	1,928	1,088	2,659
Indonesia	4,123	2,662	5,612
China	5,095	9,856	8,593
Total (world)	152,030	209,151	314,525
Imports ($ mil)			
U.S.	25,297	29,054	53,317
Canada	4,464	4,895	7,698
West Europe	11,541	18,118	39,209
Southeast Asia	31,930	29,489	58,810
Korea	3,389	5,292	12,339
Taiwan	2,523	4,691	9,493
Hong Kong	669	1,073	2,064
Singapore	1,944	1,463	3,415
Thailand	1,061	1,391	5,252
Malaysia	2,927	3,846	6,471
Philippines	1,731	1,221	2,351
Indonesia	13,305	7,311	12,770
China	5,292	5,652	14,216
Total (world)	143,290	126,408	236,737

Has there been any increase in economic integration of Japan with other Asian countries? Table 13.10 summarizes Japan's trading structure by country. As the table shows, Japan's export and import structure has changed in the past decade. In particular, Japan's exports to Asian countries increased sharply in the second half of the 1980s. In 1991, the value of Japan's exports to Asian countries (including not only East Asian countries but countries as distant as India) surpassed that to the United States. Although Japan also increased its imports from Asia, this increase kept pace with imports from other regions. As a result, Japan's trade surpluses with Asian countries have risen more rapidly than its surpluses with the United States.

A natural question is whether this evidence supports the view that Japan now has a "bias" toward trade with its Asian neighbors. Indeed, Japan's exports to the United States are influenced by various protectionist measures imposed by the United States. However, the increase in exports from Japan to Asian countries can be viewed largely as a reflection of the economic growth in the region. As investment and consumption sharply rise among the Asian Newly Industrialized Economies and Association of Southeast Asian Nations (ASEAN) countries, imports from neighboring countries, including Japan, naturally rise (see Frankel, 1991). In order to assess these different factors, a formal analysis of intraregional trade bias is needed.

13.4.2 *Intraregional trade bias*

Trade among countries can be explained largely by economic factors such as resource endowments, relative economic size, and the proximity of countries. Hence, a regression analysis with these economic factors and regional dummy variables may be used to investigate whether there is some preferential treatment among regional members. Petri (1993) and Frankel (1992) have estimated the following cross-section regression:

$$
\begin{aligned}
\log(T_{ij}) = a &+ b_1 \log((GNP_i)(GNP_j)) \\
&+ b_2 \log((GNP/POP)_i(GNP/POP)_j) \\
&+ b_3 \log(DISTANCE) + b_4 \, dum(ADJACENT) \\
&+ c_1 \, dum(EC_{ij}) + c_2 \, dum(WH_{ij}) \\
&+ c_3 \, dum(ASIA_{ij}) + u_{ij},
\end{aligned}
$$

where trade between countries i and j, denoted by T_{ij}, depends on GNP and GNP per capita in the two countries; two measures of proximity, DISTANCE and ADJACENT, a dummy variable for shared borders; and dummy variables for geographical areas (EC for European Community, WH for Western Hemisphere, and ASIA for different country groupings in Asia).

The findings in Frankel (1992, tables 2–4) can be summarized as follows. All of the estimated signs for the coefficient variables conform with theory: $b_1 > 0$, $b_2 > 0$, $b_3 < 0$, $b_4 > 0$. Estimates of the dummy variable coefficients for the EC, Western Hemisphere, and Asia indicate that for each area there is a significant regional bloc bias, that is, $c_1 >$

0, $c_2 > 0$, $c_3 > 0$. The intraregional bias result for Asian countries was robust to different groupings, including ASEAN, EAEG, Asia Pacific, and APEC.

The coefficient of the dummy variable for ASEAN is larger in magnitude than the EC or Western Hemisphere dummy variable coefficients (i.e., $c_3 > c_2 > c_1$). Frankel also found that the intraregional bias of ASEAN countries diminished during the 1980s, in contrast to the EC and Western Hemisphere effects, which increased sharply over the period. Hence, contrary to popular belief, East Asian countries have opened up rather than closed trade with countries outside the region.

13.4.3 Direct investment

While Japan continues to record large trade surpluses, and trade links with Asian countries are growing, is Japanese investment in Asia increasing as well? This is not the case, as evident from Table 13.11.

Japanese direct investment to the United States increased faster than that to Asian countries in the first half of the 1980s. The share of the United States increased from 26.8 percent in 1975 to 31.6 percent in 1980 and to 44.2 percent in 1985, while the share of Asia (defined to include Korea, Taiwan, Hong Kong, Singapore, Malaysia, Philippines, Indonesia, and Thailand) decreased from 32.8 percent in 1975 to 24.8 percent in 1980 and to 10.8 percent in 1985. Some Japanese direct investment in the United States in the first half of the 1980s, such as in the steel and automobile industries, was designed to reduce trade conflict. Other investment was motivated by a desire to diversify real estate holdings. The share of Asian countries in Japan's foreign investment rose slightly in the second half of the 1980s, as shown in Table 13.11, but was still lower than it was in 1980. Thus, Asia does not appear to be a primary target of Japan's direct investment.

13.5 Optimum currency area

13.5.1 Introduction

An optimum currency area, as originally argued by Mundell (1961), consists of a group of countries (or regions) that are affected by common economic shocks and among which labor and capital move freely. To the extent that common shocks affect a group of countries, prices would move similarly across countries. If the countries are affected by shocks asymmetrically, free factor movement would help to alleviate differentials in unemployment and growth without the need for long-term

Table 13.11. *Japanese direct investment overseas by country (millions of U.S. dollars)*

	1982	1983	1984	1985	1986	1987	1988	1989	1990	1991	1951–91
U.S.	2,738	2,565	3,360	5,395	10,165	14,704	21,701	32,540	26,128	18,026	148,554
Canada	167	136	184	100	276	653	626	1,362	1,064	797	6,454
Korea	103	129	106	134	436	647	483	606	284	260	4,398
Taiwan	55	103	65	114	291	367	372	494	446	405	3,135
Hong Kong	401	563	412	131	502	1,072	1,662	1,898	1,785	925	10,775
Singapore	180	322	225	339	302	494	747	1,902	840	613	7,168
Thailand	94	72	119	48	124	250	859	1,276	1,154	807	5,229
Indonesia	410	374	374	408	250	545	586	631	1,105	1,193	12,733
Philippines	34	65	45	61	21	72	134	202	258	203	1,783
Malaysia	83	140	142	79	158	163	387	673	725	880	4,112
Asia subtotal	1,360	1,768	1,488	1,314	2,084	3,610	5,230	7,682	6,597	5,286	49,333
Australia	370	166	105	468	811	1,222	2,413	4,256	3,669	2,550	18,613
Europe	876	990	1,937	1,930	3,469	6,576	9,116	14,808	14,294	9,371	68,636
World total	7,703	8,145	10,155	12,217	22,320	33,364	47,022	67,540	56,911	41,584	352,932
U.S. (%)	35.54	31.49	33.09	44.16	45.54	44.07	46.15	48.18	45.91	43.35	42.09
Asia (%)	17.66	21.71	14.65	10.76	9.34	10.82	11.12	11.37	11.59	21.71	13.98

Source: Ministry of Finance, *Annual Report of the International Finance Bureau,* 1992.

relative price changes among countries in the region. Under these circumstances, a common currency may be established without the pressure of relative price changes.

EC countries envision unifying their currencies by the end of this decade, as proposed in the Maastricht treaty drafted in December 1991. To assess the likelihood of success of such a union, it is natural to compare the EC countries with Canada and the United States, both nations with diverse regions. Poloz (1990) argued that real exchange rates across regions within Canada are more variable than bilateral real exchange rates among France, the United Kingdom, Italy, and Germany. By this criterion, these four countries appear more suitable than Canada for an optimum currency area. An explanation is that Canada's provinces are relatively specialized in production, while the four European countries are very similar in terms of industrial structure.

Eichengreen (1991) compared intraregional price movements in the United States (Northeast, North Central, South, and West) with those within the EC. He found that real exchange rates were more variable within the EC than were relative consumer price index (CPI) prices within the United States (except for the Netherlands and Germany in the 1980s). A major cause of the relatively high exchange rate variability in the EC has been nominal shocks to the exchange rate, although this variability was much lower in the 1980s than in the 1970s. Another factor has been the relatively greater variability of real equity share prices across countries in Europe than across U.S. regions. This also implies that regional specific shocks have been greater in Europe than in the United States.

Labor mobility helps alleviate the impact of regional shocks. In fact, interstate population movement in the United States is much greater than international population movement among EC countries, because there are fewer legal obstacles and other barriers to movement. Eichengreen showed that regional unemployment rates converge about 20 percent more rapidly in the United States than within the EC. Another factor contributing to smooth operation of a currency union is a federal fiscal mechanism. When a particular region suffers from high unemployment, federal budget expenditures directed there in the form of unemployment benefits, disaster relief, farm subsidies, or other government spending act as a form of mutual insurance. (A private market would not be able to provide such an insurance scheme.) Eichengreen (1991:24) concludes that by all of these criteria, "Europe remains further than the United States and Canada from the ideal of an optimum currency area."

Table 13.12. *Japanese and U.S. interest rate effects*

Country	Constant	Tokyo rate	New York rate	R^2	DW
Singapore	-2.29 (0.84)	0.82 (0.07)	0.43 (0.09)	.85	0.53
Australia	-6.66 (2.32)	0.74 (0.18)	2.11 (0.26)	.73	0.19
Taiwan	-4.93 (4.04)	1.91 (0.32)	0.32 (0.45)	.53	1.17
Korea	-4.08 (2.33)	1.29 (0.19)	1.16 (0.26)	.69	0.78
Hong Kong	-6.40 (1.51)	0.25 (0.15)	1.66 (0.17)	.79	0.59

Note: Standard errors are reported in parentheses. DW represents Durbin–Watson statistic.
Source: Adapted from Frankel (1992, table 7).

13.5.2 Asia as a common currency area?

The preceding discussion implies that to form a common currency area it is desirable to have countries with similar natural resource endowments and industrial structure, so that shocks are likely to be symmetric across regions. With symmetric shocks, there is no pressure for relative price changes. One way to investigate whether different regions are subject to similar shocks is to examine the co-movement of (relative) goods prices, stock prices, and interest rates.

Frankel (1992) and Chinn and Frankel (Chapter 2, this volume) investigated the influence of interest rates in the Tokyo and New York financial markets on Asian interest rates with the following time series regression:

$$i_t^A = a + b i_t^{TK} + c i_t^{NY} + e_t,$$

where the superscripts A, TK, and NY denote interest rates in Country A, Tokyo, and New York, respectively. Table 13.12, adapted from Frankel (1992), shows that Tokyo's influence is strongest in Taiwan and Singapore. Tokyo and New York rates are equally effective in Korea. New York's influence is higher in Hong Kong and Australia than is Tokyo's.

Taguchi (1994, table 17) compares the correlation between (changes in) Asian interest rates and (changes in) the Japanese interest rate with those between (changes in) Asian interest rates and (changes in) the U.S. interest rate. Among the Asian countries (Korea, Taiwan, Hong Kong, Singapore, Malaysia, Thailand, Philippines, Australia, and New Zealand) the correlation with the Japanese interest rate is consistently lower than with the United States in the periods 1980–5 and 1986–91 (except for Hong Kong in 1980–5 and Thailand and Australia in 1986–91). The correlation with Japan generally declined in the second half of the 1980s. There is little evidence that Japan's influence in the Asian region is, or is becoming, strong.

Taguchi (1994, table 19) also investigated the correlation of CPI inflation rates between Asian countries and Japan or the United States. He found that inflation correlations with Japan are in general stronger than correlations with the United States. However, the magnitude of CPI correlation with Japan is not large, with Malaysia having a correlation coefficient of .3 and other countries all less than .18. As Taguchi shows, this is much less than the price correlation among cities in Japan, between Belgium and Germany, or between France and Germany.

In addition to interest rates and inflation rates, Taguchi (1994, table 20) investigated stock price correlations between Asian countries and Japan, and those between Asian countries and the United States. Again, the influence of the United States is in general stronger than the influence of Japan for the period 1986–91. Only for Korea and Taiwan were the stock price correlations somewhat slightly higher with Japan than with the United States.

Goto and Hamada (1994) investigated how homogeneous were macroeconomic variables in the East Asian region as compared with those in Europe. They employed a principal component model to determine whether macroeconomic variables (money supply, interest rate, CPI, real GNP, and investment to GNP ratio) move together more in the case of East Asian countries than in the case of European countries. According to their analysis, the correlation of macroeconomic variables in eight East Asian nations is comparable to that in the EC. Goto and Hamada also performed a principal component analysis with real shocks (defined as the residuals from an estimated investment function) and with monetary shocks (defined as the residuals from an estimated money demand function). They concluded that real shocks are more synchronized in East Asia than in Europe, while monetary shocks are as synchronized in East Asia as in Europe. Although their sample size (annual data from 1978 to 1990) is limited, the evidence supports formation of a currency union in East Asia.

13.5.3 *Stock price correlations: Asia versus the Economic Community*

As pointed out by Eichengreen (1991), stock price movements reflect shocks to the economy, so that correlations of stock prices among different countries (or regions) suggest how well the conditions of an optimal currency area are satisfied. This section investigates the correlation of stock price movements among Asian countries in order to identify subgroups among Asian countries that seem to be more interconnected than others.

Table 13.13 shows the correlations of stock price indices of ten Asian countries – Japan, Korea, Taiwan, Hong Kong, Singapore, Thailand, Malaysia, Indonesia, Australia, and the Philippines. Observe the high correlations between Japan and Korea and between Hong Kong and the Philippines. It is also notable that some correlations are strongly negative, such as those for Japan and Hong Kong.[8]

From this table, we identify two groups of countries whose members display highly correlated stock price movement. Both groups have countries that are geographically close to one another. The first group is the Japan–Korea–Taiwan region; the second is the Singapore–Thailand–Malaysia region. The subgroups are marked by boxes in the table. For comparison, Panel B shows the stock price change correlations for the four major European countries – Germany, France, Italy, and the United Kingdom. Except for the correlation between the United Kingdom and Italy, all pairs of correlations are positive, but are not generally larger than for the Asian groupings.

Next we devise an index to average the bilateral correlations in regional subgroupings. Denote by $r(x, y)$ the correlation of two time series x and y. We construct the following two measures of "average" correlation for the three-country (x, y, z) case:

$$CR1(x, y, z) = \{r(x, y) + r(x, z) + r(y, z)\}/3,$$

$$CR2(x, y, z) = \{w(x) + w(y)\}r(x, y) + \{w(y) + w(z)\}r(y, z) \\ + \{w(x) + w(z)\}r(x, z),$$

---

[8] Since we are calculating simple correlations over a relatively short period, a trend may be influencing the result. A stock price index with a trend increase (e.g., Hong Kong) and a stock price index with a trend decrease (e.g., Japan) during the sample period will show a negative correlation. However, this is also part of the test to detect common shocks. What appears to be a trend over a short time period actually may be a series of shocks with the same sign.

Table 13.13. *Correlations of monthly stock price indices, December 1989 to September 1992*

A. Asia

	Japan	Korea	Taiwan	Hong Kong	Singapore	Thailand	Malaysia	Indonesia	Philippines
Korea	0.908								
Taiwan	0.765	0.803							
Hong Kong	-0.792	-0.726	-0.426						
Singapore	0.263	0.190	0.515	-0.239					
Thailand	0.520	0.307	0.427	-0.147	0.602				
Malaysia	0.040	-0.107	0.269	0.428	0.821	0.614			
Indonesia	0.666	0.534	0.522	-0.640	0.086	0.635	-0.001		
Philippines	-0.396	-0.384	0.030	0.831	0.605	0.129	0.684	-0.461	
Australia	0.047	0.057	0.293	0.444	0.600	0.208	0.515	-0.271	0.642

B. Europe

	Germany	France	Italy
France	0.527		
Italy	0.888	0.299	
U.K.	0.097	0.689	-0.149

Data source: Toyo Keizai Sinposha, *Economic Statistics Monthly*, various issues.

Table 13.14. *Stock price correlation index for regional groupings*

Regional grouping	Simple average, CR1	GNP weighted, CR2
Japan–Korea–Taiwan	0.826	0.836
Singapore–Thailand–Malaysia	0.679	0.661
Germany–France–Italy–U.K.	0.380	0.398

Source: Toyo Keizai Sinposha, *Economic Statistics Monthly*, various issues.

where the weights $w(x) = GNP(x)/2 \times \{GNP(x) + GNP(y) + GNP(z)\}$. CR1 represents a simple average of bilateral correlations; CR2 uses GNP weights. Both CR1 and CR2 equal 1.0 if each of the $r(\cdot, \cdot)$ is 1.0. When the bilateral correlations vary across countries, CR2 weights the correlations between countries with larger economic size more heavily.

Table 13.14 presents averages of correlations, simple and weighted, among stock prices in the selected Asian and European countries. According to these numbers, the Asian country subgroups experience common shocks to their economies to a greater extent than the group of European countries.

13.5.4 *Political economy factors*

If common shocks are no less frequently observed in East Asia than in Europe as suggested in the preceding subsections, why has there not been a similar move toward a currency union? There are several reasons. First, Japan does not seem to have made up its mind about whether yen internationalization is in its own interest. The agenda of yen internationalization was pushed by the United States during the so-called Yen–Dollar Working Group in 1983–4 (see Frankel, 1984). The United States contended that if Japan's domestic financial markets were allowed to be more open to the rest of the world and the yen to be traded worldwide, demand for the yen would increase and the yen would appreciate – an outcome commonly regarded as desirable at the time. If Japanese policymakers permit the yen to be used more internationally, further deregulation of the domestic financial markets is necessary. For example, transaction costs in the short-term money and securities market should be reduced. It would also help to issue more Treasury bills, as a safe place for short-term investment of yen funds. (The same effect could be achieved by allowing the stripping of coupons from long-term bonds and exempting these trades from the securities transactions tax.) Japanese policymakers do not appear prepared to adopt such measures quickly.

A second reason is that the yen does not yet strongly appeal to trading partners as an invoice and reserve currency. As Asian countries increase their exports to Japan as well as their imports from Japan, it would make sense for them to tie (if not peg) their currencies to the Japanese yen. But currently, Asian countries typically export more to the United States than to Japan, so that appreciation of their currencies against the dollar is not welcome. That is one reason their currencies are more closely pegged to the U.S. dollar than to the yen, a finding cited in Section 13.3. However, since Asian countries appear to be subject to common shocks, stronger trade links with Japan will enhance the advantage of their pegging to the yen.

A third reason for the lack of progress toward a yen bloc is political. The idea of Japan as a regional hegemon in a yen bloc will be politically resisted by many of its Asian neighbors, partly because of the memory of its past. Some governments of Asian countries still feel that Japan has not sufficiently apologized for its actions before and during World War II and fear that a stronger tie to the yen or the Japanese economy in general reminds the public of the infamous "co-prosperity sphere."

13.6   Concluding remarks

In this essay, issues surrounding the yen bloc have been examined from various perspectives. We have not found any intraregional trade bias among Asian nations or any strong currency ties to the yen. The increase in trade among Asian nations, though significant in the past decade, can be explained by natural proximity effects and "gravity" created by the strong increase in the economic size of Japan and its Asian neighbors. On the financial side, there is some evidence that Tokyo financial markets influence interest rates in Asian countries, but not to a greater extent that New York. Asian exchange rates are also more pegged to the dollar than to the yen. Similarly, the yen is not used extensively as an invoice or vehicle currency even in the Asian region. However, the finding that countries in Asia are subject to common shocks suggests some potential for a currency union in the region.

Movement toward closer integration in Asia has also been hampered by various political conflicts. Although the Malaysian EAEG proposal has attracted attention, the move to include Japan but to exclude the United States has met with strong opposition. Several countries in the region are still suspicious about a leading role for Japan in Asia because of the memory of its role during World War II.

References

Bilson, John F. O. (1983). "The Choice of an Invoice Currency in International Transactions." In Jagdeep S. Bhandari and Bluford H. Putnam, eds., *Economic Interdependence and Flexible Exchange Rates,* pp. 384–401. Cambridge, MA: MIT Press.

Black, Stanley W. (1991). "Transactions Costs and Vehicle Currencies," *Journal of International Money and Finance* 10:512–26.

Boltho, Andrea (1989). "Europe and United States Regional Differentials: A Note," *Oxford Review of Economic Policy* 5:105–15.

Cohen, Benjamin (1971). *The Future of Sterling as an International Currency.* London: Macmillan.

Dornbusch, Rudiger (1989). "The Dollar in the 1990s: Competitiveness and the Challenges of New Economic Blocs," *Monetary Policy Issues in the 1990s,* A symposium of the Federal Reserve Bank of Kansas City.

Eichengreen, Barry (1991). "Is Europe an Optimum Currency Area?" NBER Working Paper no. 3579. Cambridge, MA.

Frankel, Jeffrey A. (1984). *The Yen/Dollar Agreement: Liberalizing Japanese Capital Markets.* Washington, DC.: Institute for International Economics.

Frankel, Jeffrey A. (1991). "Is a Yen Bloc Forming in Pacific Asia?" In R. O'Brien, ed., *Finance and the International Economy* vol. 5, pp. 5–20 (the Amex Bank Review Prize Essays). Oxford: Oxford University Press.

   (1992). "Is Japan Creating a Yen Bloc in East Asia and the Pacific?" NBER Working Paper no. 4050. Cambridge, MA.

Frankel, Jeffrey A., and Shang-Jin Wei (1994). "Yen Bloc or Dollar Bloc: Exchange Rate Policies of the East Asian Economies." In T. Ito and A. O. Krueger, eds., *Macroeconomic Linkage* pp. 295–329. Chicago: University of Chicago Press.

Goto, Junichi, and Koichi Hamada (1994). "Economic Preconditions for the Asian Regional Integration." In T. Ito and A.O. Krueger, eds., *Macroeconomic Linkage* pp. 359–85. Chicago: University of Chicago Press.

Kawai, Masahiro (1992). "Internationalization of the Yen" [En no Kokusaika]. In Takatoshi Ito, ed., *Current Status of International Finance* [Kokusai Kin-yu no Genjo]. Tokyo: Yuhikaku.

Krugman, Paul (1984). "The International Role of the Dollar: Theory and Prospect." In John Bilson and Richard Marston, eds., *Exchange Rate Theory and Practice,* pp. 261–78. Chicago: University of Chicago Press.

Mundell, Robert (1961). "A Theory of Optimum Currency Areas," *American Economic Review* 51:657–65.

Petri, Peter (1993). "The East Asian Trading Bloc: An Analytical History." In J. Frankel and M. Kahler, eds., *Regionalism and Rivalry: Japan and the U.S. in Pacific Asia* pp. 21–48. Chicago: University of Chicago Press.

Poloz, Stephen S. (1990). "Real Exchange Rate Adjustment Between Regions in a Common Currency Area." Unpublished manuscript, Bank of Canada.

Taguchi, Hiroo (1994). "On the Internationalization of the Japanese Yen." In T. Ito and A. O. Krueger, eds., *Macroeconomic Linkage* pp. 335–55. Chicago: University of Chicago Press.

Tavlas, George S., and Yuzuru Ozeki (1992). *The Internationalization of Currencies: An Appraisal of the Japanese Yen,* Occasional Paper no. 90. Washington, DC: International Monetary Fund.

CHAPTER 14

Economic fundamentals and a yen currency area for Asian Pacific Rim countries

Michael Melvin, Michael Ormiston, and Bettina Peiers

14.1   Introduction

The success of a yen currency area for Asian Pacific Rim countries depends on the economic fundamentals related to the choice of a reserve currency. Central banks tend to peg to currencies because of trade and financial relationships with dominant partner countries that make intervention in a particular currency practical. In addition, a key reserve currency should offer the central bank (and private domestic market investors and firms) an attractive package of risk and return characteristics from a portfolio point of view.

We explore the role of the Japanese yen as a potential dominant reserve currency for other Asian Pacific Rim nations by focusing exclusively on the portfolio role a dominant currency must fulfill. The question we address is: If we formed a Pacific Rim currency area, which single currency would be preferred?

Our approach to answering this question is to rank the return distributions for each candidate currency from the point of view of central banks in each Pacific Rim country. The standard second-degree stochastic dominance approach to this problem typically suffers from ambiguities, so that unique rankings are not possible. We overcome this problem by taking a generalized stochastic dominance approach that enables us to determine unique rankings for various groups of risk-averse decision makers.

The fundamentals considered here do not provide much support for the idea of a yen currency area. We find that the portfolio analysis provides more support for a dominant U.S. dollar or Australian dollar than a dominant yen.

14.2   The Japanese yen as a candidate reserve currency

As the preceding discussion suggests, market forces, and not a government's decree, determine a currency's role.[1] A prospective dominant international money must meet two prerequisites if the market is to embrace it: a politically stable issuing country and domestic financial markets that are deep and open to the rest of the world. Japan certainly meets the first prerequisite. It has still not met the second perfectly, but has made much progress in the past decade. Tavlas and Ozeki (1992) offer an extensive review of Japanese financial market liberalization. Important policies enacted in recent years include increasing access to the Euroyen bond market since the mid-1980s, establishing offshore banking in 1986, and some deregulation of domestic financial markets starting in the mid-1980s that expanded the available assets to be traded. While Japanese financial markets are not open to the degree that U.S. markets are, it is likely that a threshold has been reached that would permit the yen to serve as a dominant international money. In this case, we turn to the oft-studied determinants of reserve currency preferences to take a fresh look at some fundamentals related to dominant currency status.

Studies of the demand for reserve currencies have focused on both a transactions demand, related to the financing and intervention needs of a central bank, and a portfolio demand, related to the mean and variance of returns. The issue of whether a dominant single currency can be identified for Asian central banks can be addressed from either perspective. While we cannot appeal to disaggregated data on actual reserve holdings on a country-by-country basis, since such data are not publicly available, we can provide suggestive measures that allow inferences to be drawn regarding the likely dominant currency. We focus on the portfolio demand.

14.3   Methodology for portfolio demand

Apart from the transactions demand for international reserve currencies, central banks care about the stability and return on their reserve portfolios. Influential studies of the portfolio approach include those of Ben-Bassat (1980, 1984), Dellas and Yoo (1991), and Jager and de Jong (1987). The portfolio demand for international reserve currencies would identify the dominant currency as the one offering the preferred distri-

---

[1] Frankel (1991a) provides an interesting historical review and current analysis of the international role of the dollar and yen.

bution of returns in terms of mean, variance, and higher moments of the return distribution. Thus, our goal in the remainder of this essay is to rank the return distributions for each currency from the point of view of central banks in each nation.

In order to provide a ranking of distributions, we use the most flexible of the stochastic dominance criteria: generalized stochastic dominance (GSD). Essentially, the GSD approach allows us to answer the following question: Given two return distributions, what type of central banker will prefer one to the other? The GSD approach assumes only that central bankers are expected utility maximizers; that is, the preferred distribution is the one that maximizes expected utility. The primary strength of this approach is that all important characteristics of the return distributions are taken into account when such distributions are ranked. Contrast this with the standard mean-variance approach to ranking risky alternatives, where only the first two moments of the return distributions are used to rank them. In this instance, other properties of the return distributions that are important to real-world decision makers, such as skewness and kurtosis, are ignored. The GSD approach accounts for such factors and, hence, provides a more reasonable ranking of risky alternatives.

Before turning to the empirical findings, we briefly describe the GSD methodology (a technical discussion is given in the Appendix). First, we use data on actual pure foreign exchange returns and uncovered returns from holding Eurocurrency deposits to estimate empirical return distributions. Second, we identify a group of decision makers by specifying upper and lower bounds on their risk-taking characteristics. Finally, by varying the group of decision makers under consideration, we determine the return distribution that is preferred to all others by all decision makers in the group. For example, we might begin by asking whether one return distribution dominates all others for all risk-averse decision makers. If such a distribution is found, we are finished. If not, we narrow the group of decision makers to, say, those that are moderately risk averse and check for dominance once again. We continue to search in this manner until we find an unambiguous ranking of return distributions.

14.4   Data and distributions

We consider the distributions for monthly data of pure foreign exchange returns and uncovered returns from holding Eurocurrency deposits. The exchange rate data are from the International Monetary Fund's *Inter-*

national Financial Statistics (line ae), except for Taiwan. The NT dollar exchange rate is taken from various issues of the Republic of China's *Monthly Bulletin of Statistics*. The Eurocurrency deposit data are bid rates on thirty-day Eurocurrency deposits as reported in the DRI data bank. The pure foreign exchange returns are calculated as the monthly percentage changes in the spot rate at annual rates: $\{[S_{i,t} - S_{i,t-1}]/S_{i,t-1}\}$ $\times$ 12, where S is the end-of-month spot exchange rate of a Pacific Rim currency against a potential dominant currency i. Each of the Pacific Rim currency exchange rates against the British pound, deutsche mark, U.S. dollar, Australian dollar, and Japanese yen were examined over the period from October 1979 to October 1991. For Taiwan, October 1991 data were not yet available, so the sample ends in September 1991.

Table 14.1 reports estimates of the mean, standard deviation, skewness, and kurtosis for the monthly exchange rate changes from the perspective of central bankers in each of the Pacific Rim countries studied. The mean return from holding yen is highest for each country, but the standard deviation of the yen return is never the lowest. Instead, it is the U.S. dollar that generally exhibits the smallest variability in returns for the Asian countries examined. (The only exceptions are with respect to Papua New Guinea, New Zealand, and Tonga, where the standard deviation of the Australian dollar return is lower, and Japan and Vanuatu, where the mark has the lowest standard deviation.) So in mean-variance terms, it is not clear that the distribution of returns from holding yen should dominate other currencies.

Table 14.2 reports descriptive statistics for the distributions of uncovered returns on Europound, Euromark, Eurodollar, Euro-Australian dollar, and Euroyen deposits. The annualized returns are calculated as $\{[(1 + (R_{i,t}/1,200))S_{i,t}/S_{i,t-1}] - 1\} \times 12$, where R is the annual yield on a Eurocurrency deposit denominated in currency i. Since the deposit data for the Australian dollar do not begin until November 1986, the data on the uncovered returns on Eurocurrency deposits cover the period from November 1986 to October 1991 (except for Taiwan, which ends in September 1991). The position of the yen is now much different from the pure foreign exchange returns listed in Table 14.1. The highest mean return for all countries comes from holding deposits denominated in Australian dollars (or British pounds for Australia). U.S.-dollar-denominated deposits generally offer the lowest volatility (exceptions are Fiji, Japan, and Tonga). Once again, it is not clear which currency agents would prefer to hold on mean-variance grounds. The GSD technique reviewed in the preceding section enables us to rank the returns associated with alternative currencies using expected utility criteria.

Table 14.1. *Descriptive statistics: pure exchange rate returns*

Domestic country; foreign currency	Mean	SD	Skewness	Kurtosis
Australia				
£	.0205	.485	0.845	4.485
DM	.0445	.519	0.972	5.503
$	.0363	.387	1.41	7.472
¥	.0847	.504	1.49	6.826
China				
£	.0969	.531	2.24	15.18
DM	.1203	.552	3.10	21.68
$	.1107	.376	5.04	37.37
A$	.0834	.466	2.23	20.99
¥	.1610	.531	2.17	12.80
Fiji				
£	.0366	.452	3.37	21.90
DM	.0605	.482	2.72	18.20
$	.0529	.353	4.47	31.57
A$	.0232	.369	2.44	22.90
¥	.1004	.452	3.19	20.20
Hong Kong				
£	.0252	.438	0.493	3.935
DM	.0471	.414	0.215	3.614
$	.0382	.192	1.75	13.07
A$	.0130	.396	−0.71	5.656
¥	.0883	.420	0.314	2.834
Indonesia				
£	.0953	.737	4.69	33.18
DM	.1170	.711	4.48	33.02
$	.1064	.575	8.31	70.92
A$	.0830	.716	5.20	41.05
¥	.1586	.724	4.65	33.14
Japan				
£	−.057	.391	−0.01	4.928
DM	−.035	.361	0.041	3.417
$	−.037	.418	−0.27	2.559
A$	−.065	.472	−1.1	5.215
Korea				
£	.0264	.486	1.44	8.875
DM	.0481	.456	0.781	6.661
$	.0382	.222	8.15	86.82
A$	.0130	.411	0.504	11.81
¥	.0894	.467	1.11	6.347

Table 14.1 (*continued*)

Domestic country; foreign currency	Mean	SD	Skewness	Kurtosis
Malaysia				
£	.0069	.374	0.396	3.866
DM	.0291	.360	0.105	3.476
$	.0213	.148	0.458	3.982
A$	−.004	.370	−0.87	5.466
¥	.0706	.380	0.471	2.944
New Zealand				
£	.0390	.498	1.81	10.68
DM	.0632	.538	1.65	8.662
$	.0575	.480	2.42	19.02
A$	.0253	.426	1.83	16.82
¥	.1037	.523	1.77	9.241
Papua New Guinea				
£	.0119	.414	1.26	7.818
DM	.0346	.412	0.482	4.719
$	.0272	.272	1.75	11.89
A$	−.004	.246	−0.97	9.608
¥	.0741	.369	0.952	4.214
Philippines				
£	.1038	.628	1.97	10.22
DM	.1278	.653	1.89	10.43
$	.1157	.461	5.28	35.80
A$	.0906	.581	2.05	14.73
¥	.1680	.634	2.05	10.51
Singapore				
£	−.033	.367	0.466	4.075
DM	−.011	.351	0.200	3.477
$	−.018	.171	−0.30	5.391
A$	−.044	.360	−1.1	5.939
¥	.0297	.351	0.527	3.076
Solomon Islands				
£	.0856	.395	0.746	4.363
DM	.1090	.413	0.228	3.555
$	.1007	.228	1.76	11.36
A$	.0731	.345	−0.17	5.642
¥	.1489	.372	0.732	3.512

Table 14.1 (*continued*)

Domestic country; foreign currency	Mean	SD	Skewness	Kurtosis
Taiwan				
£	−.037	.437	0.665	4.414
DM	−.014	.435	0.120	3.129
$	−.025	.143	−1.3	12.50
A$	−.048	.377	−0.87	6.123
¥	.0253	.436	0.525	3.102
Thailand				
£	.0066	.421	0.870	5.545
DM	.0291	.414	0.454	4.906
$	.0204	.214	7.59	70.64
A$	−.005	.415	0.409	10.44
¥	.0700	.415	1.05	5.640
Tonga				
£	.0226	.482	0.877	4.511
DM	.0465	.515	0.991	5.528
$	.0384	.382	1.42	7.617
A$	.0028	.050	−1.0	26.90
¥	.0868	.501	1.48	6.826
Vanuatu				
£	.0315	.421	1.05	5.487
DM	.0524	.365	1.81	10.89
$	.0492	.373	1.72	10.79
A$	.0219	.454	0.342	10.23
¥	.0949	.410	0.867	5.168
Western Samoa				
£	.0708	.419	0.935	5.713
DM	.0947	.449	0.524	5.286
$	.0880	.355	2.76	17.75
A$	.0582	.367	0.506	9.497
¥	.1346	.415	1.02	5.546

14.5   Dominant currencies for the Pacific Rim

We begin by ranking the distributions of pure foreign exchange returns.[2] Table 14.3 displays the results. The table lists each country, the currency

[2] The GSD program searched for dominance over the range of risk aversion coefficients between a lower bound of 0 (risk neutral) and an upper bound defined by 5/standard

Table 14.2. *Descriptive statistics: uncovered asset returns*

Domestic country; foreign currency	Mean	SD	Skewness	Kurtosis
Australia				
£	.1336	.598	0.479	3.574
DM	.0763	.536	0.403	4.062
$	.0412	.364	1.13	5.630
¥	.0685	.495	1.17	5.001
China				
£	.2548	.654	2.47	15.20
DM	.1969	.687	3.08	19.52
$	.1577	.449	6.32	43.33
A$	.2615	.584	3.10	20.37
¥	.1867	.584	2.31	13.52
Fiji				
£	.2247	.595	3.06	15.59
DM	.1666	.614	2.92	15.08
$	.1328	.499	3.88	19.37
A$	.2299	.467	3.13	18.99
¥	.1586	.570	3.53	18.25
Hong Kong				
£	.1706	.435	−0.36	3.020
DM	.1111	.415	−0.59	3.839
$	.0752	.025	−1.5	8.177
A$	.1780	.353	−0.80	4.604
¥	.1050	.409	0.021	2.416
Indonesia				
£	.2089	.425	−0.32	2.961
DM	.1494	.406	−0.56	3.840
$	.1137	.042	−0.72	3.344
A$	.2168	.356	−0.80	4.704
¥	.1430	.395	0.088	2.418
Japan				
£	.1246	.291	−0.11	2.923
DM	.0669	.326	0.010	2.493
$	.0406	.411	0.128	2.475
A$	.1406	.479	−0.85	4.238
Korea				
£	.1409	.443	−0.38	2.908
DM	.0821	.434	−0.53	3.372
$	.0459	.107	−0.62	3.229
A$	.1479	.348	−1.2	5.320
¥	.0752	.407	−0.02	2.241

Table 14.2 (*continued*)

Domestic country; foreign currency	Mean	SD	Skewness	Kurtosis
Malaysia				
£	.1786	.374	−0.34	3.091
DM	.1192	.353	−0.55	3.890
$	.0856	.110	−0.28	3.562
A$	.1883	.363	−0.84	4.517
¥	.1133	.356	0.146	2.808
New Zealand				
£	.1541	.489	0.906	5.996
DM	.0962	.507	0.795	6.201
$	.0634	.394	0.589	5.334
A$	.1610	.394	−0.63	5.730
¥	.0887	.467	1.22	7.563
Papua New Guinea				
£	.1652	.457	1.44	9.381
DM	.1060	.438	0.328	5.138
$	.0721	.264	2.85	17.72
A$	.1699	.266	0.192	8.431
¥	.0984	.391	0.918	4.443
Philippines				
£	.2299	.489	−0.13	2.748
DM	.1704	.476	−0.24	3.318
$	.1333	.176	3.45	19.69
A$	.2365	.391	−0.48	4.133
¥	.1632	.443	0.086	2.281
Singapore				
£	.1164	.354	−0.10	2.943
DM	.0575	.340	−0.32	2.829
$	.0248	.144	0.253	4.510
A$	.1266	.359	−0.99	4.999
¥	.0513	.331	0.113	2.427
Solomon Islands				
£	.2464	.369	−0.20	2.940
DM	.1876	.379	−0.39	3.766
$	.1538	.164	0.234	4.484
A$	.2548	.308	−1.1	4.961
¥	.1801	.328	0.346	2.291

Table 14.2 (*continued*)

Domestic country; foreign currency	Mean	SD	Skewness	Kurtosis
Taiwan				
£	.1083	.443	−0.14	2.615
DM	.0486	.430	−0.43	2.769
$	.0126	.188	−1.1	7.554
A$	.1192	.371	−0.88	4.846
¥	.0381	.414	0.155	2.999
Thailand				
£	.1640	.376	−0.31	3.023
DM	.1049	.362	−0.57	3.872
$	.0709	.079	0.273	2.800
A$	.1732	.343	−1.0	5.314
¥	.0983	.339	0.073	2.341
Tonga				
£	.1387	.503	0.540	3.626
DM	.0812	.527	0.410	4.047
$	.0461	.352	1.08	5.569
A$	.1388	.080	−1.6	12.29
¥	.0736	.490	1.14	4.879
Vanuatu				
£	.1583	.402	0.586	4.756
DM	.0983	.356	0.269	5.095
$	.0689	.339	0.893	6.876
A$	.1691	.419	−0.61	5.118
¥	.0927	.365	0.157	4.089
Western Samoa				
£	.1841	.402	−0.21	3.565
DM	.1267	.440	−0.54	4.426
$	.0932	.294	1.32	11.57
A$	.1925	.349	−0.21	6.062
¥	.1184	.373	0.094	3.295

whose return dominates the competition, and regions of absolute risk aversion over which the dominance ranking applies. This last column is necessary because of ambiguous rankings that arise in most cases of second-degree stochastic dominance, where all risk-averse agents will

deviation of the return. The upper bound number is considered very risk averse (see McCarl and Bessler, 1989; Raskin and Cochran, 1986).

Table 14.3. *Dominant currency preferences for Pacific Rim countries: pure foreign exchange returns*

Agents in	Dominant currency	Over risk aversion region
Australia	¥	$r \leq 1.41$
	$	$r > 1.41^a$
China	¥	$r \leq 0.78$
	$	$r > 0.78$
Fiji	¥	$r \leq 1.78$
	$	$r > 1.78$
Hong Kong	¥	$r \leq 0.74$
	$	$r > 0.74$
Indonesia	¥	$r \leq 0.61$
	$	$r > 0.61$
Japan	DM	All r
Korea	¥	$r \leq 0.63$
	$	$r > 0.63$
Malaysia	¥	$r \leq 0.86$
	$	$r > 0.86$
New Zealand	¥	All r
Papua New Guinea	¥	$r \leq 1.87$
	$	$r > 1.87^a$
Philippines	¥	$r \leq 0.57$
	$	$r > 0.57$
Singapore	¥	$r \leq 1.13$
	$	$r > 1.13$
Solomon Islands	¥	$r \leq 1.23$
	$	$r > 1.23$
Taiwan	¥	All r
Thailand	¥	$r \leq 0.80$
	$	$r > 0.80$
Tonga	¥	$r \leq 0.81$
	A$	$r > 0.81$
Vanuatu	¥	$r \leq 2.17$
	DM	$2.17 < r \leq 3.55$
	$	$r > 3.55$
Western Samoa	¥	$r \leq 1.73$
	$	$r > 1.73$

[a] The ranking switches again for extremely risk averse agents. Oscillations of this type are not uncommon in the GSD literature. In this instance, the switch may be due to a maximin type of behavior.

not agree on the preferred distribution. The nature of the ambiguities is revealed by the GSD approach used in our analysis.

By varying the degree of risk aversion, we can observe the switch in preference from one regime to another over different classes of agents. In Table 14.3 the yen generally offers the preferred return distribution from risk neutral to very low levels of risk aversion, and the U.S. dollar is preferred for low to high levels of risk aversion. The return distribution associated with the deutsche mark is preferred by all Japanese agents. The return distribution associated with the Japanese yen is preferred by all New Zealand and Taiwanese agents. The Australian dollar is preferred over the yen in Tonga once a low level of risk aversion is reached. In Vanuatu, there is a small region where the mark is preferred. Table 14.3 clearly indicates that the yen or U.S. dollar can be supported as a reserve currency for the Pacific Rim based on risk and return characteristics. The general preference switch for the dollar return distribution at very low levels of risk aversion might indicate that the dollar is a stronger candidate for reserve currency status than is the yen. This result is due to the lower volatility of dollar returns compared with that of yen returns.

Since central banks will not hold much non-interest-bearing, high-powered foreign money, the rankings in Table 14.3 for pure foreign exchange returns must be interpreted with caution. It is, perhaps, more relevant to consider the rankings of distributions of uncovered Eurocurrency returns as given in Table 14.4. Here we see that the distributions generally may be ranked in the following order: Australian dollar, for very low levels of risk aversion, and then the U.S. dollar for higher levels of risk aversion. Exceptions are Australia, where the pound is preferred at very low levels of risk aversion; Japan and New Zealand, where the pound is preferred at low levels of risk aversion; Singapore, where the pound is preferred over a narrow range of moderate risk aversion; Tonga, where the Australian dollar is preferred for all risk-averse agents; and Vanuatu, where the pound is preferred starting at low levels of risk aversion. Only six of eighteen cases deviate from the general Australian dollar and U.S. dollar preference. These results are different from those of the pure foreign exchange returns reported in Table 14.3. The difference is due to the fact that the relatively high yields on Australian dollar deposits were not fully offset by currency depreciation, so that the risk and return trade-off available with Australian dollar deposits made for an attractive return distribution when compared with the other currencies for risk neutrality and low levels of risk aversion. At moderate levels of risk aversion, the greater stability associated with the U.S. dollar returns results in

Table 14.4. *Dominant currency preferences for Pacific Rim countries: uncovered Eurocurrency deposit returns*

Agents in	Dominant currency	Over risk aversion region
Australia	£	$r \leq 1.54$
	$	$r > 1.54$
China	A$	$r \leq 1.40$
	$	$r > 1.40$
Fiji	A$	$r \leq 3.29$
	$	$r > 3.29$
Hong Kong	A$	$r \leq 1.43$
	$	$r > 1.43$
Indonesia	A$	$r \leq 1.42$
	$	$r > 1.42$
Japan	A$	$r \leq 0.21$
	£	$r > 0.21$
Korea	A$	$r \leq 1.46$
	$	$r > 1.46$
Malaysia	A$	$r \leq 1.45$
	$	$r > 1.45$
New Zealand	A$	$r \leq 2.08$
	£	$r > 2.08$
Papua New Guinea	A$	$r \leq 4.11$
	$	$r > 4.11$
Philippines	A$	$r \leq 1.42$
	$	$r > 1.42$
Singapore	A$	$r \leq 1.00$
	£	$1.00 < r \leq 1.73$
	$	$r > 1.73$
Solomon Islands	A$	$r \leq 2.12$
	$	$r > 2.12$
Taiwan	A$	$r \leq 1.66$
	$	$r > 1.66$
Thailand	A$	$r \leq 1.50$
	$	$r > 1.50$
Tonga	A$	All r
Vanuatu	A$	$r \leq 0.66$
	£	$r > 0.66$
Western Samoa	A$	$r \leq 2.82$
	$	$r > 2.82$

a preference for the U.S. dollar. A most dramatic result reported in Table 14.4 is the disappearance of the yen as offering a preferred distribution of uncovered returns on Eurocurrency deposits. On the basis of the realized returns underlying Table 14.4, the U.S. dollar is supported as the dominant currency for reasonable levels of risk aversion. This result is due to the low level of volatility relative to other currencies.

14.6 Conclusions

We have examined the distributions of returns on holding yen, Australian dollars, U.S. dollars, deutsche marks, and British pounds from the point of view of agents in selected Pacific Rim countries. Using a generalized stochastic dominance approach to ranking distributions of returns to holding currencies, we have found that the distribution associated with holding yen is preferred only by agents who are almost risk neutral. Agents with moderate or high levels of risk aversion generally prefer the distribution of returns associated with holding U.S. dollars.

The GSD findings are even more striking when we consider the distributions of returns to holding Eurocurrency deposits denominated in the candidate currencies. Any risk-averse central banker in selected Pacific Rim countries would never rank the distribution associated with the yen first. The distribution associated with the Australian dollar is generally preferred over all currencies considered for agents who are almost risk neutral. Then preferences generally shift to the U.S. dollar at moderate levels of risk aversion. Therefore, on the basis of a portfolio approach to the issue of a dominant currency for the Pacific Rim, the yen does not fare well when interest-earning assets are considered.

We realize that the economic fundamentals considered here are but part of the analysis of a Pacific Rim currency bloc. The transactions demand must also be considered along with political considerations. Evidence on the transactions demand for yen generally indicates that trade with Japan does not dominate Pacific Rim trade in a manner that would suggest a natural yen currency area. Furthermore, consideration of the sketchy evidence regarding the invoicing currency used indicates that Japanese trade is denominated in foreign currencies (see Dellas and Yoo, 1991; Tavlas and Ozeki, 1992; Ito, Chapter 13, this volume). Almost half of Japanese exports and more than three-quarters of Japanese imports are invoiced in dollars, as of 1990. As a result, the evidence does not support the use of the yen as a dominant Pacific Rim currency.

Certainly the political considerations are as important as the economic. But there is little evidence that the Japanese government has actively pursued a yen bloc for the Pacific Rim. In fact, Frankel (1991b) argues that the Japanese government has generally resisted any tendency toward the internationalization of the yen, and the push for a larger role for the yen has come from the United States. This suggests that the often-cited seignorage gains from being the dominant money producer must be quite small relative to the problems and constraints imposed on the monetary authorities of the nation issuing the money. If we consider the relatively small amount of high-powered money likely to be held by foreign agents, we should not be surprised that nations do not compete for dominant currency status in anticipation of substantial seignorage earnings. Our results suggest that the case for a yen currency area must rest on grounds other than the fundamental determinants of reserve currency demand.

Appendix

In order to provide a ranking of return distributions, we begin by assuming that all central bankers are expected utility maximizers and have preferences that can be represented by a von Neumann–Morgenstern utility function $u(x)$ that is increasing and twice differentiable. Moreover, we shall describe particular classes of central bankers by placing restrictions on their risk-taking characteristics. In particular, let $u[r_1(x), r_2(x)]$ denote the subset of central bankers whose risk preferences satisfy

$$r_1(x) \leq r(x) \leq r_2(x), \quad \text{for all } x, \tag{14.A1}$$

where $r(x)$ is the Arrow–Pratt measure of absolute risk aversion; that is, $r(x) = -u''(x)/u'(x)$. By varying $r_1(x)$ and $r_2(x)$ we can vary the group of central bankers under consideration. For example, if $r_1(x) = 0$ and and $r_2(x) = \infty$, then we would be considering all risk-averse central bankers.

Given this description of groups of central bankers, we now turn to a description of the objects of choice. We assume that central bankers choose between cumulative distribution functions (CDFs), $F(x)$ and $G(x)$, with support in the bounded interval $[a, b]$. These CDFs characterize the returns from holding various currencies or assets. The expected utility hypothesis implies that CDF $F(x)$ is preferred or indifferent to CDF $G(x)$ by a central banker with utility function $u(x)$ if and only if expected utility under $F(x)$ is greater than or equal to expected utility under $G(x)$. Formally, $F(x)$ is preferred or indifferent to $G(x)$ if and only if

$$\int_a^b u(x)\, dF(x) \geq \int_a^b u(x)\, dG(x)$$

or, equivalently,

$$\int_a^b [G(x) - F(x)]u'(x)\, dx \geq 0. \tag{14.A2}$$

The problem we consider here can now be stated precisely. Given any pair of return distributions, the objective is to find $r_1(x)$ and $r_2(x)$ such that (14.A2) is satisfied for all central bankers in the group $u[r_1(x), r_2(x)]$. Meyer (1977a) solves this problem in a general setting by proving a result that has come to be known as generalized stochastic dominance. Essentially, Meyer notes that if the expected utility from $F(x)$ is greater than or equal to the expected utility from $G(x)$ for the central banker in the group defined by $u[r_1(x), r_2(x)]$ that is least likely to prefer $F(x)$ to $G(x)$, then it must be greater for all members of the group. More precisely, the group of central bankers $u[r_1(x), r_2(x)]$ unanimously prefers or is indifferent between $F(x)$ and $G(x)$ if and only if the minimum of (14.A2) subject to (14.A1) is greater than or equal to zero.

Meyer's GSD theorem gives us a convenient way to find the central banker in a particular group that is least likely to prefer one distribution to another and thus to rank the distributions. Let $r_0(x) = -u_0''/u_0'$ denote the risk preferences of this central banker. Meyer proves that $r_0(x)$ satisfies the following conditions:

$$r_0(x) = r_1(x) \quad \text{if } \int_y^b [G(x) - F(x)]u_0'\, dx < 0, \tag{14.A3}$$

and

$$r_0(x) = r_2(x) \quad \text{if } \int_y^b [G(x) - F(x)]u_0'\, dx \geq 0. \tag{14.A4}$$

Having found $r_0(x)$, we can infer u_0' and thus determine whether or not the expected utility from distribution $F(x)$ is greater than or equal to the expected utility from $G(x)$. If it is, then all central bankers in the group $u[r_1(x), r_2(x)]$ prefer $F(x)$ to $G(x)$.

In order to implement the GSD theorem, we must (i) estimate $F(x)$ and $G(x)$ and (ii) specify $r_1(x)$ and $r_2(x)$ and calculate expected utilities. Since we do not know the functional form underlying the return distributions, we use the data to generate "empirical" distributions. These empirical distributions are used to approximate $F(x)$ and $G(x)$.[3]

We use the GSD program developed by McCarl (1988) to order the return distributions.[4] While, in general, the upper and lower bounds on the risk preference interval can be either increasing or decreasing functions of the random variable, for computational ease we assume that they are constants. That is, we assume that

$$u_0(x) = -e^{-rx}, \qquad r > 0,$$

$$u_0(x) = x, \qquad r = 0. \tag{14.A5}$$

This particular specification of upper and lower bounds has become standard in the literature dealing with GSD. It should be stressed, however, that even with constant $r_1(x)$ and $r_2(x)$ we do not *in general* assume constant absolute risk aversion utility functions. $r(x)$ can take on any shape. The only constraint is that the numerical values of $r(x)$ must fall between the constants $(r_1(x), r_2(x))$.

To interpret our results, we must have some idea of what values of the risk aversion parameter r represent risk-averse behavior. One way to illustrate the meaning of specific values of r is to calculate certainty equivalents. Suppose, for example, we consider the certainty equivalent of a risky investment yielding an annual rate of return of 20 percent with probability .5 and a zero rate of return otherwise (or an expected return of 10 percent). The certain return required for indifference between the certain payoff and the risky investment will differ with the value of r. For instance, an individual with a risk aversion parameter of 1 would be indifferent between the risky opportunity with an expected return of 10 percent and a certain return of 9.5 percent, while an individual with a risk aversion parameter of 10 would be indifferent between the risky opportunity and a certain return of 5.7 percent. Thus, it seems a risk aversion parameter of 10 can be considered indicative of extreme risk aversion. In fact, in a survey of the literature dealing with empirical investigations of the Arrow–Pratt measure of absolute risk aversion, Raskin and Cochran (1986) found that most researchers consider a risk aversion parameter of between 5 and 10 to indicate strong risk aversion in terms of the scale we use.

---

[3] Since we have no prior as to the nature of the true distribution, statistical tests for goodness of fit do not exist.

[4] Other useful references are McCarl (1988), Meyer (1977b), and Raskin and Cochran (1986).

References

Ben-Bassat, Avraham (1980). "The Optimal Composition of Foreign Exchange Reserves," *Journal of International Economics* 10:285–95.

(1984). *Reserve-Currency Diversification and the Substitution Account*, Princeton Studies in International Finance no. 53. Princeton, NJ: Princeton University Press.

Dellas, Harris, and Yoo, Chin Bang (1991). "Reserve Currency Preferences of Central Banks: The Case of Korea," *Journal of International Money and Finance* 10:406–19.

Frankel, Jeffrey (1991a). "On the Dollar and the Yen," Center for Pacific Basin Monetary and Economic Studies Working Paper no. PB91-04. Federal Reserve Bank of San Francisco.

(1991b). "Is a Yen Bloc Forming in Pacific Asia?" In Richard O'Brien, ed., *Finance and the International Economy*, vol. 5, pp. 5–20 (The Amex Bank Review Prize Essays). Oxford: Oxford University Press.

Jager, Henk, and de Jong, Eelke (1987). "The Exchange Rate Mechanism of the EMS and the ECU as a Reserve Asset," *European Economic Review* 31:1071–91.

McCarl, Bruce (1988). "Generalized Stochastic Dominance: An Empirical Examination." Unpublished manuscript, Texas A&M University, Department of Agricultural Economics.

McCarl, Bruce, and Bessler, D. (1989). "Estimating an Upper Bound on the Pratt Risk Aversion Coefficient When the Utility Function Is Unknown," *Australian Journal of Agricultural Economics* 33:56–63.

Meyer, Jack (1977a). "Choice Among Distributions," *Journal of Economic Theory* 14:326–36.

(1977b). "Further Applications of Stochastic Dominance to Mutual Fund Performance," *Journal of Financial and Quantitative Analysis* 12:235–42.

Raskin, R., and Cochran, M. (1986). "Interpretations and Transformations of Scale for the Pratt–Arrow Absolute Risk Aversion Coefficient: Implications for Generalized Stochastic Dominance," *Western Journal of Agricultural Economics* 11:204–10.

Tavlas, George S., and Ozeki, Yuzuru (1992). "The Internationalization of Currencies: An Appraisal of the Japanese Yen." International Monetary Fund Occasional Paper no. 90. Washington, DC.

Index